Communications in Computer and Information Science 352

Tai-hoon Kim Jianhua Ma Wai-chi Fang
Yanchun Zhang Alfredo Cuzzocrea (Eds.)

Computer Applications for Database, Education, and Ubiquitous Computing

International Conferences
EL, DTA and UNESST 2012
Held as Part of the Future Generation
Information Technology Conference, FGIT 2012
Gangneug, Korea, December 16-19, 2012
Proceedings

Springer

Volume Editors

Tai-hoon Kim
GVSA and University of Tasmania, Hobart, TAS, Australia
E-mail: taihoonn@hanmail.net

Jianhua Ma
Hosei University, Koganei-shi, Tokyo, Japan
E-mail: jianhua@hosei.ac.jp

Wai-chi Fang
National Chiao Tung University, Hsinchu, Taiwan, ROC
E-mail: wfang@mail.nctu.edu.tw

Yanchun Zhang
Victoria University, Melbourne, VIC, Australia
E-mail: yanchun.zhang@vu.edu.au

Alfredo Cuzzocrea
ICAR-CNR and University of Calabria, Rende, Italy
E-mail: cuzzocrea@si.deis.unical.it

ISSN 1865-0929 e-ISSN 1865-0937
ISBN 978-3-642-35602-5 e-ISBN 978-3-642-35603-2
DOI 10.1007/978-3-642-35603-2
Springer Heidelberg Dordrecht London New York

Library of Congress Control Number: 2012953702

CR Subject Classification (1998): C.2, H.4, I.2, H.3, D.2, H.5

Typesetting: Camera-ready by author, data conversion by Scientific Publishing Services, Chennai, India

Printed on acid-free paper

Springer is part of Springer Science+Business Media (www.springer.com)

Foreword

Education and learning, database theory and applications, and u- and e- service science and technology are areas that attract many academics and industry professionals. The goal of the EL, the DTA, and the UNESST conferences is to bring together researchers from academia and industry as well as practitioners to share ideas, problems, and solutions relating to the multifaceted aspects of these fields.

We would like to express our gratitude to all of the authors of submitted papers and to all attendees for their contributions and participation.

We acknowledge the great effort of all the Chairs and the members of the Advisory Boards and Program Committees of the above-listed events. Special thanks go to SERSC (Science & Engineering Research Support Society) for supporting this conference.

We are grateful in particular to the following speakers who kindly accepted our invitation and, in this way, helped to meet the objectives of the conference: Zita Maria Almeida do Vale, Hai Jin, Goreti Marreiros, Alfredo Cuzzocrea and Osvaldo Gervasi.

We wish to express our special thanks to. Yvette E. Gelogo for helping with the editing of this volume.

December 2012

Chairs of EL 2012
DTA 2012
UNESST 2012

Preface

We would like to welcome you to the proceedings of the 2012 Conference on Education and Learning (EL 2012), the 2012 International Conference on Database Theory and Application (DTA 2012), and the 2012 International Conference on u- and e- Service, Science and Technology (UNESST 2012), which were held during December 16–19, 2012, at the Korea Woman Training Center, Kangwondo, Korea.

EL 2012, DTA 2012, and UNESST 2012 provided a chance for academics and industry professionals to discuss recent progress in related areas. We expect that the conference and its publications will be a trigger for further research and technology improvements in this important field. We would like to acknowledge the great effort of all the Chairs and members of the Program Committee.

We would like to express our gratitude to all of the authors of submitted papers and to all attendees for their contributions and participation. We believe in the need for continuing this undertaking in the future.

Once more, we would like to thank all the organizations and individuals who supported this event and helped in the success of EL 2012, DTA 2012, and UNESST 2012.

December 2012 Tai-hoon Kim on behalf of the Volume Editors

Organization

General Co-chairs

Jianhua Ma	Hosei University, Japan
Wai Chi Fang	National Chiao Tung University, Taiwan
Kyung Jung Kim	Woosuk University, Korea
Yanchun Zhang	Victoria University, Australia
Alfredo Cuzzocrea	ICAR-CNR and University of Calabria, Italy

Program Co-chairs

Byeong-Ho Kang	University of Tasmania, Australia
Byungjoo Park	Hannam University, Korea
Frode Eika Sandnes	Oslo University College, Norway
Kun Chang Lee	Sungkyunkwan University, Korea
Tai-hoon Kim	GVSA and University of Tasmania, Australia
Kyo-il Chung	ETRI, Korea
Siti Mariyam	Universiti Teknologi, Malaysia

Publication Chair

Bongen Gu	Chungju National University, Korea

Publicity Chair

Aboul Ella Hassanien	Cairo University, Egypt

International Advisory Board

Ha Jin Hwang	Kazakhstan Institute of Management, Economics and Strategic Research (KIMEP), Kazakhstan

Program Committee

Abdullah Al Zoubi	Princess Sumaya University for Technology, Jordan
Alexander Loui	Eastman Kodak Company, USA
Alfredo Cuzzocrea	ICAR-CNR and University of Calabria, Italy
Ali Moeini	University of Tehran, Iran

Amine Berqia	University of Algarve, Portugal
Andrew Goh	International Management Journals, Singapore
Anita Welch	North Dakota State University, USA
Anne James	Coventry University, UK
Antonio Coronato	ICAR-CNR, Italy
Aoying Zhou	Fudan University, China
Asha Kanwar	Commonwealth of Learning, Canada
Biplab Kumer	R&D, Primal Fusion Inc., Canada
Birgit Hofreiter	University of Vienna, Austria
Birgit Oberer	Kadir Has University, Turkey
Bok-Min Goi	Universiti Tunku Abdul Rahman (UTAR), Malaysia
Bulent Acma	Anadolu University, Eskisehir, Turkey
Chan Chee Yong	National University of Singapore, Singapore
Chantana Chantrapornchai	Silpakorn University, Thailand
Chao-Lin Wu	Academia Sinica, Taiwan
Chao-Tung Yang	Tunghai University, Taiwan
Cheah Phaik Kin	Universiti Tunku Abdul Rahman (UTAR) Kampar, Malaysia
Chitharanjandas Chinnapaka	London Metropolitan University, UK
Chunsheng Yang	NRC Institute for Information Technology, Canada
Costas Lambrinoudakis	University of the Aegean, Greece
Damiani Ernesto	University of Milan, Italy
Daoqiang Zhang	Nanjing University of Aeronautics and Astronautics, China
David Guralnick	University of Columbia, USA
David Taniar	Monash University, Australia
Djamel Abdelakder Zighed	University Lyon 2, France
Dorin Bocu	University Transilvania of Brasov, Romania
Emiran Curtmola	Teradata Corp., USA
Fan Min	Zhangzhou Normal University, China
Feipei Lai	National Taiwan University, Taiwan
Fionn Murtagh	Royal Holloway, University of London, UK
Florin D. Salajan	North Dakota State University in Fargo, USA
Francisca Onaolapo Oladipo	Nnamdi Azikiwe University, Nigeria
Gang Li	Deakin University, Australia
George Kambourakis	University of the Aegean, Greece
Guoyin Wang	Chongqing University of Posts and Telecommunications, China
Hai Jin	HUST, China
Haixun Wang	IBM T.J. Watson Research Center, USA
Hakan Duman	University of Essex, UK
Hans Weigand	Tilburg University, The Netherlands

Hans-Dieter Zimmermann	Swiss Institute for Information Research, Switzerland
Hans-Joachim Klein	Christian Albrechts University of Kiel, Germany
Helmar Burkhart	University of Basel, Switzerland
Hiroshi Sakai	Kyushu Institute of Technology, Japan
Hiroshi Yoshiura	University of Electro-Communications, Japan
Hiroyuki Kawano	Nanzan University, Japan
Hongli Luo	Indiana University-Purdue University Fort Wayne, USA
Hongxiu Li	Turku School of Economics, Finland
Hsiang-Cheh Huang	National University of Kaohsiung, Taiwan
Hui Yang	San Francisco State University, USA
Igor Kotenko	St. Petersburg Institute for Informatics and Automation, Russia
Irene Krebs	Brandenburgische Technische Universität, Germany
Isao Echizen	National Institute of Informatics (NII), Japan
Jacinta Agbarachi Opara	Federal College of Education (Technical), Nigeria
Jason T.L. Wang	New Jersey Science and Technology University, USA
Jesse Z. Fang	Intel, USA
Jeton McClinton	Jackson State University, USA
Jia Rong	eakin University, Australia
Jian Lu	Nanjing University, China
Jian Yin	Sun Yat-Sen University, Japan
Jianhua He	University of Essex, UK
Jixin Ma	University of Greenwich, UK
Joel Quinqueton	LIRMM, Montpellier University, France
John Thompson	Buffalo State College, USA
Joshua Z. Huang	University of Hong Kong, SAR China
Jun Hong	Queen's University Belfast, UK
Junbin Gao	Charles Sturt University, Australia
Kai-Ping Hsu	National Taiwan University, Taiwan
Karen Renaud	University of Glasgow, UK
Kay Chen Tan	National University of Singapore, Singapore
Kenji Satou	Japan Advanced Institute of Science and Technology, Japan
Keun Ho Ryu	Chungbuk National University , Korea
Khitam Shraim	An-Najah National University
Krzysztof Stencel	Warsaw University, Poland
Kuo-Ming Chao	Coventry University, UK
Lachlan McKinnon	University of Abertay Dundee, UK
Ladjel Bellatreche	Poitiers University, France

Laura Rusu	La Trobe University, Australia
Lee Mong Li	National University of Singapore, Singapore
Li Ma	IBM China Research Lab, China
Ling-Jyh Chen	Academia Sinica, Taiwan
Li-Ping Tung	National Chung Hsing University, Taiwan
Longbing Cao	University of Technology Sydney, Australia
Lucian N. Vintan	University of Sibiu, Romania
Mads Bo-Kristensen	Resource Center for Integration, Denmark
Marga Franco i Casamitjana	Universitat Oberta de Catalunya, Spain
Mark Roantree	Dublin City University, Ireland
Masayoshi Aritsugi	Kumamoto University, Japan
Mei-Ling Shyu	University of Miami, USA
Michel Plaisent	University of Quebec in Montreal, Canada
Miyuki Nakano	University of Tokyo, Japan
Mohd Helmy Abd Wahab	Universiti Tun Hussein Onn Malaysia (UTHM), Malaysia
Mona Laroussi	Institut National des Sciences Appliquees et de la Technologie, Tunisia
Nguyen Manh Tho	Institute of Software Technology and Interactive Systems, Austria
Nor Erne Nazira Bazin	University Teknologi Malaysia, Malaysia
Omar Boussaid	University of Lyon, France
Osman Sadeck	Western Cape Education Department, South Africa
Ozgur Ulusoy	Bilkent University, Turkey
Pabitra Mitra Mitra	Indian Institute of Technology Kharagpur, India
Pang-Ning Tan	Michigan State University, USA
Pankaj Kamthan	Concordia University, Canada
Paolo Ceravolo	Universita di Milano, Italy
Peter Baumann	Jacobs University Bremen, Germany
Philip L. Balcaen	University of British Columbia Okanagan, Canada
Piotr Wisniewski	Copernicus University, Poland
Ramayah Thurasamy	University Sains Malaysia, Penang, Malaysia
Rami Yared	Japan Advanced Institute of Science and Technology, Japan
Raymond Choo	Australian Institute of Criminology, Australia
Regis Cabral	FEPRO Pitea, Sweden
Richi Nayak	Queensland University of Technology, Australia
Robert Wierzbicki	University of Applied Sciences Mittweida, Germany
Roselina Sallehuddin	University Teknologi Malaysia, Malaysia
Rozhan Mohammed Idrus	Universiti Sains Malaysia, Malaysia

William Zhu	University of Electronic Science and Technology of China, China
Xiaohua Hu	Drexel University, USA
Xiao-Lin Li	Nanjing University, China
Xuemin Lin	University of New South Wales, Australia
Yan Wang	Macquarie University, Australia
Yana Tainsh	University of Greenwich, UK
Yang Yu	Nanjing University, China
Yang-Sae Moon	Kangwon National University, Korea
Yao-Chung Chang	National Taitung University, Taiwan
Ying Zhang	The University of New South Wales, Australia
Yiyu Yao	University of Regina, Canada
Yongli Ren	Deakin University, Australia
Yoshitaka Sakurai	Tokyo Denki University, Japan
Young Jin Nam	Daegu University, Korea
Young-Koo Lee	Kyunghee University, Korea
Zhaohao Sun Hebei	Normal University, China
Zhenjiang Miao	Beijing Jiaotong University, China
Zhuoming Xu	Hohai University, China
Zhuowei Li	Indiana University, USA

Table of Contents

The Design of Experimental Nodes on Teaching Platform of Cloud Laboratory (TPCL) 1
Wenwei Qiu, Nong Xiao, Hongyi Lu, and Zhen Sun

Challenges of Electronic Textbook Authoring: Writing in the Discipline 8
Joseph Defazio

An Analysis of Factors Influencing the User Acceptance of OpenCourseWare 15
Chang-hwa Wang and Cheng-ping Chen

Applying Augmented Reality in Teaching Fundamental Earth Science in Junior High Schools 23
Chang-hwa Wang and Pei-han Chi

Anytime. Everywhere. Mobile Learning in Higher Education: Creating a GIS Course 31
Alptekin Erkollar and Birgit J. Oberer

Wireless and Configurationless iClassroom System with Remote Database via Bonjour 38
Mohamed Ariff Ameedeen and Zafril Rizal M. Azmi

KOST: Korean Semantic Tagger ver. 1.0 44
Hye-Jeong Song, Chan-Young Park, Jung-Kuk Lee, Dae-Yong Han, Han-Gil Choi, Jong-Dae Kim, and Yu-Seop Kim

An Attempt on Effort-Achievement Analysis of Lecture Data for Effective Teaching 50
Toshiro Minami and Yoko Ohura

Mobile Applications Development with Combine on MDA and SOA 58
Haeng-Kon Kim

Semantic Web Service Composition Using Formal Verification Techniques 72
Hyunyoung Kil and Wonhong Nam

Characteristics of Citation Scopes: A Preliminary Study to Detect Citing Sentences 80
In-Su Kang and Byung-Kyu Kim

Scorpio: A Simple, Convenient, Microsoft Excel Macro Based Program for Privacy-Preserving Logrank Test 86
Yu Li and Sheng Zhong

Generic Process Framework for Safety-Critical Software in a Weapon System 92
Myongho Kim, Joohyun Lee, and Doo-Hwan Bae

Threshold Identity-Based Broadcast Encryption from Identity-Based Encryption 99
Kitak Kim, Milyoung Kim, Hyoseung Kim, Jon Hwan Park, and Dong Hoon Lee

Software Implementation of Source Code Quality Analysis and Evaluation for Weapon Systems Software 103
Seill Kim and Youngkyu Park

An Approach to Constructing Timing Diagrams from UML/MARTE Behavioral Models for Guidance and Control Unit Software 107
Jinho Choi and Doo-Hwan Bae

Detecting Inconsistent Names of Source Code Using NLP 111
Sungnam Lee, Suntae Kim, JeongAh Kim, and Sooyoung Park

Voice Command Recognition for Fighter Pilots Using Grammar Tree ... 116
Hangyu Kim, Jeongsik Park, Yunghwan Oh, Seongwoo Kim, and Bonggyu Kim

Web-Based Text-to-Speech Technologies in Foreign Language Learning: Opportunities and Challenges 120
Dosik Moon

Design of Interval Type-2 FCM-Based FNN and Genetic Optimization for Pattern Recognition 126
Keon-Jun Park, Jae-Hyun Kwon, and Yong-Kab Kim

Spatio-temporal Search Techniques for the Semantic Web 134
Jeong-Joon Kim, Tae-Min Kwun, Kyu-Ho Kim, Ki-Young Lee, and Yeon-Man Jeong

A Page Management Technique for Frequent Updates from Flash Memory 142
Jeong-Jin Kang, Eun-Byul Cho, Myeong-Jin Jeong, Jeong-Joon Kim, Ki-Young Lee, and Gyoo-Seok Choi

Implementing Mobile Interface Based Voice Recognition System 150
Myung-Jae Lim, Eun-Ser Lee, and Young-Man Kwon

A Study on the Waste Volume Calculation for Efficient Monitoring of the Landfill Facility 158
Youngdae Lee, Seungyun Cho, and Jeong-Jin Kang

Design and Implementation of Program for Volumetric Measurement of Kidney 170
Young-Man Kwon, Young-Hwan Hwang, and Yong-Gyu Jung

Evaluation of Time Complexity Based on Triangle Height for K-Means Clustering 177
Shinwon Lee and Wonhee Lee

Improving Pitch Detection through Emphasized Harmonics in Time-Domain 184
Hyung-Woo Park, Myung-Sook Kim, and Myung-Jin Bae

Enhanced Secure Authentication for Mobile RFID Healthcare System in Wireless Sensor Networks 190
Jung Tae Kim

A Study of Remote Control for Home Appliances Based on M2M 198
YouHyeong Moon, DoHyeon Kim, WonGyu Jang, and SungHyup Lee

The Effect of Cervical Stretching on Neck Pain and Pain Free Mouth Opening 204
Han Suk Lee and Ho Jun Yeom

A Performance Evaluation of AIS-Based Ad-Hoc Routing (AAR) Protocol for Data Communications at Sea 211
Seong Mi Mun and Joo Young Son

Multimodal Biometric Systems and Its Application in Smart TV 219
Yeong Gon Kim, Kwang Yong Shin, Won Oh Lee, Kang Ryoung Park, Eui Chul Lee, CheonIn Oh, and HanKyu Lee

Selective Removal of Impulse Noise Preserving Edge Information 227
Young-Man Kwon and Myung-Jae Lim

High Speed LDPC Encoder Architecture for Digital Video Broadcasting Systems 233
Ji Won Jung and Gun Yeol Park

Estimation of the Vestibular-CNS Based on the Static Posture Balance: Vestibular-Central Nervous System 239
Jeong-lae Kim and Kyu-sung Hwang

A Study on a New Non-uniform Speech Coding Using the Components of Separated by Harmonics and Formants Frequencies 246
Seonggeon Bae and Myungjin Bae

A Development of Authoring Tool for Online 3D GIS Service Using LoD and Multi-mapping 252
Ran Choi, Seoung-soo Bae, Hyeon-Choel Kim, and Chang-Suk Cho

Electric Vehicle Charging Control System Hardware-In-the-Loop Simulation(HILS) with a Smartphone ... 258
Kyung-Jung Lee, Sunny Ro, and Hyun-Sik Ahn

Construction of Korean Semantic Annotated Corpus ... 265
Hye-Jeong Song, Chan-Young Park, Jung-Kuk Lee, Min-Ji Lee, Yoon-Jeong Lee, Jong-Dae Kim, and Yu-Seop Kim

Web Based File Transmission System for Delivery of E-Training Contents ... 272
Yu-Doo Kim, Mohan Kim, and Il-Young Moon

A Study on Judgment of Intoxication State Using Speech ... 277
Geumran Baek and Myungjin Bae

Research of Color Affordance Concept and Applying to Design ... 283
Pakr Sung-euk

An ANFIS Model for Environmental Performance Measurement of Transportation ... 289
Sang-Hyun Lee, Jong-Han Lim, and Kyung-Il Moon

Imaging Processing Based a Wireless Charging System with a Mobile Robot ... 298
Jae-O Kim, Sunny Rho, Chan-Woo Moon, and Hyun-Sik Ahn

An Exploratory Study of the Positive Effect of Anger on Decision-Making in Business Contexts ... 302
Jung Woo Lee, Jin Young Park, and Kun Chang Lee

Integrating a General Bayesian Network with Multi-Agent Simulation to Optimize Supply Chain Management ... 310
Seung Chang Seong and Kun Chang Lee

Data Mining for Churn Prediction: Multiple Regressions Approach ... 318
Mohd Khalid Awang, Mohd Nordin Abdul Rahman, and Mohammad Ridwan Ismail

It Is Time to Prepare for the Future: Forecasting Social Trends ... 325
Soyeon Caren Han, Hyunsuk Chung, and Byeong Ho Kang

Vague Normalization in a Relational Database Model ... 332
Jaydev Mishra and Sharmistha Ghosh

Unrolling SQL: 1999 Recursive Queries ... 345
Aleksandra Boniewicz, Krzystof Stencel, and Piotr Wiśniewski

Author Index ... 355

The Design of Experimental Nodes on Teaching Platform of Cloud Laboratory (TPCL)

Wenwei Qiu[1,2], Nong Xiao[1,2], Hongyi Lu[1,2], and Zhen Sun[1,2]

[1] State Key Laboratory of High Performance Computing
[2] School of Computer Science,
National University of Defense Technology Changsha, China
qiuwenwei11@gmail.com, xiao-n@vip.sina.com

Abstract. With the rapidly development of information technology, remote laboratory is playing an increasing important role in the experimental teaching area. However, the remote manner of experimental teaching still has some problems to be addressed. In this paper, we propose a platform called Teaching Platform of Cloud Laboratory (TPCL), which targets to provide remote teaching service for universities in China by taking advantage of the high utilization and flexible deployment of cloud computing. This work mostly focuses on the communication optimization, scalability, utilization and reliability of the experimental nodes in TPCL.

Keywords: TPCL, remote laboratory, experimental nodes, scalability, utilization.

1 Introduction

Nowadays, the Information Technology (IT) develops rapidly, all kinds of new technologies, new devices and new products emerge continuously [1-3]. In the mean time, the content of experimental teaching updates constantly.

Although traditional local experiment teaching has its advantages, it cannot well adapt to the trend of rapid growth of IT due to its time, space and quantity limitations. Some organizations cannot afford to buy advanced, costly laboratory equipment; the constructions of laboratory among different research organization are redundant; the utilization efficiency of experimental resources is low.

Remote virtual laboratory [4] uses software to simulate laboratory equipment. This solution requires no hardware devices. Furthermore, the experiments can be carried out anywhere in anytime. But the period to develop virtual laboratory may be very long and some of the hardware is difficult to simulate.

This article draws on the efficient resources utilization and flexible deployment of cloud computing [5], proposing the concept called "Teaching Platform of Cloud Laboratory (TPCL)". It targets to offer a remote experimental platform for universities and research institutes in cloud environment. This work addresses four problems of

T.-h. Kim et al. (Eds.): EL/DTA/UNESST 2012, CCIS 352, pp. 1–7, 2012.

TPCL: first, we apply "Multi-send Blocking Methods" to reduce the communication between board and server; second, we apply Dynamic Host Configuration Protocol (DHCP) to improve the scalability of the hardware; third, we apply scene preservation technique to improve the efficiency of utilization; fourth, we apply heartbeat and watchdog to enhance the reliability of the TPCL.

This paper is structured as follows. Section 2 describes the background and related work. Section 3 puts forward the architecture of TPCL. Section 4 discusses the communication, scalability, efficiency, reliability of the experimental node in TPCL. Section 5 is experimental evaluation. Finally, we draw a conclusion.

2 Background and Related Work

LAAP[6] and ViBE[7] are the examples of virtual laboratory, while our platform supplies physical devices. Relative to Remote Network Lab[8] and NetLab[9], our lab is built on the environment of cloud.

NCSU's Virtual Computing Lab[10] indicated that the approach of cloud computing is beneficial to audience. Euronet Lab[11] proposed an open system integrating different virtual lab platforms and components. NCSU's Lab and Euronet Lab are closely related to our work, what makes deference is that we aim to build an efficient, scalable, reliable and utilization-effective platform which accesses real devices in cloud environment.

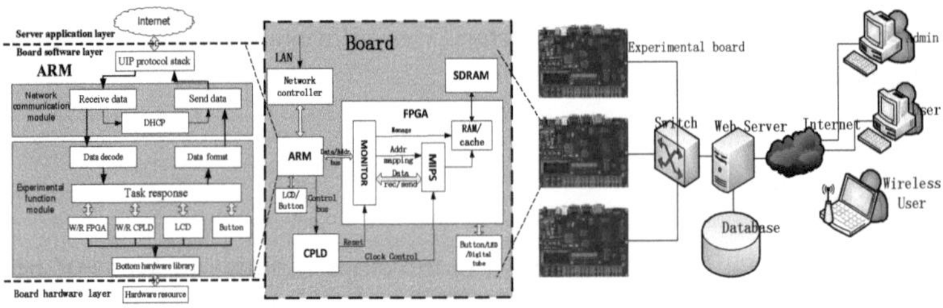

Fig. 1. TPCL Architecture

3 Overall Architecture

3.1 Deployment Frameworks of TPCL

Fig.1 shows the deployment frameworks of TPCL in the B/S mode. TPCL consists of "Tianhe sunshine" experimental board nodes, switch, Web server, database, etc. TPCL's advantages are reflected in the following aspects: 1) Accessing hardware device through browser. This advantage facilitates back-office management and future system upgrades. 2) Light-client design. It not only makes full use of the computing resources, but also enables users to carry out experiments even through mobile phones. 3)High scalability of the hardware resources. TPCL can dynamically exploit the number of hardware resources. When TPCL increases or decreases the boards, other boards will not be interrupted. 4) No fixed relationship between users and experimental board. This advantage helps to improve the utilization efficiency of board resource.

3.2 Introduction of Experimental Nodes

We employ "Tianhe sunshine VER1.3" as our experimental nodes. However, we just employ it as a test platform; its design and implementation are not the contribution of this paper. The ARM processor plays the administrator role in the hardware platform. It connects up with the Web server by network and connects down with hardware by resources library, as shown in the left of Fig. 1.

4 Design of Experimental Nodes

4.1 Communication Optimize

The problem we first meet in remote experiment is how to reduce the access delay. Between sending a command and receiving its back results, the operation passes through five delay periods: client, client to server, server, server to board, board. When the user issues an experimental command, the Web server will divide it into several subcommands to interact with the experimental board. It brings too much overhead if the Web server communicates with board once a single subcommand is issued. We denote the delay of each step as T_C , T_{CS}, T_S , T_{SB} , T_B , respectively. Assuming that Web server divides a user operation into N sub-operations, the total time can be expressed as the following equation:

$$T_{Total} = T_C + T_{CS} + T_S * N + T_{SB} * N + T_B * N \tag{1}$$

where T_C and T_S represent time-consumption on personal or high performance computer. They are negligible; T_{CS} and T_{SB} are determined by the facilities and the load of network, in the view of software programming, it rarely changes; T_B represents the subcommand time-consumption on the board, it's much lower than T_{SB} ; so the key to reduce T_{Total} in (1) is how to reduce N.

We adopt multi-send block communication to reduce operating frequency so as to reduce T_{Total} . This method caches those do not have strict timing requirements to send together. When the command requires sending information or has timing requirements, Web server calls function flush() to send cache data out, then waits for board processing finished and receives return data. It reduces the number of communication greatly and accelerates the speed of user response.

4.2 Scalability

The service-oriented architecture makes resource efficient. Therefore deploying board nodes in the cloud environment requires good scalability. Web server communicates with the board by Socket. So, it needs a scheme to dynamically allocate IP to different nodes. The adopted scheme is implemented as follows. First configure a unique MAC address for every board, and then use the address and DHCP server to allocate IP address to different boards dynamically[12].

To configure the MAC address, it needs to write the initial value of MAC address to E2PROM within the board beforehand. We have developed a tool called "MAC tools" to read and write E2PROM on the board. When the administrator prepares for the experiment, he/she uses the MAC tools to write initial value to the E2PROM. Then the board software use the MAC address value read from E2PROM to configure the MAC address in uIP protocol stack.

Allocating IP to boards by means of DHCP has four steps and its details can be seen in reference [12].

4.3 Utilization

The efficiency of resource utilization can reduce the cost of the platform constructions. How to enhance device efficiency in the cloud environment is an important research topic. The allocation policy of experimental nodes in cloud environment requires to: 1) Preserve the scene for users who have not operated the board for a certain period of time, and then release the board to allocate it to other users. Assign new equipment automatically when the user operates the board again. 2) The number of the equipments can adjust to users' needs.

Scene preservation technique stores useful data of the current experiment. They use the saved data, when necessary, to restore the board to its original state. This process has requirements in term of both accuracy and time. Scene preservation saves the configuration file that uploaded by user. Read and save the board memory, registers and other useful data when preserving scene. Use configuration file and saved data to restore the board to its original state.

4.4 Reliability

Reliability is a prerequisite to ensure the quality of cloud services. If the board disconnects with server, the board is unable to use. However, the server is unaware of the failure and still keeps the instance. As a result, serious errors will occur when the instance is assigned to users. If the board cannot automatically detect and correct the failure, the board resources cannot be made full use of.

TPCL applies "Heartbeat detection" to resolve hardware error. The experimental board software send "heartbeat" package to the Web server every 0.5 seconds. The Web server checks the number of received packages every 3 seconds. If the number is less than 1, we assume the board to malfunction.

TPCL applies "Watchdog" to resolve the board software overflow. The ARM contains two "watchdog", whose role is capturing unusual situation. It will cause the program not to feed the dog timely if the program goes into a “death cycle”. When the "watchdog" overflows, the CPU is reset, the program will be re-run.

5 Evaluation

For our experiments, the Web server adopts a DELL OPTILEX390 desktop with an Intel(R) Core(TM) i5-2400 CPU running at 3.1Ghz, 4.0GB of RAM. The server runs Windows Server 2003. The switch adopts RG-S2126S with 24 ports.

Communication Test: Take Computer Principle experiment as an example, we test the packets number and time-consumption of the operations such as download code, run, step, reset and view memory. We adopt EtherPeek NX software to capture packets.

Table 1 shows the comparison of the number of packets and delay before and after optimization among various operations. The code file selects the program obtaining the maximum from four numbers; the number of code lines is 22, and code structure has cycle. As seen from Table 1, the number of packets after optimization is reduced by about 90%. The delay is reduced by about 90%.

Table 2 shows the influence of code line on packet number and delay of downloading code, delay of run. The structure of the program has no circle. We can see that the number of packets is reduced by about 95%. The download delay is is reduced by about 93%. The running delay is reduced by about 40%.

Table 1. Number of packets and delay comparison among various operations

Operation	Packet before	Packet after	Delay before/ms	Delay after /ms
Download code	257	5	517	15
Run	2922	22	4446	871
Step	610	7	969	78
Reset	11	3	15	1.1
View memory	2055	12	1435	95

Table 2. Number of packet and delay by the influence of code line

Code line	Packet before	Packet after	Load delay before /ms	Load delay after /ms	Run delay before /ms	Run delay after /ms
8	67	5	126	0	2201	469
16	101	5	204	16	2579	812
32	165	5	375	16	3916	1483
64	291	5	532	32	6200	2840
128	550	5	891	79	11671	5524
256	1066	8	1998	126	17614	10875
512	2084	11	5305	219	23293	16622

DHCP Test: The administrator uses the MAC tools to configure the MAC address. The administrator should ensure every board has a different MAC address. Every board has a separate IP rather than a fixed IP when connecting to server each time.

Heartbeat Test: The number of packets received per second in the network under normal network is 6; and 0 under abnormal network relatively.

6 Conclusion

In this paper, we proposed the concept of TPCL, which aims to deploy a laboratory platform in cloud environment that can provide remote computer courses service for universities and research institutes with physical experiments. The Evaluation shows that the experimental nodes' communication efficiency, scalability, resource utilization, reliability have been improved.

Acknowledgement. We are grateful to the anonymous reviewers for their valuable suggestions to improve this paper. This work is supported by the National Natural Science Foundation of China (NSFC61025009, NSFC61232003).

References

1. Wang, L.Z., Laszewski, G.V.: Scientific Cloud Computing: Early Definition and Experience. High Performance Computing and Communications (2008)
2. Pattal, M.M.I., Li, Y., Zheng, J.Q.: Web 3.0: A real personal Web!More opportunities & more threats. In: Third International Conference on Next Generation Mobile Applications, Services and Technologies (2009)

3. Liu, H.B., Su, H.Y., Zhang, Y.B., Hou, B.C., Guo, L.Q., Chai, X.D.: Study on Virtualization-based Simulation Grid. In: International Conference on Measuring Technology and Mechatronics Automation, Changsha (2010)
4. Lee, H.: Comparison between traditional and web-based interactive manuals for laboratory-based subjects. International Journal of Mechanical Engineering Education (2001)
5. Vouk, M.A.: Cloud Computing – Issues,Research and Implementations. Journal of Computing and Information Technology, 235–246 (2008)
6. Meisner, J., Hoffman, H., Strickland, M., Christian, W., Titus, A.: Learn Anytime Anywhere Physics (LAAP): Guided Inquiry Web-Based Laboratory Learning. In: International Conference on Mathematics / Science Education and Technology (2000)
7. Subramanian, R., Marsic, I.: ViBE: Virtual Biology Experiments. In: 10th International Conference on World Wide Web, Hong Kong (2001)
8. Vivar, M.A., Magna, A.R.: Design, Implementation and Use of a Remote Network Lab as an Aid to Support Teaching Computer Network. In: Third International Conference on Digital Information Management, London (2008)
9. Agostinho, L., Farias, A.F., Faina, L.F., Guimarães, E.G., Coelho, P.R.S.L., Cardozo, E.: NetLab Web Lab: A Laboratory of Remote Experimentation for the Education of Computer Networks Based in SOA. IEEE Latin America Transactions (2010)
10. Schaffer, H.E., Averitt, S.F., Hoit, M.I., Peeler, A., Sills, E.D., Vouk, M.A.: NCSU's Virtual Computing Lab: A Cloud Computing Solution. Computer, 94–97 (2009)
11. Correia, R.C., Fonseca, J.M., Donellan, A.: Euronet Lab A Cloud Based Laboratory Environment. In: Global Engineering Education Conference, EDUCON (2012)
12. Rooney, T.: Dynamic Host Configuration PROTOCOL. Institute of Electrical and Electronics Engineers (2010)

Challenges of Electronic Textbook Authoring: Writing in the Discipline

Joseph Defazio

IUPUI, School of Informatics
535 W. Michigan St.
IT 465
Indianapolis, IN 46202, USA
jdefazio@iupui.edu

Abstract. Textbooks and tuition costs are continually rising in higher education. Many college administrators and faculty members work to find solutions to offset these rising costs. Teachers explore creative ways to assign course readings, assignments, and assessment instruments. Reshaping the higher education landscape, universities and colleges have adopted new and innovative modes of teaching and learning supported by extensive information technology infrastructures. The author has completed the first phase of this research design and development of a digital textbook for a gateway foundations class in the areas of media art and science. The instructional design, delivery format, and results of two semesters of data have been collected and are presented in this article.

Keywords: educational textbook, instructional design and development, information technology, e-Learning, web-based instruction, multimedia.

1 Introduction

Textbooks and tuition costs are continually rising in higher education. College administrators and faculty members work to find solutions to these rising costs. Many teachers explore creative ways to assign course readings, assignments, and assessment instruments. They struggle "to make smart decisions in the midst of a barrage of information" [1]. According to McFadden (2012) faculty are continually challenged to navigate digital opportunities without losing sight of learning outcomes, costs and wear and tear on students, teachers and institutions.

A few educational institutions acknowledge that intelligent learner empowerment has the power to revolutionize education systems consisting of the educational environment, educational content, teaching methods and evaluation in the 21st century [2]. One stellar example of this is the work currently in progress in South Korea. South Korea has increased investment in setting up a digitalized learning environment at schools nationwide based on state-of-the-art technologies offered by leading information technology firms. Educators perceive SMART education as a strong tendency to combine education to information technology and smart device development. Digital information (e.g., electronic textbooks) must be made available through these smart devices.

T.-h. Kim et al. (Eds.): EL/DTA/UNESST 2012, CCIS 352, pp. 8–14, 2012.

Authors of electronic textbooks require knowledge of instructional design processes. Within the design, there is a clear demand for writing for extra functionality such as smart searches and dynamic indexing. These qualities along with the ability to provide extra facilities are not available with paper textbooks and are crucial for the future of electronic publications if they are to compete in an educational marketplace [3]. Unfortunately, given any instructional design problem, there are an infinite number of possible solutions to a problem…and despite claims to the contrary, there is not a sufficient research base to support any instructional design model in this diverse settings [4]. The development of e-books has been led primarily by technology instead of by users' requirements, and the gap between functionality and usability is sufficiently wide to justify the lack of success of the first generation of e-books [3].

The author's research has completed the first phase of the design, development, implementation, and evaluation of a digital textbook titled, Foundations of Media Arts and Science. This e-Textbook was developed for a college-level freshman class. The instructional design, delivery format, and results of two semesters of data have been collected on the success of this e-Textbook to date. This article closes with a discussion on the design and development of a second phase; developing interactive multimedia enhancements and converting the e-Textbook for mobile technology distribution.

2 Statement of the Problem

In a typical semester, students in this course would purchase five traditional textbooks costing in excess of four hundred dollars. The goal was to revisit content from these textbooks and author a new textbook that enveloped the essence and focus for this course. Students would then purchase one e-Textbook for fewer than one hundred dollars instead of the high cost associated with the five textbooks required.

3 Media Arts and Science (New Media)

New media is defined as a blend of media, art, and science. With proper direction and academic guidance (theory into practice), media, art and science will evolve into a substantive field of study. This field uses forms of communications, design and development of applications and learning objects, and advances in technology to promote social aspects of communication, education, and corporate activity. In media, art, and science, there are many areas to review from the perspective of media, media technology, the creative use of multimedia, communication, and how these areas impact cultures.

The term convergence surfaced in the early 21st century that has fueled the coming together of communication, technology and culture. Each of these areas depends on 'new media' or media used as an art and science to move forward in today's society.

4 Challenges

Several challenges surface when authoring the e-Textbook (see Figure 1). Of all the challenges listed below the most frequent challenge was gaining permissions and rights of use for copyrighted material.

- Knowledge of hard/soft technologies used by students who access the e-Textbook
- Define the areas and topics required to produce an authoritative framework
- Research each topic for appropriate content
- Select supplemental material to enhance subject content (e.g., graphics, animation, reusable learning objects, links to video and appropriate websites)
- Write for the audience
- Gain permissions and rights of use for copyrighted material
- Review, revise and enhance writing
- Incorporate assessment tools
- Conduct usability reviews
- Publish.

5 Structure of the e-Textbook

Working with the publisher the author designed 14 units or chapters based on a 16-week long semester (see Figure 2). Units were divided into 5 topic areas that would cover diverse areas for this course. Topic areas are: 1) New Media in Perspective, 2) Design and Aesthetics, 3) Immersive Uses of New Media, 4) Creativity and Design, and 5) Intellectual Property and the Future. Within each topic, specific areas are addressed. Each area offers an interactive dictionary, graphics and animation, and links to supporting content. Online quizzes and exams are also embedded in the e-Textbook and can be scheduled by the author using an administrative feature from the publisher. Students were instructed to purchase an access code to gain entry into the e-Textbook [6].

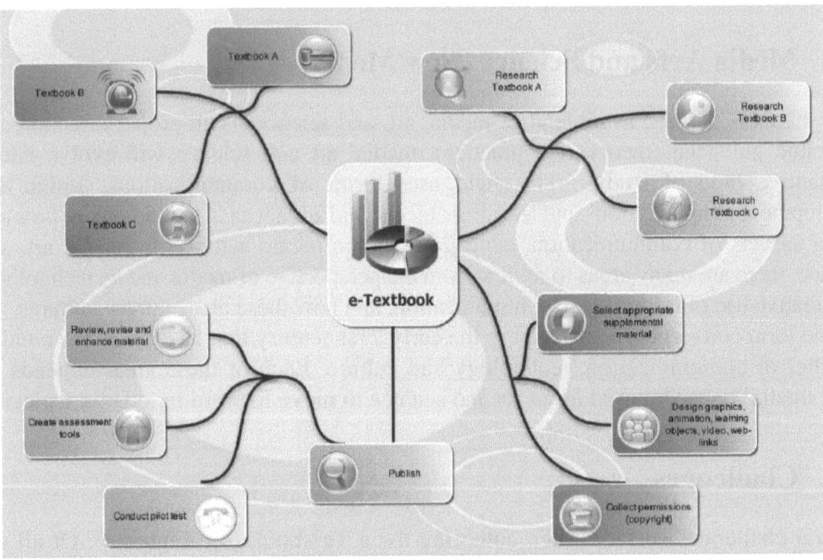

Fig. 1. e-Textbook Flowchart

Students have access to the e-Textbook 24/7. Unit readings are assigned weekly and used as supplemental content for face-to-face instruction. Figure 1 presents the textbook outline.

5.1 Research and Writing

Considerable time and research attempting to locate relevant and current sources for each unit was ongoing throughout the writing of the e-Textbook. From content gleaned, writing for the audience, freshman in higher education, was the next challenge. Since the audience for this e-Textbook was for a specific group, the process was surprisingly fluid. Using an almost conversational style of writing to deliver factual information about unit topics made the writing process flow much easier.

5.2 Permission for Rights of Use

During the research and writing process formal requests were made to obtain rights to use copyrighted material. Most of the requests were granted. Alternative sources were identified for those requested denied.

Topic 1: New Media in Perspective
Unit 1: New Media: A Historical Review
Unit 2: New Media: Theory into Practice
Unit 3: Too Many Paths; Not Enough Time
Unit 4: Technology and Society

Topic 2: Design and Aesthetics
Unit 5: New Media Tools and Toolsets
Unit 6: New Media: Design and Aesthetics
Unit 7: Storyboards, Sitemaps and Scripting

Topic 3: Immersive Uses of New Media
Unit 8: Hypermedia or Hyperinteractivity
Unit 9: Digital Storytelling: Using Games to Educate or Entertain

Topic 4: Creativity and Design
Unit 10: Digital Media: A Creative Art
Unit 11: Using Applications in Design
Unit 12: New Media: The Good, The Bad, and The Ugly

Topic 5: Intellectual Property and the Future
Unit 13: Intellectual Property and Copyright: Who Owns Your Material?
Unit 14: New Media: The Future is the Revolution

Fig. 2. e-Textbook Outline

5.3 Usability Reviews

Usability reviews were conducted through the authoring of this e-Textbook. Usability reviews consisted of review of grammar, spelling, style, and content 'voice' in each Unit.

6 Assessment

Table 1. Principles of Undergraduate Learning

Principle of Undergraduate Learning	Description
Core Communication Skills, including Writing Skills	The ability of students to express and interpret information, perform quantitative analysis, and use information resources and technology.
Critical Thinking	The ability of students to engage in a process of disciplined thinking that informs beliefs and actions. A student who demonstrates critical thinking applies the process of disciplined thinking by remaining open-minded, reconsidering previous beliefs and actions, and adjusting his or her thinking, beliefs and actions based on new information.

Each assignment was intentionally aligned with a specific PUL. Upon completion the assignments, one for each PUL, students were asked to place a mark in the corresponding area that identified their perception of how they felt they performed for that PUL. A description presented in Figure 2.

6.1 Assignment #1

This paper has a small research component. Using resources available (i.e., Google, Bing, Yahoo, IUPUI Library, etc.) create a report that presents a review of analog technology and digital technology on the same device or architecture then, produce a summary comparison. This paper must include images of each (analog and digital) device. This paper must include a reference section that lists citations and sources.

6.2 Assignment #2

This assignment assesses creativity; ingenuity and ability to develop a creative idea. The application developed must contain a title from a passage from the e-Textbook. The challenge will be; how will you incorporate these requirements into your application and ensure that the passage you select is depicted in a meaningful way?

Very Effective	Effective	Somewhat Effective	Not Effective

Fig. 3. Student scoring area for each Principle of Undergraduate Learning

Students are assessed for each assignment based on the PUL. The following scale rating is used 3 (VE) = Very Effective or a letter grade 'A', 2 (E) = Effective or a letter grade of 'B', 1 (SE) = Somewhat Effective or a letter grade of 'C' and 0 (NE) = Not Effective or a letter grade of 'D' or 'F'.

Although PULs are used to assess student learning, these principles for undergraduate learning are used by faculty to review course content and instructional delivery. For this study, the PULs served to inform and guide the second revision of the e-Textbook for this course.

7 Findings

There were 109 participants in this study. Participants were students in the Foundations of New Media class.

Table 2. Student PUL Assessment

Semester	Very Effective	Effective	Somewhat Effective	Not Effective
PUL 1	53	19	17	20
PUL 2	41	35	13	18

48% of the participants (n = 53) demonstrated very effective learning outcomes from the first e-Textbook assignment. 17% of the participants (n = 19) demonstrated effective learning outcomes. 16% of the participants (n = 17) demonstrated somewhat effective learning outcomes, and 18% of the participants (n = 20) demonstrated a deficiency learning outcomes.

For the second assignment in the e-Textbook, 37% of the participants (n = 41) demonstrated very effective learning outcomes, 32% of the participants (n = 35) demonstrated effective learning outcomes, 12% of the participants (n = 12) demonstrated somewhat effective learning outcomes and 17% of the participants demonstrated a deficiency in learning outcomes.

8 Summary

Although the principles of undergraduate learning were used to assess student learning, these PULs were also used by the author to review and improve course content and instructional delivery. For this study, the PULs served to inform and guide the second revision of the e-Textbook which is currently in progress. The next revision of this e-Textbook will include additional interactive multimedia and reusable learning objects (RLOs). Design and development of these RLOs will be constructed using multimedia design principles in Clark & Mayer's E-Learning and the Science of Instruction: Proven Guidelines for Consumers textbook [7].

Ultimately, content interaction results in changes in learner understanding, learner perceptions or even cognitive structures of the learner's mind [8]. Interactive content should help students internalize information they encounter in each topic of the e-Textbook.

References

1. McFadden, C.: Are Textbooks Dead? Making Sense of the Digital Transition. Publishing Research Quarterly 28(2), 93–99 (2012)
2. Choi, J., Lee, Y.: The Status of SMART Education in KOREA. In: Amiel, T., Wilson, B. (eds.) Proceedings of World Conference on Educational Multimedia, Hypermedia and Telecommunications, pp. 175–178. AACE, Chesapeake (2012), http://www.editlib.org/p/40742
3. Landoni, M., Diaz, P.: E-education: Design and Evaluation for Teaching and Learning. Journal of Digital Information 3(4) (2003), http://journals.tdl.org/jodi/article/view/118/85
4. Reiser, R.A., Dempsey, J.V.: Designing Effective Instruction, 3rd edn. John Wiley & Sons, Boston (2001)
5. Indiana University Purdue University Indianapolis. Principles of Undergraduate Learning (2012), http://academicaffairs.iupui.edu/plans/pul/
6. Great River Technologies, Inc. (2012), User Login Screen for the Foundations of Media Arts and Science e-Textbook, http://webcom8.grtxle.com/index.cfm?cu=newmedia
7. Clark, R.C., Mayer, R.E.: E-Learning and the Science of Instruction: ProvenGuidelines for Consumers, 3rd edn. Pfeiffer, San Francisco (2011)
8. Murray, M., Pérez, J., Geist, D., Hedrick, A.: Student Interaction with Online Course Content: Build It and They Might Come. Journal of Information Technology Education Research 11, 1 (2012)

An Analysis of Factors Influencing the User Acceptance of OpenCourseWare

Chang-hwa Wang[1] and Cheng-ping Chen[2]

[1] Department of Graphic Arts and Communications, National Taiwan Normal University, 162, Heping East Road Section 1, Taipei, Taiwan
Pw5896@ms39.hinet.net
[2] Department of Information and Learning Technology, National University of Tainan, 33. Sec. 2, Shu-Lin St. Tainan, Taiwan 700
chenjp0820@yahoo.com.tw

Abstract. OpenCourseWare (OCW) has been rapidly applied to various countries. However, many OCW users do not have enough learning motivations and some even dropped out in the middle. This study intended to investigate the factors that influence the user intention of using OCW and purposed a theoretical framework named the Theory of User Acceptance of OCW. Questionnaire survey was done to analyze the relationships among external variables, intermediate variables, and dependent variables within the theory. Correlation and multiple regression analyses were done to verify the research hypotheses. The results indicated that in terms of using OCW, the knowledge and experience influences the behavioral attitude; the effect of organization and community influences the subjective norm; and channels to elevate computer literacy influences perceived behavioral control. Moreover, the behavioral attitude, the subjective norm, and perceived behavioral control all influence the user intention. These conclusions also provide validations to the purposed theoretical framework.

Keywords: OpenCourseWare, user acceptance of information system, behavioral attitude, subjective norm, perceived behavioral control.

1 Introduction

The idea of OpenCourseWare (OCW) first introduced by Massachusetts Institute of Technology, and has been rapidly applied to various countries such as Australia, Brazil, Canada, Chile, China, Columbia, France, Japan, Taiwan, Spain, and Korea. In recent years, OCW gained enormous positive feedbacks and supports. In Taiwan, college level courses covering a wide variety of subjects have been added to OCW continuously. The terminal goal is to achieve an online lifelong learning platform. However, we found that many OCW users do not have enough learning motivations and some even dropped out in the middle. We consider that factors which influence the user resistance to the Open Course Ware should be analyzed and identified.

This study applied the Theory of Planned Behavior in User Acceptance of Information Systems proposed by Lin [1], which is modified from the Theory of

T.-h. Kim et al. (Eds.): EL/DTA/UNESST 2012, CCIS 352, pp. 15–22, 2012.

Planned Behavior first introduced by Fishbein and Ajzen in 1975 [2], to purpose the model of user intention to OCW. We hypothesized that the reason of the imperfect application of OCW in Taiwan could be users' insufficient intentions to utilize this type of material. The research purposes summarize as follows:

1. To analyze how internal and external variables affect users' intention to apply OCW,
2. To verify "Theory of User Acceptance of OCW" we purposed in this paper files of your paper to the Contact Volume Editor. This is usually one of the organizers of the conference. You should make sure that the Word and the PDF files are identical and correct and that only one version of your paper is sent. It is not possible to update files at a later stage. Please note that we do not need the printed paper.

We would like to draw your attention to the fact that it is not possible to modify a paper in any way, once it has been published. This applies to both the printed book and the online version of the publication. Every detail, including the order of the names of the authors, should be checked before the paper is sent to the Volume Editors.

2 The Development of OCW

According to Abelson [3], the Massachusetts Institute of Technology (MIT) initiated the MIT OpenCourseWare in 1999 and 2000, and formally launched in 2002. Johansen & Wiley [4] further explained that MIT OCW is founded on the idea that human knowledge is the shared property of all members of society. The main purpose of OCW is to make the educational resources open to the public. With recorded lecture and teaching materials published on the web-based platform, learners could take their initiatives to engage themselves in the materials for their own interest.

Abelson [3] also described that in February 2005, OpenCourseWare formally moved beyond MIT with the inauguration of the OCW Consortium. According to the statistics released by OpenCourseWare Consortium [5], the OCW Consortium has been adopted by numerous U. S. colleges. The number of colleges applying OCW is still growing steadily. Nevertheless, the idea of OCW was also employed in countries like Australia, Brazil, Canada, China, Korea, India, Japan, Netherland, and Taiwan [6] [7] [8] [9] [10] [11].

Taylor [8] even predicted that the innovation of OCW is not intended to threaten existing models of higher education provision, but to create a "parallel universe" capable of ameliorating the apparently insurmountable problem of meeting the worldwide demand for higher education. Actually, many higher education institutes around the world are developing OCW contents, with an aim to help variety types of learners utilize the free resources through this knowledge-sharing system.

3 User Acceptance of Information System

Many educational practitioners appraise OCW as a promise approach for continuing education [6] [11]. It was expected to equalize students' rights in receiving education, to make learning a part of their livings, and to bear in their mind the concept of lifelong learning.

With the rapid expansion of the computer technology, it has been a critical issue to study whether the information systems could be successfully introduced into the organization and whether users were willing to utilize the systems. Related theories on the adoption of the information systems have been developed in the past decade. The Adaptive Structuration Theory (AST) proposed by DeSanctis & Poole [13] and The Theory of Planned Behavior (TPB) proposed by Fishben & Ajzen [2] was two of well-known theories to structuralize different organizational changes in the application of information technologies.

Fishbein & Ajzen [2] considered that it is necessary to understand a person's intention before predicting a person's behavior. Constructed on the Social Psychology basis, they tried to explore the interdependence between a person's attitude, belief, and behavior. Ajzen [12] further analyzed the limitation of the planned behavior and proposed The Theory of Planned Behavior (TPB), hoping to predict and explain the behavior from a more appropriate approach. The theory depicts one's behavioral intention could be predicted by three intermediate variables, and the external variables proceeded. Behavioral Intention refers to the person's subjective probability to conduct certain behavior. The three intermediate variables are: attitude toward behavior (AB), subjective norm (SN), and perceived behavioral control (PBC). The external variables, however, explain the operational factors which influence the intermediate variables.

Based on TPB, Lin [1] modified related external variables according to the descriptions by Dickson & Wetherbe [14] and Hartwick & Barki [15], made those external variables be more suitable for the information systems (IS). Lin further proposed his Theory of Planned Behavior in User Acceptance of Information Systems (TPBUAIS). In TPBUAIS, the external variables are also categorized into three groups same as TPB. Among them, AB includes personal characteristics, communication and understanding, involvement in the IS, the experience of using IS, and anticipation toward using IS; SN includes The CEO support, the organized cultures, and the peer behaviors; TPB indicates in the education training, the supply of resources, and the literacy of the computer technology.

In this study, following specific characteristics of the OCW, the external variables were readjusted as the "knowledge and experience of the information system," the "organizations and community influences," and "channels to elevate computer literacy." The knowledge and experience refer to the cognition of the importance of OCW, the experiences in the usage of the web-based education platform, and the prediction of the OCW efficacy. The organizations and community influences refer to the encouragement from one's teachers or officers to utilize the OCW, the environment where the OCW was applied, and the peer influences. The channels to elevate computer literacy refer to the education training for one's information literacy, the resource to elevate one's information competency, and innate information skills.

After some adjustments, the connections between the external variables, the intermediate variables, and the applied behaviors could be constructed. According to these connections, we purposed a theoretical framework for evaluating the user intention of using OCW called "Theory of User Acceptance of OCW".

4 Methods

Based on Ajzen's Theory of Planed Behavior [12] and Lin's Theory of Planned Behavior in User Acceptance of Information Systems [1], this study purposed a "Theory of User Acceptance of OCW". Six research hypotheses were made and an online questionnaire survey was performed to validated the theory. Detailed research hypotheses are:

H1: the level of understanding and experience of using Information Systems will influence the attitude toward behavior of using OCW;
H2: the effect of organization and community will influence the subjective norm of using OCW;
H3: channels to elevate computer literacy will influence perceived behavioral control of using OCW;
H4: the attitude toward behavior of using OCW will influence the behavioral intention of using OCW;
H5: the subjective norm of using OCW will influence the behavioral intention of using OCW; and
H6: perceived behavioral control of using OCW will influence the behavioral intention of using OCW.

The following figure maps the relationships among external variables, intermediate variables, and dependent variables, as well as the locations of each purposed hypothesis.

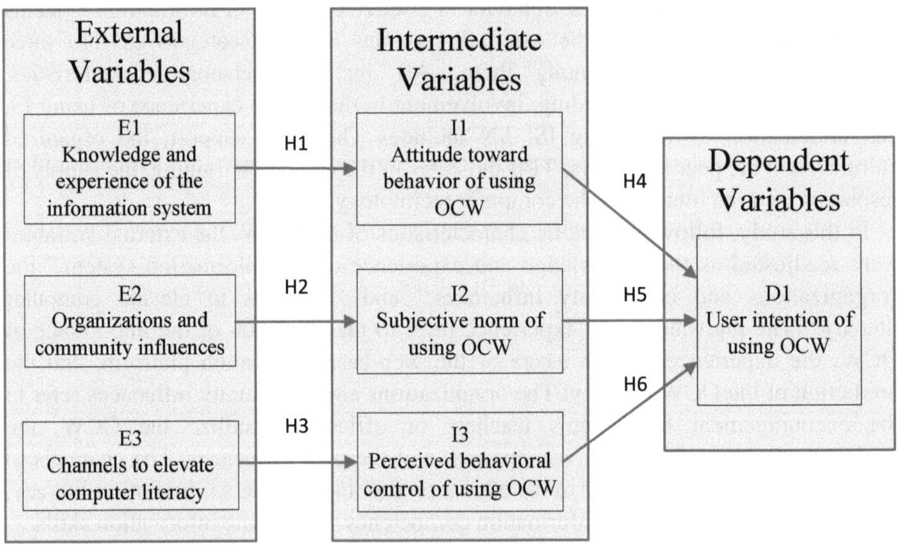

Fig. 1. The comprehensive map of the Theory of User Acceptance of OCW and embedded research hypotheses

4.1 Subjects and Instrument

The subjects of the study were those who voluntarily filled out the online questionnaire and have used the OCW before. Excluding 35 persons who filled out the questionnaire with no OCW experience, a total of 272 valid subjects were selected for the study.

An online questionnaire survey was conducted for the study. The questionnaire was developed to verify purposed research hypotheses, in which all factors to be examined were included. This questionnaire was placed on an online survey platform, My3q (http://www.my3q.com/survey/330/ocw/55307.phtml). A pilot test was done to ensure the reliability of the questionnaire. Thirty-four effective questionnaires were collected and the overall reliability were 0.872, few questions that lowered overall reliability were deleted or modified before the formal process.

4.2 Data Collection

The complete questionnaire was also placed on online My3q (www.my3q.com/survey/330/ocw/3308.phtml) to collect data for 18 days. Non OCW users were eliminated. Links to popular blogs, social networks, community networks and platforms were made to make more exposures. Besides, in order to increase the number of respondents, a drawing was available after completion of questionnaire. Ten one-hundred-dollars gift coupons of convenient store were given away. There were totally 307 respondents collected in this survey. An overall reliability of 0.940 was obtained.

5 Results and Discussions

Separate correlation analyses and a multiple regression analysis were done to verify the research hypotheses. Following are descriptions of the results of various analyses.

5.1 The Correlational Analyses

Three correlational analyses were done to examine the significances of the correlation between "knowledge and experience of using Information Systems (E1)" and "attitude toward behavior of using OCW (I1)", the correlation between "organizations and community influences (E2)" and "subjective norm of using OCW (I2)", and the correlation between "channels to elevate computer literacy (E3)" and "perceived behavioral control of using OCW (I3). Table X summarizes the results of these correlational analyses.

Table 1. Correlations between external (E) variables and intermediate (I) variables.

	I1	I2	I3
E1	.141*	--	--
E2		.153*	--
E3	--	--	.219*

*Correlation is significant at the 0.05 level (2-tailed)

As the Table shows, we found that the correlation between all three pairs of variables were significant. Such a result could explain the following research hypotheses: the knowledge and experience influences the attitude toward behavior of using OCW; the effect of organization and community influences the subjective norm; and channels to elevate computer literacy influences perceived behavioral control. Therefore, hypotheses H1, H2, and H3 were confirmed.

5.2 The Multiple Regression Analysis

This set of analysis was performed to examine the significance of the correlations between each intermediate variable and dependent variable, as well as to calculate the standardized regression coefficients. Table X and Table X summarize the results of the multiple regression analysis.

Table 2. Summary of the regression model

Model	R	R^2	Adjusted R^2	Standard Error of Estimate
1	0.665[a]	0.443	0.436	0.518

[a] Predictor : Constant, Attitude toward Behavior, Subjective Norm and Perceived

Table 3. Multiple regression table

DV	IV	Std. Coefficient	*t*	*Sig.*
	I1	.175	2.463	.014
D1	I2	.211	2.728	.007
	I3	.352	5.099	.000

The results of multiple regression analysis verified the variables that directly influence of the behavioral intention are "attitude toward behavior of using OCW", "subjective norm of using OCW, and perceived behavioral control of using OCW". As the results show in Table 3, all the variables are significant. Therefore, the corresponding hypotheses were all confirmed. That is: the behavioral attitude, the subjective norm, and perceived behavioral control all influence the user intention of using OCW. The regression coefficients for above relationships between intermediate variables and dependent variable are 0.352、0.211 and 0.175, respectively. A linear regression model can be drawn as D1 = 0.175*I1+0.211*I2 +0.352*I3.

6 Conclusion

Based on the structure of the Theory of Planned Behavior, this research examined the factors that influencing the usage of OCW, and verified the six hypotheses. After collecting data from online questionnaire survey, Pearson correlation analyses and multiple regression analysis were performed.

The results of the analyses support the Theory of User Acceptance of OCW purposed in this study. Figure X illustrates the validated relationships among external variables, intermediate variables and dependent variables, as well as their linear regression coefficients.

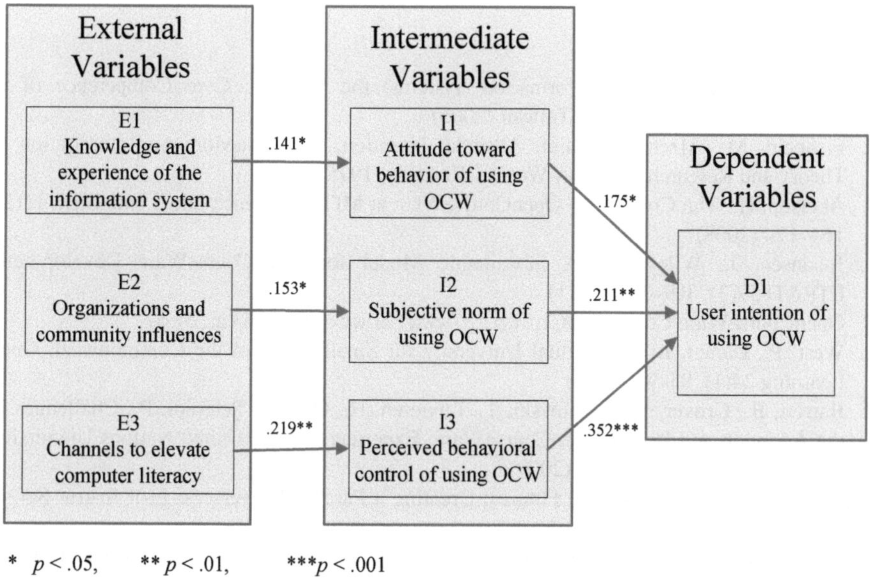

Fig. 2. Relationships among variables and corresponding regression coefficients

According to the above figure, more descriptive conclusions can be made as follows:

1. "Knowledge and experience of using Information Systems", "organization and community", and "channels to elevate computer literacy" are correlated with "attitude toward behavior", "subjective norm", and "perceived behavioral control, respectively.
2. Through influencing the attitude toward behavior, the subjective norm, and the perceived behavioral control, the knowledge and experience of using Information Systems, the organization and community, and channels to elevate computer literacy influence the user intention indirectly.
3. User intention is directly and positively influenced by the attitude toward behavior, the subjective norm, and the perceived behavioral control. Among these three internal mental variables, the perceived behavioral control is the most important factor to affect the user intention.
4. The order of the most influential dimensions of internal mental variables on user intention of using OCW is: the perceived behavioral control, the subjective norm, and the attitude toward behavior.

The above conclusions confirmed the purposed Theory of User Acceptance of OCW.

Acknowledgments. Funding of this research work is supported in part by the National Science Council of Taiwan, under research numbers NSC 99-2631-H-003-003 -.

References

1. Lin, D.C.: Management Information Systems: the Strategic Core Competence of e-Business. Best-Wise, Taipei, Taiwan (2005)
2. Fishbein, M., Ajzen, I.: Belief, Attitude, Intention, and Behavior: An Introduction to Theory and Research. Addison-Wesley, Reading (1975)
3. Abelson, H.: The Creation of OpenCourseWare at MIT. J. Science Educ. and Tech. 17(2), 164–174 (2008)
4. Johansen, J., Wiley, D.: A Sustainable Model for OpenCourseWare Development. ETR&D 59(3), 369–382 (2011)
5. OpenCourseWare Consortium, `http://www.ocwconsortium.org/`
6. West, P., Daniel, J.: The Virtual University for Small States of the Commonweal. Open Learning 24(1), 85–95 (2009)
7. Barrett, B., Grover, V.I., Janowski, T., Lavieren, H., Ojo, A., Schmidt, P.: Challenges in the Adoption and Use of OpenCourseWare: Experience of the United Nations University. Open Learning 24(1), 31–38 (2009)
8. Taylor, J.: Open Courseware Futures: Creating a Parallel Universe. e-J. of Instru. Sci. & Tech. 10(1), 1–9 (2007)
9. Kumar, M.S.: Open Educational Resources in India's National Development. Open Learning 24(1), 77–84 (2009)
10. Schuwer, R., Mulder, F.: OpenER, a Dutch Initiative in Open Educational Resources. Open Learning 24(1), 67–76 (2009)
11. Chon, E., Park, S.: An Exploration of OpenCourseWare Utilisation in Korean Engineering Colleges. BJET 42(5), E97–E100 (2011)
12. Ajzen, I.: The Theory of Planned Behavior. Organizational Behavior & Human Decision Processes 50, 179–211 (1991)
13. DeSanctis, G., Poole, M.: Capturing the Complexity in Advanced Technology Use: Adaptive Structuration Theory. Organization Science 5(2), 121–147 (1994)
14. Dickson, G.W., Wetherbe, J.C.: The Management of Information Systems. McGraw-Hill, New York (1985)
15. Hartwick, J., Barki, H.: Explaining the Role of User Participation in Information System Use. Management Sci. 40(4), 440–465 (1994)

Applying Augmented Reality in Teaching Fundamental Earth Science in Junior High Schools

Chang-hwa Wang and Pei-han Chi

Department of Graphic Arts and Communications,
National Taiwan Normal University, Taipei, Taiwan
pw5896@ms39.hinet.net, 60072022h@ntnu.edu.tw

Abstract. Augmented reality (AR) has educational values which have been used for system development with the purpose of learning. In this paper, we present an AR system of learning the relationship of the earth revolving around the sun. This system was tested on 12-to-14-years-old students. We comprehended student satisfaction by using an AR system in the classroom. Student satisfaction was measured by Technology Acceptance Model (TAM), Informational System Success Model (ISS Model) and student satisfaction in learning. To understand learning achievement, students had pre and post tests respectively. The results showed that this AR system improved learning achievement; also, students had high satisfaction of this system. Besides, there was a positive relationship between technology (device) satisfaction and learning achievement.

Keywords: Augmented Reality, earth science, technology satisfaction, learning achievement.

1 Introduction

Recently, students have been learning auxiliary audio-visual contents on computers or with specific technology. Many researches indicate that students learn more effectively with the increase of e-learning environment because students, in general, like interactive learning [1] [2] [3]. Hrastinski indicated if learner has an opportunity to control their learning environment, they would have more interest and willing to learn in classes [4]. Moreover, during the learning process, they become positive and active learners.

An AR system is the combination of the virtual and real world. In addition to visualization, users can interact with virtual objects [5]. When students use an AR system in the classroom, we can observe whether or not students are willing to learn by using this system. Previous researches showed that AR systems have educational values because students enjoyed the interaction with virtual objects which is also effective to improve students' learning performance [6] [7] [8]. Hence, AR systems would become helpful tools for learning.

T.-h. Kim et al. (Eds.): EL/DTA/UNESST 2012, CCIS 352, pp. 23–30, 2012.

2 Using AR in the Classroom

According to previous studies [8] [9] [10] [11]. Yuen, Yaoyuneyong, & Johnson defined that AR has three characteristics: (a) it is the combination of real world and virtual elements, (b) it is interactive in real-time, and (c) it is registered in three dimensions[12]. Thus, AR has some potential to influence instruction and learn knowledge from different fields[6].

Billinghurst indicated that AR systems are proved to be beneficial in education. For instance, students learn by smooth interactions and the extension of new teaching and learning strategies. Aside from that, students are immersed in dynamic learning contents [13]. Several researches have used AR systems in education, including mathematics, science, language, and medicine.

It has been an important research area as for the acceptance of new information technologies recently. By understanding their perceived usefulness, perceived ease of use, and intention of using of Technology Acceptance Model (TAM) from Davis [14]. Yusoff, Zaman, & Ahmad used the basic TAM model to investigate the acceptance of MR technology in education [15]. As the participants perceived the system to be useful, they would have developed stronger intentions of using the same technology in the future.

According to DeLone and McLean's IS success model, there are six dimensions: Information Quality, System Quality, Service Quality, Use, User Satisfaction, and Perceived Net Benefit [16]. Through the ISS Model, we could understand user satisfaction of equipment and adjust it based on their degrees of satisfaction. Fujita-Starck & Thompson divided learning satisfaction into four aspects, including course quality, institution quality, environment quality, and service system supporting [17]. This study investigated student satisfaction in the following main aspects: user attitude, user satisfaction, and learning satisfaction. Moreover, eight secondary aspects are discussed; namely, perceived usefulness, perceived ease of use, technology anxiety, and intention of user attitude; system quality and information quality for user satisfaction; course quality and environment quality for learning satisfaction.

3 Construction and Arrangements of AR System

In Taiwan's junior high school, most students learn the concept of spatial and several changes of geographical phenomenon in classroom with traditional lecture. The lack of physical demonstrations and hands-on experience, these spatial concepts seem to be difficult to understand. We believe that it is possible to increase student learning motivations and interests by employing adequate technology-supported tools. From this point of view, the technology of AR seems to be appropriate for designing innovative strategies that help student understanding the spatial concepts. We thus developed an AR toolkit particularly used as the facilitations for understanding the seasonal and day/night rotations. The toolkit includes both hardware and software. Specifically, hardware equipment includes a computer and a webcam. The software used for creating and displaying AR effects are D' Fusion™. It is easy-to-use and compatible with various operating systems.

The AR toolkit consists of two parts. The physical part is a sun-earth module that allows students to move it around by hands. The virtual part is the AR that displayed on computer screen. A webcam serves as the interface between the two parts. When the webcam captures the markless pattern on the tellurion in the physical sun-earth module, three images are displayed on the computer screen simultaneously. These images include the shadow variation, the AR displayed of rotation and revolution, and the day-night variation. On the top of the screen, it shows the date and time. Students can observe the day-night variation while rotating the terrestrial globe (Rotation). When users rotate the black disk (Revolution), it shows the seasonal variation on the screen. The physical and virtual orientations are shown in Figure 1.

Fig. 1. Physical (right picture) and virtual (left picture) orientations of the AR context

4 Method

4.1 Research Questions

Previous researches related to the use of AR systems in learning were tended to focus on students learning motivation and effects. The purpose of this study, however, tries to investigate student satisfaction and their relation to learning achievement Specific research questions are as follows:

(a) How do students accept the AR-facilitated earth science learning?
(b) How satisfied are students while AR system?
(c) What are the relationships among user acceptance of the AR system, user satisfaction, learning satisfaction, and learning effects?

4.2 The Experiment

An experiment was done to examine the effects of the AR-facilitated learning. Basic earth science concepts of seasons and day/night turns were selected as the learning content because these spatial concepts seem to be difficult to be taught by lecture alone and were proper for using AR as the facilitating tool. Eighty-nine junior high school students from age of 12 to 14 participated in the experiment. None of them had previous experience of using AR. Students were assigned to small groups. Each group contained 2 to 3 members. Before students started operating the AR toolkit, a pretest was done and regular classroom lecture was provided in a traditional form. That is, students learned basic concepts of the day-night and seasonal variations before the AR demonstration and hands-on experience were given. After the lecture, teacher explained the correct steps of operating the AR toolkit. Each group was given a learning worksheet on which problem-solving questions were presented. With the assistance of on-site tutor, each group started operating the AR toolkit and tried to solve the problems and answered the questions on the worksheet. After the experiment, students needed to complete a questionnaire and a posttest. Pictures of the experimental activities are shown in Fig 3.

Fig. 2. Students operated the AR system in groups with the assistance of tutors

4.3 Instrument and Data Collection

A questionnaire of student satisfaction and a test of learning content were the instrument for collecting data. The factors examined on the questionnaire include user attitude, user satisfaction, and learning satisfaction. The questionnaire comprised 34 questions, 18 for user attitude, 8 for user satisfaction, and 8 for learning satisfaction. A reliability of Cronbach's $\alpha = .942$ was obtained. A 5-point Likert scale was applied to gather student feedback, ranging from 1 to 5, from strongly disagree to strongly agree. Sample items in the questionnaire are shown in Table 1.

Table 1. Sample items of the questionnaire

Factor	Aspect	Sample item
User attitude	Perceived usefulness	Operating this AR system can improve my learning efficiently.
	Perceived ease of use	I think operating this AR system is easy.
	Technology anxiety	Operating this AR system makes me nervous.
	Intention to use	I like the course design with the combination of this AR system.
User satisfaction	System quality	I feel satisfied with the speed of this AR system.
	Information quality	I feel satisfied that this AR system presents course contents clearly.
Learning satisfaction	Course quality	I think the whole course contents are clearly understandable.
	Environment quality	I feel satisfied with the venue.

5 Result and Discussion

5.1 Descriptive Statistics

Descriptive data of means and standard deviations of each factor are shown in Table 2.

Table 2. Descriptive Statistics

Factor	Secondary aspects	M	SD
User attitude	Perceived usefulness	4.36	0.66
	Perceived ease of use	3.98	0.85
	Technology anxiety	3.55	1.12
	Intention to use	2.49	0.86
User satisfaction	System quality	2.35	0.83
	Information quality	4.28	0.77
Learning satisfaction	Course quality	3.30	0.78
	Environment quality	3.11	0.89

The highest score of the questionnaire was the factor of perceived usefulness（M=4.43） while the lowest score was the factor of technology anxiety. However, the means of all these three factors were above 3.50. This thus indicated that students had a positive attitude toward the use of this AR toolkit.

5.2 Correlational Analyses

We used part correlation analysis to evaluate if learning gains was significantly correlated with user attitude, user satisfaction, and learning satisfaction, respectively.

The part correlation, or semi-partial correlation, is used for to correlate partialled scores on one variable with ordinary scores on another. It has the effect of reducing the correlation between the partialled variable and the variable partialled from it to zero. In our case, each category of user attitudes and overall user attitude are dependent variables (1), and learning gain is the predicting variables, in which the interaction effect of pretest performance (3) and posttest (2) should be partial out (i.e. the results of (2)-(3) would be greater for the low-pretest-score students, and smaller for the high-pretest-score students). The formula used to perform the part correlation of this study is illustrated as follow, and Table 3 lists the results of all 4 sets of the part correlation:

$$r_{1(2.3)} = \frac{r_{12} - r_{13} r_{23}}{\sqrt{1 - r_{23}^2}} \tag{1}$$

Table 3. Pearson correlation analysis of user attitude and learning achievement

		User attitude	User satisfaction	Learning satisfaction	Overall satisfaction
Learning gain	*r*	.267	.143	.166	.235
	t	2.615	1.344	1.569	2.246
	p	.011	.182	.120	.027

According to part correlation analysis, we found that the pairs of user satisfaction–learning gain, and learning satisfaction–learning gain were not significant. However, the significant results were found in the pairs of user attitude–learning gain and overall satisfaction–learning gain.

6 Conclusion

We found that students had high acceptance of employing AR toolkit in learning basic earth science. More specifically, students felt that operating the AR toolkit was not too complicated therefore students didn't feel confused or anxious. They seemed to have high interests to use AR for learning in the future. In terms of the user satisfaction, students felt satisfied with the quality of the AR toolkit as well as the information embedded. They thought that AR-facilitated instruction could improve the understanding of spatial concepts and be easier to acquire the course contents. In terms of learning achievement, students got higher scores in the posttests than they did in pretests which indicated their learning achievement improved. Thus, it was obviously helpful for students.

Moreover, user attitude and overall satisfaction were significantly correlated with learning gains. This indicated that the learning gain would be higher if students satisfied with the AR orientation. Nevertheless, the differences between individual students were not discussed in this study. For further research, we suggest that other demographic variables, such as age, gender, and learning styles that associated with the use of AR system in the classroom.

Acknowledgments. Funding of this research work is supported in part by the National Science Council of Taiwan (under research numbers NSC 100-2515-S-003 -008 – and NSC 101-2515-S-003 -008 -) and Department of Graphic Arts and Communications, National Taiwan Normal University. We also thank the logistic supports from Mr. Xin-xing Lai from Tu-Cheng Junior High School, and Miss Yu-shi Li and her colleagues from Yu-ying Elementary School in New Taipei City of Taiwan.

References

1. Lee, S.H., Choi, J., Park, J.-I.: Interactive E-Learning System Using Pattern Recognition and Augmented Reality. IEEE Transactions on Consumer Electronics 55(2), 883–890 (2009)
2. Hatziapostolou, T., Paraskakis, I.: Enhancing the Impact of Formative Feedback on Student Learning Through an Online Feedback System. EJEL 8(2), 111–122 (2010)
3. Ali Karime, A., Hossain, M.A., Rahman, A.S.M.M., Gueaieb, W., Alja'am, J.M., El Saddik, A.: RFID-based interactive multimedia system for the children. Multimed Tools Appl. 59, 749–774 (2012), doi:10.1007/s11042-011-0768-3
4. Hrastinski, S.: A theory of online learning as online participation. Computers & Education 52(1), 78–82 (2009), doi:10.1016/j.compedu.2008.06.009
5. Chehimi, F., Coulton, P., Edwards, R.: Augmented Reality 3D Interactive Advertisements on Smartphones, vol. 6, p. 21. IEEE Computer Society (2007)
6. Balog, A., Pribeanu, C., Iordache, D.: Augmented Reality in Schools: Preliminary Evaluation Results from a Summer School. In: WASET International Conference on Technology and Education, ICTE 2007, vol. 24, pp. 114–117 (2007)
7. Larsen, Y.C., Buchholz, H., Brosda, C., Bogner, F.X.: Evaluation of a portable and interactive augmented reality learning system by teachers and students. In: Augmented Reality in Education 2011, pp. 47–56 (2011)
8. Kaufmann, H., Schmalstieg, D.: Mathematics and Geometry education with collaborative augmented reality. Computers & Graphics 27, 339–345 (2003)
9. Azuma, R., Baillot, Y., Behringer, R., Feiner, S., Julier, S., MacIntyre, B.: Recent advances in augmented reality. Computers & Graphics 21(6), 1–15 (2001)
10. Zhou, F., Duh, H.-L., Billinghurst, M.: Trends in augmented reality traching, interaction and display: A review of ten years in ISMAR. In: 7th IEE/ACM International Symposium on Mixed and Augmented Reality, ISMAR, pp. 193–202. IEEE, Cambridge (2008)
11. Höllerer, T.H., Feiner, S.K.: Mobile Augmented Reality. In: Karimi, H.A., Hammad, A. (eds.) Telegeoinformatics: Location-Based Computing and Services, pp. 392–421. CRC Press (2004)
12. Yuen, S., Yaoyuneyong, G., Johnson, E.: Augmented reality: An overview and five directions for AR in education. JETDE 4(1), 119–140 (2011)
13. Billinghurst, M.: Augmented Reality in Education. New Horizons for Learning (2002), `http://www.it.civil.aau.dk/it/education/reports/ar_edu.pdf`

14. Davis, F.D.: Perceived usefulness, perceived ease of use, and user acceptance of information technology. MIS Quarterly 13(3), 319–340 (1989)
15. Yusoff, R.C.M., Zaman, H.B., Ahmad, A.: Evalustion of user acceptance of mixed reality technology. Australasian Journal of Educational Technology 27(8), 1369–1387 (2011)
16. DeLone, W.H., McLean, E.R.: The DeLone and McLean model of information systems success: A ten-year update. JMIS 19(4), 9–30 (2003)
17. Fujita-Starck, P.J., Thompson, J.A.: The Effects of Motivation and Classroom Environment on the Satisfaction of Noncredit Continuing Education Students. In: The Annual Forum of the Association for Institutional Research, University of Hawaii, New Orleans, LA, vol. 26 (1994)

Anytime. Everywhere. Mobile Learning in Higher Education: Creating a GIS Course

Alptekin Erkollar[1,*] and Birgit J. Oberer[2]

[1] Halic University, Istanbul, Turkey
erkollar@etcop.com
[2] Kadir Has University, Cibali, Istanbul, Turkey
birgit.oberer@khas.edu.tr

Abstract. The course concepts introduced in this contribution were implemented in 2011 in a university in Turkey and show an approach for integrating mobile learning modules in higher education. The results of the course show the advantages as well as potential for improvement of the system and the use of it in higher education.

Keywords: mobile learning, European Union.

1 Introduction

Social media are popular for education, not least because the young adults who attend courses at university are familiar with these systems and most of them use it frequently. Social media have been integrated into the daily practices of many users, and supported by different websites, tools, and networks. Implementing mobile services in education as mobile learning modules is an innovative process at many levels of universities. E-learning developers and course instructors have to be aware of the changing user preferences, technological issues, and the new tools available in order to be able to determine how to benefit from them [1, 2, 3, 12].

2 Mobile Learning

The term 'mobile' refers to the possibility of taking place in multiple locations, across multiple times, and accessing content with equipment, such as smart phones or tablets [4, 5, 6, 7].

The field of wireless technologies is developing exceedingly fast. Most of the developments contribute to the greater feasibility of mobile learning and to the richness of the courseware that can be developed for mobile learning. All of this has greatly facilitated the development of mobile learning and contributed to the richness and complexity of courseware on mobile devices [3].

---

* Corresponding author.

T.-h. Kim et al. (Eds.): EL/DTA/UNESST 2012, CCIS 352, pp. 31–37, 2012.

Mobile learning can be used to enhance the overall learning experience for students and teachers [6, 8, 9, 10, 11].

The fields of wireless technologies and of mobile telephony are moving ahead with amazing speed. Today, the industry of providing news feeds and sports feeds to mobile phones is commonplace in most countries of the world. The techniques of sending these feeds to mobile devices can be used to provide mobile learning. It is crucial that education and training are not left behind by these developments [3]

3 Case Study: Integrating Mobile Learning Modules in Course Design

3.1 Course Requirements

The designed course is intended for bachelor students from different faculties, such as natural sciences, engineering, social sciences, and law. To be able to attend the 'Geographic Information Systems (GIS)' course there are no perquisites, and it is not mandatory to attend introduction courses, such as 'Introduction to Information Systems (IS)' or 'Management Information Systems (MIS)'. In the last two semesters, the course was given as a lecture with only few assignments that the students had to work on, and no student projects. The student performance was sufficient (more than 80% of all students attending the course had a BB or higher grade). Nevertheless, the performance for the 'Geographic Marketing' course, GIS is a perquisites, was significantly insufficient. Students had a basic knowledge about GIS topics when attending the 'Geographic Marketing' course, but they had no idea at all as to how to apply the knowledge generated.

To overcome the difficulties with the non-project related design of the GIS course, the instructor decided to integrate mobile learning modules in education in a pilot course in the spring term of 2011.

3.2 Course Content

The main focus of the course is placed on showing students the basics of geographic information systems (14 weeks at 3 hours). The main course topics are geographic information systems, global positioning systems, geodata, and location based services (see table 1).

Before integrating mobile modules, the course design focused on lecture, offline assignments, and readings as teaching methods.

Table 1. Course content and teaching methods (before and after the integration of mobile learning modules)

BEFORE mobile learning module integration		
Week	**Content**	**Teaching method**
1-2	GIS principles	lecture
3-4	GIS techniques	lecture
5	GIS analysis	Lecture, assignments
6-8	Managing GIS	lecture, reading
9-10	Global positioning systems	lecture
11-14	Selected topics	lecture
AFTER mobile learning module (MLM) integration		
Week	**Content**	**Teaching method**
1	Introduction	lecture
2-3	GIS principles: Representing geographic data Geo-referencing	Lecture, MLM
4-7	GIS techniques: Geographic data modeling GIS data collection Geographic databases Geo-web GIS Software	Lecture, MLM
6-9	GIS analysis: Map design Geo-visualization	Lecture, MLM, student project
10	GIS management. Managing GIS	Lecture, MLM
11-12	Applications	Field analysis, MLM
13	Geomarketing: introduction	Lecture, MLM
14	Selected topics	

With the integration of mobile learning modules (MLM), the teaching methods primarily used a focus on lectures and MLM, supported by MLM based field analysis and student projects.

For mobile learning modules (MLM), mobile devices, such as tablets or smart phones, are used to reach the learning goals that were defined.

In the GIS course that was designed, students were given a tablet for the whole course to work on their mobile learning modules: this includes working on their individual assignments as well as on their group projects.

A sample group project of the students, who had to work using mobile devices to support their work, is shown in table 2.

Table 2. Student project including MLM

Student project: GIS data collection & cartography and map production

PART	MAIN QUESTION?	WHAT TO DO?
Part 1	How can GIS data be COLLECTED?	Analyze primary and secondary sources
Part 2	What are the principles of MAP DESIGN?	Find out purpose, available data, map scale, …
Part 3	What are typical MAP COMPOSITION LAYOUTS?	Analyze body, title, scale, ..
Part 4	What is MAP SYMBOLIZATION?	
Part 5	What are MAP SERIES?	

(!) MLM:

Use your tablet and find sample applications and evaluate them.

Use your tablet and prepare a sample base map (choose the design and layout)

Include symbolization and map series

Use your tablet for sharing your designed map with your instructor and the other groups in your course.

For the regular course stream, the mobile learning modules were mainly used for working on the following topics: representing geographic data and geo-referencing, geographic data collection, geographic databases and GIS software and managing GIS. For the student projects, tablets were used to encourage students to actively participate with the MLM, such as for searching readings on the general student project topic; for communicating with other group members and for preparing project presentations and documentation. Figure 1 shows sample presentations and reports prepared by students on their tablets.

For the effective searching of project related literature and sources, students obtained a basic introduction on scientific work, literature research, and Internet technologies. For communicating with each other in the group, students used Google+ as a communication tool. At the beginning of the course, Google+ was introduced to students and they started a learning by doing process on how to use Google+ effectively for their project management.

Google+ has the potential to improve students' collaboration through circles, conduct research for projects with sparks, improve the student-instructor relationship by using this kind of social media to get in touch with each other, and support blended learning with the hangout functionality.

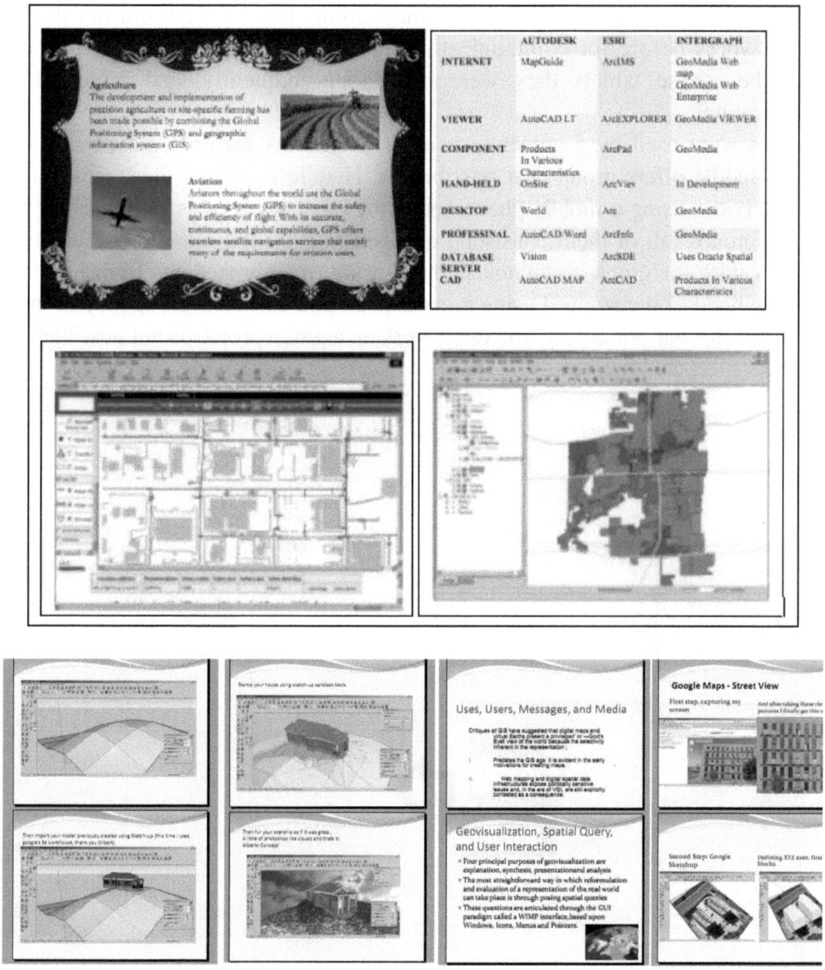

Fig. 1. Students' presentations & reports

3.3 Research Results

The instructor created and frequently used a GIS circle on Google+ for communicating with all the students, and sub circles for all the student groups working on projects; Hangouts were used for the online office hours of the instructor, explaining assignments, talking about projects, group work or communicating with students completing their projects, facing problems, or needing some kind of support.

The instructor used sparks, which is a customized way of searching and sharing that follows an interest-based approach, to share results with the GIS circle or any sub circle or selected students.

An evaluation at the end of the course, where questionnaires were used, showed that 97% of all the students worked with their tablets on social media networks, mainly Google+, for group internal communication, 40% of them did not use social media networks before for communicating on course related issues, mainly because without the course tablets they were not online frequently, and preferred email communication.

Huddles were used by 5 students groups (14 students each); 2 groups did not use huddles. Huddle offers group chat possibilities. Huddle is part of the 'mobile' feature, offering services using a mobile phone, including other services as well, such as instant upload. 3 groups (all of them consisting of business students) found it useful using the Huddles feature for group communication. 1 group (mainly students from law faculty) tried to use huddles but stopped using it in the main phase of their group project 'because with this group, chat possibility structured work on a group project is not possible'.

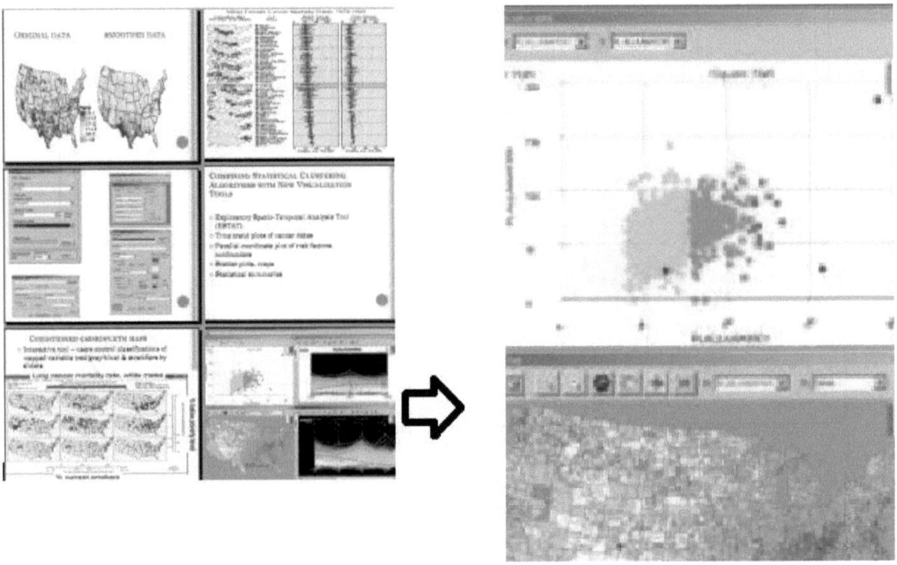

Fig. 2. Student projects. GIS systems, students worked on their tablets

All students attending the GIS course used hangouts as an instant videoconferencing tool with their GIS circles, or selected contacts in circles. Hangouts offer video conferencing with multiple users; small groups can interact on video. 54% of all students will use hangouts for upcoming courses as well. 8% already used hangouts for the courses they attended in spring term 2011 as well.

In comparison to the course results from previous years, students worked interactively, worked on different GIS systems online and tried to apply them in their projects (some visualization examples are given in figure 1 and figure 2).

4 Conclusions

Almost any mobile service can be adopted for educational issues. It needs some flexibility mainly from the instructors to use mobile learning modules in education and to motivate students to use these modules, while not focusing on the restrictions, limitations, and additional workload but rather on the benefits that these components could offer for use in education.

References

1. Erkollar, A., Oberer, B.: Trends in Social Media Application: The Potential of Google+ for Education Shown in the Example of a Bachelor's Degree Course on Marketing. In: Kim, T.-H., Adeli, H., Kim, H.-K., Kang, H.-J., Kim, K.J., Kiumi, A., Kang, B.-H. (eds.) ASEA 2011. CCIS, vol. 257, pp. 569–578. Springer, Heidelberg (2011)
2. Kurkela, L.J.: Systemic Approach to Learning Paradigms and the Use of Social Media in Higher Education. IJET 6, 14–20 (2011)
3. Keegan, D., Dismihok, G., Mileva, N., Rekkedal, T.: The role of mobile learning in European education. Work Package 4, 227828-CP-1-2006-1-IE-MINERVA-M, European Commission (2006)
4. Shafique, F., Anwar, M., Bushra, M.: Exploitation of social media among university students: a case study. Webology 7(2), article 79 (2010), `http://www.webology.org/2010/v7n2/a79.html`
5. Rao, N.M., Sasidhar, C., Kumar, V.S.: Cloud Computing Through Mobile Learning. International Journal of Advanced Computer Science and Applications 1(6), 42–43 (2010)
6. Hylen, J.: United Nations Educational, Scientific and Cultural Organization (UNESCO), Turning on Mobile Learning in Europe. Illustrative Initiatives and Policy Implications. UNESCO Working Paper Series on Mobile Learning, France (2012)
7. Dykes, G., Knight, H.: United Nations Educational, Scientific and Cultural Organization, UNESCO (2012), Mobile Learning for Teachers in Europe. Exploring the Potential of Mobile Technologies to Support Teachers and Improve Practices, UNESCO Working Paper Series on Mobile Learning, France
8. Kukulska-Hulme, A., Sharples, M., Milrad, M., Arnedillo-Sanchez, I., Vavoula, G.: Innovation in Mobile Learning: A European Perspective. International Journal of Mobile and Blended Learning 1(1), 13–35 (2009)
9. Pachler, N.: Mobile Learning towards a research agenda. WLE Centre, Institute of Education, occasional papers in work-based learning 1, UK (2007)
10. Sarrab, M., Elgamel, L., Aldabbas, H.: Mobile Learning (M-Learning) and Educational Environments. International Journal of Distributed and Parallel Systems 3(4), 31–38 (2012)
11. Sorensen, A.: Social Media and personal blogging: Textures, routes and patterns. MedieKultur: Journal of Media and Communication Research 25(47), 66–78 (2009)
12. Asabere, N.Y., Enguah, S.E.: Integration of Expert Systems in Mobile Learning. International Journal of Information and Communication Technology Research 2(1), 55–61 (2012)

Wireless and Configurationless iClassroom System with Remote Database via Bonjour

Mohamed Ariff Ameedeen and Zafril Rizal M. Azmi

Universiti Malaysia Pahang, LebuhrayaTun Razak, 26300 Gambang, Kuantan, Pahang, Malaysia
{mohamedariff,zafril}@ump.edu.my

Abstract. Wireless communication protocols are fast replacing wired communication methods in the world nowadays, especially with the ever-growing popularity of mobile devices. One such wireless communication protocol that has a unique characteristic of not requiring any sort of configuration is Bonjour, an Apple proprietary zero-configuration protocol that are currently used in Apple manufactured devices such as the Apple MacBook, iPads and iPhones. This paper aims to utilize this unique wireless communication protocol in an intelligent classroom environment (iClassroom) where the teachers and students communicate wirelessly using their mobile devices through the iClassroom system that requires no configuration.

Keywords: Wireless, Bonjour, Intelligent Classroom, Remote Database.

1 Introduction

Wireless communication protocols have been the focus of plenty of researches in the past decade, be it the IEEE 802.11 wireless protocol [1], the infrared protocol [2], RFID [3] protocol as well as the Bluetooth [4] protocol. Each of these protocols shares a common limitation; they all require some amount of configuration before they could be implemented or even accessed.

The emergence of Bonjour [5, 6], a wireless networking protocol developed by Apple, provides a new zero-configuration network protocol allowing devices to automatically discover each other without the need to enter IP addresses or configure DNS servers. Bonjour also allows automatic assignment of IP addresses without the use of a DHCP server. In short, Bonjour is highly expected to be the future of wireless networking, pushing more established technologies to the sideline.

Intelligent classrooms or iClassrooms are also a major trend in the researchers community nowadays [7-10]. However, to the extent of the authors' knowledge, a vast majority to all of the proposed iClassroom solutions requires a certain amount of technical know-how and configuration to be applied before the iClassroom could be implemented.

The purpose of this research is to apply the Bonjour protocol together with a remote database to create an iClassroom environment that requires no wires and no configurations that could be implemented with minimal to zero know-how on the part of the users.

T.-h. Kim et al. (Eds.): EL/DTA/UNESST 2012, CCIS 352, pp. 38–43, 2012.

This paper begins with providing the preliminary information in the Foundation section followed by the body of the research in the third section. Finally, a brief discussion and conclusion to the paper is provided in the fourth section.

2 Foundation

In this chapter, preliminary information regarding the technologies and the equipment used to undertake this research is introduced in order for the readers to easily understand the contents of this paper.

2.1 Bonjour

Bonjour is a zero-configuration (or *zeroconf*) [11] protocol proprietary to Apple products and comes shipped as a default in Apple's personal computer operating system OS X as well as Apple's mobile operating system iOS. This protocol is most commonly used in everyday applications such as printer discovery, file sharing, music players, web browsers and other day-to-day applications. A simple example of the capabilities of Bonjour is when a Bonjour enabled personal computer intends to print a document; all Bonjour enabled printers around the computer would be automatically detected and configured. The user only needs to press print and the document will be printed on the printer of the user's choice. Another example of the capabilities of Bonjour is the *AirPlay* technology from Apple where any display from Apple devices (MacBooks, iPhones or iPads) could be mirrored in real-time to an *AppleTV* device without any wires. Although prominently used in daily routines, Bonjour commonly works behind the scenes as it creates a local area network connection independently without any input from the user.

Due to the purpose of this paper – utilizing the Bonjour protocol rather than dissecting it, only a brief introduction to Bonjour is provided. For a more comprehensive information on Bonjour, please refer to [5, 6].

2.2 Equipment and Peripheral Devices

For the purpose of this research, the equipment and peripheral devices used are selected in order to allow a seamless integration between one another and allow unobstructed communication through the Bonjour zero-configuration protocol. The devices used are as follows:

Apple Macbook Air. The Apple Macbook Air is used as a central computer and controller for the teacher to access the iClassroom system. This central computer will then be the focal point-of-access for all the iPads. The Macbook Air will also be a sole point of communication to the remote database in the Apple TimeCapsule.

Apple iPad. The Apple iPad serves as the interactive tablet device used by the students to access the iClassroom system. The iPads will be standalone for most parts, where all the offline contents can be viewed and accessed at any times. However, in order to access the online contents, the students will have to be in proximity of the teachers MacBook Air, to unlock the online functions. The iPads will also not be able to access directly to the remote database.

Apple Time Capsule. The Apple Time Capsule device serves as the location for the remote database used by the iClassroom system. The database is only accessible by the teacher's MacBook Air. The reason for having the database as a separate entity and not in the MacBook Air itself is so that multiple MacBook Airs may connect to a single TimeCapsule device should there be more than one classroom.

3 Bonjour-ed iClassroom

The Wireless and Configurationless iClassroom System with Remote Database via Bonjour or here forth referred to as *Bonjour-ed* is targeted for any level of classroom environment be it in a primary education environment up to tertiary education environment. This is because of its unique zero-configuration environment that allows users of limited technological backgrounds to operate with absolute ease.

For each classroom environment, it is assumed that there would be one instructor with numerous students. As such, the instructor would be in control of the central notebook computer (or in this case, the Apple Macbook Air) while each student will be in charge of a tablet computer (or in this case, an Apple iPad).

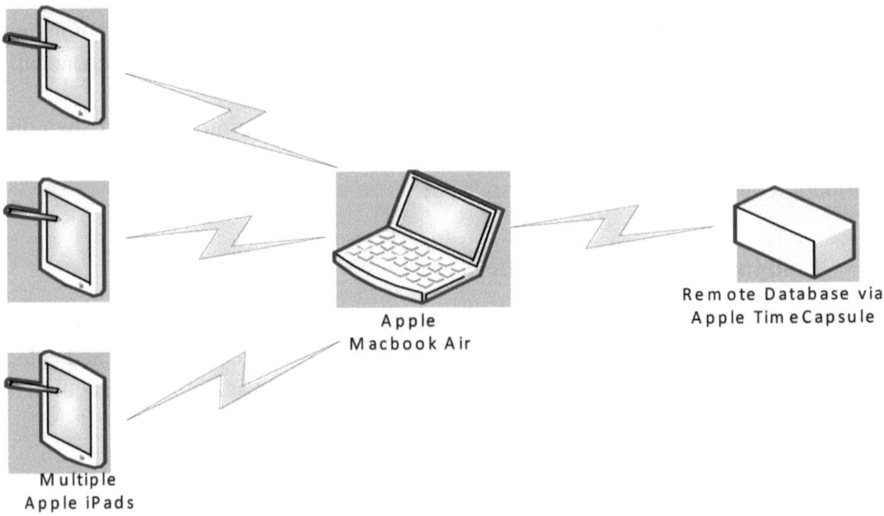

Fig. 1. An overview of the Bonjour-ed iClassroom system

Each classroom should also feature an external storage device capable of the Bonjour protocol for storing the remote database (in this case, the Apple Time Capsule). Figure 1 shows a depiction of this scenario with three tablet computers connecting with the notebook computer wirelessly, while the notebook computer accesses the remote database in the external storage wirelessly as well. The three tablet computers used in Figure 1 serves only as an example of how the connection is made, not as a limitation to how many simultaneous connections can be made between the tablet computers and notebook computer.

Bonjour-ed works typically by just activating the application on the tablet computers and the notebook computer. The Bonjour-ed application on the notebook then automatically discovers the tablet computers around it that have been installed with Bonjour-ed, and establishes a connection – all without the need for any configuration. After the connection has been made, the instructors may communicate with the students through the various modules that exist in the Bonjour-ed system. There are five initial modules that exist in the Bonjour-ed system, some *online* (requires connection between the tablet computers and notebook computer) and some *offline* (does not require any connection and may operate ad-hoc). Each of the modules would also take advantage of touch-screen input from the tablet computers as the interface. The modules are further explains in the forthcoming sections.

3.1 iTextbook

The iTextbook module in Bonjour-ed is the primary module that operates *offline*. This module is typically located on the tablet computers and allows the students to read and understand the material as they would with a conventional textbook. The responsibility of the instructor in this module is non-existent as the students will be working independently similarly to a normal textbook.

3.2 iExercise

The iExercise module is similar to the iTextbook module where it is available *offline* and the students could work at their own pace on the exercises that exist in the module. The instructor's responsibility is minimal and they may be involved as much as they want to be. The students will work on the exercises, and the instructor may access the completed exercises wirelessly whenever the Bonjour connection is established.

3.3 iAssignment

iAssignment is an *online* module where the instructor sends out assignments either individually or broadcasted to groups of students wirelessly after a connection has been established. The module also allows the submission of the assignments once it has been completed where the notebook computer will accept incoming connection from the tablet computers, wirelessly accept the submission of all the assignments, archives it it, and store it in the remote database.

3.4 iExamination

The iExamination module is a completely *online* module that requires active connection to be established before it is launched. In this module, the instructor would have to prepare the examination questions, and release the questions wirelessly to the students. The students have to be within certain proximity of the lecturer's notebook computer to be able to access the module – so that they could be monitored by the instructor. The iExamination module also freezes all other modules when it is active, so that the students would not be able to refer to their iTextbooks while the examination is in progress. When the examination is completed, the exam scripts would be automatically checked and the marks, together with the students' individual answer scripts will be sent to the remote database via the instructor's notebook.

3.5 iReminder

Finally, the iReminder module serves as a virtual to-do list that could be set by the instructor for each individual student. For example, if Student A is weak in Chapter 2 of the subject while Student B is weak in Chapter 4, the instructor could customize their iReminder modules to remind Student A to study Chapter 2 and Student B to study Chapter 4. The students would not be able to set any reminders for themselves, but they would be able to mark any items as done (this function may be disabled by the instructor if needed). The instructor may also set reminders such as deadlines for assignments, or dates for examinations in this module.

4 Discussion and Conclusion

Bonjour-ed is currently in the final stages of implementation and rigorous in-house testing before it could be implemented in a real-life classroom. The real-life implementation is planned in two stages; Stage 1 where a case study in a university classroom is conducted to test the acceptance of the iClassroom system and Stage 2 where an entire classroom of a primary school (children aged between 10 and 11) is adopted to conduct a year-long test implementation.

The test implementation in Stage 1 would provide valuable feedback regarding the interface of the system as well as the durability of the system. A test scenario involving university students will undoubtedly allow each module of Bonjour-ed to be tested to the maximum of its capabilities, and this would be very valuable for us to address any supposed vulnerabilities that is contained in the system.

Stage 2 will offer a real-life situation that is closer to the intended users of this system. The main selling-point of Bonjour-ed referred in this paper is the ease-of-use, where minimum to zero knowledge of the underlying technologies used in this system is required for the operation. Teachers and students should be able to interact wirelessly using the Bonjour-ed iClassroom with absolute ease as it requires no configuration of any kind. This will prove to be the stern test that the system needs before it could be released as a fully functional iClassroom system.

One apparent limitation that may seem obvious in this paper is the requirement of this system to use only Apple manufactured devices. This is because Bonjour, the zero-configuration communication protocol used as the backbone of this system, is an Apple proprietary protocol. However, a future plan for this system is to extend it to be available on other platforms i.e. Windows and Android. This tentatively could be achieved using the native *zeroconf* technology [11] that Bonjour is based on.

References

1. Cali, F., Conti, M., Gregori, E.: IEEE 802.11 wireless LAN: capacity analysis and protocol enhancement. In: Proceedings of Seventeenth Annual Joint Conference of the IEEE Computer and Communications Societies (1998)
2. Adams, N., et al.: An infrared network for mobile computers. In: Mobile & Location-Independent Computing Symposium (1993)
3. Gao, X., Gao, Y.: TDMA Grouping Based RFID Network Planning Using Hybrid Differential Evolution Algorithm. In: Wang, F.L., Deng, H., Gao, Y., Lei, J. (eds.) AICI 2010, Part II. LNCS, vol. 6320, pp. 106–113. Springer, Heidelberg (2010)
4. Harte, L.: Introduction to Bluetooth. Althos (2009)
5. Apple, Bonjour Overview (Networking, Internet, & Web: Services & Discovery) Apple (2006)
6. Lee, W.-M.: Beginning Ipad Application Development. Wrox Press Ltd., Birmingham (2010)
7. Winer, L.R., Cooperstock, J.: The Intelligent Classroom: changing teaching and learning with an evolving technological environment. Computers & Education (2002)
8. Franklin, D., Hammond, K.: The intelligent classroom: providing competent assistance. In: Proceedings of the Fifth International Conference on Autonomous Agents. ACM, Montreal (2001)
9. Ferreira, M.: Intelligent classrooms and smart software: Teaching and learning in today's university. Education and Information Technologies 17(1), 3–25
10. Xie, W., Shi, Y., Xu, G., Xie, D.: Smart Classroom - An Intelligent Environment for Tele-education. In: Shum, H.-Y., Liao, M., Chang, S.-F. (eds.) PCM 2001. LNCS, vol. 2195, pp. 662–668. Springer, Heidelberg (2001)
11. Jae Woo, L., et al.: z2z: Discovering Zeroconf Services Beyond Local Link. In: 2007 IEEE Globecom Workshops (2007)

KOST: Korean Semantic Tagger ver. 1.0

Hye-Jeong Song[1,3], Chan-Young Park[1,3], Jung-Kuk Lee[2,3], Dae-Yong Han[2], Han-Gil Choi[4], Jong-Dae Kim[1,3], and Yu-Seop Kim[1,3,*]

[1] Dept. of Ubiquitous Computing, Hallym University, 1 Hallymdaehak-gil, Chuncheon, Gangwon-do, 200-702 Korea
{cypark,kimjd,hjsong,yskim01}@hallym.ac.kr
[2] Dept. of Computer Engineering, Hallym University, 1 Hallymdaehak-gil, Chuncheon, Gangwon-do, 200-702 Korea
percussive@gmail.com, handae01@naver.com
[3] Bio-IT Research Center, Hallym University, 1 Hallymdaehak-gil, Chuncheon, Gangwon-do, 200-702 Korea
[4] Dept. of Ubiquitous Game Engineering, Hallym University, 1 Hallymdaehak-gil, Chuncheon, Gangwon-do, 200-702 Korea
gksrlf0820@hallym.ac.kr

Abstract. Despite that the semantic annotated corpus data is necessary in semantic role labeling of natural language processing, the data set is not quite enough in Korean language. Semantic role labeling is to tag a semantic role on the given sentential constituent. This paper proposes a S/W tool, named as KOST (KOrean Semantic Tagger), to help the construction of the Korean semantic annotated corpus data including both Korean Proposition Bank (PropBank) and Sejong semantic annotated corpus. Human annotators can give a proper semantic tag easily to the given argument phrase with help of KOST. KOST shows a syntactic tagged sentence and highlights its predicate words. KOST also shows a frame structure of the given predicate word. With the given frame structure, human taggers can find the proper tag very easily. A Korean syntactic annotated corpus made by Korean Electronics and Telecommunications Research Institute (ETRI) is used for the target syntactic tagged corpus of semantic annotation.

Keywords: Korean PropBank, Semantic Role Labeling, Semantic Tagged Corpus, Sejong Semantic Annotated Corpus.

1 Introduction

Semantic role labeling [1] is one of the critical elements in semantic analysis of the natural language processing. Given a sentence, the task consists of analyzing the propositions expressed by some target verbs of the sentence. In particular, for each target verb all the constituents in the sentence which fill a semantic role of the verb have to be recognized. Typical semantic arguments include Agent, Patient, Instrument etc. [2] However, research on the semantic role labeling for Korean language is not as

* Corresponding author.

T.-h. Kim et al. (Eds.): EL/DTA/UNESST 2012, CCIS 352, pp. 44–49, 2012.

active as other languages since Korean language does not have a large amount of semantic annotated corpus. The most commonly used semantic analysis corpus is the Proposition Bank (PropBank)[3]. University of Pennsylvania built the Korean PropBank [4]. However, this corpus is insufficient to be utilized effectively, due to its small size and to the fact that it does not fit the Korean language analysis since its tag system is based on the Penn Treebank of English. This paper intends to realize an annotation tool in order to construct a Korean version of the PropBank and also Sejong semantically annotated corpus. Sejong corpus has its own tag system adjusted for the Korean language.

KOST, KOrean Semantic Tagger, is a S/W tool to help human annotators to map a semantic role to a given sentential constituent. KOST firstly shows a whole sentence and its syntactic structure showing its dependency relation between predicate and argument words[5]. KOST highlights the predicate words and human annotators than decide a proper semantic role of an argument phrase of the highlighted predicate. For the convenient annotation, KOST retrieves the predicate's case frame structure defined in Korean PropBank frame files and concurrently the structure defined in Sejong predicate case frame dictionary[6]. If an annotator cannot find the matched case frame in dictionaries, then he/she can refer example sentences explained in the dictionaries.

2 Related Study

Most of the researches related to semantic role labeling attempts to find semantic roles of arguments of given predicate. [1, 7. 8] PropBank consists of two main linguistic components. One is a verb dictionary including case frame structure of each verb. And the other is a corpus data having semantic role information mapped into the syntactic annotated corpus.

Korean semantic role labeling researches have tried to find an appropriated semantic role of the given argument phrase, mainly focused on an adverbial phrase. [9, 10] Due to the lack of available semantic annotated corpus data, the researches could not go further.

Cornerstone and Jubilee are PropBank annotation tool [11]. Cornerstone is an XML editor that enables the annotator to create and edit the frame file, and Jubilee is a tool for the annotation task that displays several grammar and semantic information at once. The two tools are successfully utilized in various PropBank projects.

This paper realizes KOST, a tool similar to Jubilee, that can display a series of information and execute the annotation task simultaneously, enabling the annotator to construct the Korean PropBank and Sejong semantic annotated corpus concurrently.

3 Structure of KOST

The main role of KOST is to construct a Korean PropBank and Sejong semantic annotated corpus. (Fig. 1) KOST shows a sentence and its dependency structure. It also highlights predicate word in the sentence and annotators should give a proper semantic role to the argument word directly dependent to the predicate. It also enables a convenient search of the PropBank frame files and the Sejong case frame dictionary without the need to directly open the XML-formatted dictionary files.

In Fig. 1, the top most window shows a raw sentence and a big window of left side shows dependency structure of the raw sentence. KOST highlights a predicate with yellow color. The right side shows the retrieved results from Korean PropBank frame files and Sejong dictionary with the predicate as a query. The upper one is from PropBank frame files and the lower one is from Sejong dictionary.

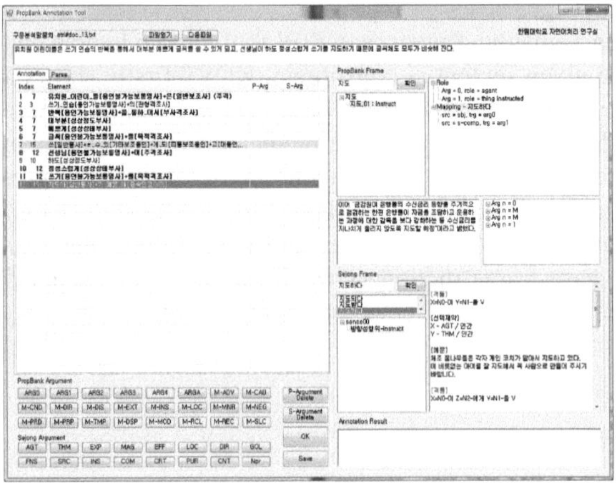

Fig. 1. KOST main view

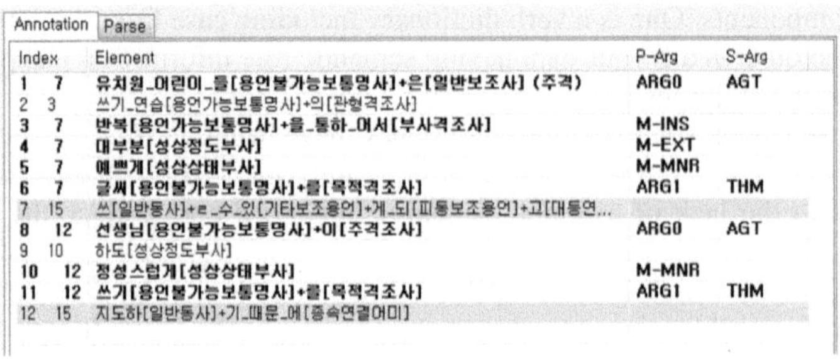

Fig. 2. Annotation Tab

The 'annotation' tap on the left side is a screen that can manage the annotation task (fig.2). Words in direct dependency relation with the predicate have to be given PropBank semantic role and Sejong semantic role. The words are shown in bold letters. When tagging Sejong semantic role, only the words with 'case prepositions' can be annotated.

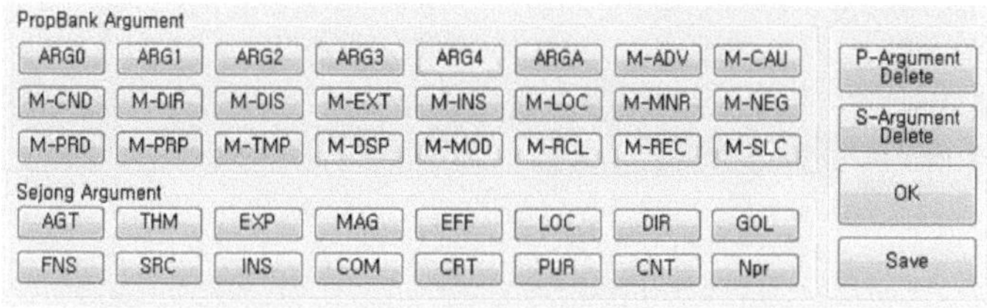

Fig. 3. PropBank and Sejong argument insert/delete button

At the bottom of the 'annotation' tap, the argument buttons of PropBank and Sejong is deployed (fig. 3). The annotation can be done by clicking one of argument buttons after selecting the word to be annotated from the Annotation tap.

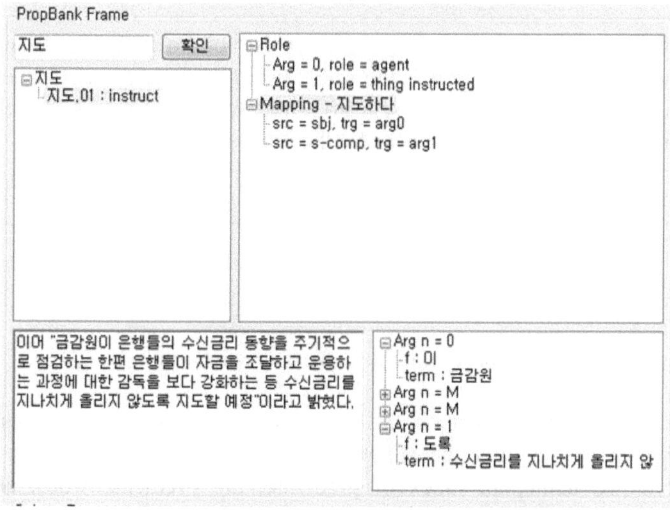

Fig. 4. Windows for PropBank frame file

At the right side of Fig. 1, the windows showing the PropBank frame file and Sejong case frame dictionary are positioned. When clicking on the verb highlighted in yellow, the tool automatically searches the PropBank frame file and Sejong case frame dictionary. The tree shown just below the search window in Fig. 4 is branches according to word senses with its English translation. When the user clicks on the desired sense, the role and mapping appears on the right window. The role explained each argument's characteristics and the mapping shows the connectivity between syntactic constituent and its semantic role. The example sentence is shown on the bottom left side, and the annotation result of the sentence is shown on the bottom right.

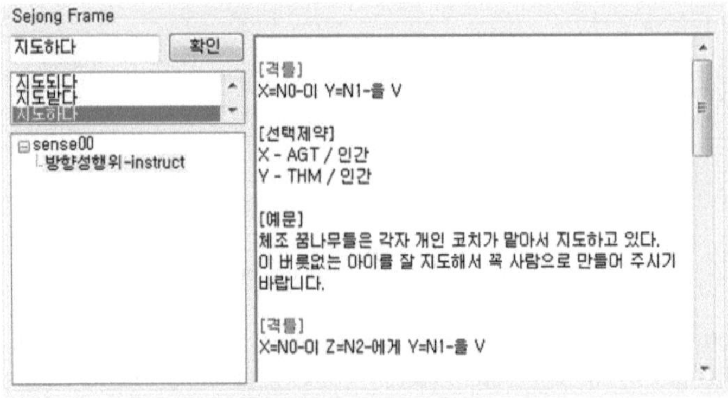

Fig. 5. Windows for Sejong case frame dictionary

The Sejong case frame dictionary is shown at the bottom of the PropBank frame file (Fig.5). Beneath the search window is the whole list of the Sejong case frame dictionary, and beneath that is the tree separated by word senses which annotators can select. On the right, case frames and example sentences for the selected sense are shown.

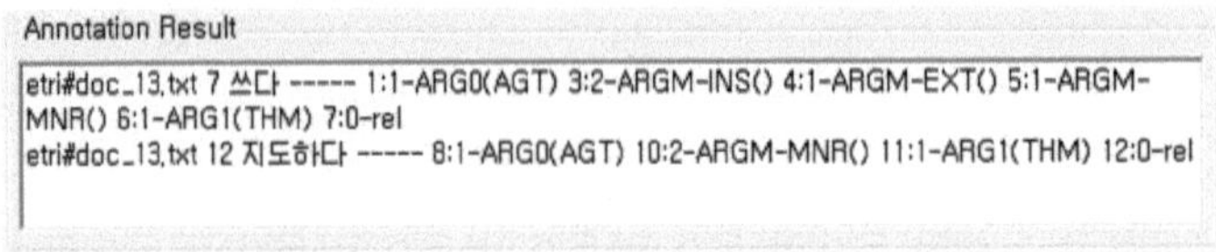

Fig. 6. A Window for the annotation results

The annotation result is shown in the Annotation Result window by pressing the ok button shown in Fig. 3 after the annotation task is completed (Fig. 6). The result consists of a file name, an index of predicate, the predicate word, an index of argument word, the number of words dependent to the argument word including the argument word itself, PropBank role, and Sejong role. The annotation result can be saved as a text file by clicking on the save button in Fig. 3.

4 Conclusion

This paper describes KOST, a tool for KOrean Semantic Tagging, that can construct a Korean semantic annotated corpus, the Korean PropBank and Sejong corpus, which are to be used for the semantic role labeling of Korean. To annotate on the syntactically annotated corpus, the dependency relation of the words is firstly analyzed. Also the tool enables the annotator to conveniently construct a corpus by aiding the search the PropBank frame file and Sejong case frame dictionary.

Automation of part of semantic annotation task is highly recommended as a further research. KOST will be able to recommend proper semantic roles to the given argument with machine learning methodology. Additionally, tools for editing frame files should be developed for making the frame files more robust.

Acknowledgments. This research was supported by Basic Science Research Program through the National Research Foundation(NRF) funded by the Ministry of Education, Science and Technology(2010-0010612).

References

1. Palmer, M., Gildea, D., Xue, N.: Semantic Role Labeling. Morgan & Claypool Publishers (2010)
2. Carreras, X., Marquez, L.: Introduction to the CoNll-2005 shared Task: Semantic Role Labeling. In: Procs. of the 9th Conference on Computational Natural Language Learning(CoNLL), pp. 152–164 (2005)
3. Palmer, M., Gildea, D., Kingsbury, P.: The Proposition Bank: An Annotated Corpus of Semantic Roles. Computational Linguistics 31(1), 71–105 (2005)
4. Linguistic Data Consortium, http://www/ldc.upenn.edu
5. Electronics and Telecommunications Research Institute, `http://www.etri.re.kr`
6. 21st Century Sejong Project, `http://www.sejong.ac.kr`
7. Xue, N., Palmer, M.: Calibrating Features for Semantic Role Labeling. In: Procs of EMNLP 2004 (2004)
8. Gildea, D., Jurafsky, D.: Automatic Labeling of Semantic Roles. Computational Linguistics 28(3), 245–288 (2002)
9. Kim, B., Lee, Y., Na, S., Kim, J., Lee, J.: Bootstrapping for Semantic Role Assignmen of Korean Case Marker. In: Procs. of Korea Computer Congress, Kangwon, Korea, pp. 4–6 (2006)
10. Kim, B., Lee, Y., Lee, J.: Unsupervised Semantic Role Labeling for Korean Abverbial Case. J. of KIISE 34(2), 95–107 (2007)
11. Choi, J.D., Bonial, C., Palmer, M.: Multilingual Propbank Annotation Tools: Cornerstone and Jubilee. In: Procs. of NAACL-HLT 2010, Los Angeles, pp. 13–16 (2010)

An Attempt on Effort-Achievement Analysis of Lecture Data for Effective Teaching

Toshiro Minami[1,2] and Yoko Ohura[3]

[1] Kyushu Institute of Information Sciences, 6-3-1 Saifu, Dazaifu, Fukuoka 818-0117 Japan
minami@kiis.ac.jp
[2] Kyushu University Library,
minami@lib.kyushu-u.ac.jp
[3] Kyushu Institute of Information Sciences,
ohura@kiis.ac.jp

Abstract. The eventual goal of the study in this paper is to find inspiring tips for effective teaching by analyzing lecture data. As a case study, we take a course in a junior college and investigate the relations between effort and achievement of the students. We take two types of data for measuring effort of students; attendance and homework. The former one is for representing the students' "superficial" efforts and the latter for representing the students' "intentional" efforts. We take the term-end examination score for measuring the student's achievement. In this paper, we first try to find what kind of efforts the students put in terms of effort by comparing the attendance and the homework data. Then we investigate the relations between the efforts and achievement and try to find if the efforts of students really give good amount of influence to their achievements. As a result of the analysis we have found even with some amount of efforts, students learn just a little bit in achievement in terms of practically applicable skills. We need further investigation in order to give more clear influencing factor in effort-achievement analysis of lecture data.

1 Introduction

It is one of the most important issues for university professors to make their lectures more effective. Due to the popularization of university and other environmental changes, the university students have changed in their study skills, eagerness to study, way of life, and many other aspects.

In order to catch up with such changes, universities and university professors, or lecturers, have been trying to change their lecture styles as well. The FD (Faculty Development) activity has been popular already and universities give a number of opportunities to their lecturers to learn about their teaching skills, re-consider their way of teaching, discuss and exchange their thought about teaching, etc. In addition to these activities, it is now very popular in universities to ask their students to tell about the courses including their evaluations and opinions. The results of such inquiries are statistically processed and are feed-backed to the lecturers.

However such efforts are not sufficient enough for improving the effects of lectures so that the university graduates are sufficiently well-educated as a high-quality workers.

T.-h. Kim et al. (Eds.): EL/DTA/UNESST 2012, CCIS 352, pp. 50–57, 2012.

Thus it must be very profitable if the lecturers get more knowledge about the students on their learning styles, eagerness to studying, and others. The motivation underlying in the study of this paper is to invent new tools that are useful in finding some inspiring tips for more effective lectures, by analyzing objective data rather than subjective opinions, such as lecture data.

In the paper [2], the authors analyzed the relation between effort and achievement scores, where the effort score consists of the scores for daily exercises and for term-end examination. In this paper, we take a course in a junior college and investigate the relations between effort and achievement of the students as well; with more detailed analysis. We deal with two types of data for measuring effort of students, attendance and homework, separately. The former one can be considered to represent the students' "superficial" efforts and the latter one to represent the students' "motivated" efforts. We take the score of the term-end examination for measuring the students' achievement.

The papers [1] and [3] presented case studies on analysis methods of library data, especially of circulation records, which are supposed to use in every library. An aim of this paper is to demonstrate the usefulness of the new approach toward data analysis; use of lecture data instead of library data with similar but different analysis methods. This approach includes not only extracting useful tips for student education and learning process assistance but also exploring useful analysis methods through various case studies from different points of view.

We firstly try to find what kind of efforts the students put in terms of effort by comparing the attendance and the homework data. Then we investigate the relations between the efforts and achievement and try to find if the efforts of students really give good amount of influence to their achievements. As a result of the analysis we found even with some amount of efforts, students learn just a little bit in achievement in terms of practically applicable skills. In order to make clear about this issue we need further investigation in order to give more clear influencing factor in effort-achievement analysis of lecture data.

The rest of this paper is organized as follows: First of all in Section 2, we give an overall description about the data for effort-analysis and our analysis method. Then in Section 3, we start with the comparative study on two measures for efforts; one for attendant and one for homework. Then follows the analysis of the influence of the efforts upon the achievements, which are measured by the scores of the term-end examination, which is described in Section 4. And finally in Section 5, we conclude our discussions and present our possible future works.

2 Overview of the Data for Analysis

The data for analysis in this paper are the scores of term-end examination, attendance, and homework for the class of "Information Retrieval Exercise" in 2009 for a junior college. The attending students are in the year 2 students and thus those going to graduate from the junior college. The course is one of the compulsory courses for the students willing to obtain the librarian certificate. The number of students of the class is 35.

The most important aim of the course is to let the students become expert information searchers in the sense they have enough knowledge about information retrieval, or

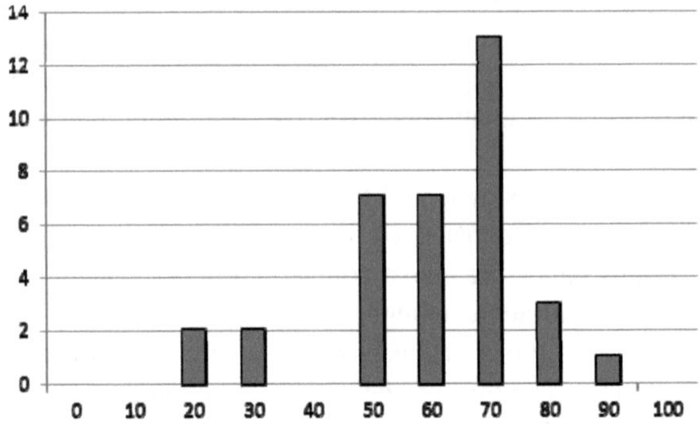

Fig. 1. Distribution of Term-end Examination Scores

search, finding, and have enough skills in finding appropriate search keywords based on the understanding of the aim and background of the retrieval.

The term-end examination consists of 3 problems/questions. The first question is on finding the Web sites of search engine and summarize their characteristic features, together with discussing appropriate and efficient methods in information retrieval. The second question is on finding the Web sites on e-books and on-line material services. The third question is to find and discuss about the information criminals in the Internet environment. The aim of these questions is to evaluate the skill on information retrieval including the planning and summarizing skills that are supposed to be learned and trained in the course. The scores of term-end examination represent the evaluation results of this aim.

The distribution of the scores for term-end examination is shown in Figure 1. The average score is 65.5. The characteristic difference of examination score in comparison with homework score lies that the former evaluates the performance in a limited time, whereas the latter evaluates the potential performance ability using much longer time-period. The peak frequency lies in the 70s, i.e. score class of B. Note that A is from 80 to 100, full mark, and B for 70-79, C for 60-69, and no units for less than 60. In this respect 11 students (31%) did not reach to the passing level. However they all had succeeded in obtaining the units of the course because in the final scores, in which the scores for attendance and homework are added.

Figure 2 shows the distributions of the attendance and homework scores. The attendance scores are calculated based on the attending counts with some modifications in the reason such as late arrival to the lecture room and others. In this case, the peak frequency lies in the 90s because most students attended fairy good. The average score is 88.1.

One reason of this good attendance might be that this course is a compulsory in obtaining the librarian certificate. Another reason might be that the attendants are all women students in a junior college; they are generally more diligent than men students and also than the four-year university students because they are more motivated in general.

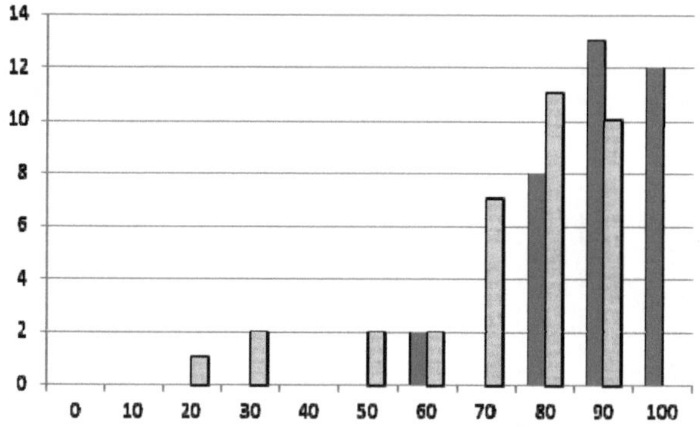

Fig. 2. Distribution of Attendance (left) and Homework (right) Scores

However two students are exception in this class. It happens often that a couple of students in a class are not diligent enough to obtain the unit and thus obtain the certificate of librarian. Mostly these couple of students once lose the unit in the first evaluation score, and the supervising professors worried so much and they try hard to contact the losing students, encourage the students to prepare for the second term-end examination, which is the final chance for the students to obtain the unit. And eventually most students are succeeded in passing the examination and in obtaining the librarian's certificates.

The right bar-graph of Figure 2 shows the distribution of the homework scores, which are calculated based on the submitted counts of homeworks together with the evaluation of their qualities. As was pointed out previously, students can spend relatively longer hours to complete the homeworks than when they solve the similar problems during examinations. The skills needed in doing homeworks and solving examinations are basically the same ones.

Thus the evaluation criteria are basically the same between the examination score and the homework score. The students who need a long time in solving problems would might take better scores for homework than those for examination, and the one who has good performance in information retrieval and summarization might have relatively better score for examination than that for homework .

3 Evaluation of Student's Effort

Our main interest in this paper is to find the relationship between the effort and the achievement of students. We take the scores for attendance and homework as the indexes for measuring the student's effort, whereas the examination score as the index for achievement.

To start with such an analysis, we compare the two kinds of effort indexes of attendance and homework. Figure 3 shows the correlation between the homework score and attendance score. The x-axis indicates the homework score and the y-axis the attendance score. Their correlation coefficient is 0.53.

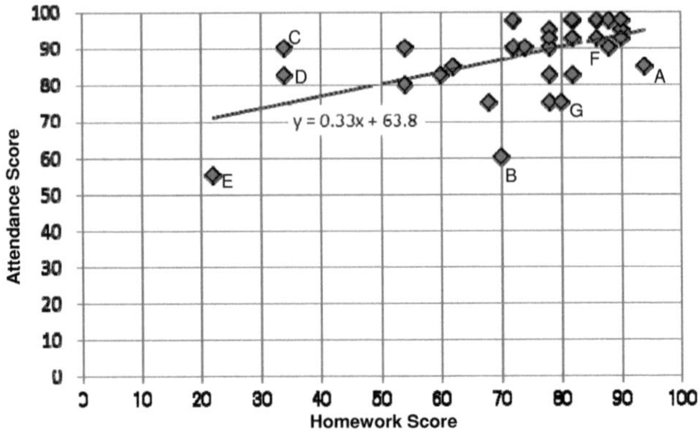

Fig. 3. Correlation between Homework Score (x-axis) and Attendance Score (y-axis)

The linear approximation to this correlation is represented as $y = 0.33x + 63.8$, which is shown in the figure. The students located in the upper part of this approximation line have lower homework score than they are supposed to have; which means they need more "real effort" in the course. On the other hand the students located in the lower part of the line are the students who do relatively more effort in doing homework. The number of students in the upper part is 23 (66%, 2 out of 3), and that in the lower part is 12 (1 out of 3).

From these data we can see that majority of students are rather attendance-oriented rather than homework-oriented, which might indicate that many students may be satisfied with just attending diligently. We would need more evidence to finally conclude this observation. However, if it is true, we, the lecturers need to put more effort in changing the students' thought so that they put more efforts in learning seriously rather than just let them look like studying in a superficial sense like just attending the classes.

As we see Figure 3, we find that most students are located in the area with 50 to 90 in homework score and 70 to 100 in attendance score. The center of this area is the same as the average values of 73.8 for the homework score and 88.1 for the attendance score.

We are interested not only in the students as a whole but also the students who are away from the central cluster. Three students marked C, D and E are located away left from the central cluster. The student E submits homework only 3 times (23%) and the student C, 5 times (38%). They seem to hate submitting homeworks. To have a look of the data of students in more detail, we have found an interesting fact. The student E has a good examination score 81, thus this student obtained the unit with total score 60 eventually. So we may conclude that this student E has potentially good ability in learning. She could get a very high total score in A rank, say 80 or more. However in some unknown reason(s) she did not, or could not, do homework diligently. This is not specifically occurred only in this class. It is not rare to find one or two students are like student E. Even though they have good potential ability to get good final scores, they will not put sufficient efforts to learning. We need more research why they are like this and how the lecturer helps them to be more diligent in learning.

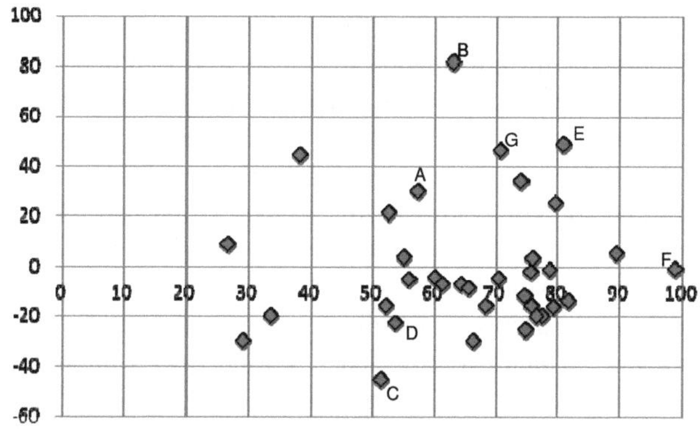

Fig. 4. Correlation between Examination (x-axis) and Effort (y-axis) Scores

On the other hand, the students A and B are those who do better performance in the homeworks in comparison with that in attendance. The student A has the best score 94 in homework, even though the attendance score is not maximum. To have a closer look at the data, she is basically a good student. She submitted all the homeworks and got the highest score. The attended 12 times out of 13, and appeared the classroom late once or twice in some reasons. Thus the attendance score is a little bit lower than the maximum.

The student B has very low score in attendance. She attended only 8 times. However she submitted the homeworks 11 times, and thus her homework score is close to the average. She submitted the homeworks more times than her attendance. This probably because the students are encouraged to submit the homeworks even when they could not attend the classes. The students are able to know the homework assignment by downloading the lecture material via Internet from the homepage of the course. The student B is diligent enough to check the homework assignments and actually did and submitted them even when she did not attend the class in some reasons.

4 Correlation Analysis between Effort and Achievement

In this section we analyze the relation between effort and achievement. First of all we would like to define an integrated measure for the student's effort. As has shown in Figure 3, a student's attendance score (y) is roughly approximated for her homework score (x) using the linear formula $y = 0.33x + 63.8$. Thus the standard homework score (x) can be estimated from the attendance score (y) by $x = (y - 63.8)/0.33$. We define the effort score of a student as the difference of the actual homework score from this standard homework score; i.e. Effort score $= x - (y - 63.8)/0.33$. This definition intends to represent how much the student put intentional effort in comparison with the standard effort.

Figure 4 shows the correlation between the term-end examination scores, i.e. achievements, and the effort scores, i.e. overall efforts. As we can see the correlation coefficients are nearly 0; to be precise, 0.06. This is a surprising fact because the students who seem to put effort in doing homeworks and others may not show good performance in the term-end examination, which is against the lecturer's intention and prediction. As has been explained in Section 1, what required in answering to the problems of the examination are the skills for information search such as making the appropriate keywords, deciding which information to use, summarizing them, and put some of their opinions, which are basically what they have done in doing the homeworks.

It is true that the limitation of time to spend for the problem is much different from doing homeworks and solving examinations. So they might feel a kind of panic when they solve the examination problems, and thus they could not do things in an ordinary style as they can do in everyday homeworks.

If this explanation is appropriate, then it means that against the lecturer's intention and hope, students just do their exercises like a routine-work without intending to learn something new and without trying to learn as much as they can. What they can obtain during the lectures and the time doing homeworks are just the knowledge and some memory of experiences of doing something without obtaining some kind of accumulated skills that might remain and help them afterword during their lifetime. As a conclusion, we have an issue to be investigated, from this finding; how can we find the practical way(s) of teaching student so that they are able to obtain the real skills that will last for a long time.

Let us check how the students marked from A to G in Figure 3 appear in Figure 4. Student A who takes the maximum homework score and thus located at the rightmost place in Figure 3 is located in a mid-upper place, where she gets the ormal examination score, or achievement even though she submitted homeworks rather diligently. Student B takes relatively high homework score in comparison with the attendance score, thus she takes the maximum effort score and is located at the topmost place in an middle area in terms of examination score. So, even though she was not a good student according to attendance, but more willing to do homeworks and gets a relatively good examinatiion score as a result. Student C and D are in a sense opposite to student B; they attend well but poor in doing homeworks. Their examination scores are not very bad, but smaller than the student B. Student E takes the maximum examinaton score and thus located at the rightmost place in Figure 4. She locates in the right-top area in Figure 3. Even if not taking the highest homework score, she is very eager in attending and doing homeworks, and as the result she takes a very good examination score. Student F also gets relatively good effort score in comparison with her attendance and achieves a good examination score like student E.

5 Concluding Remarks

In this paper we have presented a case study with the aim of obtaining some helpful tips for more effective lectures by analyzing lecture data. We take the attendance and homework scores as the indexes of students' effort and the examination score as the index of students' achievement. As a result of the analysis, we found that even though the attendance score and the homework score have some amount of correlation, but they have difference each other basically. Another finding is that the effort score and achievement score have little correlation in our case, which may indicate the students may do exercises during the lectures not for obtaining useful knowledge and skills but for just doing without intending to learn as much as they can. We have to investigate more about this issue and we have to find an effective way of teaching so that the students are able to truly learn in the lectures.

We have to keep investigating this issue in this approach toward this direction. Our future plans on this topic include, (1) to analyze in more detail in order to get more detailed and more effective results, (2) to collect other lecture data and compare the implications of various courses, and (3) to generalize the analysis methods so that they are applicable to wider lecture data.

References

1. Minami, T.: Expertise Level Estimation of Library Books by Patron-Book Heterogeneous Information Network Analysis – Concept and Applications to Library's Learning Assistant Service. In: The 8th International Symposium on Frontiers of Information Systems and Network Applications (FINA 2012), pp. 357–362 (2012), doi:19.1109/WAINA.2012.184
2. Minami, T., Ohura, Y.: Toward Learning Support for Decision Making: Utilization of Library and Lecture Data. In: Watada, J., Watanabe, T., Phillips-Wren, G., Howlett, R.J., Jain, L.C. (eds.) Intelligent Decision Technologies, Vol. 2. SIST, vol. 16, pp. 137–147. Springer, Heidelberg (2012)
3. Minami, T., Baba, K.: Investigation of Interest Range and Earnestness of Library Patrons from Circulation Records. In: Proc. International Conference on e-Services and Knowledge Management in IIAI-AAI 2012, pp. 25–29. IEEE CPS (2012), doi:10.1109/IIAI-AAI2012.15

Mobile Applications Development with Combine on MDA and SOA

Haeng-Kon Kim

School of Information Technology, Catholic University of Daegu, Korea
hangkon@cu.ac.kr

Abstract. Service Oriented Architecture and Model Driven Architecture are both considered as the frontiers of their own domain in the mobile applications world. Following components - which was the greatest step after object oriented - SOA is introduced, focusing on more integrated and automated software solutions. On the other hand – and from the designers' point of view - MDA is just initiating another evolution. MDA is considered as the next big step after UML in designing domain. Model driven architecture (MDA) is a method which can build abstract model for business logic, and generate the ultimate complete application based on the abstract model. SOA and MDA are program process representation method which can describe the behavioral process of software formally. In this paper, we give a model of mobile applications development process based on these. This model might be useful in the mobile applications development process with the semantic information from the extended MDA diagram.

Keywords: Model driven architecture (MDA), procedure blueprint, Mobile service.

1 Introduction

SOA is a paradigm that utilizes services as fundamental elements for developing mobile applications. In order to gain the full benefits of such technology, an effective approach to modeling and designing these complex distributed systems is required. In fact there is not a suitable approach to SOA-based development and little works have been done on this area and most of them are for special applications and specific domains. To exploit the benefits of SOA effectively and duly, we propose an approach that involves MDA into the context[1,2]. Service-oriented architecture (SOA) is an approach to loosely coupled, protocol independent, standards-based distributed computing where software resources available on the network are considered as Services[3]. SOA is believed to become the future enterprise technology solution that promises the agility and flexibility the business users have been looking for by leveraging the integration process through composition of the services spanning multiple enterprises. Business logic (i.e. application functionality) developers can more or less effortlessly integrate a new middleware into their system, will a widespread adoption be possible. Developers responsible for the integration of the middleware into the overall system should be able to concentrate on middleware

T.-h. Kim et al. (Eds.): EL/DTA/UNESST 2012, CCIS 352, pp. 58–71, 2012.

concerns and not have to cope with the business logic as well. The overall architecture and flow of MDA is shown as in figure 1.

In this paper, we present a model-driven approach to SOA modeling and designing for mobile applications. The paper proposes a new approach to modeling and designing service-oriented architecture for mobile applications. In this approach the PIM of the system is created and then the PSM based on SOA is generated (this PSM is a PIM for next level). Then the final PSM based on a target platform (such as mobile applications) is generated. These models are generated with transformation tools in MDA and an approach to the model driven development for e-business applications on SOA is presented. The goal of the approach is to minimize the necessary human interaction required to transform a PIM into a PSM and a PSM into code for a SOA. The separation of concerns introduced on the PSM layer is mirrored on the code layer by the use of Java annotations, allowing the same business code to run in different domains simply by exchanging the annotations and thus decoupling application code and SOA middleware. With the development of mobile applications, Business services on mobile became more and more important in the business cooperation on collaborative. The emergence of mobile services make enterprises enable to share resources and business process through service composition. Furthermore, a single mobile service has been unable to satisfy the complex requirement from industry and business application now. So the service composition is proposed. And it soon becomes a hot topic of research in recent years. A mobile service development process is to model the behaviors of single mobile service and the composition of multiple services[4].

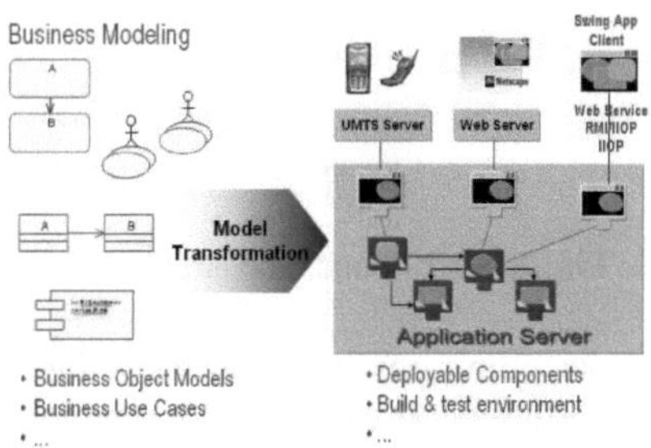

Fig. 1. Overall Flow of MDA and SOA in our work

In the traditional development process, there are a lot of systematic development methods. These methods are already not enough for the current application environment of mobile service.

In this paper, we also give a development process model based on MDA and SOA procedures to satisfy the requirement of semantic in the current construction and composition for mobile applications. This model might be useful in the mobile applications development process with the semantic information from the extended MDA diagram.

2 Related Works

2.1 SOA-Based System Development

As shown in figure 2, generating a profile for service-oriented architecture is the first step to produce such a framework. This profile enables the designer to describe the platform specific model based on SOA. Profiles are standard techniques for extending UML. By using profiles for precise modeling, we ensure that the designed model can be used in different views of MDA with the same concepts, as we are following the MDA for defining standard models.

In this way, the SOA application development infrastructure and operation infrastructure can be merged into a single and unified SOA infrastructure. The development infrastructure may include: Modeling, function and policy specification, analysis, design, code generation, verification and validation. The operation infrastructure may include: Code deployment, code execution, policy enforcement, monitoring, communication, and system reconfiguration. The architecture consists of four phases: modeling, assembling, deployment, and management. Furthermore, runtime governance activities are performed to provide guidance and oversight for the target SOA application. The activities in the four phases are performed iteratively: Architecture. Modeling: This phase models the user requirements in a system model with a set of services;

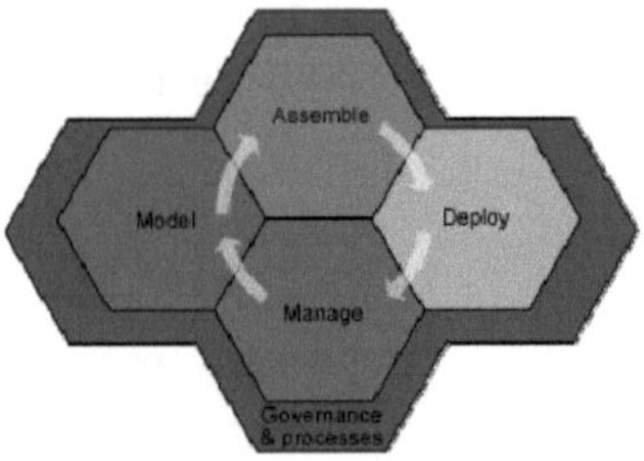

Fig. 2. SOA Foundation Architecture

- **Assembling:** This phase composes applications using services that have been created or discovered at runtime according to the model specified in the previous phase;
- **Deployment:** In this phase, the runtime environment is configured to meet the application's requirements, and the application is loaded into that environment for execution;
- **Management:** After the application is deployed, the services used in the application are monitored. Information is collected to prevent, diagnose, isolate, and/or fix any problem that might occur during execution. These activities in management phase will provide the designer with better know-ledge to manage the application.

2.2 MDA-Based System Development

Figure 3 show the MDA process that includes: Computation Independent Model (CIM): describes concepts of a given domain but does not describe the software system. Platform Independent Model (PIM): describes software behavior that is independent of some platform. Platform Specific Model (PSM): describes software behavior that is specific for some platform. The first step in using MDA is to develop a CIM which describes the concepts for a specific domain.

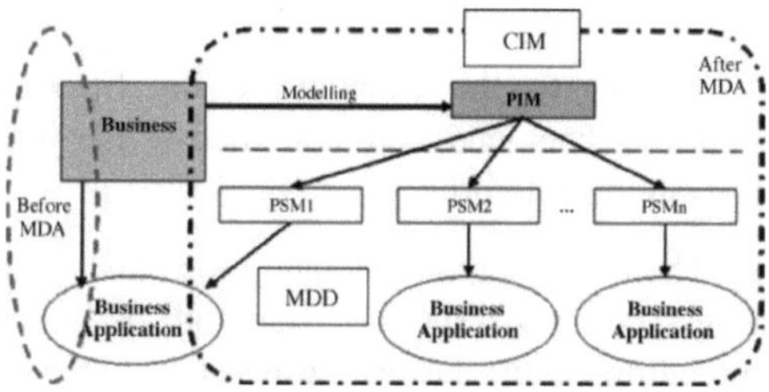

Fig. 3. MDA Foundation Architecture

2.3 Mobile Application Development

Handheld devices are evolving and becoming increasingly complex with the continuous addition of features and functionalities. The rapid proliferation of the Internet Protocol (IP)-based wireless networks, the maturation of cellular technology, and the business value discovered in deploying mobile solutions in different sectors like education, enterprise, entertainment, and personal productivity are some of the drivers of these changes. Computing and communication technologies are converging, as with communications-enabled Personal Digital Assistants (PDAs) and smart phones, and the mobile landscape is getting swamped with devices having a variety of different form factors[5]. Mobile applications are a natural extension to the current wired infrastructure. Traditional mobile applications like email and Personal Information Management (PIM) have been widely adopted in the enterprise and consumer arenas. A plethora of applications targeting the consumer is now available in the market. Mobile applications enabling Business to Business (B2B) and Business to Consumer (B2C) transactions are rapidly becoming mainstream along with other shrink-wrap software products.

Definitions of mobile applications vary. A mobile application is any application that runs on a handheld device, like a personal digital assistant or a smart phone, and connects to the network wirelessly. The following is a model for categorizing

mobile applications and includes additional categories to account for the recent changes in wireless technology.

• **Applications that Are Stand-Alone:** These applications run on the handheld device itself without connecting to the network. An example of a standalone application is a calculator running on a Windows Pocket PC.

•**Applications that Connect to the Backend through Synchronization Software:** These applications use synchronization software like Microsoft Active Synch to connect to a parent computer or network. An example of such an application is Microsoft Outlook for Pocket PC that synchronizes data between the handheld device and the host computer through synchronization software.

• **Applications that Connect to the Backend through a Wide-Area Wireless Network:** These applications use either circuit-switched or packet-switched wide-area wireless networks to connect to a data source or other network resource. An example of such an application is a stock-ticker application that streams real-time information about the stock rates to handheld devices using cellular data transfer.

• **Applications that Connect to the Backend Using Special Networks:** These applications connect to the back-end through special networks like Specialized Mobile Radio (SMR) or paging networks.

• **Other Applications:** There applications include those that connect to the back-end using short-range wireless networks, such as Bluetooth or infrared. Another way to categorize mobile applications could be on the basis of the layering of the system, which is based on the software and hardware infrastructure.

• **Mobile Application Layer:** This layer includes the application software that is responsible for user authentication and privacy, for establishing the communication partners, and for determining the constraints on data and other application services.

• **Client-Side Devices:** This layer constitutes the hardware on which a mobile application with varying capabilities executes.

• **Mobile Content Delivery and Middleware:** This layer includes mobile middleware that integrates heterogeneous wireless software and the hardware environment, and that hides the disparities to expedite development at the application layer. There are a rich set of content delivery and application programming interfaces available from Microsoft, Sun, and other leading companies in the mobile application domain that developers can use out of the box for rapid application development.

3 Mobile Applications Development with Combine on MDA and SOA

3.1 Mobile Service

Mobile services are obviously at the heart of Service-oriented architecture, and the term *service* is widely used. “A service is a discoverable resource that executes a repeatable task, and is described by an externalized service specification.″ the key concepts behind services are as followings;

- **Business Alignment:** Services are not based on IT capabilities, but on what the business needs. Services business alignment is supported by service analysis and design techniques.
- **Specifications:** Services are self-contained and described in terms of interfaces, operations, semantics, dynamic behaviors, policies, and qualities of service.
- **Reusability:** Services reusability is supported by services granularity design decisions.

- **Agreements:** Services agreements are between entities, namely services providers and consumers. These agreements are based on services specification and not implementation.
- **Hosting and Discoverability:** As they go through their life cycle, services are hosted and discoverable, as supported by services metadata, registries and repositories.
- **Aggregation:** Loosely-coupled services are aggregated into intra- or inter-enterprise business processes or composite applications.

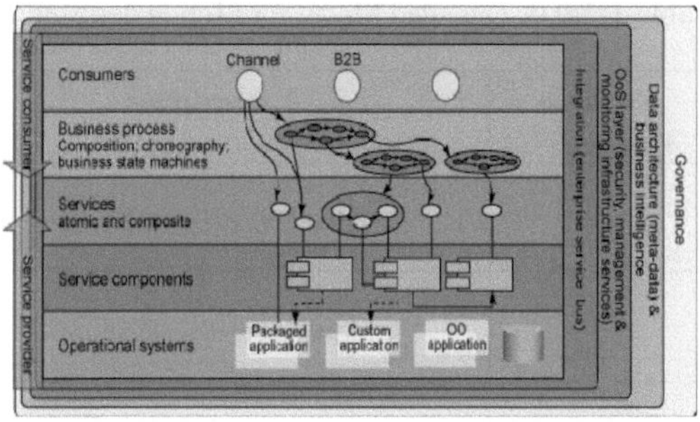

Fig. 4. Categories of Mobile Services in this paper

These combined characteristics show that SOA is not just about "technology", but also about business requirements and needs. The development and update process of software is the top-down, step-by-step refinement process of the model. And the life cycle is a process that driven by a model convention. Model construction, model mapping and model refinement technologies are the core of MDA. In MDA, model is a specification of system structure, function or behavior. The specification was given usually by diagram language, such as UML, and nature language.

We considered that strict formalization should be using in the MDA modeling as in figure 4. As the support platform of the MDA development, UML provides a large number of predefined structure, semi-formal definition and support tools. It provides rich visual model elements and graphical representations. These elements and representations are used to describe the software system. But sometimes UML will not be able to satisfy the requirements of system, because it lacks of rigorous semantics. For example, it could not express the relationship between state, properties, and method, etc. And the definition of state diagram information is not precise enough. So a modeling language that precise in syntax and semantics is needed to work with UML in MDA process. It is used to ensure the consistency in different period of software life cycle.

3.2 PIM Model for Mobile Application

In this paper, we modeling language to extend the UML based MDA modeling process with SOA. Specially, we made this extending mainly in the domain of Mobile service development. We combine UML withSOA, as the modeling language for the mobile service development process based on MDA. In this way, we hope to improve the model's accuracy, consistency, and to eliminate ambiguity in MDA process. And at same time, we hope to improve the quality of the mobile service development. We give a model of Mobile service development process based on MDA and SOA. The main work is to bind a process modeling language in the MDA. This modeling language is an extending on UML, through procedure descriptions as table 1. We will describe the extending of use case diagram, sequence diagram and class diagram in UML as an example. The extending of other UML diagrams will not be introduced here cause of page spaces.

Table 1. MDA extended Model for Mobile descriptions

Extended Diagram	Description
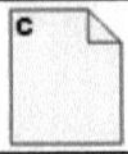	Mobile Contents Descriptor
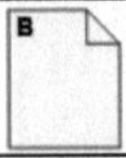	Mobile business Descriptor
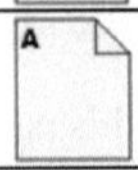	Mobile Application Descriptor
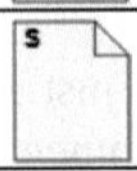	Mobile Service Descriptor
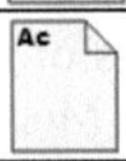	Mobile Collection Application(App.)
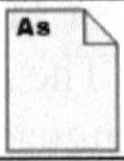	Mobile Search Application(App.)

(1) The Extending of the User Case for Mobile Application

Use case diagram for mobile application is corresponding to the Mobile Abstract Big Diagram (MABA) in the description level. MABA is an overview structure of the process behavior. It is independent of the programming language, and irrelevant to process control and data flow implementation details [3]. It is the basis and key of procedure subsequent development. Combination of user case and MABA would be a better representation of the entire development modeling process. The specific implementation is shown in Figure 5. In figure 5, user A is a participant, use case *A* is a set of actions sequences for user *A*. <<user>> express the interactive relationship between user *A* and system. Description B+C expresses the use case diagram extending, including Business and Content of mobile applications to be developed. It contains the following three aspects:

- The name of use case diagram extending: User Case-extended
- Use case diagram of UML corresponding to the contents and business of the mobile applications: B+C as Business and Concept structure
- The content of the concept structure: *Contl, Cont 2*

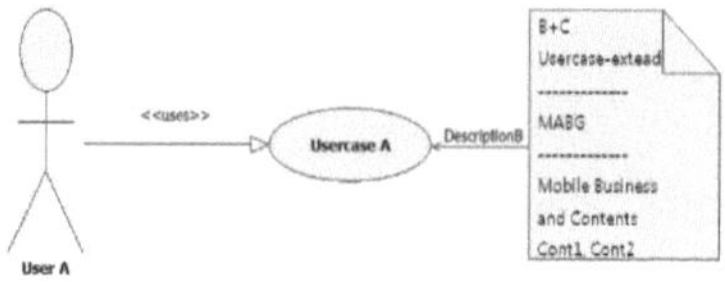

Fig. 5. Use case diagram extending for mobile applications

(2)The Extending of the Sequence Diagram for Mobile Application

Sequence diagram for mobile application is corresponding to Mobile Abstract Big Diagram (MABA). MABA depends on and is the results of control refinement. MABA contains the control flow implementation detail of process. It expresses the global logic structure of detailed design process. The sequence diagram is a dynamic modeling approach. It is used to confirm and rich the logic of use imagery. Combination of sequence diagram and MABA would describe the sequence better in the development process. The extending of sequence diagram is shown in Figure 6. In the figure 6, target 1,2 and 3 is a sequence objects that are set of actions sequences for user *A*. Description A expresses the mobile application description to be developed. It contains the following three aspects:

• The content of the concept structure: seq*1,seq 2*

There are three objects and four massages. Description A expresses the sequence diagram extending, including extending content. *Seql and seq2 are* contents of the logic structure.

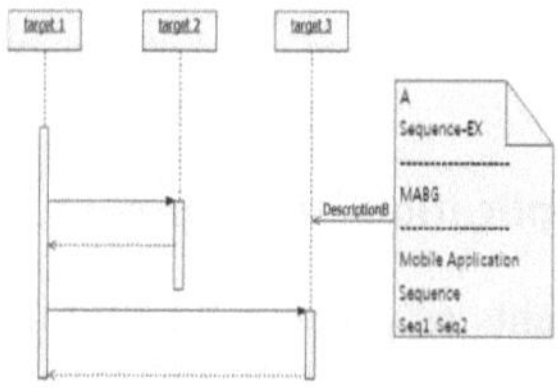

Fig. 6. Sequence diagram extending for mobile applications

(3) The Extending of Class Diagram for Mobile Application

Class diagram is corresponding to the Mobile Abstract Big Diagram (MABA). The MABA uses formal language expression on logic control structure. MABA contains all implementation details of control flow and data flow. Class diagram shows class, interfaces, static structure and relationships. It describes the structural design of the system. Combination of class diagram and MABA would describe the components relationship and implementation details more precisely. The specific implementation is shown in Figure 7.

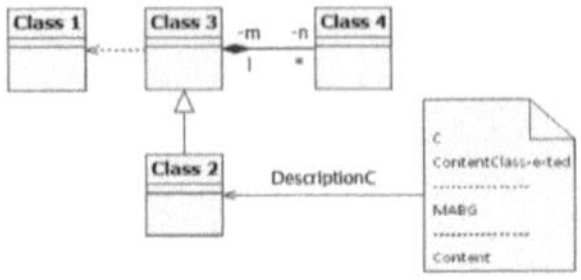

Fig. 7. Class diagram extending for mobile contents

(4) The Extending of Services for Mobile Application

Compared to the source code, it has a better structure. Now, we will introduce the development process from requirements analysis, software design and software implementation. The service use case diagram extending is shown in Figure 8. When users finish an action, service1 and service2 will be called. When service1 running, it will call two son service, service 11 and service 12. Here, it also needs to expand the use case diagram. The difference is that the extending of each service is according to MDA and SOA.

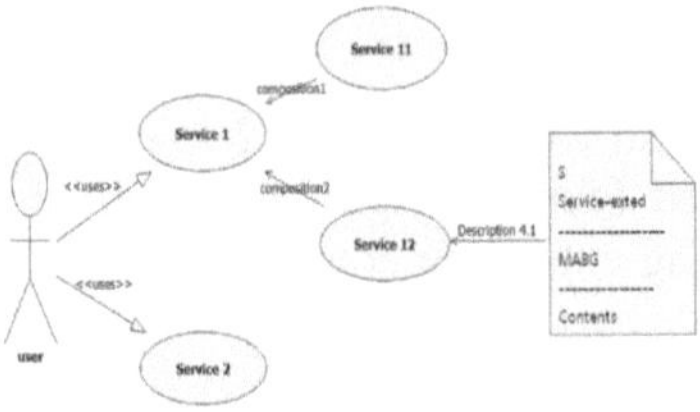

Fig. 8. Mobile Service use diagram extending

3.3 Process for Mobile Application Development

There are several key components of process for mobile applications with MDA and SOA framework;

- **Message:** Message represents the data required to complete some or all parts of a unit of work. They are autonomous and have enough information to be self-governing. It is the information required by the operation within a service to send a useful response back to the requestor.
- **Operation:** An operation represents the logic required to complete a task by processing the message. It is thus a unit of processing logic that acts on the data provided by the message to carry out a task. An operation is largely defined by the message it receives and sends.
- **Service:** W3C defines service as an "abstract resource that represents a capability of performing tasks that form a coherent functionality from the point of view of providers and requesters." In service-oriented architecture, services are autonomous, yet not isolated from each other. These services can evolve independently but still maintain some level of commonality and standardization. Service is a group of related operations.

• **Business Process:** A business process is a set of rules that governs how a task is completed. In service-oriented architecture, a business process is accomplished when a set of operations within services collaborate, to form the logic and process flow, and to complete a unit of automation. It actually follows the basic SOA process as followings;

- **Model** includes business analysis and design (requirements, processes, goals, key performance indicators) and IT analysis and design (service identification and specification).
- **Assemble** includes service implementation and the building of composite applications.
- **Deploy** includes application deployment and runtimes such as Enterprise Service Buses (ESB).
- **Manage** includes the maintenance of the operating environment, service performance monitoring, and service policy enforcement.

It also includes interactions modeling between services and activity diagrams, collaboration modeling between services and sequence diagrams. To complete a task as in figure 9, system send information to call service1 and it needs a coordinate of service11 and service12. After the complete of service11 and service12, the complete information will be returned to the system service. Then call service2, after it complete, the whole task will be completed. It lacks of semantic information. The development process which presented in this paper combines UML with procedure blueprint to modeling. It provides a common language to describe the service. The language can be modeling for service, service-oriented architecture and service-oriented solutions. The three layers structure allows developer to understand the whole process intuitive and better grasp the idea of mobile service development. It is also helpful for developers to monitoring throughout the development process as followings;

Step 1; Conditional steps which test occurrence of a specific case in the model
Step 2: Functional steps which perform a change in the model

Details of each step are as follows:

1. Start is the very first node of the diagram. A state without any input and only one exit.
2. Print defined with *<<code>>* stereotype and prints out an informative message.
3. Initial check of the input model, where we check whether input model contains at least one UML package and four classes and Initial check of the input model
4. Selecting input model components and iterate over them.
5. Copying the selected model into the target model.
6. Initial check of the selected element which checks whether this element has at least 3 connecting edges.
7. Applying SOA profile to the selected element, which has passed the initial checking.

4 Case Study

At present, there are many researches on MDA-based Mobile services development. However, there is not a complete development framework. In this paper, we propose a mobile service development process based on MDA with SOA. It can be divided into three layers structure. They are concept structure, logic structure and implementation structure. Mapping rules between the three layers structure is proposed in reference. In this paper, we will not detailed introduce.

Logic structure is dependent on concept structure. It is the refining of concept structure. It is concerned with the control structure of programming language. In logic structure, developer can make a more detailed design of the system. Here can detailed description control flow information. Implementation structure is based on logic structure. It is the data flow refinement of logic structure. It contains all the details of the source code.

In this section, we introduced the mobile service development process and apply the suggested method to develop Intelligent Subway train Guidance Application (ISGA). The system's main function is to guide the DaeGu metropolitan in Korea as subway train on-line intelligent information and provide the GPS information for it. Figure 9 shows the ISGA structure.

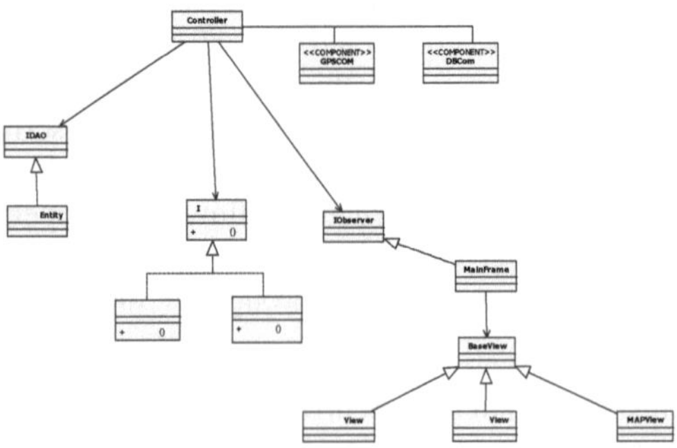

Fig. 9. Subway train Guidance Application system structure

Based on the brief requirements, we can drive and get the requirement's use case diagram and sequence diagram extending of the ISGA system as in Figure10 and Figure11 using the extended descriptions. First is the expansion of the use case diagram. It gives the relationship between the three parts. But it does not give the specific implementation details. When the ISGA broke out, intelligent application will give subway detail information. And the three services will respond to this information. The Sequence extending is shown as figure 12. It gives the implementation details. When ISGA gives subway information, GPS detection service will test environment subway information.

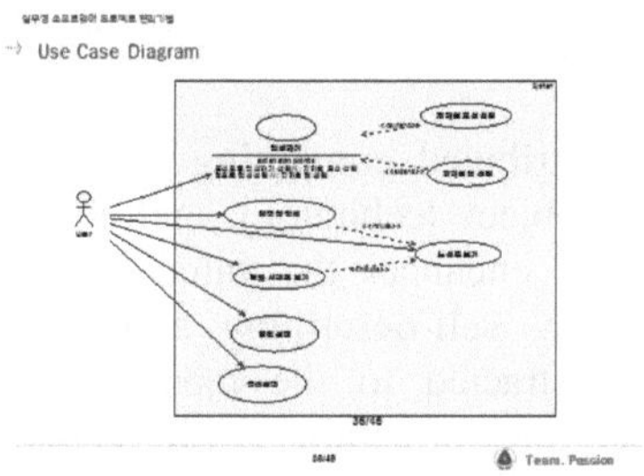

Fig. 10. Use case extending diagram

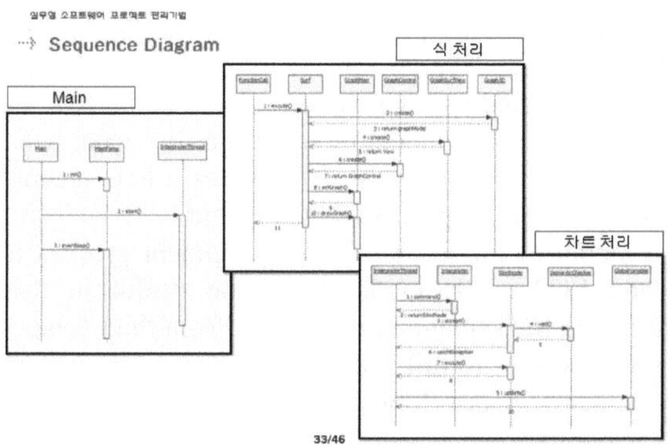

Fig. 11. Sequence extending diagram

Figure 13 show the component extended diagram for mobile applications. It will use for Reuse or With Reuse in the future to adapt the same domain development. Figure 13 show the our final product execution examples with MDA and SOA approaches. As part of evaluation, we can gain the quality and productivity to develop the mobile application compare to traditional approaches.

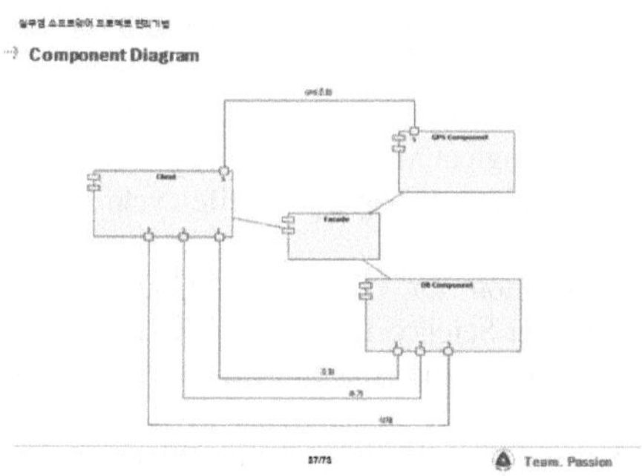

Fig. 12. Component extending diagram

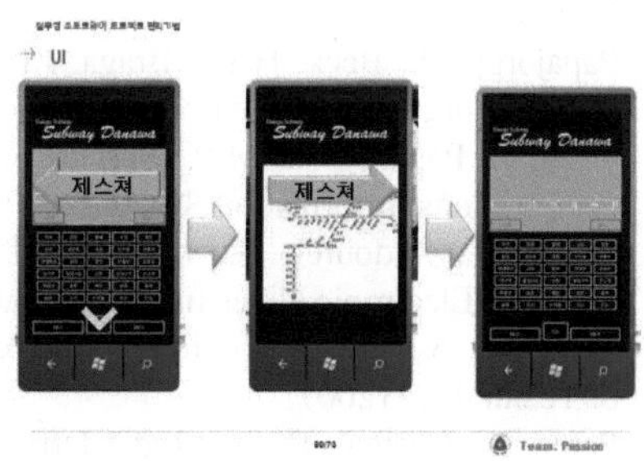

Fig. 13. ISGA Execution Examples

5 Conclusion and Future Works

Mobile service is a new distributed computing technology. It emerged with the development of distributed object technology and the extending of e-commerce applications. It integrates and enhances the value of applications in the network. Mobile services are adaptive, self-describing and modular In MDA, software development behavior is abstracted to the model analysis. Coding work done automatically by the model transformation. So it realized the separation between function design and implementation technology. The impact of technology change on the system is minimized. The value of model is to maximize reflected. System is driven by model. Software development and update process is the top-down and gradual refinement process of model. MDA and SAO convergence design methodology is a series of related principles, theory, methods and techniques. It is suitable for program process development. This development method focuses the developer's attention, knowledge, experience, skills and creativity on procedure blueprint development. It also is a modeling language for visual behavioral procedure analysis, detailed design and construction. It provides a new technology, theory and solution for the software behavior process development.

In this paper, a model of mobile service development process is given based on procedure MDA and SOA. This model might be useful in the Mobile service development process with the semantic information from the extended MDA diagram. In future, we will focus on how to fully combine the three-layer structure of procedure blueprint and mobile services development process, and will also develop software tools to support the modeling.

Acknowledgement. This work was supported by the Korea National Research Foundation (NRF) granted funded by the Korea Government (Scientist of Regional University No. 2012-0004489)

References

1. Motogna, S., Lazar, I., Parv, B., Czibula, I.: An Agile MDA Approach for Service-Oriented component. Electronic Notes in Theoretical Computer Science 253, 95–110 (2009)
2. Papajorgji, P., Beck, H.W., Braga, J.L.: An architecture for developing service-oriented and component-based environmental models. Ecological Modelling 179, 61–76 (2004)
3. Yang, J., Papazoglou, M.P.: Service components for managing the life-cycle of service compositions. Information Systems 29, 97–125 (2004)
4. Andre, P., Ardourel, G., Attiogbe, C.: Adaptation for Hierarchical Components and Services. Electronic Notes in Theoretical Computer Science 189, 5–20 (2007)
5. Jha, A.K.: A Risk Catalog for Mobile Applications. A thesis submitted to Florida Institute of Technology (2007)
6. Perez, B., Correal, D.: A Model Driven Approach to the Analysis of Quality Scenarios within Self-Adaptable SOA Systems. Electonic Notes in Theoretical Computer Science 281, 113–126 (2011)

7. Zmuda, D., Psiuk, M., Zielinski, K.: Dynamic monitoring Framework for the SOA execution environment. In: International Conference on Computational Science(ICCS), vol. 1, pp. 125–133 (2012)
8. Holzinger, A., Kosec, P., Schwantzer, G., Debevc, M., Hofmann-Wellenhof, R., Fruhauf, J.: Design and development of a mobile computer application to reengineer workflows in the hospital and the methodology to evaluate its effectiveness. Journal of Biomedical Informatics 44, 968–977 (2011)
9. Malek, S., Edwards, G., Brun, Y., Tajalli, H., Garcia, J., Krka, I., Medvidovic, N., Mikic-Rakic, M., Sukhatme, G.S.: An architecture-driven software mobility framework. The Journal of Systems and Software 83, 972–989 (2010)
10. Medvidovic, N., Edwards, G.: Software architecture and mobility:A roadmap. The Journal of Systems and Software 83, 885–889 (2010)

Semantic Web Service Composition Using Formal Verification Techniques*

Hyunyoung Kil[1] and Wonhong Nam[2]

[1] Korea Advanced Institute of Science & Technology, Daejeon 305-701, Korea
hkil@kaist.ac.kr
[2] Konkuk University, Seoul 143-701, Korea
wnam@konkuk.ac.kr

Abstract. Web service is a software system designed to support interoperable machine-to-machine interaction over a network. The web service composition problem aims to find an optimal composition of web services to satisfy a given request by using their syntactic and/or semantic features when no single service satisfies it. In particular, the semantics of services helps a composition engine identify more correct, complete and optimal candidates as a solution. In this paper, we study the web service composition problem considering semantic aspects, i.e., exploiting the semantic relationship between parameters of web services. Given a set of web service descriptions, their semantic information and a requirement web service, we find the optimal composition that contains the shortest path of semantically well connected web services which satisfies the requirement. Our techniques are based on semantic matchmaking and two formal verification techniques such as boolean satisfiability solving and symbolic model checking. In a preliminary experiment, our proposal efficiently identify optimal compositions of web services.

Keywords: Formal Verification, Model Checking, SAT, Web service composition, Semantic web.

1 Introduction

Web services are software systems to support machine to machine inter-operations over internet. Recently, many researches have been carried out for the web service standard, and these efforts significantly have improved flexible and dynamic functionality of *service oriented architectures* in the current semantic web services. However, a number of research challenges still remain; e.g., automatic web service discovery, web service composition and formal verification for composed web services. Given a set of available web services and a user request, a *web service discovery problem* is to automatically find a web service satisfying the request. Often, the client request cannot, however,

* Corresponding author: Wonhong Nam. This research was supported by the MKE(Ministry of Knowledge Economy), Korea, under the ITRC(Information Technology Research Center) support program supervised by the NIPA(National IT Industry Promotion Agency): NIPA-2012-H0301-12-3006.

T.-h. Kim et al. (Eds.): EL/DTA/UNESST 2012, CCIS 352, pp. 72–79, 2012.

be fulfilled by a single pre-existing service. In this case, one desires *web service composition (WSC)* which combines some from a given set of web services to satisfy the requirement, based on their syntactic and/or semantic features.

Semantics is one of the key elements for the automated composition of web services since this machine-readable description of services can help a composition engine find a correct, complete, consistent and optimal candidates as a solution. In general, semantic description is mainly represented with an ontology which is a formal knowledge base specified with a set of concepts within a domain, properties of each concepts, and the relationships among those concepts. Based on the ontology, programs can reason about the entities within the domain and find more candidate web services which are not only syntactically but also semantically appropriate for composition. As a result, we can obtain a composite service with high quality.

In this paper, we propose two efficient techniques to find an *optimal* composition for the semantic web service composition problem. Given a set of web services, their semantic descriptions and a requirement web service, our algorithms identify the *shortest sequence of web services* such that we can legally invoke the next web service in each step and achieve the desired requirement eventually. We first reduce the composition problem into a *reachability problem* on a *state-transition system* where the shortest path from the initial state to a goal state corresponds to the shortest sequence of web services. To solve the reachability problem, we employ a state-of-the-art SAT solver [1] and a symbolic model checker [2]. We report on a preliminary implementation and experiment for our solutions, which demonstrate that our techniques efficiently identify optimal compositions for 7 modified versions of examples created by a test-set generator adopted for the WSC'09 competition [3].

2 Semantic Web Service Composition

First, we formalize the notion of web services and their composition we consider in this paper. A *web service* is a tuple $w = (I, O)$ where I and O are respectively a finite set of *input parameters* and a finite set of *output parameters* for w. Each input/output parameter $p \in I \cup O$ is a concept referred to in an ontology Γ through OWL-S [4] or WSMO [5]. We assume that when a web service w is invoked with all the input parameters $i \in I$, w returns all the output parameters $o \in O$.

To decide invocation relationship from $w_1(I_1, O_1)$ to $w_2(I_2, O_2)$ in the composition, it is necessary to semantically compare outputs O_1 of the caller w_1 with inputs I_2 of the callee w_2. For this, we need to compute a semantic similarity between two parameters; that is, we have to find a relationship between two knowledge representations encoded using Γ. A causal link [6] describes the semantic matchmaking between two parameters with the matchmaking function $Sim_\Gamma(p_1, p_2)$ which identifies the matching level of p_1 and p_2 based on a given ontology Γ. In a number of web service composition models [7,8,9], Sim_Γ is reduced to the following matching levels.

- *exact* if two parameter p_1 and p_2 are equivalent concepts; i.e., $\Gamma \models p_1 \equiv p_2$.
- *plug-in* if p_1 is sub-concept of p_2; i.e., $\Gamma \models p_1 <: p_2$.
- *subsume* if p_1 is super-concept of p_2; i.e., $\Gamma \models p_1 :> p_2$.
- *disjoint* if p_1 and p_2 are not compatible.

The *exact* matching means that p_1 and p_2 can substitute for each other since they refer to equivalent concepts. The *plug-in* matching is also a possible match to substitute p_1 for p_2 everywhere since p_1 is more specific than p_2. In other words, p_1 is more informative than p_2. The *subsume* matching is the converse relation of the plug-in matching. The *Disjoint* matching informs the incompatibility of two web service parameters. Thus, it cannot give any contribution to connect the services.

We assume that the ontology Γ is given, e.g., specified in OWL. Given two web services $w_1(I_1, O_1)$ and $w_2(I_2, O_2)$, we denote $w_1 \sqsupseteq_I w_2$ if w_2 requires less informative inputs than w_1; i.e., for every $i_2 \in I_2$ there exists $i_1 \in I_1$ such that $i_1 <: i_2$. Given two web services $w_1(I_1, O_1)$ and $w_2(I_2, O_2)$, we denote $w_1 \sqsubseteq_O w_2$ if w_2 provides more informative outputs than w_1; i.e., for every $o_1 \in O_1$ there exists $o_2 \in O_2$ such that $o_2 <: o_1$. A *web service discovery problem* is, given a set W of available web services and a request web service w_r, to find a web service $w \in W$ such that $w_r \sqsupseteq_I w$ and $w_r \sqsubseteq_O w$.

However, it might happen that there is no single web service satisfying the requirement. In that case, we want to find a sequence $w_1 \cdots w_n$ of web services such that we can invoke the next web service in each step and achieve the desired requirement eventually. Formally, we extend the relations, $\sqsupseteq_I$ and $\sqsubseteq_O$, to a sequence of web services as follows.

- $w \sqsupseteq_I w_1 \cdots w_n$ (where $w = (I, O)$ and each $w_j = (I_j, O_j)$ and $I, O, I_j, O_j \subseteq \Gamma$) if $\forall 1 \leq j \leq n$: for every $i_2 \in I_j$ there exists $i_1 \in I \cup \bigcup_{k<j} O_k$ such that $i_1 <: i_2$.
- $w \sqsubseteq_O w_1 \cdots w_n$ (where $w = (I, O)$ and each $w_j = (I_j, O_j)$ and $I, O, I_j, O_j \subseteq \Gamma$) if for every $o_1 \in O$ there exists $o_2 \in \bigcup_{1 \leq j \leq n} O_j$ such that $o_2 <: o_1$.

Finally, given a set of available web services W, an ontology Γ and a service request w_r, a *semantic web service composition problem* $WC = (W, \Gamma, w_r)$ we focus on in this paper is to find a sequence $w_1 \cdots w_n$ (every $w_j \in W$) of web services such that $w_r \sqsupseteq_I w_1 \cdots w_n$ and $w_r \sqsubseteq_O w_1 \cdots w_n$. The optimal solution for this problem is the shortest sequence among them.

3 Semantic Web Service Composition with Formal Verification

To solve a semantic web service composition problem with formal verification techniques, we first explain how the problem can be reduced into a reachability problem on a state-transition system. Then, we present our first algorithm based on symbolic model checking. For the second technique based on boolean satisfiability solving, we explain our encoding of the problem to a Conjunctive Normal Form (CNF) formula which is true if and only if there exists a path of length k from an initial state to a goal state of the state-transition system. Finally, we propose our second algorithm to find an optimal solution for the problem.

3.1 Reduction to Reachability Problem

Given a semantic web service composition problem $WC = (W, \Gamma, w_r)$, the problem can be reduced into a reachability problem on a state-transition system. A *state-transition system* is a tuple $S = (X, \Sigma, T)$ where

- X is a finite set of *boolean variables*; a *state* q of S is a valuation for all the variables in X.
- Σ is a set of *input symbols*.
- $T(X, \Sigma, X')$ is a *transition predicate* over $X \cup \Sigma \cup X'$. For a set X of variables, we denote the set of primed variables of X as $X' = \{x' \mid x \in X\}$, which represents a set of variables encoding the successor states. $T(q, a, q')$ is *true* iff q' can be the next state when the input $a \in \Sigma$ is received at the state q.

Given a set $W = \{w_1, \cdots, w_n\}$ of web services where for each j, $w_j = (I_j, O_j)$, we denote as Γ_p a set of concepts of parameters such that there exists $p \in \bigcup(I_j \cup O_j)$ and $p \in \Gamma_p$. Then, we can construct a state-transition system $S = (X, \Sigma, T)$ corresponding with W as follows:

- $X = \{x_1, \cdots, x_m\}$ where $m = |\Gamma_p|$; each boolean variable x_j represents whether we have the parameter $p_j \in \Gamma_p$ at a state.
- $\Sigma = W$.
- For each j, $T(q, w_j, q') =$ *true* where $q = (b_1, \cdots, b_m)$, $q' = (c_1, \cdots, c_m)$ (each b_k and c_k are *true* or *false*), and $w_j = (I_j, O_j)$ iff (1) for every $i \in I_j$, there exists b_k in q such that b_k is *true* and $x_k <: p_i$, (2) if b_l is *true*, c_l is also *true*, and (3) $\forall o \in O_j$: for every variable c_k in q' if t_o is a sub-concept of x_k (i.e., $t_o <: x_k$), c_k is *true*. Intuitively, if a web service w_j is invoked at a state q where we have data instances being more informative than inputs of w_j, we proceed to a state q' where we retain all the data instances from q and acquire outputs of w_j as well as their supertypes.

In addition, from a given requirement web service $w_r = (I_{w_r}, O_{w_r})$, we encode an *initial state predicate* $Init(X)$ and a *goal state predicate* $G(X)$ as follows:

- $Init(q) =$ *true* where $q = (b_1, \cdots, b_m)$ iff $\forall i \in I_{w_r}$: for every variable b_j in q, if x_j is a super-concept of i (i.e., $i <: x_j$), b_j is *true*.
- $G(q) =$ *true* where $q = (b_1, \cdots, b_m)$ iff for every output parameter $o \in O_{w_r}$, there exists b_j in q such that b_j is *true* and x_j is a subconcept of o (i.e., $x_j <: o$).

Intuitively, we have an initial state where we possess all the data instances corresponding to the input of w_r as well as one corresponding to their supertypes. As goal states, if a state is more informative than the outputs of w_r, it is a goal state. Finally, given a type-aware web service composition problem $WC = (W, \Gamma, w_r)$, we can reduce WC into a reachability problem $R = (S, Init, G)$ where the shortest path from an initial state to a goal state corresponds to the shortest sequence of web services. We omit a formal proof for our reduction due to space limitation.

3.2 WSC Algorithm Using Symbolic Model Checking

Our first method to solve the semantic WSC problem is based on symbolic model checking. Given a semantic WSC problem instance, we reduce it to a reachability problem instance and then solve the reachability problem using symbolic model checking with binary decision diagrams (BDDs) [10]. The standard symbolic model checking method

Algorithm 1: Symbolic model checking algorithm for the WSC problem

Input : a set W of web services, an ontology Γ and a requirement web service w_r.
Output: a sequence of web services.

1 $(S, \mathit{Init}, G) := \mathit{ReduceToReachabilityProb}(W, \Gamma, w_r)$;
2 BDD $\rho := \mathit{false}$;
3 BDD $\tau := \mathit{Init}$;
4 **while** $\tau \neq \mathit{false}$ **do**
5   **if** $\tau \wedge G \neq \mathit{false}$ **then return** $\mathit{ConstructWSSeq}(\mathit{ConstructPath}())$;
6     $\rho := \rho \vee \tau$;
7     $\tau := \mathit{PostImage}(S, \tau) \wedge \neg\rho$;
8 **return** *null*;

to solve the reachability problem is a fixed-point algorithm that can be implemented using BDDs which represent a set of states of the state-transition system. Algorithm 1 presents our symbolic model checking algorithm for the semantic WSC problem. The BDD ρ represents a set of states the algorithm has already explored, and the BDD τ denotes a set of states it visits for the first time in each loop. The algorithm begins with the set of initial states (line 3). In each iteration, if there exists any state in a set of states represented by $\tau \wedge G$ (i.e., we reach any goal state in the corresponding iteration), then the algorithm terminates with a path from the initial state to a goal state. Otherwise, the set of states represented by τ is stored to ρ (line 6) and we compute a set of new states (line 7). The function *PostImage* is a standard post image computation in the symbolic model checking technique [11]. When given a predicate τ representing a set of states, the function returns a predicate for the set of possible next states of τ. When the *while* loop terminates (i.e., there does not exist any new state), the algorithm returns *null* which means there is no solution path. As a symbolic model checker to solve this problem, we employ Cadence SMV [2].

3.3 Encoding to CNF Formula

Now, we study how to construct a formula $[[R]]_k$ which is true if and only if there exists a path $q_0 \cdots q_k$ of length k for a given reachability problem $R = (S, \mathit{Init}, G)$. The formula $[[R]]_k$ is over sets $X_0, \cdots, X_k$ of variables and $W_1, \cdots, W_k$ where each X_j represents a state along the path and W_j encodes a web service invoked in each step. It essentially represents constraints on $q_0 \cdots q_k$ and $w_1 \cdots w_k$ such that $[[R]]_k$ is satisfiable if and only if q_0 is the initial state, each q_j evolves according to the transition predicate for w_j, and q_k reaches to a goal state. Formally, the formula $[[R]]_k$ is as follows:

$$[[R]]_k \equiv Init(X_0) \wedge \bigwedge_{0 \leq j < k} T(X_j, W_{j+1}, X'_{j+1}) \wedge G(X_k)$$

Since each X_j is a finite set of boolean variables, Σ and W_j are finite, and *Init*, T and G are predicates, we can easily translate $[[R]]_k$ into a CNF formula which is the standard input format for conventional SAT solvers.

Algorithm 2: WSC algorithm via SAT

Input : a set W of web services, an ontology Γ and a web service w_r.
Output: a sequence of web services.

1 $(S, \mathit{Init}, G) := \mathit{ReduceToReachabilityProb}(W, \Gamma, w_r)$;
2 **for** $(k := 1; k \leq |W|; k := k + 1)$ **do**
3     $f := \mathit{ConstructCNF}(S, \mathit{Init}, G, k)$;
4   **if** $((\mathit{path} := \mathit{SAT}(f)) \neq \mathit{null})$ **then**
5   **return** $\mathit{ConstructWSSeq}(\mathit{path})$;
6 **return** *null*;

3.4 WSC Algorithm Using SAT Solver

Our second technique to solve the semantic WSC problem is to employ a boolean satisfiability solver [1]. Algorithm 2 presents the WSC algorithm via SAT solving. Given a set W of web services, an ontology Γ and a requirement web service w_r, the algorithm first reduces them into a state-transition system, and initial and goal predicates (line 1). For each loop, it constructs a CNF formula for k which is true if and only if there exists a path of length k from an initial state to a goal state of the state-transition system. The algorithm then checks the formula with an off-the-shelf SAT solver, zChaff [1] (line 4). If the formula is satisfiable, the SAT solver returns a truth assignment; otherwise, it returns *null*. Once the algorithm finds a path of the length k, it extracts a web service sequence from the path, and returns the sequence.

4 Experiments

We have implemented prototype tools for two algorithms in Section 3. Given a semantic ontology in a OWL file, and a set of available web services and a query web service in WSDL files, our tools generate a optimal web service sequence in BPEL to satisfy the request. To evaluate which method identify an optimal solution more efficiently, we have experimented on several modified problem instances of sample examples which are produced by the web service test set generator employed in Web Services Challenge [3]. We employ Cadence SMV [2] and zChaff [1] as an off-the-shelf model checker and an off-the-shelf SAT solver, respectively. All experiments have been performed on a PC using a 2.93GHz Core i7 processor and 4GB memory.

Table 1 presents the comparative result of our experiment that includes 7 examples, i.e., $e_1, \cdots, e_7$. The table shows the number of web services and the number of parameters which each problem includes, and the length of the optimal solution. It also presents the total execution time in seconds for the symbolic model checking (SMC) and the SAT solver (SAT). '–' means that the corresponding tool cannot finish the task in a given timeout (600 seconds) or terminates due to out-of-memory. Overall, the SAT-based algorithm has outperformed the symbolic model checking technique.

Table 1. Experiment result

Problem	Parameters	Web services	Solution length	SMC	SAT
e_1	100	30	3	0.2	0.1
e_2	110	110	2	6.4	0.1
e_3	120	120	2	22.0	0.1
e_4	500	100	5	–	2.1
e_5	1,000	150	9	–	14.8
e_6	2,000	300	7	–	46.9
e_7	5,000	300	7	–	106.2

5 Conclusion and Future Work

For the semantic web service composition problem, we have proposed two novel solutions that find the shortest sequence of web services to satisfy a given requirement considering semantic aspect. To identify the optimal solution, the techniques are based on a semantic matchmaking of service parameters and a boolean satisfiability solving and symbolic model checking. Our preliminary experiments present promising results where the tools find the shortest sequence efficiently, and it shows that the SAT-based algorithm has outperformed the symbolic model checking technique.

There are several directions for future work. First, we want to optimize the current version of our implementation and to support various semantic aspects. Second, we plan to study other efficient model checking methods for this problem, e.g., counter-example guided abstraction refinement [12].

References

1. Zhang, L., Malik, S.: The Quest for Efficient Boolean Satisfiability Solvers. In: Brinksma, E., Larsen, K.G. (eds.) CAV 2002. LNCS, vol. 2404, pp. 17–36. Springer, Heidelberg (2002)
2. The Cadence SMV model checker, `http://www.kenmcmil.com/smv.html`
3. Kona, S., Bansal, A., Blake, B., Bleul, S., Weise, T.: WSC-2009: a quality of service-oriented web services challenge. In: The 11th IEEE Conference on Commerce and Enterprise Computing, pp. 487–490 (2009)
4. Martin, D.: OWL-S: Semantic Markup for Web Services (2004), `http://www.w3.org/Submission/OWL-S`
5. Fensel, D., Kifer, M., de Bruijn, J., Domingue, J.: Web Service Modeling Ontology (WSMO). W3C member submission (2005)
6. Russell, S., Norvig, P.: Artificial Intelligence: a modern approach. Prentice-Hall (1995)
7. Paolucci, M., Kawamura, T., Payne, T.R., Sycara, K.: Semantic Matching of Web Services Capabilities. In: Horrocks, I., Hendler, J. (eds.) ISWC 2002. LNCS, vol. 2342, pp. 333–347. Springer, Heidelberg (2002)
8. Zhang, R., Arpinar, I.B., Aleman-Meza, B.: Automatic composition of semantic web services. In: Proceedings of the 10th International Conference on Web Services, pp. 38–41 (2003)

9. Sirin, E., Parsia, B., Hendler, J.A.: Filtering and selecting semantic web services with interactive composition techniques. IEEE Intelligent Systems 19(4), 42–49 (2004)
10. Bryant, R.E.: Graph-based algorithms for boolean function manipulation. IEEE Transactions on Computers 35(8), 677–691 (1986)
11. Clarke, E., Grumberg, O., Peled., D.: Model checking. MIT Press (2000)
12. Clarke, E., Grumberg, O., Jha, S., Lu, Y., Veith, H.: Counterexample-guided Abstraction Refinement. In: Emerson, E.A., Sistla, A.P. (eds.) CAV 2000. LNCS, vol. 1855, pp. 154–169. Springer, Heidelberg (2000)

Characteristics of Citation Scopes: A Preliminary Study to Detect Citing Sentences

In-Su Kang[1] and Byung-Kyu Kim[2,*]

[1] Kyungsung University, Pusan, South Korea
[2] Korea Institute of Science and Technology Information (KISTI), Daejeon, South Korea
dbaisk@ks.ac.kr, yourovin@kisti.re.kr

Abstract. Citing sentences are gaining much attention in citation-based summarization and article review generation which depend on precisely identifying the scope of citing sentences. This article presents characteristics of citing sentences and citation scopes, which were obtained from the manual analyses of numerous citing sentences.

Keywords: Citing Sentence, Detection of Citing Sentences, Citation Scope Unit.

1 Introduction

Recently, *citing sentences* receive a growing attention in understanding academic articles cited. The following shows an example of citing sentences which provide a peer's review on the article cited as *'Li et al. (2012)'*.

Li et al. (2012) proposed a SVM-based ensemble method for imbalanced data. They used VQ algorithm to segment the majority class to create less-skewed ... The method showed the best performance for the well-known UCI datasets.

A collection of such citing sentences from several different papers citing the same article could be used to generate an article review [4], or to produce an article summarization [1,3]. In addition, Athar and Teufel [2] employed citation context to discern positive and negative article reviews.

However, detecting the scope of citing sentences within a full-text article is not trivial, since citing sentences may not have explicit citation markers. For example, the first sentence in the above is explicitly indicated to cite something by a citation marker *'Li et al. (2012)'*, while the next sentences implicitly cite the same article without apparent marks. Earlier approaches to identifying citing sentences relied on either citation cue phrases [4] or coreference-chain [3], reporting performances less than 80% in F1.

* Corresponding author.

T.-h. Kim et al. (Eds.): EL/DTA/UNESST 2012, CCIS 352, pp. 80–85, 2012.

As a preliminary study to identify citing sentences, we have attempted to manually analyze numerous citing sentences to determine different types of citation areas and some characteristics of citing sentences. This article presents the results of such analyses.

2 Data

We collected a set of 56 recent articles in PDF format published in 50 different academic journals which belong to broadly science and engineering fields. Next, a total of 1048 citing sentences with one or more explicit *citation markers*[1] such as '(Croft, 2011)' or '[23]' was identified. For each citation marker found, the sentence containing the marker and its adjacent sentences were analyzed to determine the boundaries that the citation marker spans. This process corresponds to locating a group of citing sentences referring to a particular previous work. We call such group of citing sentences *citation area*, *citation scope* or *citation context.*

3 Characteristics of Citation Areas

Our analysis has identified five types of citation-scope units: phrase, clause, sentence, multi-sentence, and the others. The following (a) through (e) show real examples for such units sequentially, with citation markers bold-faced and citation-scope underlined.

(a) *Using BioEdit(**Hall 1999**), we collated the total sequences and then aligned them visually.*
(b) ***Lee et al. (2008)** presented symmetrical BVR light curves in the observing season in 2005, while Zhu & Qian (2009) obtained an asymmetrical V light curve with a strong O'Connell effect.*
(c) *The first GA approach for the structure learning is introduced by **Larranaga et al.** at 1996 **[12]**.*
(d) *Hoffmann's light curves were reanalyzed by **Kaluzny (1986)** with the Wilson Devinney binary model (WD; Wilson & Devinney 1971). His solutions showed that WZ Cep is a contact binary with the components of unequal surface temperatures.*
(e) *Fig. 13. Import of copper ore **[14]**.*

In the above, *'(Hall 1999)'* of (a) was cited only to refer to a term *'BioEdit'*. *'Lee et al. (2008)'* of (b) affects only the main clause, regardless of the subordinate clause *'while'* leads. In (c), the whole sentence is all about *'Larranaga et al. [12]'*. In (d), the second sentence continues to describe the work of *'Kaluzny (1986)'* which was cited in the previous sentence. In (e), a figure (not shown here) from *'[14]'* and its caption are about *'[14]'*.

[1] Citation markers mean in-text citations.

Table 1. Distribution of citation-scope units

Citation-scope unit	Frequency	%
Phrase	111	10.6%
Clause	82	7.8%
Sentence	788	75.2%
Multi-sentence	54	5.2%
Others	13	1.2%
Total	1048	

Table 1 shows distribution of citation-scope units. As expected, a single sentence is mostly used to cite other's works. However, sub-sentential citation scopes such as phrases and clauses attain close to 20%, meaning that roughly 20% of sentences with citation markers may have parts unrelated to the works cited. This implies that citation-based summarization approaches [1,3] could be improved by detecting sub-sentential citation scopes. In addition, the cases encompassing multiple sentences were relatively not frequent.

Table 2. Detailed statistics of citation-scope units

Citation-scope unit	Sub-category	Frequency	%
Phrase	Noun phrase	104	93.7%
	Adverbial phrase	6	5.4%
	Noun phrase(chapter titles)	1	0.9%
Clause	Clause	77	93.9%
	Embedded clause	5	6.1%
Sentence	Sentence	788	100.0%
Multi-sentence	Citation spans next sentences	32	59.3%
	Citation spans previous sentences	6	11.1%
	Citation spans equation/table/fig.	16	29.6%
Others	Figure	7	53.8%
	Equation	4	30.8%
	Table	2	15.4%
Total		1048	

Table 2 shows detailed statistics of citation-scope units. As for phrasal citation scopes, the noun phrase was the dominant linguistic construction. Regarding clausal citation scopes, subordination and coordination were more common than embedded structures. The following (f) corresponds to the use of subordination with citing sentences.

(f) *Motivated by previous studies in [1], we introduce a new notion of…*

For multi-sentential cases, citing sentences having citation markers were likely to precede other related citing sentences rather than to follow them. In the following (g) and (h), citation markers *'(Lee et al., 2007b)'* and *'[25]'* respectively span the previous and next sentence.

(g) *Lee et al. reported GC as a lysozyme stabilizer ~. Lysozyme hydrolyzes GC and then ~ (Lee et al., 2007b)*

(h) *The direct effect of staurosporine ~ was published by our group [25]. In that paper, we proposed that ~.*

Table 3. Citation pattern rules in BNF notation with non-terminal nodes uppercased

PATTERN ::= P1 | P2 | P3 | P4 | P5 | P6

P1 ::= BE? PROPOSED
P2 ::= NUMEROUS (RESEARCHER | STUDY)
P3 ::= OTHER PROPOSED
P4 ::= PREVIOUS (METHOD | RESEARCHER | STUDY)
P5 ::= (her | his | their | OTHER 's) (METHOD | STUDY)
P6 ::= RECENTLY

BE ::= are | been | is | was | were
METHOD ::= algorithm | approach | method | solution | strategy | technique
NUMEROUS ::= a few | a large number of | a lot of | a series of | little | many | numerous | several
OTHER[2] is defined by *a noun phrase excluding ones containing 'I', 'my', 'we', 'our'*
PREVIOUS ::= earlier | old | others | previous | recent
PROPOSED ::= analyzed | created | demonstrated | described | developed | devised | discovered | elaborated | employed | exploited | explored | expressed | found | inspired | introduced | investigated | made | motivated | noticed | observed | proposed | published | questioned | reported | reviewed | showed | studied | suggested | used
RECENTLY ::= in recent years | recently | to date | until now | past decades
RESEARCHER ::= investigator | researcher | scholar
STUDY ::= analysis | article | conclusion | finding | idea | literature | paper | proposal | report | research | result | study | theory | thought | work

Table 3 shows citation cue patterns obtained from our 1048 citing sentences. The following are some examples matched for each of six different patterns P1 through P6 in Table 3, where rules were written in BNF(Backus-Naur Form) notation with non-terminal nodes uppercased.

[2] This symbol was specially defined by a natural language sentence due to inconveniences in writing it in BNF notation.

s1: *The quantum white noise theory has* ***been developed*** *based on ...*
Motivated *by the previous studies in [1], ...*
... ***reported*** *by Rassow et al. in 1978 [30].*

s2: *Until now,* ***several studies*** *have been completed ... [20-26].*
A large number of papers *have been published ...*
Strategies ... have advanced through ***numerous studies*** *[3].*

s3: ***Kabli et al. proposed*** *a chain-model GA to search for ...*
Shimada et al. introduced *SS-OCT for this purpose [2].*
In 2002, ***Fried et al. demonstrated*** *that ...*

s4: *This explains why* ***previous investigators*** *(Djurasevic et al. 1998 ...) ...*
Recent study *has suggested that ...*
... widely used by ***earlier researchers*** *[4-7].*

s5: ***Their analysis*** *showed that ...*
His solutions *showed that ...*
Their findings *...*

s6: ***Recently***, *Lee et al. proposed a new sequence-based genetic operator [19] ...*
To date, *several PKC inhibitors have been developed ...*
Over the ***past decades***, *various technologies for ...*

The pattern rules may represent necessary features that sentences citing other works should have. For example, the first sentence of *s2* has two rules P6 and P2 matched for *'until now'* and *'several studies'*, as well as a citation marker *'[20-26]'*. Thus, that sentence could be converted into a feature representation [0, 1, 0, 0, 0, 1, 1] for machine learning (ML), assuming that we are using [P1, P2, P3, P4, P5, P6, ExistenceOfCitationMarkers] as feature elements.

4 Conclusion

This article provided some aspects of citing sentences and their scopes. The boundaries that citation markers encompass could be categorized into five types: phrase, clause, sentence, multi-sentence, and others. Distributional statistics of such citation scopes suggest the need for citation-based summarization approaches to determine sub-sentential citation scopes such as phrases and clauses, as well as multi-sentence regions. Citation cue patterns presented in Table 3 could be employed in rule-based and ML-based approaches to identifying citing sentences.

Acknowledgments. This research was supported by Kyungsung University Research Grants in 2012.

References

1. Abu-Jbara, A., Radev, D.: Coherent Citation-based Summarization of Scientific Papers. In: Proceedings of ACL, pp. 500–509 (2011)
2. Athar, A., Teufel, S.: Detection of Implicit Citations for Sentiment Detection. In: Proceedings of ACL, pp. 18–26 (2012)
3. Kaplan, D., Iida, R., Tokunaga, T.: Automatic Extraction of Citation Contexts for Research Paper Summarization: A Coreference-chain Based Approach. In: Proceedings of the 2009 Workshop on Text and Citation Analysis for Scholarly Digital Libraries, pp. 88–95 (2009)
4. Nanba, H., Kando, N., Okumura, M.: Classification of Research Papers Using Citation Links and Citation Types: Towards Automatic Review Article Generation. In: Proceedings of the 11th SIG Classification Research Workshop, pp. 117–134 (2000)

Scorpio: A Simple, Convenient, Microsoft Excel Macro Based Program for Privacy-Preserving Logrank Test

Yu Li and Sheng Zhong

Computer Science and Engineering Department
State University of New York at Buffalo, Amherst, NY 14260, USA
{yli32,szhong}@buffalo.edu

Abstract. Survival analysis is frequently used for dealing with survival outcomes in biological organisms. However it is a tedious process to compare survival curves step by step. In this study, we designed and developed a user-friendly, cloud-storage based Microsoft Excel program, named Scorpio, for privacy preserving logrank test model. Our program can be applied to Microsoft Excel immediately which is widely used by clinics and biomedical scientists. Therefore, it can be more easily to use and avoid incorrect manipulation by mistake when people compute survival curves comparison statistic manually.

Keywords: Survival curves, Cloud-storage, Microsoft Excel.

1 Introduction

Since the explosive growth of biomedical research in recent years, biomedical scientists have come up with the idea of using these electronic medical data for incorporate research. With the development of privacy preserving and cryptograph technology, there is a trend that developing computer methods and programs to help biomedical staffs collecting the massive data and calculating the complicated models.

Survival analysis is very useful for studying different kinds of event like disease onset, earthquakes, stock market crash etc[1]. Survival analysis also can be used to predict after observing a set of individuals at some specifically time point and continuous monitoring them for fixed intervals of time. In biomedical field, survival analysis mainly means observing time to death of experimental subject. Obviously, if having more experimental data they can get a more precise model. Therefore, biomedical researchers want to combine the data from different institutes to build a better survival function comparison models[2]. For the privacy and security issues, computer scientist can use privacy preserving method to protect the data from revealing to anyone. In order to compare the survival curves without revealing the data, [2] has come up with a privacy preserving model that can protect the data privacy.

However it is a tedious process to compare survival curves step by step. In biomedical field, Microsoft Excel is widely used due to its friendly user-interface

T.-h. Kim et al. (Eds.): EL/DTA/UNESST 2012, CCIS 352, pp. 86–91, 2012.

and easy operation. Compared with other statistical computing softwares like SAS and SPSS etc, although most of these softwares have a strong data management ability, the usage of them will be complicated for biomedical people who have not been trained professionally. Microsoft Excel has been widely applied in Medical institutes no matter it is used for store experimental data or create survival curves. It can help biomedical scientists to analyze and make better decisions. Besides these, Microsoft Excel has a strong ability to let VBA(Visual Basic for Applications) or Macro develop programs to manipulate Excel. Therefore, most of biomedical scientists are more willing to use Microsoft Excel to store the data obtained from the experiment. Consequently, many scientists have developed programs which can apply to Microsoft Excel immediately and automatically. In [3], Hitoshi Sato presented a package of macro programs named PK_MOMENT to automatically calculate non-compartmental pharmacokinetic parameters on Microsoft Excel spreadsheet. In [4], Zhang presented PKSolver, a freely available menu-driven add-in program for Microsoft Excel written in Visual Basic for Applications (VBA), for solving basic problems in pharmacokinetic (PK) and pharmacodynamic (PD) data analysis. In [5], Brown presented a simple, easily understood methodology for solving biologically based models using a Microsoft Excel spreadsheet. In [6], A user-friendly, inexpensive EXCEL-based program to find potential phosphorylation sites in proteins is presented by S.Wera.

In this paper, we develop a user-friendly, cloud-storage based Microsoft Excel program, named Scorpio, for privacy preserving logrank test model. Since the program does not require any programming skills or any use of VBA or Macro language, once the data from all institutes are ready, the program can be run automatically. In the rest of this paper, we describe the method of creating privacy preserving logrank test of survival curves, data storage and collection method as well as the design and implementation of our program.

2 Methods

Logrank test is a standard comparison test of survival curves. When a research institute wants to raise a computation for logrank test, he needs to collect data from different medical institutes. However, some biomedical data are very sensitive. In [2], the authors have come up with a privacy preserving secure sum method which can protect the data from revealing to others.

Based on the privacy preserving logrank test model presented in[2], we develop a program that can automatically collect data from each participate medical institute and add these data to the initial file immediately. After collecting all the data, the program then calculate the quotient of the number of events occurring divided by the number of individuals that are alive in each interval. Then each medical institute can get the value automatically. After that each institute can calculate the expected number of deaths. Then the first institute who raises the comparison can get the final logrank test statistic and inform all other participants.

Specifically we use cloud-based storage to collect the data from each institute. Cloud-based storage can let everybody who has the permission reach the file from anywhere. In this part, as shown in figure 1, our program first let party 1 add a random number on its Windows Excel file which contains the survival data and upload the file into the server, then party 2 downloads this file and add its own data to the existing data, then upload the file to the server. Every party processes like this until the last party is done. Therefore our program which executed by first party can get the sum of actual data after minus the random number. After that program can automatically call Microsoft Excel Macro we developed to calculate the value we need. After that party 1 can get the final logrank test statistic result and let other participated institutes know.

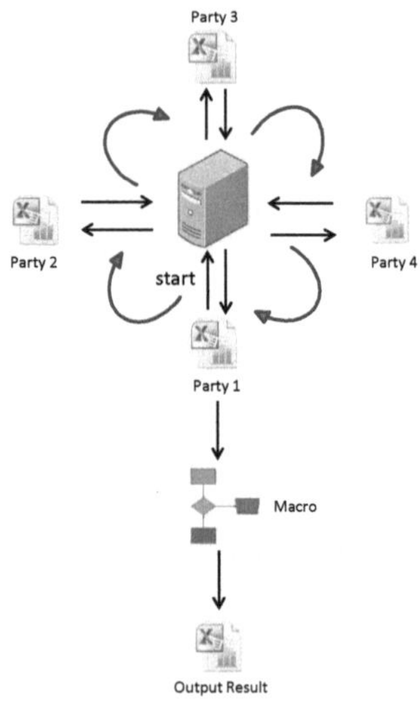

Fig. 1. The flow chart of our program, assume there are four parties participate in this calculation

3 Program Description

3.1 Software Design

The program is developed using C# combined with Microsoft Excel VBA. Microsoft Excel is universal available and very convenient in Bio-medical research institute. We assume every medical institute uses Microsoft Excel to store the survival data. Our program adds a random number to the original data of first institute. Then the first institute raises the requirement of computation for the survival curve comparing logrank test. Our program will automatically upload the file to the server and add other institutes' data to the existing data. Therefore, every institute who participates the computation will not know others' survival data. Although this can be done manually, it will be very tedious and waste a lot of time to click the button when calculate the value using Excel. However our program can easily read the input file and calculate the logrank survival comparison automatically without revealing data to others.

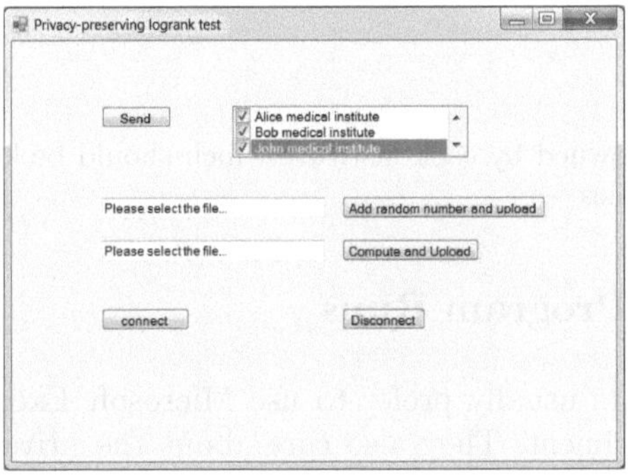

Fig. 2. The program user interface for privacy preserving logrank test

3.2 How to Use Scorpio

At first, we should set up a server that can store the file and send message to each institute. We use socket programming to let the server continue listening to the sockets. When the server received a request, it can set up a connection and send message to this address. After one institute sets up a server that use for store the file, the institute who wants to participate the logrank test calculation runs the program we developed as shown in figure 2. First, every institute should connect to the server. Then one biomedical institute who wants to raise the calculation chooses the participants, and click the send button to uploads its file which has been added a random number on the data. Then each participant will receive a message in turn. After that the program will download the file and add their own data on the previous data in the file and upload it. After all participant finishing adding their data, the first institute can get the whole sum data with the random number he added.

3.3 Computation of Survival Curves Comparing Using Logrank Test

Then the first party can compute the survival curve comparing using logrank test. After the program collecting the data from all medical institutes, the program minus the random number which has been added to the original data and get the whole alive and death number of every intervals. The program then calculate the summation of all alive and death number respectively. Then the program can get the value that we need to calculate the logrank statistic. Our program calls the Microsoft Excel VBA to run the whole process automatically. It can prevent incorrect manipulation by mistake when people do it manually. So our program is easy and convenient to use.

(a) Original data from institute 1

	A	B	C
1	Time to infection	dj	nj
2	0-50	11	18
3	51-100	0	7
4	101-150	2	7
5	151-200	4	5
6	201-250	0	1
7	251-300	0	1
8	301-350	0	1
9	351-400	0	1
10	401-450	0	1
11	451-500	0	1
12	>500	1	1

(b) Original data from institute 2

	A	B	C
1	Time to infection	dj	nj
2	0-50	14	24
3	51-100	5	10
4	101-150	2	5
5	151-200	1	3
6	201-250	1	2
7	251-300	0	1
8	301-350	1	1
9	351-400	0	0
10	401-450	0	0
11	451-500	0	0
12	>500	0	0

(c) Original data from institute 3

	A	B	C
1	Time to infection	dj	nj
2	0-50	3	8
3	51-100	2	5
4	101-150	0	3
5	151-200	2	3
6	201-250	0	1
7	251-300	0	1
8	301-350	0	1
9	351-400	0	1
10	401-450	0	1
11	451-500	0	1
12	>500	1	1

Fig. 3. Original data owned by each institute which should be keep confidential from revealing to other parties

4 Samples of Program Runs

The medical scientists usually prefer to use Microsoft Excel to store the data that gets from experiment. They also care about the privacy issue when they want to combine the data from different medical institute to do some research. Our Scorpio program is specially designed for medical scientists to combine their survival data to generate comparing survival curves using logrank test. The input data is as figure 3 shows. The medical scientists just only need to type the alive and death number into different time intervals. After the program collects all required data from other institutes, the first party use the macro we provide can get the final logrank test statistic result as shown in figure 4.

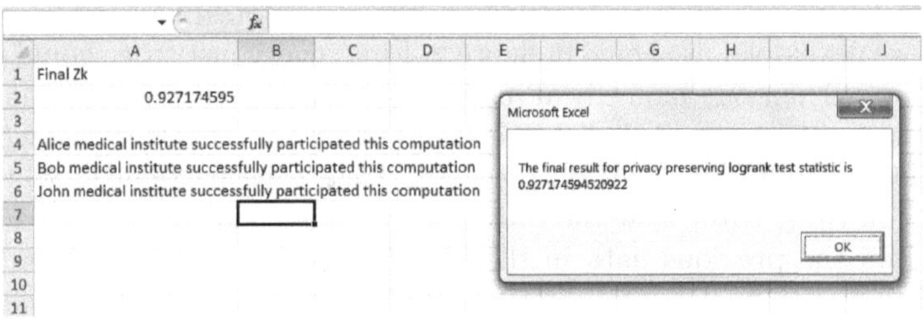

Fig. 4. The final result for privacy preserving logrank test statistic after program finish running

5 Conclusion

In this paper, we have designed a simple, convenient Microsoft Excel Macro based privacy preserving program for survival curves comparison using logrank test. In order to make it easy to use and protect the data privacy, the program can be applied to Microsoft Excel immediately which is widely used by clinics and biomedical scientists. The program also can protect privacy of the data by adding random number to the original data. Experiments on the real medical data has shown the effectiveness of our proposed program.

References

1. Allison, P.D.: Survival analysis using SAS: A practical guide. SAS publishing (2010)
2. Chen, T., Zhong, S.: Privacy-Preserving Models for Comparing Survival Curves Using the Logrank Test. Computer Methods and Programs in Biomedicine (2011)
3. Sato, H., Sato, S., Wang, Y.M., Horikoshi, I.: Add-in macros for rapid and versatile calculation of non-compartmental pharmacokinetic parameters on Microsoft Excel spreadsheets. Computer Methods and Programs in Biomedicine 50(1), 43–52 (1996)
4. Zhang, Y., Huo, M., Zhou, J., Xie, S.: PKSolver: An add-in program for pharmacokinetic and pharmacodynamic data analysis in Microsoft Excel. Computer Methods and Programs in Biomedicine 99(3), 306–314 (2010)
5. Brown, M., et al.: A methodology for simulating biological systems using Microsoft Excel. Computer Methods and Programs in Biomedicine 58(2), 181–190 (1999)
6. Wera, S.: An EXCEL-based method to search for potential Ser/Thr-phosphorylation sites in proteins. Computer Methods and Programs in Biomedicine 58(1), 65–68 (1998)

Generic Process Framework for Safety-Critical Software in a Weapon System

Myongho Kim[1], Joohyun Lee[2], and Doo-Hwan Bae[1]

[1] Software Graduate School, Korea Advanced Institute Science & Technology, Korea
[2] LIG Nex1, Seongnam, KyoungGi Province, Korea
myonghokim91@gmail.com, joohyunlee@lignex1.com

Abstract. A modern weapon system has deployed much more software to control its capability than before. Therefore, the importance of software safety has been more recognize in the system safety by various stakeholders such as developers and users. In the future, software safety will be the most critical portion of the weapon system. Advanced countries in the defense area such as USA and European countries have already established the standards for software safety and forced to use them in deploying new products in the both commercial and defense areas. However, the Korean government and government agencies haven't established any appropriate software safety standard yet. The purpose of this paper is to suggest a new software safety process framework based on international software safety standard and the Korean acquisition process. This will be used to make the basic line of the software safety standard in Korea.

1 Introduction

The past several decades have seen a rapid increase in the use of software in safety-critical systems such as the avionics, medical, nuclear, transportation, and military industries [12]. Today, digital computer systems have autonomous control over safety-critical functions in nearly every major technology, both commercially and within Government systems [1].

To accomplish the software safety in a safety-critical complex weapon system, software safety engineering activities have to be integrated with the other engineering activities: system safety engineering, system engineering, software engineering. And software safety activities are planned and managed by risk management process. Furthermore, software safety process has to comply with the government regulations of weapon system acquisition process. However, the Korean government and government agencies haven't established any software safety standard yet. In this paper, we propose a generic software safety process framework which complies with the Korea regulations: Defense Acquisition Management Regulation, Weapon System Software Development and Management Guideline. To describe this framework, BPMN (Business Process Modeling Notation) 2.0 is used.

The remainder of this paper is organized as follows: In section 2, we briefly present the characteristics of the weapon system. Section 3 proposes the 'generic process

T.-h. Kim et al. (Eds.): EL/DTA/UNESST 2012, CCIS 352, pp. 92–98, 2012.

framework for safety-critical software in a weapon system'. Finally, in Section 4, we discuss the future work.

2 Characteristics of Weapon System

In developing the generic process framework for safety-critical software in the weapon system, it is essential to understand the common characteristics of weapon systems. The brief overview of these will help you understand the framework.

There are two main characteristics of the weapon system: safety-criticality and mission-criticality. Each detailed feature is described in the following.

Safety-criticality in safety-critical systems [13] : Failure may cause injury or death to human beings. Weapon systems are intended to cause destruction on targets. However, the key phrase is "to intended targets", meaning that the weapon system should not cause harm to its own users. For example, a torpedo is incapable of differentiating signals from its target and from its mother ship. Thus, system developers incorporate a feature in the design such as arming after a safe distance.

Mission-criticality in mission critical systems [13] : Failure will cause significant loss in terms of money, trust, or defense capabilities of a nation or of a military entity. For example, if a particular weapon does not work in a combat airplane or in a ship, the airplane or ship will be subject to destruction by the enemy. It is similar to real-time systems.

Thus, weapon system software needs to be managed and handled by considering these characteristics. Especially when it comes to "generic process framework for safety-critical software", the features of safety-critical systems need to be taken into consideration.

3 Proposed Generic Process Framework for Safety-Critical Software in a Weapon System

3.1 Overview

The important issue is that software safety process should be taken into account as well as system safety process, software engineering process, system engineering process and project management process. And, all activities related to software safety have to be reflected in the integrated master plan & integrated master schedule. The relationship of process area is as below;

The framework has been constructed in consideration of the weapon acquisition process in Korea and has three features as follow:

First, safety engineering process is classified by three phases, which are planned and managed by safety risk management process. Second, safety risk management process closely interacts with both system engineering process and project management process. Third, software safety requirements led by software safety engineering process are combined with system safety requirements in the light of hardware, human factor and emergent properties. After that, software safety requirements baseline is established by trade-off study of system engineering process.

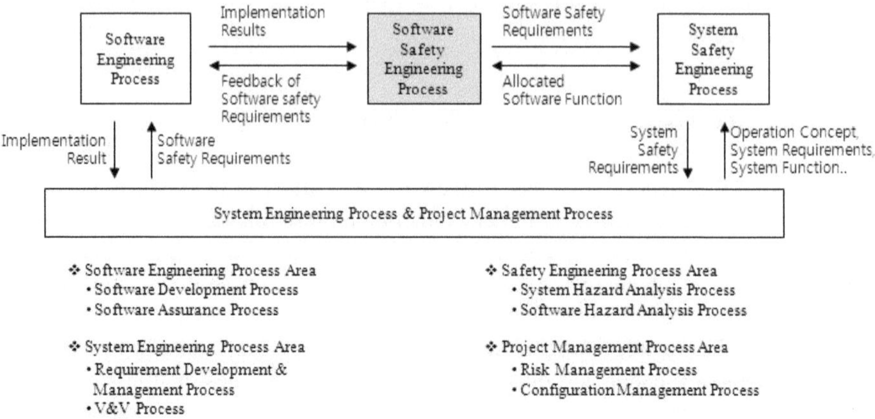

Fig. 1. The Relationship of process areas related to software safety

And all changes after the baseline should be managed through configuration management process, risk management process, and requirement management process.

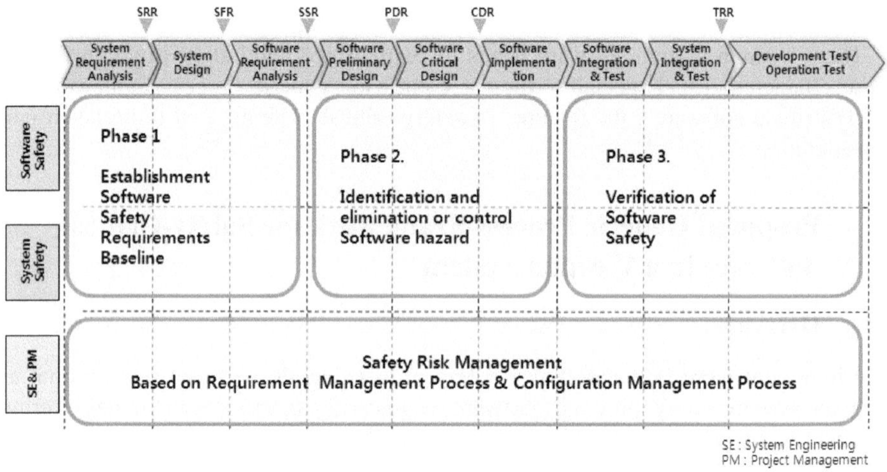

Fig. 2. Process Framework for Safety-Critical Software

3.2 Safety Risk Management

Safety risk management process consists of 3 sub-processes.

- Risk planning process : This process provides the organized, integrated safety risk plan to identify and assess hazard considering the other plan.
- Identification & assessment of hazard and management of safety risk process : This process consists of 2 activities. First, it examines a situation and identifies the area of

potential risk. Second, it determines the severity with software control categories[2] and potential severity. This process includes activities as below:

- Define acceptance of risk
- Make risk management plan focus on software requirement
- System requirements are properly allocated to software requirements.

- Management of safety risk process : This process monitors and controls all activities related to software safety activities and assesses the residual risk to establish the lifecycle risk management plan.

3.3 Phase 1 : Establishment of Safety Requirements Baseline

The main purpose of Phase 1 is to draw PHL(Preliminary Hazard List). Based on this, software safety requirements should be decided through Phase 1. The technique and model of analysis is various, the important issue is to select an appropriate technique considering all aspects: characteristics of system, time, resource, maturity of technique etc.

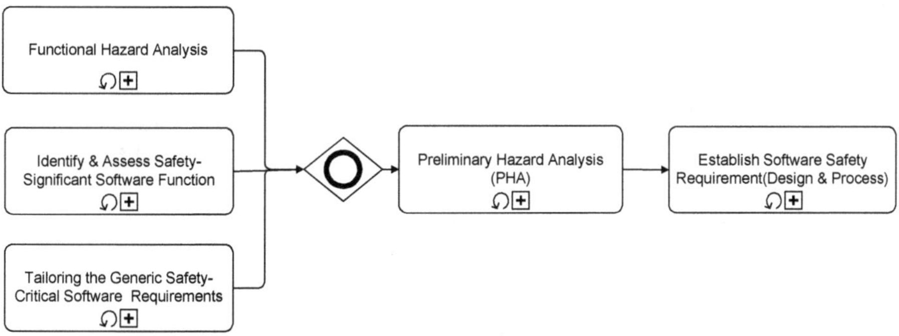

Fig. 3. Phase 1. Establishment of Safety Requirements Baseline

- Functional Hazard Analysis

- Evaluate hazards against system function requirements
- Evaluate all safety-critical functions identified by each domain expert

- Identify & assess safety-significant software function

- Identify safety-significant software function
- Assess for severity to determine software criticality and level of rigor allocation

- Tailoring the generic safety-critical software requirements

- Use historical data & existing generic requirements and guidelines
- Tailor generic and domain specific software requirements

- Preliminary Hazard Analysis(PHA)
  - Identify & system/software level causal factors
  - Apply HRI and prioritize hazards
  - Apply risk assessment criteria and categorize hazards
  - Link hazard causal factors to requirements
  - Develop design recommendations
- Establish software safety requirement
  - Identify & system/software kevel causal factors
  - Apply HRI and prioritize hazards
  - Apply risk assessment criteria and categorize hazards
  - Link hazard causal factors to requirements
  - Develop design recommendations

3.4 Phase 2 : Identification and Elimination or Control Hazard

In phase 2, Software safety engineer have to do SHA(Software Hazard Analysis) in accordance with the development maturity. The data of SHA(Software Hazard Analysis) is used for SHA(System Hazard Analysis).

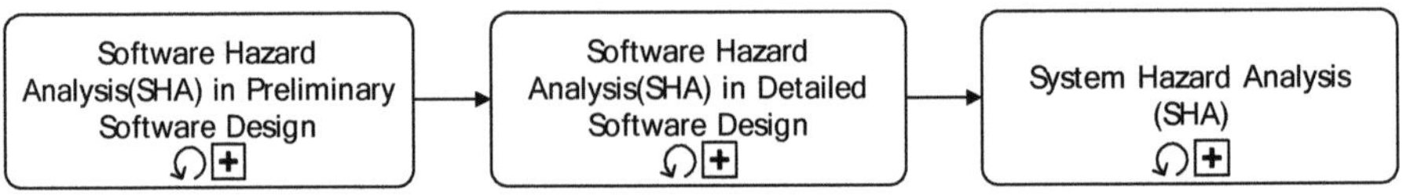

Fig. 4. Phase 2. Identification and elimination or control hazard

- Software Hazard Analysis (SHA) In Preliminary Software Design
  - Trace Top Level Safety Requirements to Software Design
  - Link Hazard Causal Factors to Software Architecture.
  - Analyze Design of CSCI
- Software Hazard Analysis (SHA) In Detailed Software Design
  - Perform in-depth hazard causal analysis (ex: "What-If" Type Analysis & Safety-Critical Path Analysis, Link Hazard Causal Factors to Actual Code)
  - Analyze Final Implementation of Safety requirements
- System Hazard Analysis (SHA)
  - Analyze Interface Requirements to ensure Implementation of Safety Requirements
  - Examine Causal Relationship of Multiple Failure Modes (Hardware, Software, Human, Emergency Properties)
  - Determine Compliance with Safety Criteria
  - Derive Control Requirement to Minimize Hazard Effects
  - Assist to produce Safety Test case & Procedures

3.5 Phase 3 : Verification and Validation of Software Safety

In phase 3, The software safety requirement is verified and validated by various predetermined methods: test, demonstrate, analysis and inspection. And then, Residual risk is assessed to establish the lifecycle risk management plan.

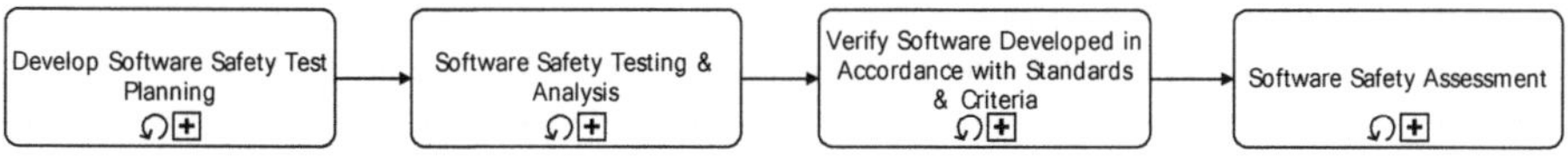

Fig. 5. Phase 3. Verification and Validation of Software Safety

- Develop Software Safety Test Planning

- Develop Software safety Test Plan.
- Integrate Software Safety Test plan to Software Test plan & System Test Pan.

- Software Safety Testing & Analysis

- Perform Software Safety Testing & Analysis
- Retest of Failed Requirements

- Verify Software Developed in Accordance with Standards & Criteria

- Examine evidence of safety-significant Requirements implementation.

- Software Safety Assessment

- Assess Results of Software Hazard Analysis, Safety & IV&V Tests
- Review Safety-Critical Software Requirements Compliance Assessment
- Assess Residual Risk of System Modifications

4 Conclusion and Future Work

The purpose of this framework is to provide a process guideline to achieve safe software. To accomplish this purpose, considering all activities related to software safety, we propose a generic process framework with a set of system engineering, software engineering and project management, and the framework is consistent with the weapon system acquisition regulation in Korea.

The proposed generic process framework for safety-critical software in weapon systems is not completed yet. The framework will be verified and revised by software engineers and system engineers through real application to safety critical software development. Also, gathered data will be used to improve the process framework.

References

1. Joint Software Systems Safety Engineering WorkGroup : Joint Software Systems Safety Engineering Handbook (Version 1.0, Published August 27, 2010)
2. Department of Defense : MIL-STD-882E System Safety (May 11, 2012, Superseding MIL-STD-882D, February 10, 2000)

3. Department of Defense : DoDI 5000.02 Operation of the Defense Acquisition System (December 8, 2008)
4. Defense Acquisition Program Administration : Defense Acquisition Management Regulation (June 20, 2012)
5. Defense Acquisition Program Administration : Weapon System Software Development and Management Guideline (August 28, 2012)
6. Federal Aviation Administration : Acquisition Management Policy (revised July 2012)
7. Federal Aviation Administration : System Safety Handbook (December 30, 2000)
8. Federal Aviation Administration : Safety Risk Management Guidance for System Acquisitions (December 2008)
9. National Aeronautics and Space Administration : NASA/SP-2010-580 System Safety Handbook (Version 1.0, November 2011)
10. National Aeronautics and Space Administration : NASA-STD-8719.13B Software Safety Standard (July 8, 2008)
11. National Aeronautics and Space Administration : NASA-GB-8719.13 Software Safety Handbook (March 31, 2008)
12. Walker, E.: DOD Software Tech News, Tech Views - Challenges Dominate Our Future (2011)
13. Demir, K.A.: Challenges of weapon systems software development. Journal of Naval Science and Engineering 5(3) (2009)
14. Stuebing, H.G.: A Software Engineering Environment(SEE) for Weapon System Software. IEEE Transactions on Software Engineering SE-10(4) (July 1984)

Threshold Identity-Based Broadcast Encryption from Identity-Based Encryption

Kitak Kim, Milyoung Kim, Hyoseung Kim, Jon Hwan Park, and Dong Hoon Lee

Graduate School of Information Security, Korea University, Seoul, Korea
{kitak,us61219,ki_myo,decartian,donghlee}@korea.ac.kr

Abstract. In threshold identity-based encryption, a sender encrypts a message under identities of a pool of users and assigns a threshold t to the ciphertext, and sends the resulting ciphertext to these users. The cooperation of at least t users among them is required to decrypt the given ciphertext. We propose a construction method for threshold identity-based broadcast encryption from any existing identity-based encryption.

1 Introduction

In a threshold encryption scheme, the sender can encrypt the message and send to an authorized group of users. It is required that at least t of receivers cooperate to decrypt the given ciphertext. Threshold cryptosystem is suitable when the decryption ability is controlled and distributed to the authorized group of users such as an electronic voting and a key escrow system. In dynamic threshold identity-based broadcast encryption, the encrypter can choose the set of intended users who are potentially able to decrypt the ciphertext and also control the threshold value.

Desmedt and Frankel first introduced a concept of the threshold cryptosystem [1]. To the best of our knowledge, there are two threshold identity-based broadcast encryption schemes which satisfy two properties: the security under the adaptive corruption model and the dynamic threshold value. In [2] the authors proposed a threshold identity-based broadcast encryption scheme that satisfies above two properties. However the security was proven in the random oracle model [3]. In [4] the authors gave threshold broadcast encryption schemes both public-key and identity-based setting. The identity-based scheme in [4] satisfied above two properties. However they also used the random oracle model to prove the security.

We propose a construction method for dynamic threshold identity-based broadcast encryption from any existing identity-based encryption. A threshold identity-based broadcast encryption scheme generated by our construction method is secure under the adaptive corruption model and the standard model if the underline identity-based encryption is secure under these models. Among the previous works, the schemes in [2] and [4] are secure under the adaptive corruption model. Unfortunately, those schemes are secure in the random oracle model. A demerit of our work is a length of ciphertext. The ciphertext-size of our scheme is s+O(1) where s is the number of users in the authorized set of user. The ciphertext-size of the schemes in [2] and [4] are

T.-h. Kim et al. (Eds.): EL/DTA/UNESST 2012, CCIS 352, pp. 99–102, 2012.

O(n) and n-t+O(1), respectively, where n is the number of all users and t is the threshold value. In some situation such that t is less than s/2 and s equals n, our scheme is more efficient than the schemes in [2] and [4].

2 Preliminaries

2.1 Threshold Identity-Based Broadcast Encryption

Threshold identity-based broadcast encryption consists of seven algorithms.

- Setup(λ, n): Takes as input a security parameter λ and a number of receivers n. It outputs a master key mk and the public paramters params. The master key is kept secret and public parameters are widely distributed.
- Ext(ID, mk): Takes as input the identity of a user ID and mk. It outputs a user's key set (uvk_{ID}, usk_{ID}), where uvk_{ID} and usk_{ID} are the verification key and the private eky of the user, respectively. The private key is given to the user and kept secret. The verification key of the user is widely distributed.
- Enc(params, S, t, M): Takes as input params, a user's identity set S, a threshold t and a message M. It generates the ephemeral encryption key K. It outputs a ciphertext C on the message M.
- ValCT(params, S, t, C): It checks the validity of the ciphertext with respect to params, S, t. It outputs 1 if the ciphertext is valid. Otherwise, outputs 0.
- ShaDec(params, S, t, usk_{ID}, C): It outputs a decryption share σ_{ID} of the user ID.
- ShaVer(params, S, ID, σ_{ID}): It checks the validity of the decryption share σ_{ID} with respect to ID. It outputs 1, if a decryption share is valid. Otherwise, outputs 0.
- Com(params, S, t, T, Γ, C): Takes as input params, S, t, a subset $T \subset S$, where $|T|=t$, a collection of t decryption shares Γ, and C. It first checks the validity of given decryption shares using the ShaVal algorithm. If there is not an invalid decryption share, it outputs a message M. Otherwise, outputs 0.

These algorithms have to satisfy the correctness, when C is corresponded to a user set S and a threshold t, then

$$\forall M\text{: VerCT(params, S, t, C)=NULL, ShaVer(params, S, ID, }\sigma_{ID}\text{, C)=NULL for } ID \in S \text{ and Com(params, S, t, T, }\Gamma\text{, C)=M, where } \sigma_i\text{=ShaDec(params, S, t, }usk_{ID}\text{, C) and C=Enc(params, S, t, M).}$$

2.2 Identity-Based Encryption

Identity-based encryption consists of four algorithms.

- Setup(λ): It outputs a public parameters $params_{IBE}$ and mk_{IBE}. The master key is kept secret and public parameters are distributed.
- Ext($params_{IBE}$,mk_{IBE},ID): It outputs a private eky d_{ID}.
- Enc($params_{IBE}$,ID,M): It outputs a ciphertext C.
- Dec(params,d_{ID},C): It outputs the message M.

Theses algorithms have to satisfy the correctness, when d_{ID} is the private eky generated by algorithm Ext where ID is the public key, then

$$\forall M\text{: Dec}(params_{IBE}, d_{ID}, C)=M \text{ where } C=\text{Enc}(params_{IBE}, ID, M).$$

Bilinear Pairings. Let G_1 and G_2 be two cyclic groups of prime order p. We assume that g is a generator of G_1. Let $e{:}G_1\times G_1\rightarrow G_2$ be a function that has the following properties:

1. Bilinear: for all u, v $\in G_1$ and a, b$\in Z$, we have $e(u^a,v^b)=e(u,v)^{ab}$.
2. Non-degenerate: $e(g,g)\neq 1$.
3. Computable: there is an efficient algorithm to compute the map e.

3 Threshold Identity-Based Broadcast Encryption

In this section, we introduce a construction method for TIBBE from any existing IBE scheme and a bilinear pairing. A TIBBE scheme Π=(Setup, Ext, ValCT, ShaDec, ShaVer, Com) can be constructed by given any identity-based encryption scheme Π_{IBE}=($Setup_{IBE}$, Ext_{IBE}, Enc_{IBE}, Dec_{IBE}), and a bilinear pairing e and strongly unforgeable one-time signature scheme Σ. We use Shamir's secret sharing scheme [5] to control the threshold ability.

- Setup(λ, n): Choose a bilinear pairing e: $G_1\times G_1\rightarrow G_2$. Choose a prime p such that $|p|=\lambda$. Choose two cryptographic hash functions, H_1: $\{0,1\}^*\rightarrow Z_p$ and H_2: $Z_p\rightarrow G_1$. Run <$params_{IBE}$, mk_{IBE}> ←$Setup_{IBE}(\lambda)$. Choose a strongly unforgeable one-time signature Σ=(Gen, Sign, Vrfy). Choose random g, u and v of G_1. Set params←<$params_{IBE}$,n,g,u,v,H_1,H_2,e,Σ> with the description of underlying identity-based encryption scheme, and mk←mk_{IBE}. Output <params, mk>.
- Ext(ID, mk): Run d_{ID}←ExtIBE($params_{IBE}$, mk_{IBE}, ID). Generate a one-time signature key pair for ID such as (ssk_{ID}, svk_{ID})←Gen(λ). Set (uvk_{ID}, usk_{ID})←(svk_{ID}, (d_{ID}, ssk_{ID})). Output (uvk_{ID}, usk_{ID}).
- Enc(params, S, t, M): Without loss of generality, let S be the set $\{ID_1, \ldots, ID_s\}$ for s=|S|. Choose a polynomial $P[X]=\alpha+\alpha_1X+\ldots+\alpha_{t-1}X^{t-1}\in Z_p[X]$, for random coefficients $\alpha, \alpha_1, \ldots, \alpha_{t-1}\in Z_p$. Choose a random $k\in Z_p$. Compute C_M←$Me(H_2(P(0)),g)^k$ and C_0←g^k. Run C_{IDi}←Enc_{IBE}($params_{IBE}$, ID_i, $P(H_1(ID_i))$) for $ID_i\in S$ and $i\in\{1, \ldots, s\}$. Generate a one-time signature key pair (ssk, svk)←Gen(λ). Compute σ←Sign(ssk, (C_M, C_0, C_{ID1}, …, C_{IDs})) and C_σ←$(u^{svk}v)^k$. Set C←<svk, C_M, C_0, C_{ID1}, …, C_{IDs}, C_σ σ>. Output C.
- ValCT(params, S, t, C): Return 1, if Vrfy(svk, (C_M, C_0, C_{ID1}, …, C_{IDs}), σ)=1 and $e(g, C_\sigma)=e(C_0, u^{svk}v)$. Otherwise, return 0.
- ShaDec(params, S, t, usk_{IDi}, C): Run s_{IDi}←Dec_{IBE}($params_{IBE}$, d_{IDi}, C_{IDi}). Choose a random k_i of Z_p. Compute σ_i←Sign(ssk_{IDi}, s_{IDi}), C_{sIDi}←$(u^{svkIDi}v)^{ki}$ and C_i←g^{ki}. Set the decryption share of ID_i as σ_{IDi}←(uvk_{IDi}, s_{IDi}, σ_i, C_{sIDi}, C_i). Output σ_{IDi}.
- Com(params, S, t, T, Γ, C): Without loss of generality, let T be $\{ID_1, \ldots, ID_t\}$. Returen 0 if ValCT(params, S, t, C)=0 or ShaVer(params, S, uvk_i, σ_{IDi})=0 for each $ID_i\in T$ and $\sigma_{IDi}\in\Gamma$. Otherwise, Compute the value s ←

$\Sigma_{i=1}^{t}(P(H_1(ID_i))\cdot\Pi_{j=1,j\neq i}^{t}-H_1(ID_j)/(H_1(ID_i)-H_1(ID_j)))$. Compute $M\leftarrow C_M/e(H_2(s), C_0)$. Output M.

Correctness. We define the Lagrange coefficient $\Delta_{i,S}$ for $i\in Z_p$ and a set S, of elements in $\{0, 1\}^*$:

$$\Delta_{i,S(x)}=\Pi_{j\in S,j\neq i}(x-H_1(j))/(H_1(i)-H_1(j))$$

We will show that our TIBBE scheme satisfies the correctness. We assume that ValCT algorithm and ShaVer algorithm return 1 for all inputs.

$$C_M/e(H_2(s), C_0)=(M\cdot e(H_2(P(0)),g)^k)/(e(H_2(\Sigma_{i=1}^{t}(P(H_1(ID_i))\cdot\Delta_{IDi,T}(0))),g^k))$$
$$=(M\cdot e(H_2(P(0)),g)^k)/(e(H_2(P(0)),g^k))=M.$$

4 Conclusion

We proposed the construction method for threshold identitybased broadcast encryption from any identity-based encryption. Our construction is first scheme which is secure under the full security model. However, the length of ciphertext depends on the number of user included the authorized broadcast set. Reducing the ciphertext size under the full security model is the interesting problem in this area.

Acknowledgement. This work was partially supported by Defense Acquisition Program Administration and Agency for Defense Development under the contract.

References

1. Desmedt, Y., Frankel, Y.: Threshold Cryptosystems. In: Brassard, G. (ed.) CRYPTO 1989. LNCS, vol. 435, pp. 307–315. Springer, Heidelberg (1990)
2. Chai, Z., Cao, Z., Zhou, Y.: Efficient id-based broadcast threshold decryption in ad hoc network. In: Ni, J., Dongarra, J. (eds.) IMSCCS (2), pp. 148–154. IEEE Computer Society (2006)
3. Bellare, M., Rogaway, P.: Random oracles are practical: A paradigm for designing efficient protocols. In: Denning, D.E., Pyle, R., Ganesan, R., Sandhu, R.S., Ashby, V. (eds.) ACM Conference on Computer and Communications Security, pp. 62–73. ACM (1993)
4. Daza, V., Herranz, J., Morillo, P., Ràfols, C.: CCA2-Secure Threshold Broadcast Encryption with Shorter Ciphertexts. In: Susilo, W., Liu, J.K., Mu, Y. (eds.) ProvSec 2007. LNCS, vol. 4784, pp. 35–50. Springer, Heidelberg (2007)
5. Shamir, A.: How to share a secret. Commun. ACM 22(11), 612–613 (1979)
6. Waters, B.: Efficient Identity-Based Encryption Without Random Oracles. In: Cramer, R. (ed.) EUROCRYPT 2005. LNCS, vol. 3494, pp. 114–127. Springer, Heidelberg (2005)

Software Implementation of Source Code Quality Analysis and Evaluation for Weapon Systems Software

Seill Kim and Youngkyu Park

Defense Agency for Technology and Quality
Cheongyang P.O. Box 276, Seoul 130-650, South Korea
{ksismo,youngkyupark}@dtaq.re.kr

Abstract. DESIS(DEfense Software Information System) is being developed to manage and maintain weapon systems software as a whole in defense area. Main goal of the system is to evaluate software quality of weapon systems, analyze whether to violate copy right, and to service technical information. In this paper, we present product quality evaluation function of weapon systems software. First, we developed procedure according to ISO/IEC-9126 to evaluate product quality of weapon systems software. Product quality characteristics have been defined by ISO/IEC-9126, specifically Maintainability for main characteristic, and analyzability, changeability, stability, and testability for minor characteristic. We have obtained common metrics by comparing and analyzing metrics from 3 state analysis softwares in order to establish quality measure metric of sub characteristic. Based on that, we established quality metrics per sub characteristics that let us decide where to attain Maintainability, quality objective, utilizing quality metrics. In addition, we set up desired value broken down by weapon systems classification based upon weapon systems software characteristic. As future work, we will calibrate desired value reflecting development capability and environment of domestic weapon systems software.

1 Introduction

DESIS(DEfense Software Information System) is being developed to manage and maintain weapon systems software as a whole in defense area. Main goal of the system is to evaluate software quality of weapon systems, analyze whether to violate copy right, and to service technical information.

Hundreds of weapon systems softwares are managed in DESIS. Since it takes 5 to 10 years for weapon systems development, source code managed in DESIS is written in Ada, C, and etc. Approximately 30% of those are written in C/C++.

3 static analysis tools are available in DESIS, capable of analyzing C/C++, JAVA, Ada.

In this paper, we describe quality analysis and evaluation functionality among many functions in DESIS. We applied quality characteristics and minor characteristics according to ISO/IEC-9126 to evaluate product quality of weapon systems software.

T.-h. Kim et al. (Eds.): EL/DTA/UNESST 2012, CCIS 352, pp. 103–106, 2012.

As for product quality characteristics, we have chosen maintainability because weapon systems software needs to be maintain 20 to 30 years until they are discarded. Minor characteristics are analyzability, changeability, stability, and testability.

We applied metrics from commercial-off-the-shelf static analysis software to set up quality indicator and metric per minor characteristics.

Since every static analysis software has different metrics and methodology, we established common metrics by comparing and analyzing metrics from 3 static analysis tools. We defined derived metric as common metric, and based on that, we defined quality metric per 4 minor characteristics.

Next, we established metric derived value of SW product of weapon systems. We added scale value in order to adjust desired value, for SW quality is different. Software code quality evaluation functionality has been implemented in DESIS.

In this paper, we describe quality evaluation framework in section 2, quality evaluation functionality implementation in section 3, conclusion and future work in section 4.

2 Quality Evaluation Framework

2.1 Quality Characteristics and Critera

We defined SW quality characteristic for weapon systems based on ISO/IEC 9126-1. Since SW quality evaluation function is applicable to software source code, we defined maintainability as quality characteristics.

Table 1. Quality Characteristics

Quality Characteristics	Definition
Maintainability	The ease with which a product can be maintained
Analyzability	The ease with which a product can be analyzed for diagnosis
Changeability	The quality of being changeable
Stability	The state of being stable
Testability	The degree to which

2.2 Quality Evaluation Characteristics and Measure Criteria

We compared metrics from 3 different commercial-off-the-shelf static analysis software in order to establish quality measure criteria of SW source of weapon systems. Since every static analysis software has different measure criteria and metric, we need common metric that can be applied. Table 2 shows the common metrics.

Table 2. Common metrics of commercial-off-the-shelf static analysis software

No	language	metric	METRIC		
			A사	B사	C사
1	C	Comment Density	Total Comments /Exe. Lines	FICRO	Comment Density
2		…			

2.3 Quality Evaluation Indicator for Minor Characteristics

We established metrics in order to evaluate quality of minor characteristics using common metrics. We used weighted value from NASA to set up indicator. Metric for C was different from C++, and scale factor has been added for each weapon systems.

In the Case of C

$$\text{Analyzability} = VG \times W\_SA + STMT \times W\_SA + ASOS \times W\_SA + CD \times W\_SA$$

$$\text{Changeability} = NP \times W\_SC + NOLV \times W\_SC + STMT \times W\_SC + VF \times W\_SC$$

$$\text{Stability} = NP \times W\_SS + OSTMT \times W\_SS + NOGV \times W\_SS + NOFI \times W\_SS$$

$$\text{Testability} = VG \times W\_ST + NP \times W\_ST + NNL \times W\_ST + NOFO \times W\_ST$$

here, W_SA , W_SC , W_SS , W_ST are Scale Factors.

In the Case of C++

$$\text{Analyzability} = WMC \times W\_SA + STMT \times W\_SA + DIT \times W\_SA + CD \times W\_SA$$

$$\text{Changeability} = WMC \times W\_SC + RFC \times W\_SC + SIX \times W\_SC + PubMR \times W\_SC$$

$$\text{Stability} = WMC \times W\_SS + LCOM \times W\_SS + CBO \times W\_SS + DIT \times W\_SS$$

$$\text{Testability} = RFC \times W\_ST + CBO \times W\_ST + DIT \times W\_ST + NOM \times W\_ST$$

here, W_SA , W_SC , W_SS , W_ST are Scale Factors.

To obtain the quality characteristic Maintainability from above, Maintainability is

$$\text{Maintainability} = \text{Analyzability} \times W\_V + \text{Changeability} \times W\_V + \text{Stability} \times W\_V + \text{Testability} \times W\_V$$

here, W_V is Weight Value

From above, the total Maintainability is

Total_Maintainability = Maintainability × WW_F

here, WW_F is a Scale Factor for Weapon Systems.

3 Implementation of Quality Evaluation Functionality

The functionality for managing quantitatively quality analysis and evaluation of weapon systems software has been implemented into software system. Administrator of the system can confirm the software user registered, and let the static analysis software analyze. When analysis has been initiated, each analysis software check coding rule, conduct static analysis, derive common metrics, and conduct quality evaluation. When those jobs are finished, it present final results to the screen.

4 Conclusion

In this paper, we present product quality evaluation function of weapon systems software. First, we developed procedure according to ISO/IEC-9126 to evaluate product quality of weapon systems software. Product quality characteristics have been defined by ISO/IEC-9126, specifically Maintainability for main characteristic, and analyzability, changeability, stability, and testability for minor characteristic. We have obtained common metrics by comparing and analyzing metrics from 3 state analysis softwares in order to establish quality measure metric of sub characteristic. Based on that, we established quality metrics per sub characteristics that let us decide where to attain Maintainability, quality objective, utilizing quality metrics. In addition, we set up desired value broken down by weapon systems classification based upon weapon systems software characteristic.

With our quality evaluation method, we conducted 50 case studies by evaluating 50 weapon systems source code, and validated the results.

Desired value of quality characteristics in this paper reflects cases from public sector, making it unrealistic in defense weapon systems software. Thus, in the future, we will reflect domestic weapon systems software developmental capability and environment, and calibrate desired value as necessary.

References

1. Kim, S.-I., Kim, H.-S., Lee, I.-L.: A Study on the Management System Design for Technical Information of the Weapon Embedded Software. The Korea Society of Computer and Information 14(11), 123–134 (2009)
2. ISO 9126, Information Technology - Software product quality (1998)
3. Rosenberg, L.H.: Applying and Interpreting Object Oriented Metrics, NASA
4. Hudli, R., Hoskins, C., Hudli, A.: Software Metrics for Object Oriented Designs. IEEE (1994)
5. McCabe & Associates, McCabe Object Oriented Tool User"s Instructions (1994)

An Approach to Constructing Timing Diagrams from UML/MARTE Behavioral Models for Guidance and Control Unit Software

Jinho Choi[1,2] and Doo-Hwan Bae[1]

[1] Dept. of Computer Science, College of Information Science and Technology, Korea Advanced Institute of Science and Technology (KAIST)
[2] Agency for Defense Development (ADD)
Daejeon, Republic of Korea
{jhchoi,bae}@se.kaist.ac.kr

Abstract. Timing-related issues need to be managed from early design phase for successful development of GCU (Guidance and Control Unit) software. UML/MARTE behavioral models can specify timing information in the multiple viewpoints. Among UML behavioral models, UML timing diagrams are useful to show timing information intuitively. We propose an approach to constructing timing diagrams with MARTE annotations from the state machine and sequence diagrams with MARTE annotations. The proposed approach consists of the consistency checking step to get well-formed UML/MARTE models and the model transformation step to construct timing diagrams.

1 Introduction

GCU (Guidance and Control Unit) software used in military avionics systems is rapidly growing in complexity and size. A GCU is a safety-critical and real-time embedded system, and GCU software controls GCU resources and communicates with other subsystems and also executes flight-related functions [1]. Furthermore, diverse experts in the fields of aerospace, electronics, mechanics and computer science attend to develop a GCU. To develop GCU software successfully, timing-related issues such as timing constraints and execution scenarios should be specified and analyzed from early design phase [1][4].

The UML (Unified Modeling Language) is a general purpose modeling language for visualization and understanding of software structures and behaviors [2]. However, UML is hard to specify timing characteristics of RTES. To solve limitations of UML, MARTE (Modeling and Analysis of Real-Time Embedded systems) profile is adopted [3]. MARTE provides predefined stereotypes and tagged values for real-time embedded software.

UML sequence diagrams and UML state machine diagrams are frequently used for describing interactions between objects and behavior of objects, respectively. Since UML timing diagrams show intuitive specifications for timing constraints and have been used widely in electronic domain [4], timing diagrams are useful for providing a

T.-h. Kim et al. (Eds.): EL/DTA/UNESST 2012, CCIS 352, pp. 107–110, 2012.

common understanding and effective communications to stakeholders attended in the development of GCU software.

We observe that timing diagrams can be constructed from sequence diagrams and state machine diagrams because sequence diagrams and state machine diagrams have relevant information to timing diagrams such as timing ruler values, lifelines, states, events and durations. We propose an approach to constructing timing diagrams with MARTE annotations (TDs/MARTE) from sequence diagrams with MARTE annotations (SDs/MARTE) and state machine diagrams with MARTE annotations (SMDs/MARTE). With the proposed approach, we can save modeling time for TDs/MARTE and can easily understand and analyze timing behavior of RTES. This research is extended with our previous work [5].

2 An Approach to Constructing Timing Diagrams

Figure 1 shows the overall approach for constructing timing diagrams. SDs/MARTE and SMDs/MARTE are input to the TDs/MARTE construction process. The TDs/MARTE construction process consists of two steps such as the consistency checking and the model transformation. We explain UML/MARTE behavioral modeling, consistency checking and model transformation as follows:

UML/MARTE Behavioral Modeling for RTES

We propose guidelines for UML/MARTE behavioral modeling to describe behavior of RTES for event-driven or timing-triggered systems (e.g., a GCU). Since UML is informal, guidelines are necessary to use UML/MARTE in RTES domain. We assume that temporal behaviors are performed under the synchrony hypothesis. Figures 2 and 3 show an example of SD/MARTE and SMDs/MARTE for Counter and Displayer. The SD/MARTE in Figure 2 shows message interchange between Counter and Displayer every 50 milliseconds. Lifelines, messages, time observations, execution specifications and MARTE annotations are used to specify SDs/MARTE. SMDs/MARTE in Figure 3 describe the overall behavior of Counter and Displayer. In SMDs/MARTE modeling, states, events, actions, and MARTE annotation are used.

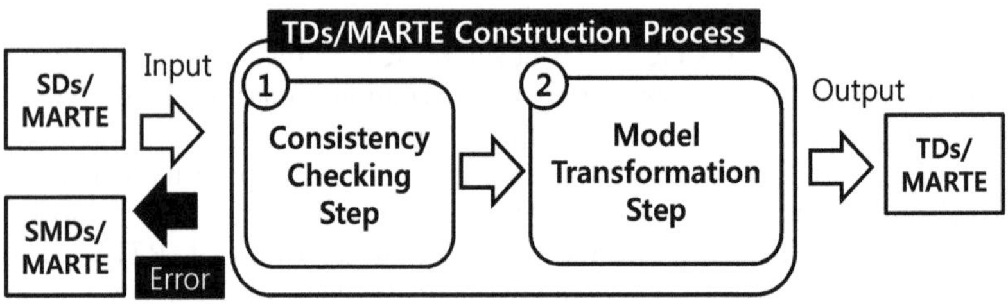

Fig. 1. Overall approach

Consistency Checking for SDs/MARTE and SMDs/MARTE

UML/MARTE inconsistency exists naturally between an UML model and MARTE annotations (intra-model), and between SDs/MARTE and SMDs/MARTE (inter-model).

In the consistency checking step, we check UML/MARTE consistency using a rule-based method to get well-formed UML/MARTE behavioral models. To this end, we defined 20 Rules and developed the UMCA (Uml/Marte Consistency Analyzer) tool to detect the inconsistency points automatically. Figures 2 and 3 do not have inconsistency points.

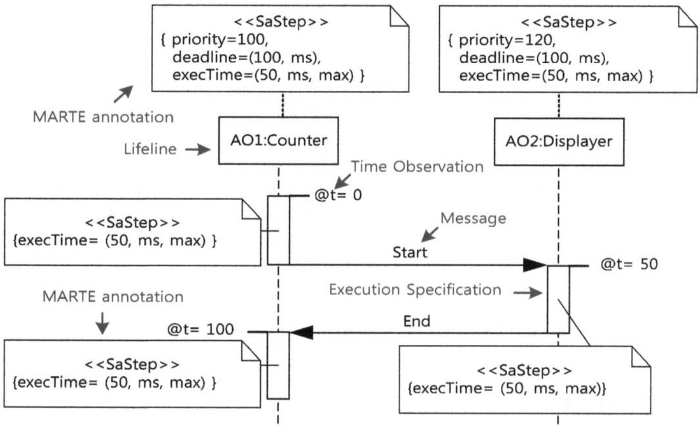

Fig. 2. Example of SD/MARTE

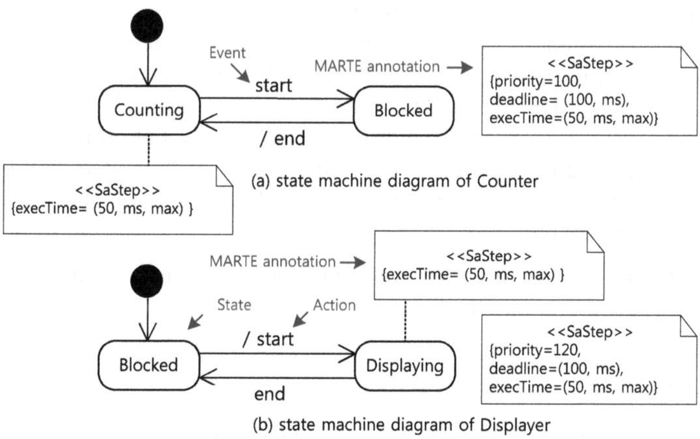

Fig. 3. Example of SMD/MARTE

Model Transformation for TDs/MARTE

We construct TDs/MARTE using four transformation rules. Rule 1 is for construction of timing ruler. Time unit is determined from MARTE annotations. In Figures 2 and 3, time unit is milliseconds. In Rule 2, lifelines of TDs/MARTE are extracted from SDs/MARTE. Counter and Displayer are selected from Figure 2. Rule 3 is for construction of states. States of TDs/MARTE are extracted from SMDs/MARTE of the lifelines selected in Rule2. Counting, Blocked, Displaying states are extracted from Figure 3. In Rule 4, durations and events are constructed from SDs/MARE and SMDs/MARTE. In previous our work [5], we proposed the algorithm to specify durations and events in TDs/MARTE. After applying four transformation rules, we can construct the TD/MARTE as shown in Figure 4.

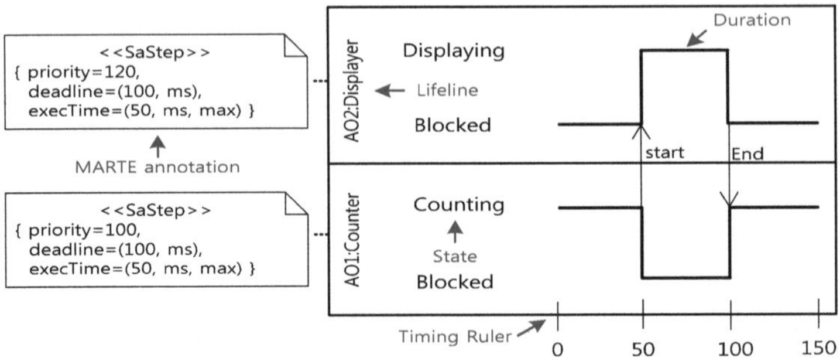

Fig. 4. TD/MARTE constructed from Figures 2 and 3

3 Conclusion

We presented an approach to constructing TDs/MARTE from SDs/MARTE and SMDs/MARTE for GCU software in military avionics systems. UML/MARTE modeling guidelines are presented to specify UML/MARTE models in GCU software domain. The consistency checking step makes consistent SDs/MARTE and SMDs/MARTE to construct error-free TDs/MARTE. The model transformation step constructs TDs/MARTE from the consistency-checked SDs/MARTE and SMDs/MARTE. We have three plans. First, we will apply the proposed approach in GCU software domain. Second, we will refine and extend guidelines for UML/MARTE behavioral modeling. Last, we will develop an automated tool for constructing TDs/MARTE.

Acknowledgments. This research was sponsored by the Agency for Defense Development under the grant UD100031CD.

References

1. Choi, J., Jee, E., Kim, H.-J., Bae, D.-H.: A case study on timing constraints verification for a safety-critical, time-triggered embedded software. Journal of KIISE: Software and Applications 38(12), 647–656 (2011) (in Korean)
2. Unified Modeling Language: Superstructure, version 2.4.1 (ptc/2011-08-06), OMG (2011), `http://www.omg.org`
3. UML Profile for MARTE: Modeling and Analysis of Real-Time Embedded Systems, version1.1 (formal/2011-06-02), OMG (2011), `http://www.omg.org`
4. Fowler, M.: Uml Distilled: A Brief Guide to the Standard Object Modeling Language, 3rd edn. Addison-Wesley (2004)
5. Choi, J., Jee, E., Bae, D.-H.: Toward Systematic Construction of Timing Diagrams from UML/MARTE Behavioral Models for Time-Triggered Embedded Software. In: The 6th IEEE International Conference on Software Security and Reliability, pp. 118–127 (June 2012)

Detecting Inconsistent Names of Source Code Using NLP

Sungnam Lee[1], Suntae Kim[2,*], JeongAh Kim[3], and Sooyoung Park[4]

[1] Defense Acquisition Program Administration, Seoul, South Korea
[2] Dept. of Computer Engineering, Kangwon National University, Sam-Cheok, South Korea
[3] Dept. of Computer Education, Kwandong University, South Korea
[4] Dept. of Computer Science & Engineering, Sogang University, Seoul, South Korea
dapalee@korea.kr, stkim@kangwon.ac.kr, clara@kd.ac.kr, sypark@sogang.ac.kr

1 Introduction

Software developers use refactoring in order to improve quality of source code. Refactoring is a disciplined technique for restructuring an existing body of code without changing its external behavior[3]. For example, 'Extract method' is the one of the refactoring approaches to improving readability of the large-scale method by splitting them into several small-scale methods. In refactoring, code smell indicates any symptom in the source code that possibly causes a deeper problem. Although inconsistent names of source code elements as one of the code smells are crucial, it is hardly achieved by going through the whole source code. Furthermore, it generally can be handled by several developers that understand the source code and also is easy to pass without checking because it does not affect software execution.

There has been some work to improve source code readability (e.g., see [1][5]). Most studies are based on software metric, measuring extent of readability using several indicators such as line length of a method, number of comments and keywords. Although the approach is helpful to characterize quality of the source code, software developers do not have any concrete hints or guidelines while naming source code elements.

In order to address the above issues, we propose NLP(Natural Language Process) based approach to identifying inconsistent names of Java source code elements such as classes and methods. This approach is comprised of three steps. 1) It starts from tokenizing all names of source code elements into words. Then, the words are analyzed by NLP parser[6] to decide POS(Part of Speech). 2) After then, the words are classified into semantic and syntactic synonyms by using WordNet[7] and Levenshtein Distance Algorithm[4] respectively. 3) Inconsistent names are detected by applying the proposed rules. The major contributions of this paper are summarized into two. 1) It is possible for developers who have no background on the source code to identify inconsistent names. 2) The quality of the source code can be improved by investigating inconsistent names throughout entire source code. This paper provides possible approaches for the issues as a position paper.

* Corresponding author.

T.-h. Kim et al. (Eds.): EL/DTA/UNESST 2012, CCIS 352, pp. 111–115, 2012.

2 Background

This section describes Java naming convention which is a coding style while writing java program, and types of inconsistent name code smells.

2.1 Java Naming Convention

Naming conventions make program more understandable by making them easier to read. The guideline published from Sun Microsystems(now, Oracle) [2] introduces Java naming convention on how to name each source code elements such as classes or methods as below:

- **Classes** and **Interfaces** should be a noun phrase and its first letter should be capital.
- **Methods** should be a verb phrase and starts with the lowercase.
- **Attributes** and **Parameters** should be a noun phrase with a lowercase first letter.
- **Constants** should be a noun phrase with all uppercase with words separated by underscores.

In addition to this, words composing of the code element names including classes, attributes, methods and parameters should be separated by the uppercase letter. Whereas words for constants should be separated by underscores. In the case of the class name *WhitespaceTokenizer*, it is a noun phrase composing of two words *Whitespace* and *Tokenizer*. For the method name *getElementNameForView()*, *get*, *Element*, *For* and *View* are the composing words and make a verb phrase.

2.2 Inconsistent Name Code Smell

Inconsistent name code smell is any symptom caused by naming source code elements inconsistently in terms of syntax or semantics, and it eventually makes source code harder to read and maintain. This is mainly attributed to property of software projects where many developers should be involved. In addition, a human can name source code elements inconsistently though there is only one developer in the project.

Inconsistent name code smell can be divided into three. First, a semantic inconsistent name smell indicates a case of words having a same intended meaning but different words which are synonyms. For example, in methods *abortParsing()* and *stopParsing()*, *abort* and *stop* are considered as semantic inconsistent names. Second, a syntactic inconsistent name is a case of words having a similar letter sequences composing of name. It is easily observed in source code because abbreviated and short forms of variables are generally used while writing a program. For example, *args*, *arg0* and *arg1* are short forms of an argument, and also *param* meaning a parameter is another example. Although these words are not searched in a dictionary, they are easily found in source code. Third, a POS(Part of Speech) inconsistent name smell means a word used with diverse POSes. In the class *CheckAbort*, for example, *Abort* is used as noun, but the word is used as verb in the method *abort()*. This case indicates that a word has different POS usage. In addition, if an attribute name is *aborted*, it should be a noun according to the java naming convention. However, it is also POS inconsistent name because it is an adjective.

3 Detecting Inconsistent Names Using NLP

An approach to detecting inconsistent names in source code is composed of three steps. 1) All source code elements are tokenized into individual words based on Java naming convention, and then NLP(Natural Language Process) parser analyzes POS of each word. 2) POS-tagged words are classified into words having the same root word, semantic synonyms and syntactic synonyms. 3) At last, inconsistent names are detected by the proposed rules.

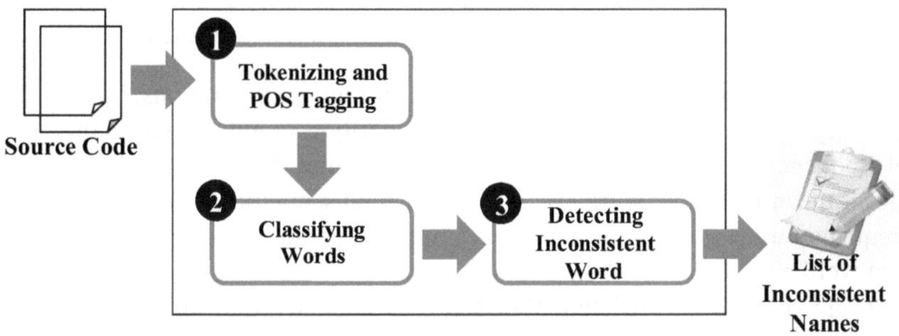

Fig. 1. Overview of An Approach

Step 1. Tokenizing and POS Tagging: This step is intended to tokenize all names from source code elements including classes, attributes, methods and parameters. It is based on Java naming convention mentioning that a new word in a name should start with the uppercase first letter. Suppose that there is a class composed of two words whitespace and tokenizer. Then, we can name the class *WhitespaceTokenizer* with two captialized first letters of two words. For constants, words are separated by underscores.

To analyze POS of each word, a blank between words should be inserted. In addition, words from method names should have a period at the end of the last word for making a complete sentence. It is because a method name should be a verb phrase. The method *getWordSet()*, for example, can be converted into 'get word set.' for NLP parser. It is crucial for the parser to analyze POS accurately for words that may be used as a noun as well as a verb. In this paper, we applied Stanford Parser[6], which is very fast and accurate.

Step 2. Classifying Synonyms: In this step, POS-tagged words are classified into words having the same root word, semantic synonyms and syntactic synonyms. As an example of a root word, *Abort* is the root of *aborting*, *aborted* and *aborts*. For finding roots of all words, we adopted WordNet[7]. WordNet is a lexical database in English, providing not only a root word, but also synonyms according to POSes and senses of a word. To find semantic synonyms observed in a source code, POS-tagged words are searched in WordNet. For example, *Abort* as a noun has synonyms like termination, ending and conclusion. If those synonyms are found in the source code, they can be classified into semantic synonyms.

For identifying syntactic synonyms, Levenshtein Distance Algorithm[4] has been applied. This algorithm measures distance between two words, counting alphabetic differences and dividing them with the number of letters. For example, distance between *kitten* and *sitting* is three(*kitten* $\rightarrow$ *sitten* $\rightarrow$ *sittin* $\rightarrow$ *sitting*). The distance is computed as $1 - (3/6) = 0.5$, meaning 50% syntactic similarity between two words. In this paper, if a word has over 80% similarity, we recognized two words as syntactic synonyms.

Step 3. Detecting Inconsistent Words: The basic approach to detecting inconsistent words is achieved by majority rule, meaning that a word used frequently throughout the source code is more acceptable then rarely used words. The following describes an approach to detecting semantic, syntactic and POS inconsistent names.

Detecting Semantic Inconsistent Words. For all semantic synonyms, find words that have high semantic similarity. Semantic similarity is computed based on the order of frequency among senses in WordNet. The former the order is in the sense, the closer meaning of two words is. Among the high semantic similar synonym, more frequently used word is considered as a base word, others are detected as inconsistent words.

Detecting Syntactic Inconsistent Words. Less frequently used words among the syntactic synonyms are considered as syntactic inconsistent words. As an exception, this rule is not applied to noun words having the same root word and words that can be searched in a dictionary. Suppose there are '*String accent*' and '*String[] accents*' as attributes. The two words *accent* and *accents* are syntactic synonym and have the same root word, which is meaningful to understand the source code. While *accent* and *accept* are syntactic synonym, meaning is totally different. Except those words, syntactic inconsistent word such as *args* or *param* can be easily detected.

Detecting POS Inconsistent Words. Two approaches can be applied to detect POS inconsistent words. First, words that have a big gap in frequencies of POS usages can be detected in POS inconsistent words. When 90% of *Abort* is used as a verb, the remainder is considered as POS inconsistent words. Second, POS inconsistent words can be investigated by checking results of NLP parsing based on Java naming convention. For example, as attribute names should be noun or noun phrase, it is a POS inconsistent word if adjective is used as an attribute.

4 Conclusion

In this paper, we have presented an approach for detecting inconsistent words. This approach enables developers who have no background on the source code to identify inconsistent names so that it supports to improve software maintainability. This paper suggested three types of inconsistent names, and steps and rules for detecting the inconsistent names based on NLP. As a position paper, this paper proposed rough approach to achieving the goal. As future work, tool support is currently under construction and several case studies are planned.

References

1. Buse, R., Weimer, W.: A Metric for Software Readiability. In: Proceedings of International Symposium on Software Testing and Analysis (ISSTA), Seattle, WA, pp. 121–130 (2008)
2. Code Conventions for the Java Programming Language: Why Have Code Conventions, Sunmicro Systems (1999), http://www.oracle.com/technetwork/java/index-135089.html
3. Fowler, M.: Refactoring: Improving the Design of Existing Code. Addison-Wesley (1999)
4. Levenshtein, V.I.: Binary codes capable of correcting deletions, insertions and reversals. Soviet Physics Doklady 10(8), 707–710 (1966)
5. Posnett, D., Hindle, A., Devanbu, P.: A Simpler Model of Software Readiability. In: Proceedings of International Confernce on Mining Software Repository(MSR), Honolulu, Hawaii, pp. 73–82 (2011)
6. The Stanford Parser: A statistical parser, Home page (2012), http://nlp.stanford.edu/software/lex-parser.shtml
7. WordNet: A lexical database for English, Home page (2012), http://wordnet.princeton.edu/

Voice Command Recognition for Fighter Pilots Using Grammar Tree

Hangyu Kim[1], Jeongsik Park[2,*], Yunghwan Oh[1], Seongwoo Kim[3], and Bonggyu Kim[4]

[1] Computer Science Department, Korea Advanced Institude of Science and Technology, Daejeon, South Korea
[2] Department of Intelligent Robot Engineering, Mokwon University, Daejeon, South Korea
[3] LIG Nex1, Daejeon, South Korea
[4] Agency for Defence Development, Daejeon, South Korea

{hgkim,yhoh}@cs.kaist.ac.kr,
parkjs@mokwon.ac.kr,
kim.seongwoo@lignex1.com,
bongq@add.re.kr

Abstract. This research copes with the voice command recognizer for fighter pilots. The voice command is composed of several connected words in the fighter system. And the recognizer automatically separates the command into individual words and implements isolated word recognition for each word. To improve the performance of the command recognizer, the error correction using grammar tree is proposed. The isolated word recognition error is corrected in the error correction process. Our experimental result shows that the grammar tree significantly improved the performance of the command recognizer.

1 Introduction

With the development of the air force military technology, fighter pilots can perform various missions in cockpit. Generally, fighters are controlled with button interface. But it is inconvenient for a pilot to control a lot of buttons in cockpit whenever the pilot uses a specific function of a fighter. In comparison with the button interface, the voice may provide much more convenience for pilots because they do not need to use buttons except for starting the voice command.

However, the voice command recognition is not an easy task in the pilot system because the command is composed of several connected words with a short pause between isolated words. In general, the voice command recognizer segments the input signal into separated words and implements isolated word recognition for each separated word. In this process, even if only one word within a command is misrecognized, the command recognition result is regarded to be incorrect.

---

[*] Corresponding author.

T.-h. Kim et al. (Eds.): EL/DTA/UNESST 2012, CCIS 352, pp. 116–119, 2012.

In general, pilots' voice command is not a random combination of words. Instead, the command obeys a specific grammar corresponding to the functions of the fighters. For this reason, it is expected to correct a number of errors occurring in the isolated word recognition, by applying the linguistic grammar for command sequences to the speech recognition system. In this research, grammar tree is used to describe the grammar of the voice command and is employed for the post processing of recognition system to correct the illegal errors.

2 Voice Command Recognizer

As described above, the voice command recognizer recognizes a command by separating it into individual words and implementing isolated word recognition to each separated word [1]. The block diagram of the recognizer is shown in Fig. 1.

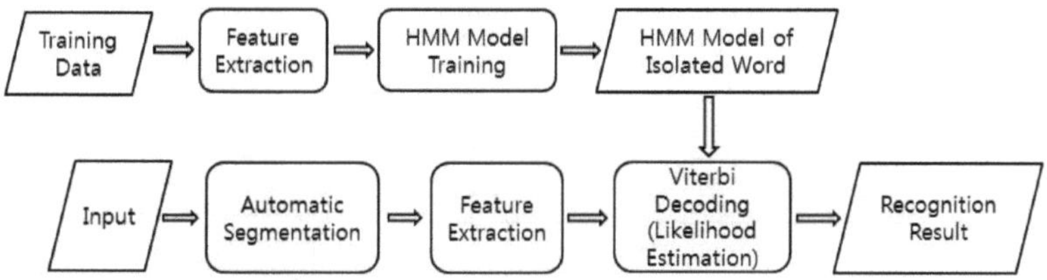

Fig. 1. The block diagram of the voice command recognizer.

In this research, HMM (Hidden Markov Model) based speech recognition algorithm is used. In the training process, the feature of the training data is extracted and it is trained into the HMM model. The MFCC (Mel-Frequency Cepstrum Coefficient) feature which is widely used for speech recognition is used in this research [2]. Baum-Welch algorithm is used for HMM model training [3]. By the end of the training process, a set of HMM models where a model represents an isolated word is obtained. In the recognition process, the input test data is segmented into isolated words. The pause detection with energy and zero crossing rate is used for automatic segmentation. Then the MFCC feature of each separated word is extracted and the likelihood between this feature and each HMM model is computed using Viterbi decoding algorithm [3]. The model that has the biggest likelihood is selected as the result of the isolated word recognition. Finally, the voice command recognition result is obtained by connecting the results of the isolated word recognition together.

3 Error Correction Using Grammar Tree

If series of the isolated word recognition results is directly used as the command recognition result, the accuracy of the recognition system will be small because even only one isolated word recognition error causes the incorrect command recognition result.

The voice commands used in fighters are not random combinations of the words. Instead, the commands obey a specific grammar. By applying the grammar to the recognition result, the illegal recognition error can be found and further it can be corrected.

To describe the grammar, the grammar tree is used [4]. In the grammar tree, the root node represents the starting and the leaf node represents the ending of a command. The node represents each word lies between root node and leaf node. For the adjacent two words in a command, the former word becomes the parent node of the latter word. The first word of a command becomes the child node of the root node and the last word of a command becomes the parent node of the leaf node. Fig. 2 shows an example of a grammar tree. The 'NUM' node represents numbers. As the command may need number with several digits, the 'NUM' node has self-loop. Only when a series of words passes the grammar tree, it is considered as a correct command; otherwise, the series of words is considered to be illegal and the error is corrected using the grammar tree.

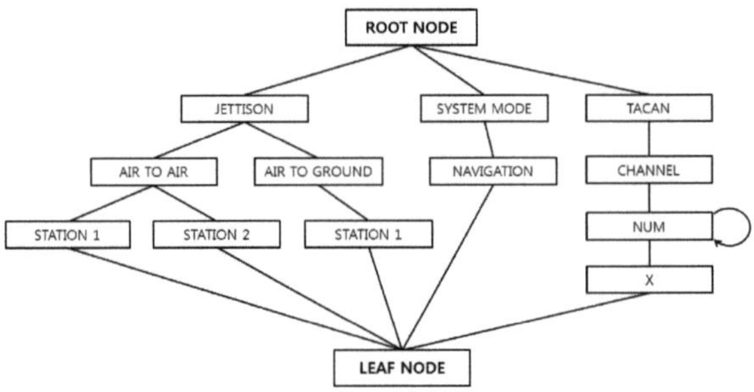

Fig. 2. An example of grammar tree

With the help of the grammar tree described above, the recognition error that does not obey the grammar can be corrected. The proposed error correction works as follows. First, during the isolated word recognition, not only the model with biggest likelihood is selected but also the several models that have big likelihoods are selected as the candidates of the recognition result. In this research, 15 candidates are selected. After all isolated word recognition finished, all the combinations of commands that can be composed by all candidates are found and the combination that can pass the grammar tree and has the biggest likelihood is selected as the final result of the error correction. The likelihood of a command is defined as the summation of the likelihoods of the words in the command where the likelihood of each word can be obtained in isolated word recognition. In this way, the final result always obeys the grammar and the most probable command is obtained. Thus, the error occurred in isolated word recognition may be corrected and the improvement in accuracy is expected.

4 Experiment Result

To evaluate the performance of the proposed system, the command recognition experiment was implemented. The training data and test data for the experiment were recorded via the microphone used in fighters. All speech data has resolution of 16 bit and sampling rate of 10 kHz. There are totally 194 words in the command set. All 194 words were pronounced by 30 different speakers for 5 times for training. The test set of 183 commands containing all possible commands were used for recognition experiment. For the recognition experiment, two speakers pronounced the test cases for 2 times and 3 times respectively. The recognition result in Table 1 showed that the performance of recognizer improved significantly by applying proposed error correction technique using grammar tree.

Table 1. The Result of the Voice Command Recognition Experiment

Speaker No.	Test Data	Recognition Accuracy	
		Before Using Error Correction	After Using Error Correction
1	183 commands x 3 times	65.94%	94.17%
2	183 commands x 2times	69.95%	90.98%
Avg.	183 commands x 5times	67.54%	92.90%

5 Conclusion

In this study we proposed a technique for voice command recognizer in cockpit. As the voice command is composed of several words, the words are automatically separated and each word is recognized via HMM-based isolated word recognizer. In order to improve the accuracy of the command recognition, we proposed error correction using grammar tree. To evaluate the efficiency of the proposed technique, we performed voice command recognition experiment. The recognition result showed that the performance improved significantly owing to error correction technique. Our voice command recognizer will provide much more convenience for fighter pilots.

Acknowledgments. This work was partially supported by Defense Acquisition Program Administration and Agency for Defense Development under contract.

References

1. Perera, K.A.D., Ranathunga, R.A.D.S., Welivitigoda, I.P., Withanawasam, R.M.: Connected speech recognition with an isolated word recognizer. In: Proceesings of the Intenational Conference on Information and Automation, Colombo, Sri Lanka, pp. 319–323 (2005)
2. Rabiner, L., Juang, B.H.: Fundamentals of Speech Recognition. Prentice Hall (1993)
3. Rabiner, L.: A tutorial on hidden Markov models and selected applications in speech recognition. Proceedings of the IEEE 77(2), 257–286 (1989)
4. Vijay-Shanker, K.: Using descriptions of trees in a tree adjoining grammar. Journal of Computational Linguistics 18(4), 481–517 (1992)

Web-Based Text-to-Speech Technologies in Foreign Language Learning: Opportunities and Challenges

Dosik Moon

Hanyang Cyber University, Dept. of English, 17 Haengdang-dong,
Seongdong-gu, Seoul, Korea
dmoon@hycu.ac.kr

Abstract. Exposure to the input of the target language is crucial for successful foreign language learning. However, learners in English as a foreign language (EFL) contexts are placed in input poor environments because English is neither their native nor official language and there is a limited number of native speaker teachers available. With the rapid development of information technology, text-to-speech (TTS) synthesizers, computer programs converting written text into spoken words, provides great potential for offering learners with varied and easily accessible spoken language input. As the quality of the TTS speech sound is beginning to reach actual real human speech sound, a growing number of English instructors have been exploring ways to incorporate TTS programs in their classes. This paper intends to explore the current development of TTS technology, to identify possible opportunities and challenges of employing TTS technology in EFL contexts, and to discuss pedagogical implications and future research directions.

Keywords: Text-to-Speech, EFL, Foreign language learning, Web-based learning.

1 Introduction

Learning a foreign language is a complex and time consuming process, involving a variety of factors. Theories of second language acquisition have claimed that language input and interaction are two critical external factors determining successful foreign language learning. One of the main roles of language teachers, therefore, is often considered the maximization of their students' exposure to the target language meaningfully. However, learners in EFL contexts, where English is neither their native nor official language and the insufficient number of native speaker teachers is available, have resulted in difficulties in learning English due to limited opportunities for exposure to the target language and interaction. In particular, the lack of sufficient spoken language input presents a severe challenge for EFL learners to acquire speaking and listening skills. As a way to solve this problem, audio equipment such as audiocassette and videocassette players or more advanced devices like CD/DVD/mp3 players has been widely adopted, but these devices have not fully meet EFL learners' needs due to cost effectiveness, technological inconveniences, and unreliability of native speakers ' teaching methods[1].

T.-h. Kim et al. (Eds.): EL/DTA/UNESST 2012, CCIS 352, pp. 120–125, 2012.

Recently, with the rapid development of information technology, various web-based technologies have emerged as alternatives to traditional audio equipment. Among such technologies, text-to-speech synthesizers, computer programs converting written text into spoken words, can provide a new way for learners to experience varied and easily accessible spoken language input. The early TTS programs did not attract much interest from language teachers due to the unnatural voice and poor intelligibility. However, as the quality of TTS speech sound is beginning to reach the actual human speech sound, a growing number of English instructors have been exploring ways to incorporate TTS programs in their classes [2]. Given this situation, this paper intends to explore the current development of TTS technology, to identify possible opportunities and challenges of employing TTS technology in EFL contexts, and to discuss pedagogical implications and future research directions.

2 Current Development of TTS

A TTS synthesizer is a computer program designed to convert written text to speech automatically. It was originally developed to help visually challenged people read texts on the computer. When the TTS synthesizer was first released, it did not attract much attention from language teachers. Its speech output was of low quality, and thus teachers believed that this new technology could not account for the full complexity of human language, nor be used as speech models for foreign language learners [3].

However, the quality of TTS sound has dramatically improved as a new approach to TTS technology called concatenative speech synthesis emerged. The current TTS programs, through the selection of a string of human utterances from a large pre-recorded human voice database, create natural voices which sound nearly human. As a result, TTS technologies are now widely applied in a range of new and innovative applications, such as desktop speech systems, computer voice interfaces, audio books, electronic dictionaries, etc. [1] [4]. Furthermore, a growing number of English teachers adopt TTS to provide spoken input to their students.

Table 1. Unique Features of Popular Free TTS Programs

TTS	Features	Web address
Paralink	Quickly converts text into speech	text-to-speechtranslator.paralink.com
Text2Speech	No limit on number of letters to be converted	www.text2speech.org
Odiogo	Create automatic podcast from blogs and websites	www.odiogo.com
iSpeech	Natural sounding voices	www.ispeech.org
ImTranslator	animated characters read the text	imtranslator.com

These days, a great variety of TTS programs are available on the Web to be used for free or available through a fee. Many of these programs allow users to select voice and accent ranging from female to male and American to British. Users can also control the speed of speech. Most programs offer online TTS conversion, and some allow users to download it on computer or other media device. Thus, users can choose the service according to their needs. Unique features of some of the most popular free online TTS programs are presented as follows (see Table 1).

3 How TTS Works?

A TTS program is similar to other PC applications such as a word processer or a web browsing program in that the programs contain an interface for a text shown on screen. For example, if a user uses a TTS synthesizer developed by AT&T, he or she first selects the voice and language ranging from female to male, native to non-native, and slower to faster speakers. Then, the user copies a text from any text-based program, such as HTML files or Microsoft Word files, pastes the text in a text box of the TTS program, clicks the SPEAK button, and then each sentence is individually generated with the selected voices After this, the user can listen to a book or a newspaper. Since most TTS programs highlight each word as it is being read aloud, users can follow along on the screen. When the user presses the DOWNLOAD button, an audio file is made and saved on the user's computer (see Fig 1) [5].

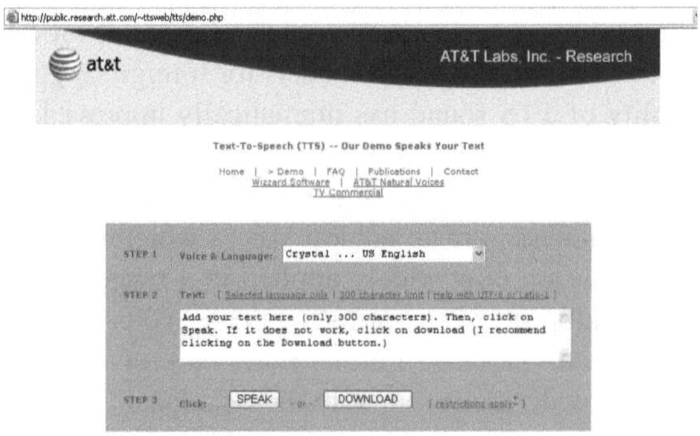

Fig. 1. A demo offered by AT&T, free to use for non-commercial purposes

Recently developed TTS programs presented in Table 1 are equipped with more sophisticated functionalities. For example, Paralink TTS programs has animated characters read the text, highlighting each word as it is being read aloud, so a listener can follow along on the screen (see Fig 2). iSpeech can read any kind of text, including web documents, word documents, emails, and PDFs, save as MP3 files and add these sound file to web pages, wikis or blogs. Furthermore, these files are accessible through mobile devices, so users can listen to text files anywhere and at anytime. These unique features of TTS provide several advantages over traditional speech recording devices which can be summarized as follows [3]:

- TTS allows language teachers far more flexibility and adaptability in authoring audio materials.
- TTS offers highly precise and adjustable speech rate control.

- TTS can add variations to listening comprehension using different voices.
- TTS files are easy to copy and distribute without lowering sound quality.
- TTS is more cost-effective.

Fig. 2. A demo offered by Paralink TTS

These advantages of TTS programs provide learners with opportunities to learn English more effectively.

4 Opportunities for English Language Learners

The aforementioned unique functions of TTS can present several opportunities for learners to develop writing and reading skills as well as listening and speaking skills in individualized and autonomous manners. These opportunities can be used for several different purposes in learning English:

- Learners can listen to any text on any topic of their own choice by creating audio versions, wav or mp3 files, from any text.
- Learners can be exposed to comprehensible input by adjusting the speed and pace of the audio according to their own needs.

- Learners can practice the pronunciation of vocabulary they have difficulty with by creating pronunciation exercises for themselves.
- Learners can practice speaking by creating mini dialogues using various types of English accents.
- Learners can revise their writing while listening to TTS reading aloud their drafts while revising them.

In fact, research on the effectiveness of TTS-based on language teaching suggests that TTS has overall positive effects on English learning. For example, TTS has been proved to help learners improve in pronunciation and to help them enhance vocabulary and reading comprehension [6] [7]. Meanwhile, another study found that TTS helped learners to develop L2 writing skills because while a TTS program read their written work aloud, they could hear the problems of their writing instead of simply seeing them [8].

5 Challenges to English Language Learners

Although TTS programs provide learners with numerous possible opportunities, they also have several pitfalls. Despite the improved voice quality, some programs still create mispronunciation of certain types of words, and more seriously, the TTS speech still has its limitations in terms of naturalness, pleasantness and expressiveness [1]. These problems can cause several challenges to learners in the following ways:

- Learners may misinterpret some words pronounced differently.
- Learners need to have the text ready to be able to hear it.
- Voices sounding artificial may cause learners to lose their interest in using TTS for learning English.

Due to these demerits, some teachers are still hesitant in integrating TTS in their classes. This is understandable, given that little research has been done that fully explores the capacities that this technology has to offer its students. So far, most studies explored the effects of TTS in conjunction with other software such as a tutoring system or accent reduction software. Therefore, the effectiveness of TTS in English learning has not been clearly demonstrated yet. Subsequently, more strictly controlled studies are needed to confirm the potential effects of TTS in EFL contexts. Also, understanding language learners' views and needs on the use of TTS will be beneficial in directing the future development of this technology.

On the other hand, in order for TTS to have been effectively implemented in EFL contexts, the following recommendations can be made. First, EFL teachers need to create an environment that allows learners to use TTS in a more personalized and autonomous manner. In this environment, learners can work individually with TTS with access to both aural and visual input, controlling the input at their own pace by adjusting or changing certain features of TTS, such as the speed rate and the synthetic voices. Second, since some TTS programs do not work properly, teachers need to provide guidance for learners in selecting a reliable TTS program. Particularly, if TTS is used for low level learners, teachers should monitor learners' learning process and provide proper feedback that TTS malfunctions because they have difficulty in evaluating the quality of TTS. .

6 Conclusion

Based on the discussion in this paper, it can be concluded that TTS technologies have a great potential to facilitate successful foreign language learning by providing varied and easily accessible spoken language input. They can be used as supplementary or alternative providers of input for EFL learners because the currently available TTS tools provide speech sounds that approximate the natural human voice. The TTS programs can also promote learners' autonomy by allowing them to learn on their own pace. The capacity of TTS to provide different forms of input can make language learning more varied and dynamic Taken into account the fact that technology is constantly improving, it is possible that TTS technology will be a common feature of EFL learning. However, it is important to note that TTS technology is no panacea since they are still evolving.

References

1. Guoquan, S.: Using TTS voices to develop audio materials for listening comprehension: A digital approach. Bri. J. Edu. Tech. 41, 632–641 (2010)
2. Proctor, C.P., Dalton, B., Grisham, D.L.: Scaffolding English language learners and struggling readers in a universal literacy environment with embedded strategy instruction and vocabulary support. J. Lit. Res. 39, 71–93 (2007)
3. Ehsani, F., Knodt, E.: Speech technology in computer-aided language learning: Strengths, and limitations of a new call paradigm. Lang. Lea. Tech. 2, 45–60 (1998)
4. Handley, Z.: Is text-to-speech synthesis ready for use in computer-assisted language learning? Spe. Com. 5, 906–919 (2009)
5. AT &T Labs, Inc., `http://www2.research.att.com/~ttsweb/tts/demo.php`
6. Sisson, C.: Text-to-speech in vocabulary acquisition and student knowledge models: A classroom study using the REAP intelligent tutoring system. Technical Report, CMU-LTI (2007)
7. Kiliçkaya, F.: Improving pronunciation via accent reduction and text-to-speech software. In: 1st Proceedings of the WorldCALL 2008 Conference, Japan, pp. 135–137 (2008)
8. Kirstein, M.: Universalizing universal design: Applying text-to-speech technology to English language learners' process writing. Doc. diss (2006)

Design of Interval Type-2 FCM-Based FNN and Genetic Optimization for Pattern Recognition

Keon-Jun Park, Jae-Hyun Kwon, and Yong-Kab Kim

Department of Information and Communication Engineering,
Wonkwang University, 344-2, Shinyong-dong, Iksan-si, Chonbuk, 570-749 South Korea
{bird75,kojman,ykim}@wonkwang.ac.kr

Abstract. A new category of fuzzy neural networks with multiple outputs based on an interval type-2 fuzzy c-means clustering algorithm (IT2FCM-based FNNm) for pattern recognition is proposed in this paper. The premise part of the rules of the proposed network is realized with the aid of the scatter partition of the input space generated by the IT2FCM clustering algorithm. The number of the partition of input space equals the number of clusters, and the individual partitioned spaces describe the fuzzy rules. The consequence part of the rules is represented by polynomial functions with an interval set along with multiple outputs. The coefficients of the polynomial functions are learned by the back-propagation (BP) algorithm. To optimize the parameters of the IT2FCM-based FNNm, we consider real-coded genetic algorithms. The proposed network is evaluated with the use of numerical experimentation for pattern recognition.

Keywords: Modeling and Optimization, Fuzzy Neural Networks (FNN), Interval Type-2 FCM clustering algorithm, Genetic Algorithms (GAs), Pattern Recognition.

1 Introduction

Fuzzy neural networks (FNNs) [1, 2] have emerged as one of the active areas of research in fuzzy inference systems and neural networks. These networks are predominantly designed for the integration of these two fields. Typically, FNNs are represented by fuzzy "if–then" rules, while back propagation (BP) is used to optimize the parameters. The generation of the fuzzy rules and the adjustment of their membership functions were conducted by trial and error and/or on the basis of the operator's experience. The designers find it difficult to develop adequate fuzzy rules and membership functions to reflect the essence of the data.

Zadeh [3] introduced the concept of a type-2 fuzzy set as an extension of type-1 fuzzy sets. Mizumoto and Tanaka [4] studied the set of theoretical operations of type-2 fuzzy sets and discussed the properties of membership grades of such sets. In contrast to type-1 fuzzy sets, in type-2 fuzzy sets, the membership grades are not numeric values but are fuzzy sets defined in the unit interval. Mendel and Karnik [5, 6], studied the theory of type-2 fuzzy logic systems. Their theories are also described in the form of fuzzy if–then rules.

T.-h. Kim et al. (Eds.): EL/DTA/UNESST 2012, CCIS 352, pp. 126–133, 2012.

In this paper, we present the structure of fuzzy neural networks with multiple outputs based on an interval type-2 fuzzy c-means (IT2FCM) clustering algorithm formed by expanding the conventional FCM clustering algorithm [7]. The premise part of the rules of this network is realized with the aid of the scatter partition of the input space generated by the IT2FCM clustering algorithm. The consequence part of the rules is represented by polynomial functions with an interval set along with multiple outputs for pattern recognition. The coefficients of the polynomial functions are learned by the BP algorithm. We also optimize the parameters of the networks using real-coded genetic algorithms (GAs) [8]. The proposed network is evaluated through numerical experimentation.

2 Design of IT2FCM-Based FNNm

The structure of IT2FCM-based FNNm emerges at the junction of interval type-2 FCM clustering algorithm and fuzzy neural networks. In this section, the form of fuzzy if-then rules along with their development mechanism is discussed.

2.1 IT2FCM Clustering Algorithm

A interval type-2 fuzzy set, denoted here by $\tilde{A}$, is characterized by a type-2 membership function $\mu_{\tilde{A}}(x)$ of the form

$$\tilde{A} = \int_{x\in X} \mu_{\tilde{A}}(x)/x = \int_{x\in X}\left[\int_{u\in J_x} 1/u\right]\Big/x,\ J_x \subseteq [0,1]\cdot \tag{1}$$

The domain of a secondary membership function is called the primary membership of *x*. In (1), J_x is the primary membership of *x*, where $J_x \subseteq [0,1]$ for $\forall x \in X$. The amplitude of a secondary membership function is called a secondary grade.

An example of a footprint of uncertainty (FOU) is shown in the form of the shaded regions in Fig. 1.

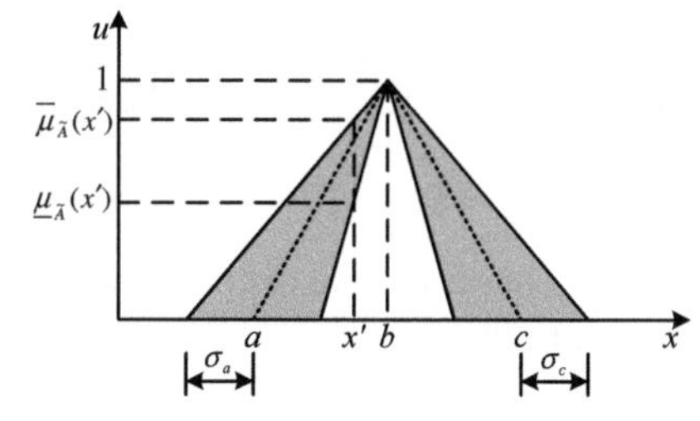

Fig. 1. Interval type-2 fuzzy set: *a*, *b*, and *c* are membership parameters, and σ_a and σ_c are the uncertainties of *a* and *c*, respectively

An upper membership function $\overline{\mu}_{\tilde{A}}(x)$ and a lower membership function $\underline{\mu}_{\tilde{A}}(x)$ are two type-1 membership functions that form the bounds for the FOU of the type-2 fuzzy set. Hence, (1) can be rewritten in the following form:

$$\tilde{A} = \int_{x\in X}\left[\int_{u\in[\underline{\mu}_{\tilde{A}}(x),\overline{\mu}_{\tilde{A}}(x)]} 1/u\right]\Big/ x \cdot \tag{2}$$

The IT2FCM clustering algorithm is an extension of the existing FCM clustering algorithms [7]. It is developed by incorporating the concept of the interval type-2 fuzzy sets. The upper part and lower part of the uncertainty about the degree of representation are expressed by adjusting the fuzzification factor. Each cluster has a different uncertainty, which obtained by the standard deviation of the data belonging to the maximum membership grade of each cluster. The process is as follows.

[Step 1] Initialize the membership matrix **U** with random values between 0 and 1.

[Step 2] Calculate c fuzzy cluster centers **v***i*, $i = 1,\ldots,c$,.

[Step 3] Compute the cost function.

[Step 4] Compute a new **U**.

[Step 5] Calculate the standard deviation σ_i from each maximal membership grade in the membership matrix **U**.

[Step 6] Adjust the uncertainty.

$$\overline{m}_i = m + (1+\rho_i)\sigma_i,\ \underline{m}_i = m - (1+\rho_i)\sigma_i \tag{3}$$

where $\overline{m}_i$ and $\underline{m}_i$ are the *i*-th upper and lower fuzzification factor, respectively.

[Step 7] Calculate fuzzy cluster center $\overline{\mathbf{v}}_i$ and $\underline{\mathbf{v}}_i$.

[Step 8] Compute new $\overline{\mathbf{U}}$ and $\underline{\mathbf{U}}$.

2.2 Structure of IT2FCM-Based FNNm

The structure of the IT2FCM-based FNNm involves the IT2FCM clustering algorithm in the premise part and neural networks present in the consequence part of the rules. The overall topology of the network is illustrated in Fig. 2.

IT2FCM-based FNNm is based on the fuzzy scatter partition of the input spaces. In this sense, each rule can be viewed as a certain rule of the following format:

$$R^j : If\ \ x_1\ and \cdots and\ x_d\ is\ \tilde{F}_j\quad Then\ y_{sj} = f(x_1,\ldots,x_d)\cdot \tag{4}$$

As far as inference schemes are concerned, we distinguish the following cases:

Case 1 (Simplified Inference):

$$f = W_{jo}^{s}\cdot \tag{5}$$

Case 2 (Linear Inference):

$$f = W_{jo}^{s} + \sum_{k=1}^{d} W_{jk}^{s} x_k \cdot \tag{6}$$

To be more specific, R^j is the j-th fuzzy rule, while $\tilde{F}_j$ denotes the j-th membership grades using the IT2FCM clustering algorithm. $W^s_{jk} = [w^s_{jk} - s^s_{jk}, w^s_{jk} + s^s_{jk}]$, $k = 0,\cdots,d$ are consequent parameters of the rule and s is the number of outputs.

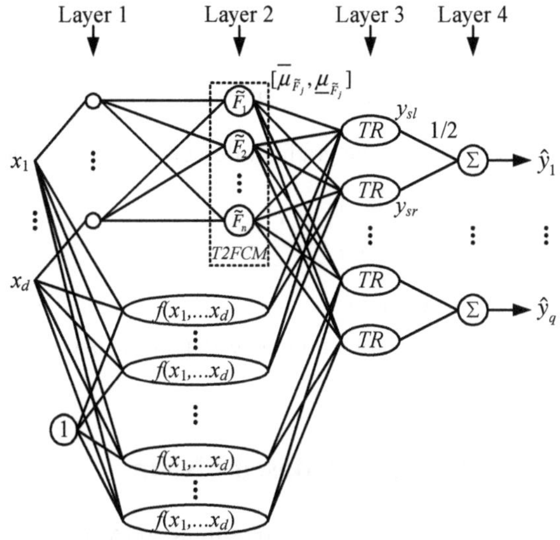

Fig. 2. The structure of the IT2FCM-based FNNm

The functionality of each layer is described as follows.

[Layer 1] The nodes in this layer transfer the inputs.

[Layer 2] The nodes here are used to calculate the membership grades using the IT2FCM clustering algorithm. The firing strengths are as follows.

$$\hat{f}_j = [\overline{\hat{f}}_j, \underline{\hat{f}}_j] = [\overline{\mu}_j, \underline{\mu}_j] = [\overline{u}_i, \underline{u}_i], \quad j = i \cdot \tag{7}$$

[Layer 3] The nodes in this layer are used to conduct type reduction.

Note that the leftmost point y_{sl} and the rightmost point y_{sr} depend upon the values of $\hat{f}_j$. Hence, using the Karnik-Mendel (KM) algorithm, y_{sl} and y_{sr} can be expressed as follows:

$$y_{sl} = \frac{\sum_{j=1}^{n} \hat{f}^l_j y^l_{sj}}{\sum_{j=1}^{n} \hat{f}^l_j}, \quad y_{sr} = \frac{\sum_{j=1}^{n} \hat{f}^r_j y^r_{sj}}{\sum_{j=1}^{n} \hat{f}^r_j}. \tag{8}$$

Here, $\hat{f}^l_j$ and $\hat{f}^r_j$ are the upper and lower firing sets that affect y_{sl} and y_{sr}, respectively.

[Layer 4] The nodes in this layer compute the outputs.

The output $\hat{y}_s$ is an interval set, so we need to defuzzify (decode) it by taking the average of y_{sl} and y_{sr}.

2.3 Learning Algorithm

The parametric learning of the network is realized by adjusting the connections of the neurons and, as such, it could be realized by running a standard BP algorithm. The performance index E_p is based on the Euclidean distance.

As far as learning is concerned, the connections are changed (adjusted) in a standard manner,

$$w^s_{jk}(p+1) = w^s_{jk}(p) + \Delta w^s_{jk}, \quad s^s_{jk}(p+1) = s^s_{jk}(p) + \Delta s^s_{jk} \tag{9}$$

where this update formula follows the gradient-descent method, namely,

$$\Delta w^s_{jk} = \eta\left(-\frac{\partial E_p}{\partial w^s_{jk}}\right), \quad \Delta s^s_{jk} = \eta\left(-\frac{\partial E_p}{\partial s^s_{jk}}\right) \tag{10}$$

with η being a positive learning rate.

To accelerate convergence, a momentum coefficient α is commonly added to the learning expression.

3 Optimization of IT2FCM-Based FNNm

It has been demonstrated that genetic algorithms (GAs) [8] are useful global population-based optimizers. GAs are shown to support robust search in complex search spaces. Given their stochastic character, such methods are less likely to get trapped in local minima (which becomes quite a common problem in case of gradient-descent techniques). The search in the solution space is completed with the aid of several genetic operators with reproduction, crossover, and mutation being the standard ones. Let us briefly recall the essence of these operators. Reproduction is a process in which the mating pool for the next generation is chosen. Individual strings are copied into the mating pool according to the values of their fitness functions. Crossover usually proceeds in two steps. First, members from the mating pool are mated at random. Secondly, each pair of strings undergoes crossover as follows; a position l along the string is selected uniformly at random from the interval [1, l-1], where l is the length of the string. Swapping all characters between the positions k and l creates two new strings. Mutation is a random alteration of the value of a string position. In real coding, mutation is defined as an alternation at a random value in special boundary. Usually mutation occurs with a small probability. Those operators, combined with the proper definition of the fitness function, constitute the main body of the genetic optimization.

In order to optimize the parameters of the IT2FCM-based FNNm, we determined the fuzzification and uncertainty coefficients associated with the corresponding clusters, the learning rate, and the momentum coefficient as the parameters. Each chromosome is coded using real numbers (instead of binary numbers). This type of coding is helpful from the point of view of the effectiveness of the overall search process.

4 Experimental Studies

We discuss numerical example in order to evaluate the advantages and the effectiveness of the proposed approach. We use the Wisconsin Diagnostic Breast Cancer (WDBC) dataset [9]. Features are computed from a digitized image of a fine needle aspirate (FNA) of a breast mass. A computer program determined 30 real-valued input features (attributes) found in each of two types (benign or malignant) of diagnosis. For the evaluation of the performance of the network, the random sub-sampling method was applied. The random sub-sampling was performed with 5 data splits of the data set. Each split was randomly selected from the training examples and the test examples with the ratio of 7:3.

We experimented with the networks using the parameters outlined in Table 1.

Table 1. Initial parameters

	Parameter	Value
GAs	Generation	100
	Population size	50
	Crossover rate	0.65
	Mutation rate	0.1
IT2FCM-based FNNm	Fuzzification coefficients	$1.0 < m_i \leq 2.5$
	Uncertainty coefficient	$-1.0 \leq \rho_i \leq 1.0$
	Learning rate	$0.0 \leq \eta \leq 0.01$
	Moment coefficient	$0.0 \leq \alpha \leq 0.001$

Table 2. Performance of the IT2FCM-based FNNm

No. of Clusters	Inference (Case)	CR		PI	
		Training	Testing	Training	Testing
5	1	91.86±0.70	92.63±1.21	0.058±0.00	0.056±0.01
	2	96.53±0.33	95.91±0.72	0.039±0.00	0.041±0.01
10	1	92.41±0.54	92.51±1.82	0.055±0.00	0.059±0.01
	2	96.03±0.21	95.67±1.52	0.041±0.00	0.042±0.01
15	1	92.21±0.59	93.10±0.64	0.057±0.00	0.055±0.01
	2	95.28±0.54	95.67±1.68	0.042±0.00	0.042±0.01
20	1	93.02±1.09	91.58±1.52	0.053±0.00	0.061±0.01
	2	95.03±0.65	94.62±1.12	0.042±0.00	0.048±0.00

Table 2 summarizes the performance for the IT2FCM-based FNNm before optimization, and Table 3 shows the performance for the IT2FCM-based FNNm using genetic optimization. From Table 3, we select the network that has ten fuzzy rules (clusters) and a linear inference engine. This network exhibits CR = 98.49±0.40, PI = 0.048±0.00 for the training datasets and CR = 98.48±1.41, PI = 0.046±0.01 for the testing datasets.

Fig. 4 presents the optimization procedure for the CR and PI for the use of ten rules in Case 2 (Linear Inference), as obtained by genetic optimization. These figures depict the average values using random subsampling.

Table 3. Performance of the optimized IT2FCM-based FNNm

No. of Clusters	Inference (Case)	CR		PI	
		Training	Testing	Training	Testing
5	1	96.28±0.76	94.62±0.76	0.059±0.04	0.071±0.03
	2	98.69±0.57	97.89±0.98	0.042±0.01	0.047±0.01
10	1	96.18±0.84	95.67±1.68	0.054±0.04	0.061±0.04
	2	98.49±0.40	98.48±1.41	0.048±0.00	0.046±0.01
15	1	95.78±0.78	95.91±1.24	0.044±0.02	0.047±0.02
	2	98.74±0.40	97.54±0.96	0.043±0.00	0.053±0.01
20	1	96.43±0.67	96.37±0.76	0.038±0.01	0.039±0.01
	2	98.54±0.57	98.01±1.14	0.039±0.00	0.047±0.01

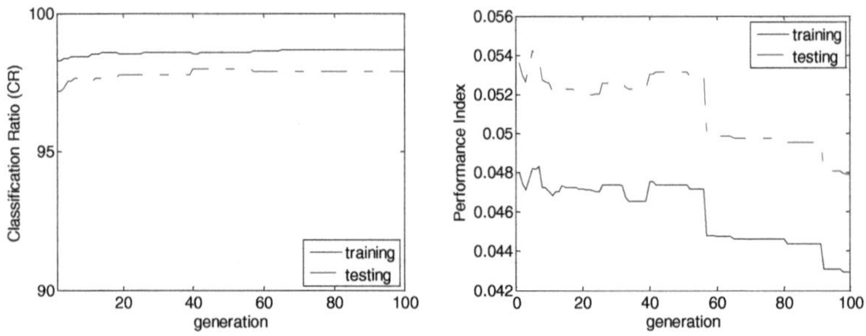

(a) CR (b) PI

Fig. 3. Optimization process for the selected network

Table 4 shows the performance of the proposed model to compare with the performance of some other models reported in the literature. The comparison shows that the proposed model has a good result.

Table 4. Comparison of performance with previous models

Model	Classification Ratio (%)
SVM	96.68±2.40
Bayes Net	95.81
RVM	97.20±1.86
MLP	85.92±3.02
MPANN[10]	98.1
DigaNN[11]	97.9
RBF2 [12]	97.13±1.80
Our model	98.48±1.41

5 Conclusions

In this paper, we have introduced fuzzy neural networks based on the interval type-2 fuzzy c-means clustering algorithm for pattern recognition and discussed its optimization using real-coded genetic algorithms.

The input spaces of the proposed networks were divided as the scatter form using IT2FCM clustering algorithm to generate the fuzzy rules. By this method, we could alleviate the problem of the curse of dimensionality and design fuzzy neural networks that are compact and simple. We also used genetic algorithms for parametric optimization of the proposed networks.

From the results in the previous section, we were able to design preferred networks. Through the use of a performance index, we were able to achieve a balance between the approximation and generalization abilities of the resulting network for pattern recognition. Finally, this approach would find potential application in many fields.

References

1. Yamakawa, T.: A Neo Fuzzy Neuron and Its Application to System Identification and Predition of the System Behavior. In: Proceeding of the 2nd International Conference on Fuzzy Logic & Neural Networks, pp. 447–483 (1992)
2. Buckley, J.J., Hayashi, Y.: Fuzzy neural networks: A survey. Fuzzy Sets Syst. 66, 1–13 (1994)
3. Zadeh, L.A.: The concept of a linguistic variable and its application to approximate reasoning-I. Information Science 8, 199–249 (1975)
4. Mizumoto, M., Tanaka, K.: Some Properties of Fuzzy Sets of Type-2. Information and Control 31, 312–340 (1976)
5. Karnik, N., Mendel, J., Liang, Q.: Type-2 Fuzzy Logic Systems. IEEE Trans. On Fuzzy Systems 7, 643–658 (1999)
6. Mendel, J.M.: Uncertain Rule-Based Fuzzy Logic Systems: Introduction and New Directions. Prentice-Hall, NJ (2001)
7. Bezdek, J.C.: Pattern Recognition with Fuzzy Objective Function Algorithms. Plenum Press, New York (1981)
8. Golderg, D.E.: Genetic Algorithm in search, Optimization & Machine Learning. Addison-Wesley (1989)
9. UCI Machine Learning Repository: Data Sets, http://archive.ics.uci.edu
10. Abbass, H.A.: An evolutionary artificial neural networks approach for breast cancer diagnosis. Artif. Intell. in Med. 25(3), 265–281 (2002)
11. Anagnostopoulos, I., Maglogiannis, I.: Neural network-based diagnostic and prognostic estimations in breast cancer microscopic instances. Medical & Biological Engineering & Computing 44(9), 773–784 (2006)
12. Young, Z.R.: A Novel Radial Basis Function Neural Network for Discriminant Analysis. IEEE Trans. Neural Networks 17(3), 604–612 (2006)

Spatio-temporal Search Techniques for the Semantic Web

Jeong-Joon Kim[1], Tae-Min Kwun[2], Kyu-Ho Kim[2,*], Ki-Young Lee[2], and Yeon-Man Jeong[3]

[1] Department of Computer Science and Information Engineering, KonKuk University, Seoul, Korea
jjkim9@db.konkuk.ac.kr

[2] Department of Medical IT and Marketing, Eulji University, Seongnam, Korea
tmkwun@gmail.com, {khkim,kylee}@eulji.ac.kr

[3] Department of Information and Telecommunication, Gangneung-Wonju National University, Wonju, Korea
ymjeong@gwnu.ac.kr

Abstract. Recently, a study on geo semantic web has been actively conducted. Geo semantic web is intelligence geography information web service technology that is combined geospatial web with semantic web. It can efficiently provide by integrating various geospatial and non-geospatial information. However, spatial-time data processing as a whole is suffering from a shortage of study. Moreover related standard is not established. Therefore, in this paper, we propose ontology, querying, reasoning about spatio-temporal data processing that applying various related processing technology and progress. Also, it is demonstrated effectiveness of system by applying to virtual scenario that requires spatio-temporal.

Keywords: Spatio-Temporal, Semantic Web, Ontology, SPARQL, Inference.

1 Introduction

Recently, a study on geo semantic web has been actively conducted. Geo semantic web is intelligence geography information web service technology that is combined geospatial web with semantic web. It can provide efficiently by integrating various geospatial and non-geospatial information. The OGC proposed the standard about GeoSPARQL[1] of spatial query for geo semantic web standards development and W3C is proposed the standard about GeoRSS, Geo OWL[2] of spatial ontology.

However, spatio-temporal data process including temporal element is suffering from a shortage of study as a whole, also related standard is not established. In addition, up to now study has a problem that is only possible independent inference separated by space and time.

Therefore, in this paper we propose spatio-temporal data process that is available to spatio-temporal data process for ontology, query and inference through the application

* Corresponding author.

T.-h. Kim et al. (Eds.): EL/DTA/UNESST 2012, CCIS 352, pp. 134–141, 2012.

of ontology processing technology and a variety of related theory and technology. Also, it is demonstrated effectiveness of system by applying to virtual scenario that requires spatio-temporal.

2 Related Works

2.1 Ontology Language

2.1.1 RDF/OWL

RDF[3] is proposed by W3C to overcome the limitation of XML, and retain interoperability on Semantic Web. RDF is a basic unit which is consisted of subject, predicate and object. Its resource is described by a graph, which is a set of triple. Subject and object is represented as an ellipse and if it is literal value is represented as a rectangle. The predicate is represented by a graph model connected to arrows.

OWL[4] is ontology language based on DAML+OIL. It has been designated as a W3C Recommendation in 2004. OWL was created to complement existing RDF, which had not represented part. Typically, Disjoint, Complement, Cardinality, symmetric, transitive relationships can be represented.

2.1.2 GeoRSS / Geo OWL

GeoRSS, Geo OWL was proposed by W3C in 2004 for representing geographic information identification, location and geospatial information on ontology through Geospatial Vocabulary of the Incubator Group Report. GeoRSS Feature Model is presented to use point, line, box, polygon by representing geographic attribute in Geospatial Vocabulary. GeoRSS included element that represented the location information, it was a technique which can apply namespace with existing xml document. Also, Geospatial Vocabulary suggested Geo OWL , it helps to represent spatial ontology using not only GeoRSS but also syntax of GML.

2.1.3 Temporal RDF

Temporal RDF[5] was Temporal RDF Graph Model proposed by Gutierrez, et al. who defined Graph Model about linear, discreate, absolute time in 2005. Temporal RDF proposed *T* of time factor, it was expressed through $(s,p,o) : [t]$. Also, it was expressed through $\{(s,p,o) : [t] | t1 \leq t \leq t2\}$. Using Temporal RDF Graph was able to inference temporally.

2.2 Query Language

2.2.1 SPARQL

SPARQL[6] was Query Language and presented at W3C in 2008. In addition, it was proposed to distribute semantic web for effectively access and navigate. If you have an experience using database, you can adapt more easily. Because it has many similarity between SQL used in existing relational database and method of SPARQL.

2.2.2 GeoSPARQL

GeoSPARQL was presented to extend SPARQL of semantic web architecture standard query language. It proposed to standard geometry type and standard geospatial operators for processing. GeoSPARQL can search the wanted RDF triple information by describing the RDF triple patterns alike SPARQL. In case of geospatial relational operators except relate operator, it support to spatial predicate through predicate extension of existing SPARQL. Relate operator which is one of the spatial relationship operators and spatial analysis operators support to extension of Filter Function in existing SPARQL.

2.2.3 SPARQL-ST

SPARQL-ST[7] was proposed spatio-temporal query language for support to existing SPARQL's problem which does not support spatio-temporal query by Wright State University's Matthew Perry in 2011. To make the spatio-temporal Ontology, time and space RDF triple structure was added to the SPARQL's RDF triple structure using Temporal RDF, OWL Time Ontology and GML described in the above 2.1.3. However, it had a problem which was only possible detached inferences about time, space unlike integrative inference that proposed in this paper.

2.3 Inference

2.3.1 SWRL

SWRL[8] was proposed at W3C in May 2004 to purpose OWL's utility extension including Horn-like Rules, OWL DL and Unary/Binary Datalog RuleML which was Sub-language of OWL lite and RuleML. SWRL must be written in grammar of Human-readable format.

SWRL syntax basically is as follows.

$$antecedent \Rightarrow consequent$$

SWRL simple example is as follows.

$$hasParent(?x1,?x2) \wedge hasBrother(?x2,?x3) \Rightarrow hasUncle(?x1,?x3)$$

3 Spatio-temporal Semantic Web

3.1 Spatio-temporal OWL

Geo OWL was proposed as a spatial ontology standard, but now OWL2 is suggested as a recommendation. Therefore, we propose ST-OWL based on contents of defined OWL2, GML and XML. The following shows polygon and circle which is one of the Spatio-Temporal OWL schema definition.

```
...
<complexType name="SpatioTemporalPolygon">
  <complexContent>
    <extension base="gml:AbstractSurfaceType">
      <sequence>
        <choice>
          <element name="t1" ref="xsd:datetime />
          <element name="t2" ref="xsd:datetime />
        </choice>
        <element name="posList" ref="gml:posList />
      <sequence>
    </extension>
  </complexContent>
</complexType>
...
```

```
...
<complexType name="SpatioTemporalCircle">
  <complexContent>
    <extension base="gml:AbstractSurfaceType">
      <sequence>
        <choice>
          <element name="t1" ref="xsd:datetime />
          <element name="t2" ref="xsd:datetime />
        </choice>
        <element name="posList" ref="gml:posList />
      <sequence>
    </extension>
  </complexContent>
</complexType>
...
```

```
Prefix(:=<http://www.w3.org/2001/XMLSchema#>
Prefix(:=<http://www.opengis.net/gml/3.2#>)
Prefix(:=<http://www.spatio-temporal.com/ver/0.1#>)
    Annotation( rdfs:label "Spatio-Temporal OWL Example" )
)

Declaration( Class( :Building ) )
Declaration( NamedIndividual( :ABCBuilding ) )
Declaration( DataProperty( :location ) )
Declaration( DataProperty( :constructionDate ) )
Declaration( DataProperty( :repairDate ) )

// Point
DataPropertyAssertion( :location :ABCBuilding "31.1012412 -12.1241221"^^st:Point )

// Polygon
DataPropertyAssertion( :location :ABCBuilding "31.1012412 -12.1241221 31.121142 -12.1136211
                                               31.0911002 -12.114532 31.0114214 -12.142124
                                              31.5232212 -12.164323"^^st:Polygon )

DataPropertyAssertion( :constructionDate :ABCBuilding "1999-12-20T11:20:12"^^st:Datetime )
DataPropertyAssertion( :repairDate :ABCBuilding "2005-11-05T10:02:09"^^st:Datetime )
```

Time and space information is required to construct ontology on spatial information. In case of time, it consist instance time, interval time. Instance time has one time point. Interval time has two time points. Spatial information supports most of the GML's data type. The following shows simple example of ST-OWL's point and polygon which is composed Functional Syntax form.

This example briefly shows about the ABC building in Yeouido-do, Republic of Korea. Construction date and location to object is declared Property. Also, it can confirm prefix to expand spatio-temporal after receiving inheritance on XML Schema and GML.

3.2 Spatio-temporal SPARQL

It is proposed to contents on ST-SPARQL to enable spatial query based on ST-OWL as defined above. ST-SPARQL's basic structure is shown in Figure 1.

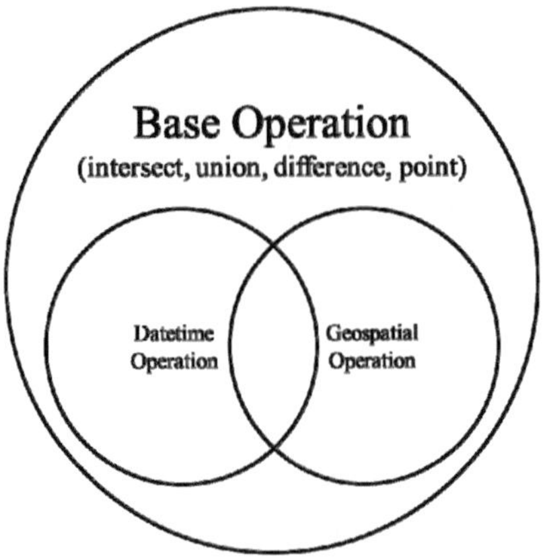

Fig. 1. Spatio-Temporal SPARQL's basic structure

As you can see Figure 1, Spatio-Temporal SPARQL uses GeoSPARQL of OCG recommendation by extending. ST-SPARQL processing architecture is divided into three parts. At first, it has a base operation for spatial query. Base operation consists intersect, difference, point. Since it targets specific coordinates in the case of point, it does not use geospatial operation. Secondly, it is divided date-time operation for selecting time and geospatial operation for selecting space.

The following shows syntax which is supported in the Spatio-Temporal SPARQL

```
...
SELECT [ATTRIBUTE]
WHERE
...
        [S] [BASE OPERTATION] ( [GEOSPATIAL OPERATION] ( [LAT LONG] ),
                  [DATETIME OPERATION] ( begin( [T1 YYYY/MM/DD hh24:mm:ss] ),
                                               end( [T2 YYYY/MM/DD hh24:mm:ss] )))
...
```

Filter operation is supported in SPARQL. But we don't use the filter operation due to complexity of the query. Base operation does not require a single local search. So omission of the base operation is possible. A few examples are as follows. First, the example of ST-SPARQL "Select established building in the Gang-nam district of Seoul city between 12 may 1999 and 10 march 2005" is as follows.

```
...
SELECT ?location ?constructionDate ?buildingName
WHERE
...
        ?location ?datetime st:polygon(40.157623 -74.855347 41.077281 –73.586426
                                      42.027521 –71.582426 40.217ABC4 –71.482334),
                      st:interval(begin(1999/03/15, 14:20:00),
                                  end(1999/03/18, 13:10:00))
        ?location ?datetime buildingName ?buildingName
...
```

The next example of Spatio-Temporal SPARQL "Select established building at the intersection of the Gang-nam district and the Song-pa district until 1 March 2008 from 2 September 2005" is as follows.

```
...
SELECT ?location ?constructionDate ?buildingName
WHERE
...
        ?location ?time st:intersect(st:polygon(40.157623 -74.855347 41.077281 –73.586426,
                                     41.142421 -78 342343 42.124122 -77.412412),
                            st:polygon(40.157623 -74.855347 41.077281 –73.586426,
                                     41.142421 -78 342343 42.124122 -77.412412),
                                 st:interval(begin(1999/03/15, 14:20:00),
                            end(1999/03/18, 13:10:00)))
        ?location ?time name ?buildingName
...
```

In the above example, We can see used st:polygon of geospatial operation two times. Specific building is displayed to user after intersecting polygon of match the date-time operation in two areas.

3.3 Inference for the Spatio-temporal Semantic Web

We have considered a number of ways for spatio-temporal inferences. Because of our goal of the spatio-temporal inferences, we defined operators and inferences rule for basic relation inferences such as Table 1 based on RCC8 and Temporal Inferences.

Table 1. Spatio-Temporal relation operators

Spatio-Temporal Relation Operator	
st:Equals(ST_1, ST_2)	*st:Intersect* (ST_1, ST_2)
st:Within(ST_1, ST_2)	*st:Disjoint*(ST_1, ST_2)

ST includes spatial *G* and interval time *T* or instance time *t*. The following briefly shows that each operator is represented by SWRL Rule.

$$isEquals(ST_1(t_1),ST_2(t_2))\ \&\ isEqual(ST_1(G_1), ST_2(G_2)) => \mathbf{Equals(ST_1(G_1, t_1), ST2(G_2, t_2))}$$

$$isContain(ST_2(T_2), ST_1(T_1))\ \&\ isContain(ST_1(T_1), ST_2(T_2))\ \&\ isContain(ST_2(G_2), ST1(G_1)) \\ \&\ isContain(ST_1(G_1), ST_1(G_2)) => \mathbf{Intersect(ST_1, ST_2)}$$

$$isContain(ST_2(T_2), ST_1(T_1))\ \&\ isNotIntersect(ST_1(G_1), ST_2(G_2)) => \mathbf{Within(ST_2, ST_1)}$$

$$isNotIntersect(ST_1, ST_2) => \mathbf{Disjoint(ST_1, ST_2)}$$

In the above example, we are defined inference rule that is only possible spatio-temporal integration inference.

4 Scenario

To verify temporal-spatial data is proposed in this paper, Scenario is follows.

"We should find a landing place because the plane has a problem during moving to berlin."

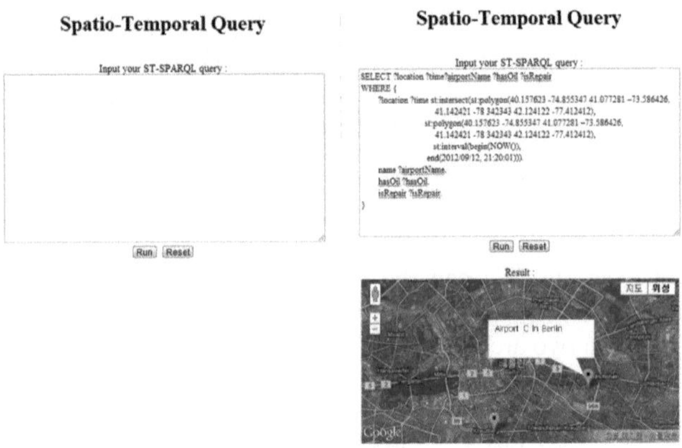

Fig. 2. The result of experiment

When we perform the above query, we can display the closest airports by using spatial-temporal data about airport with current location. Also, we can find the information that is possible to maintain and refueling instantly. We create spatial information about airport in random places for virtual scenario, Spatio-Temporal SPARQL query experiment results directly tagged on Google Map. This experiment is used to expand the Apache Jena2. For the experiment, proposed SWRL Rule is change to Jena Rule.

Client is consisted of Spatio-Temporal SPARQL query input section and result section. Jena Rule and Ontology is imported from outside.

As you can see the experimental results of Figure 2, you can see that it printed airport which is accorded with condition in location after intersecting polygons is consisted of each locations. Also, if you click on each tag, you can see the information about appropriate airport.

5 Conclusion

Recently, interest in Semantic Web providing an efficiently by integrating a variety of Geospatial and non-Geospatial information has increased steadily. However, the current standard for spatio-temporal semantic web is not established, related research is underway with several organizations, association and standardization. In this paper, we organized the research on up-to-date spatio-temporal semantic web. And we proposed standard about ontology language, inference rule, and query. It is compatible with current standard. Finally, it is verified by the simulation to target the building in specific area.

References

1. Perry, M., Herring, J.: GeoSPARQL - A Geographic Query Language for RDF Data, http://www.opengeospatial.org/
2. Lieberman, J., Singh, R., Goad, C.: GeoOWL Geospatial Ontology language Document Overview, http://www.w3.org/2005/Incubator/geo/XGR-geo-20071023/
3. Brickley, D., Guha, R.V.: RDF vocabulary description language 1.0: RDF schema, http://www.w3.org/tr/rdf-schema/
4. W3C OWL Working Group, OWL 2 Web Ontology Language Document Overview, http://www.w3.org/TR/owl2-overview/
5. Gutierrez, C., Hurtado, C.A., Vaisman, A.A.: Temporal RDF. In: Gómez-Pérez, A., Euzenat, J. (eds.) ESWC 2005. LNCS, vol. 3532, pp. 93–107. Springer, Heidelberg (2005)
6. Prud'hommeaux, E., Seaborne, A.: SPARQL Query language Document Overview, http://www.w3.org/TR/rdf-sparql-query/
7. Perry, M., Jain, P., Sheth, A.P.: SPARQL-ST: Extending SPARQL to Support Spatio-temporal Queries (2011)
8. Horrocks, I., Patel-Schneider, P.F., Boley, H., Tabet, S., Grosof, B., Dean, M.: SWRL Rule Document Overview, http://www.w3.org/Submission/SWRL/

A Page Management Technique for Frequent Updates from Flash Memory

Jeong-Jin Kang[1], Eun-Byul Cho[2], Myeong-Jin Jeong[3,*], Jeong-Joon Kim[4], Ki-Young Lee[2], and Gyoo-Seok Choi[5]

[1] Department of Information and Communication, Dong Seoul University, Korea
jjkang@du.ac.kr
[2] Department of Medical IT and Marketing, Eulji University, Seongnam, Korea
pinichi@naver.com, kylee@eulji.ac.kr
[3] Department of Environmental Health & Safety, Eulji University, Seongnam, Korea
jmj123@eulji.ac.kr
[4] Department of Computer Science and Information Engineering, KonKuk University, Seoul, Korea
jjkim9@db.konkuk.ac.kr
[5] Department of Computer Science, Chungwoon University, Hongseong, Korea
lionel@chungwoon.ac.kr

Abstract. Flash Memory as the next generation of storage device with a wide variety of benefits is getting more popular. Because overwritten of Flash Memory's characteristic doesn't work, Data updating in the flash memory should be carried out efficiently. When frequent updates occur in flash memory, there are drawbacks that the update rate may be very slow. By managing frequent updates on flash memory, this paper focuses on improve performance of Flash Memory.

Keywords: Frequent Updates, Page Management, Flash Memory.

1 Introduction

Electronic devices in embedded systems with built-in miniaturized products are gaining recently popularity. Flash memory is the non-volatile memory that recorded data does not clear so it has various advantages such as fast operation speed, small size and light of weight. Accordingly flash memory spotlighted as the next generation mass storage device is currently being used in various fields, such as laptops, digital cameras [1]. Also, in recent Years as Secondary Storage, SSD (Solid State Drive) composed of Flash Memory is being spotlighted rather than HDD (Hard Disk Drive) [2].

In case we update algorithm to update the files in the flash memory, To Update algorithms in FTL (Flash Translation Layer) have a lot of erasing operations and recording operations. So Sequential Update rather than Random Update is more suitable. However there is LPRM (Logical Page Re-Mapping) Algorithm to indicate

* Corresponding author .

T.-h. Kim et al. (Eds.): EL/DTA/UNESST 2012, CCIS 352, pp. 142–149, 2012.

the effect, current random updates as much as sequentially updates [3]. The number of updates increases as much as the number of invalid page increases due to updating frequently. Increased invalid page, Re-mapping among mapping tables is done. It cause mapping rate to delay. As a result when pages update, the update rate eventually slows and it needs method previously. When frequent updates of the Flash Memory' characteristics are done. In this paper, it is suggested to efficient Page management by improving the mapping table.

2 Related Works

2.1 Flash Memory

Flash memory has features of small, light of weight and non-volatile so many products in the form of storage have been used widely. There is the kind of flash memory and it consists of NAND-type and NOR-type. The basic structure of flash memory consists of a large number of blocks. A block size is 16KB and a block consists of 32 Pages. In addition, a page size is 528 KB. Of these, 512 Byte is area to store data and 16byte is spare area [4-5]. The most important feature of flash memory is HDD doesn't have Erase Operation but Flash memory has Erase Operation and Computational speed of flash memory for each operation is different. Table 1 is time required for each operation in a variety of storage devices [6].

Table 1. The time required for each operation in a variety of storage devices

	Read	Write	Erase
NAND Memory	12μs/512B	200μs/512B	2ms/16KB
NOR Memory	150ns/1B	200μs/1B	1s/16K
DRAM	100ns/1B	100ns/1B	
HDD	12.4ms/512B	12.4ms/512B	

Because Flash memory can't operate Overwritten to modify a particular Sector, the corresponding block is cleared and operate overwrite operation. These issues solve problems through "Erase Before Write operation". So Page Management of Flash memory is very important. Because "Erase Before Write" operation execute and Invalid page occurs [7].

2.2 LPRM (Logical Page Re-Mapping) Algorithm

Flash memory structure is suitable for sequential recording, the application consists of sequential records accordingly. However, through LPRM algorithm, Not only be slow relative to speed of random updates but sequential record speed through LPRM algorithm The difference of record speed is reduced. Figure 1 is one example of the LPRM algorithm.

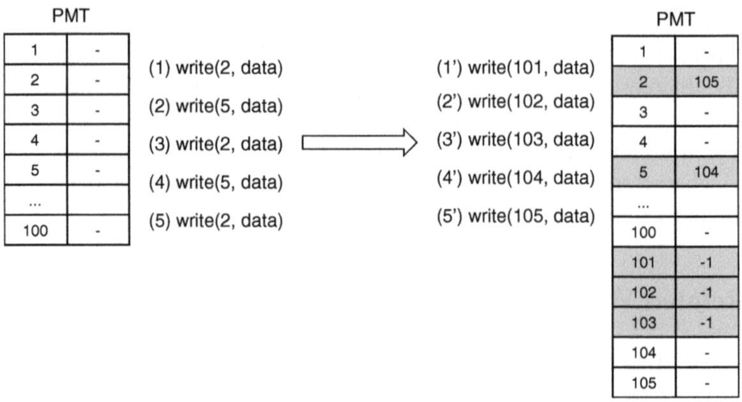

Fig. 1. Example of operating the LPRM algorithm

Because the process (1) ~ (5) represent random update, It can be seen that each of the data from the page 2 and the page 5 repeatedly written. The Process (1')~(5') in sequential update represent, it can be seen that each of data is written from the page 101 sequentially. That is, Data written by Process (4) and (5) in the process (1)~(5) can be finally stored Page 5 and Page 2. Finally, the data stored in this process correspond to data (4')~(5') in process (1')~(5'), data (1)~(3) is disappeared. But because in Process (1')~(5') the data is updated sequentially , Process (1')~(3') has data of corresponding data.

PMT has a role in the mapping-table that mapping the page. For example, if the process (1) is successful, to run the process (1') and PMT of right to map page record in a table format. At First If the data is written on the page 2, the data correspond page 101. So number 2 of left area in PMT will be recorded on 101 of the right side. If the process (2) is successful, the process (2') will be executed and number 5 of left area in PMT will be recorded on 102 of the right side. Because in the Process (3) page 2 is overwritten with the new data, number 2 of left area in PMT will be recorded on 103 of the right side and page 101 which have been mapped and page 2's relationships will be disconnected. How to determine the relationship was broken, 101 page map –1. In this way, the mapping of the page mapping is not placed difference.

Like Figure 2, the data pages in the table space exist. The table space mapping Page information is stored. When the page written newly data is update, a page which is mapped by LPRM algorithm is determined primarily on the ReMT (ReMapping Table) update. Then, PMT point mapped page. Mapped page will be added to the LPRM area. When the same page is updated several times in ReMT, The number of invalid page increases. Then, ReMT manages it.

In LRPM algorithm, ReMT Table informs information to map page for ID and valid page detail. When mapped page frequently occurs writing invalid page would continue to grow but LPRM algorithm doesn't have management for invalid pages.

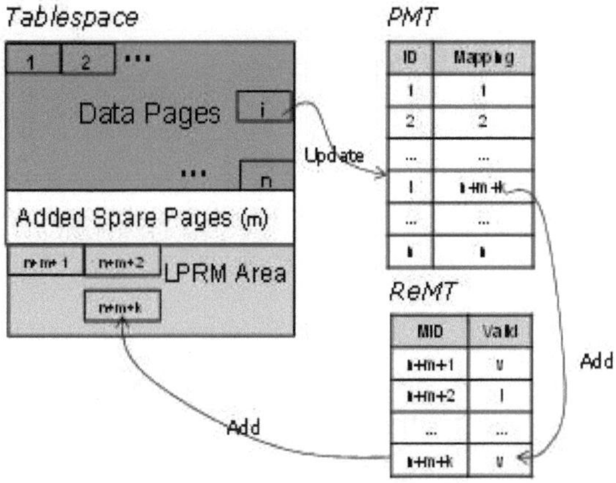

Fig. 2. Mapping table for LPRM algorithm

3 Proposed Algorithm

If link is broken, A page in the mapping table follows the pointer type. Because the overall balance was broken and cost of time to re-map cost it a lot. Time to cost a lot means to update-cost a lot. Eventually, it is closely related with the update rate. In other words, When the mapping state between mapping table is broken and page be updated with new data re-map on that page, Cases that the existing mapped page by PMT has been re-mapped are a lot. When Remapping Page can't map invalid page because this page is invalid page Reassign the newly mapped page. In this case, the time of remapping page will occur. And if there is invalid page in middle of ReMT because invalid page should be remapped when the overall memory updates, this affects memory usage.

Like Figure 3, ReMT page is divided into two categories in order that new proposed algorithm improves the shortcoming of these existing algorithms. Invalid page and valid page more than a certain threshold with the possibility of invalid page is Risk Group and other page classified as Normal Group consist of ReMT table.

First, Criterion is necessary to divide ReMT into two categories. Risk Group represents the sum of invalid page and the number of valid pages that contain risk group and Formula (1) indicates this. Because already invalid page is unable to write a record longer, it include Risk group without condition so the problem does not occur. But if valid page is contained Risk Group, valid page only to satisfy certain conditions mentioned above must be included in the Risk Group.

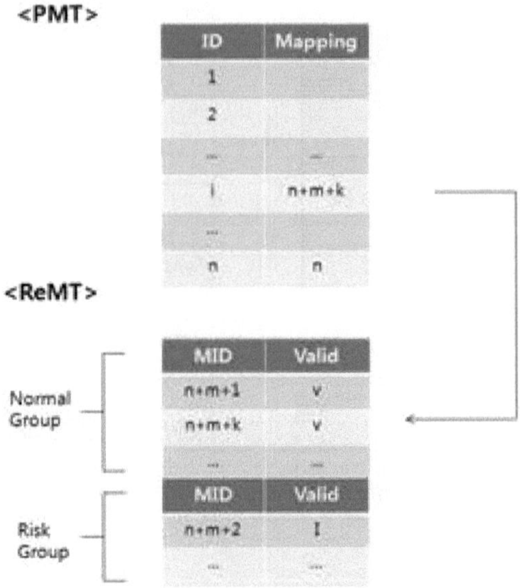

Fig. 3. Proposed mapping table

Formula (2) is valid pages to be included in the risk group it is possible to indicate whether it is discriminant. It is indicated sum of valid page's renewal as over sum of total valid pages, multiplying the coefficient called expectation coefficient (e).

$$n(Page\ of\ Risk Group) = n(Valid\ Page\ Included\ Danger\ Group(d\_p)) + n(Invalid\ Page(i)) \tag{1}$$

$$Threshold = \frac{\sum(the\ renewal\ umber\ of\ Validpage(v))}{\sum n(Validpage)} \times Expectation Coefficient(e) \tag{2}$$

According to the following conditions As ReMT is separated Risk Group and Normal Group, Mapping priority for normal groups rather than risk group put priority. When it is mapped Risk Group because the possibility of re-mapping it exist, the update date can lead to degradation. By Placing to Normal Group, you can get the effect of making the degradation prevention of update rate and remapping time.

In addition, as other purpose in order to manage efficient page Risk Group and Normal Group, we divide efficient page management's aspect, if the amount of valid page contained and invalid page consist of 30% of the entire page, we reset Mapping Table by Garbage Collection.

The following show some of the pseudo code of algorithm proposed in this paper.

```
Struct ReMT{ int MID;
             boolean Valid;}
typedef Struct New_ReMT
{ int Count;
Struct ReMT remt;} New_ReMT
```

Fig. 4. Pseudo code of a proposed new mapping table structure

```
New_ReMT Risk_G;
New_ReMT Normal_G;
check_DangerG ( )
{  if (Normal_G.remt.Valid == 'FALSE'){
Risk_G.Count = Normal_G.Count;
Risk_G.remt.MID = Normal_G.remt.MID;
Risk_G.remt.Valid = Normal_G.remt.Valid;}
if ( Normal_G.remt.Valid == 'TRUE'
&&Normal_G.remt.Count >D){
Risk_G.Count = Normal_G.Count;
Risk_G.remt.MID = Normal_G.remt.MID;
Risk_G.remt.Valid = Normal_G.remt.Valid;}    }
```

Fig. 5. Pseudo code representation of the function to check for Risk Group

Figure 4 shows proposed structure of Mapping table and Figure 5 is function to check to relocate page to risk group of the page to configure the normal group.

4 Performance Evaluation

In this Chapter, in order to compare the performance of the newly proposed algorithm with the LPRM algorithms, we compare update speed and amount of memory usage is taken into consideration at the time of renewal of the most important factors.

Experiments are performed in a mobile environment and H/W consist of CPU 1.2 GHz, RAM DDR2 1GB, Database use contacts2.db is provided within the mobile phone book DB. The total number of phonebook's Records is 5000. We make comparison Update speed and memory usage of LPRM and proposed algorithm. Like Figure 6, it compares Update rates about total records of LPRM Speed and Proposed algorithm speed.

When update rate is 5 %, LPRM's time is 3500ms and Proposed algorithm is 2900ms and The proposed algorithm showed a 82.8% speed improvement than the LPRM. When update rate is 10 %, LPRM's time is 6700ms and Proposed algorithm is 5400ms and The proposed algorithm showed a 80.5% speed improvement than the LPRM. When update rate is 15 %, LPRM's time is 9400ms and Proposed algorithm is 7600ms and The proposed algorithm showed a 80.8% speed improvement than the LPRM. When update rate is 20 %, LPRM's time is 12200ms and Proposed algorithm is 9700ms and The proposed algorithm showed a 79.5% speed improvement than the LPRM. According to each of the update rate, on average, update rate of proposed algorithm is faster than that of LPRM about 19.1%.

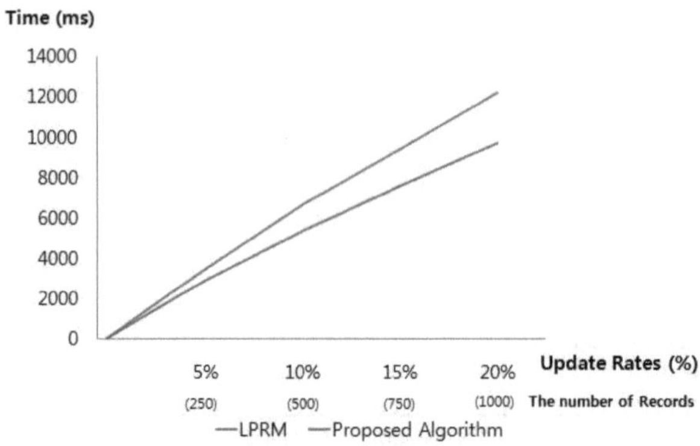

Fig. 6. The comparison of updating rates of LPRM and Proposed Algorithm

Like Figure 7, it compares amount of Memory usage of LPRM algorithm and Proposed algorithm. We know that LPRM algorithm will be update evenly by sequential update. But Propose Algorithm is not updated evenly. It will be updated when Risk Group is over 30%. Because of Preprocessing process divided by Risk Group and Common Group, We know that Proposed Algorithm approximately increase 5.7% of memory usage.

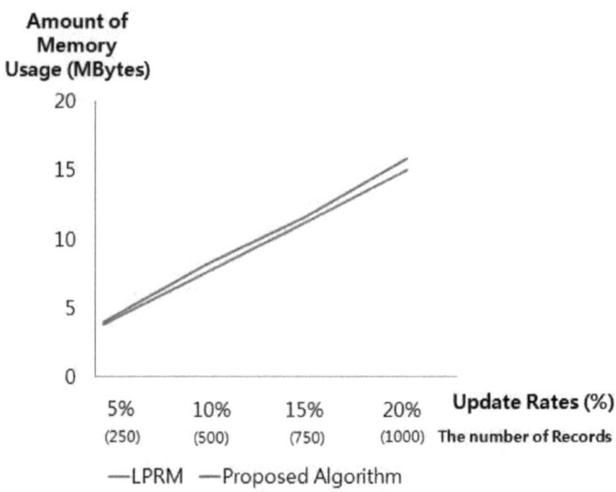

Fig. 7. The comparison of amount memory of LPRM algorithm and the Proposed algorithm

5 Conclusion

In this paper, to supplement LPRM algorithm for invalid page management drawback, we propose a new algorithm. Invalid page and valid page have high possibility of invalid page to be classified as a risk group and the other page to be classified as a normal group divide into 2 mapping table, we expect that renewal time increased due to the unnecessary link and the frequent updates of pages reduce. Proposed algorithm update looked better performance than existing methods in terms of speed, In Memory usage, performance seemed similar to the increase in the number of new code, because the memory usage is not more prominently good performance the proposed algorithm than LPRM techniques Parts to be improved are needed.

References

1. Dirik, C., Jacob, B.: The Performance of PC Solid-State Disks (SSDs) as a Function of Bandwidth, Concurrency, Device Architecture, and System Organization. In: ISCA, Austin (2009)
2. Lee, S., Moon, B., Park, C., Kim, J., Kim, S.: A Case for Flash Memory SSD in Enterprise Database Applications. In: Proc of the ACM SIGMOD, pp. 1075–1086 (2008)
3. Min, K., An, K., Jang, I., Jin, S.: A System Framework for Map Air Update Navigation Service. ETRI Journal 33, 476–486 (2011)
4. NAND vs. NOR Flash Memory: Technology Overview, http://www.chips.toshiba.com
5. NAND Flash Spare Area Assignment Standard, http://www.samsung.com
6. Yim, K.: A Novel Memory Hierarchy for Flash Memory Based Storage Systems. Journal of Semiconductor Technology and Science 5, 262–269 (2005)
7. Baek, S., Choi, J., Lee, D., Noh, S.H.: Performance Characteristics of Flash Memory: Model and Implications. In: Lee, Y.-H., Kim, H.-N., Kim, J., Park, Y.W., Yang, L.T., Kim, S.W. (eds.) ICESS 2007. LNCS, vol. 4523, pp. 162–173. Springer, Heidelberg (2007)

Implementing Mobile Interface Based Voice Recognition System

Myung-Jae Lim[1], Eun-Ser Lee[2], and Young-Man Kwon[1,*]

[1] Department of Medical IT and Marketing, Eulji University,
553, Sanseong-daero, Sujeong-gu, Seongnam-si, Gyeonggi-do, 461-713, Korea
[2] Department of Computer Engineering, Andong National University
Seongcheon-dongn 1375 Gyeongdong-ro, Andong-si Gyeongsangbuk-do, 760-749, Korea
{lk04,ymkwon}@eulji.ac.kr, eslee@andong.ac.kr

Abstract. Recently, as supply of smart phone is widely spreading, various voice applications for user's convenience are under development. However, since Google Android-based smart phone delivered by Korean manufacturer processes voice recognition through Google server, it has a weakness to take long time to be processed and need activation of internet. This paper implemented Android-based voice recognition system using continuous HMM without having to use Google server. As the result of evaluation for proposed voice recognition system and Google's voice recognition system, the proposed system showed similar voice recognition performance but its processing speed is proved to be better than Google's.

Keywords: Mobile HCI, Voice Recognition, CHMM, Android OS.

1 Introduction

Recently as ubiquitous market is rapidly growing, various HCI(Human Computer Interaction) technologies have been actively under development. Moreover, convenience and various functions focused on portability depending on ubiquitous environment are highlighted and accordingly various types of user interface technologies are under development[1]. Therefore, voice interfaces are provided for mobile device users and developer's convenience. Since transferring information via voice is natural and easy to be understood and especially it has a strength making it possible to process with visual based task simultaneously, researches for voice recognition are actively under development[2]. However, as Android based mobile device delivered by Korea market has no built-in voice engine and it processes voice recognition via Google server, it takes a long and internet needs to be activated. Therefore, Android device users using Android applications and developers for Android application suffer from inconvenience more severely.

This paper implemented Android based Korean language voice recognition system without having to pass through Google server in a way that creates voice recognition

[*] Corresponding author.

T.-h. Kim et al. (Eds.): EL/DTA/UNESST 2012, CCIS 352, pp. 150–157, 2012.

model using CHMM and integrates C-language based HTK with Android using Java JNI and Android NDK[8][9].

2 Related Works

2.1 HMM(Hidden Markov Model)

HMM algorithm, under an assumption that voice can be modeled by Markov process, calculates parameters for Markov model in a process of learning voice and then makes a standard Markov model and compares inputted voice and stored standard Markov model and finally determines recognized words for the highest similarity of standard Markov model [4]. HMM algorithm is a double probability processing technique to estimate unpredictable process by predictable processes. This technique makes it possible to set standard patterns to phonemes and syllable. Since HMM algorithm is possible to use words and sentences for input voice, it is strong for independence of speaker and continuous voice recognition.

2.2 Continuous HMM

Continuous HMM uses a specific vector extracted from voice signal as it is. Continuous HMM uses Gaussian Mixture Model to calculate Maximum Likelihood for signals which are observed to estimate parameters of model. In case of continuous HMM, a probability to observe an input vector O_t at status and time can be expressed by Gaussian Mixture Model, GMM as shown in formula (1)[5]

$$b_j(O_t) = \sum_{k=1}^{M} c_{jk} N(O_t, \mu_{jk}, U_{jk}), 1 \le j \le N \tag{1}$$

Here, M is the number of Gaussian mixture consisting of GMM, c_{ik} is a weight for k^{hh}

Gaussian mixture, μ_{ik} and U_{ik} average vector and covariance matrix at status j and k th Gaussian mixture respectively. N is a whole state. Baum- Welch reestimation algorithm to calculate $b_i(O_t)$ from learning data is following: Provided that the number of status is N and the length of symbol is T, forward probability is $\alpha_t(i)$ (i=1,2,...,N ; t=1,2,..., T) and backward probability is $\beta_t(i)$ (i=1,2,..., N; t= T, $T-1$,...,0), probability $\gamma_t(j,k)$ which is likely to become status j $t$at time is defined as following:

$$\gamma_t(j,k) = \left[\frac{\alpha_t(j)\beta_t(j)}{\sum_{i=1}^{N}\alpha_t(j)\beta_t(j)}\right]\left[\frac{c_{jk}N(O_t,\mu_{jk},U_{jk})}{\sum_{m=1}^{M}c_{jm}N(O_t,\mu_{jm},U_{jm})}\right] \tag{2}$$

A formula to estimate model parameters, c_{ik}, μ_{ik}, U_{ik} using 3 probability variables (α, β, γ) is following:

$$\overline{c_{jk}} = \frac{\sum_{t=1}^{T} \gamma_t(j,k)}{\sum_{t=1}^{T}\sum_{k=1}^{M} \gamma_t(j.k)} \tag{3}$$

$$\overline{\mu_{jk}} = \frac{\sum_{t=1}^{T} \gamma_t(j,k) \cdot O_t}{\sum_{t=1}^{T} \gamma_t(j.k)} \tag{4}$$

$$\overline{U_{jk}} = \frac{\sum_{t=1}^{T} \gamma_t(j,k) \cdot (O_t - \mu_{jk})(O_t - \mu_{jk})^T}{\sum_{t=1}^{T} \gamma_t(j.k)} \tag{5}$$

2.3 Java JN and Android NDK

Android application is able to interconnect functions and libraries which are made of C and C++ language not by Java through Java JNI(Java Native Interface) and NDK(Native Development Kit).[8][9] In other word, theoretically Android application can call C or C++ code with more or less portability from Java Virtual Machine (JVM). JNI is included in JVM as shown in Fig. 1 and provides an interface to load Native Method and execute it.

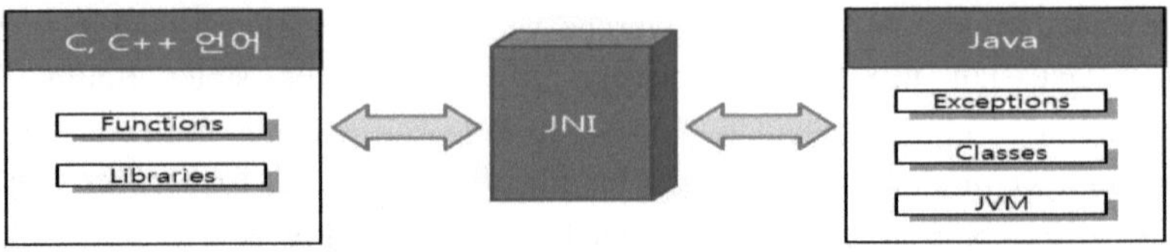

Fig. 1. C-based Library and JNI to connect Java

Although Java is a limitation of platform-dependent performance, the use of JNI can result in performance enhancement in a way that makes C or C++ codes for segments pr functions whose processing speed might be slow due to use of Java. In addition, JNI is also used when big and important codes are already made by C or C++ and user doesn't want to re-write same codes with Java. This paper is able to shorten processing time for voice recognition without having to write same codes by connecting existing C-code based HTK using JNI.

3 Android Based Voice Recognition System

3.1 Extracting Voice Characteristics

Since not only voice is variably changing depending on gender, age and pronunciation although it is same language and but also its characteristics are also changing when it is pronounced by a single or by words and texts, it's important to extract characteristics to express voice well.

A procedure to extract a specific vector MFCC(Mel Frequency Cepstral Coefficients) used by this paper is shown in Fig. 2. The inputted voice signal is converted into digital signal and the converted signal is divided into block unit of frame being wrapped by hamming window. After that, all processes are carried out in a frame unit. The size of frame is 20ms and 10 ms is used to move frame. Voice signal for one frame is converted into frequency area using FFT(Fast Fourier Transform) The frequency bandwidth is divided by several filter banks and then energy is calculated for each bank. The final MFCC is calculated by applying log to band energy and doing DCT(Discrete Cosine Transform) MFCC coefficient uses 12 items from to and MFCC coefficient becomes 13 MFCC as frame log energy is additionally used apart from previous 12 MFCC. Although use of several frames rather than use of a single frame may result in better performance to model voice signal containing 13 MFCC, the total number of frames is increased, several frames need to be expressed by minimum parameter.

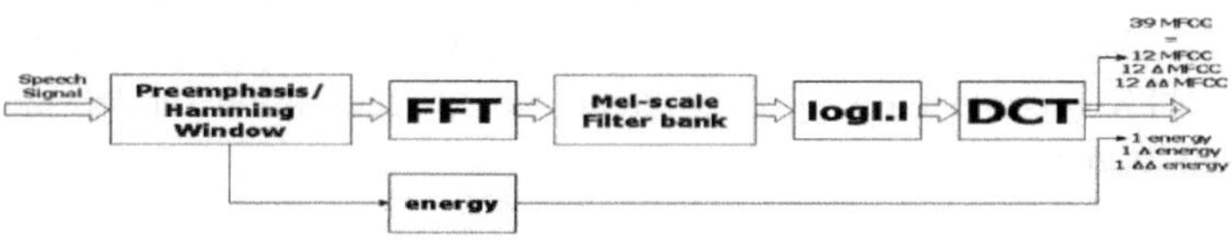

Fig. 2. Procedure to extract specific vector

Below Fig. 3 shows procedure for HMM training. This training uses "Korean language increase mike voice recognition recite-typed sentence DB" A total of 689 people pronounced 50 sentences respectively and trained a total of 34,447 voices. In general, HTK is used for HMM training from voice DB. HTK is a portable tool kit used to make and adjust HMM. It consists of C-based libraries, module and tools and widely used for voice recognition system using HMM.

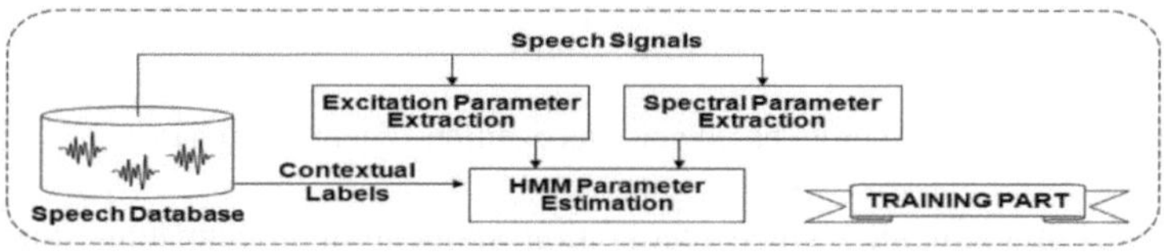

Fig. 3. HMM training

3.2 Procedure for Voice Training

This paper used a context dependent triphone model considering both front and rear phonemes among phonemes modeling as a recognition unit for HMM training[7]. Triphone model has its strength to reflect phonemic phenomenon within word more efficiently than phonemes model. In order to estimate reliable model parameters, a certain level of learning data for each triphone model needs to be acquired. In order to solve this insufficiency of learning data, all triphone models make phonemic phenomenon which shares transition probability and state parameters. This paper structured a total of 895 tied-state triphone in this paper and defined phonemes-based 5 state left-to-right mode. 4 mixtures, 39 means . covariance are extracted based on Gaussian continuous density function for each model and used for parameters. A procedure to extract isolated word from each phonemes model is carried out in a way that first learns HMM for phoneme unit using re-estimation algorithm from training data. During recognition phase, it refers to pronunciation dictionary in recognition phase and assembles model of words to be recognized using phonemes model. Once a word model is structured, probability of observation for inputted specific vector is calculated using inputted forward algorithm and then a model with the highest probability is founded and then the result of recognition is printed out.

3.3 Android Based Voice Recognition System

Android based Korean language voice recognition system suggested by this paper consists of Java-based Android module to execute voice recognition result recording voice and HTK module built by C to create voice recognition model and execute voice recognition as shown in Fig. 4.

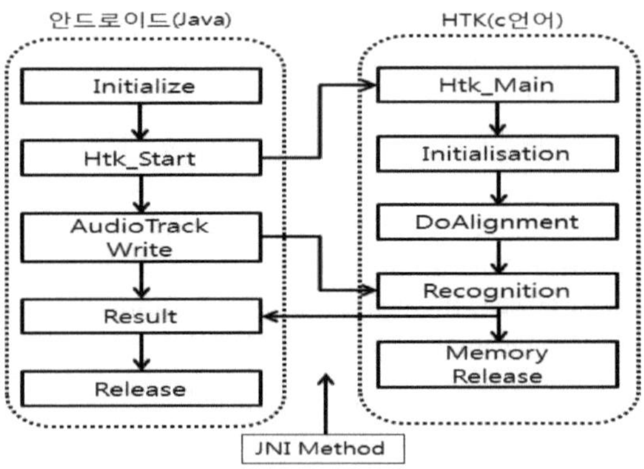

Fig. 4. Android based voice recognition system flow chart

This paper implemented voice recognition application in Samsung smart phone Galaxy S2 to test Korean voice recognition as shown in Table. 1.

In order to implement Android based Korean voice recognition system, 2 distinctive libraries are created using Android NDK. The first library, as an initialization library, executes initialization of HTK, setting model parameters and releasing memory. The second one, as HTK recognition library, executes recognition by most fitted words or sentence with already created model by analyzing inputted voices from Android module. Development environment for Android based voice recognition system is shown in Table. 1.

Table 1. Media construction

OS	Android 2.3(Gingerbread)
CPU	Dual core 1.2GHZ
MEMORY	RAM 1GB, 16GB storage

Application is built to output recognized sentence once a voice is inputted through built-in mike in terminal. Fig. 5 shows a screen shot to execute Android based voice recognition system and operate it.

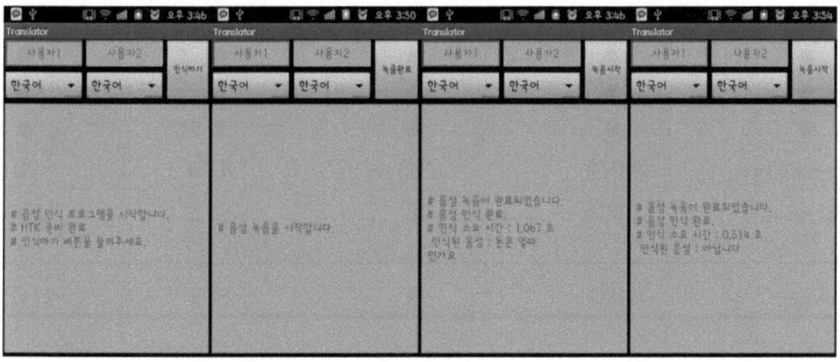

Fig. 5. A screen to execute Android based voice recognition system

4 Experiments and Results

4.1 How to Experiment

In order to evaluate built-in Android based Korean voice recognition system performance, voice recognition rate and time for execution are compared to Google voice recognition system. For this experiment, 40 recognition targets for the experiment are selected and a total of 400 sentences are used by 10 times of pronunciation for each sentence for this experiment.

4.2 Comparison of Execution Time and Recognition Rate for Voice Recognition System

Execution time for voice recognition system is verified to take average 4.068 seconds for Google voice recognition system and 1.513 seconds for the proposed voice recognition system respectively. Since Google voice recognition system is carried out in a way that inputted voice from a terminal is transferred to Google server under internet environment and the recognized result is returned to the terminal, it takes a long. However, as the proposed voice recognition system is equipped with built-in voice recognition library, processing time is verified to be short and its execution time is shortened.

Table 2. Execution time for voice recognition system (sec) and recognition rate (%)

Test Sentence	Google method		This method	
	Time	Recog. Rate	Time	Recog .Rate
sentence1	3.822	100	1.99	100
sentence2	3.635	90	1.091	90
sentence3	4.331	100	1.557	80
•	•	•	•	•
•	•	•	•	•
•	•	•	•	•
sentence39	4.019	100	1.438	90
sentence40	3.874	90	1.572	100
Avg	4.068	93	1.513	91.75

Recognition rate for voice recognition system is shown to be average 93% for Google voice recognition system and 91.75% for the proposed voice recognition system as shown Table 2. As Google server recognizes voice by word, a long sentence "Take subway as buses are under traffic jam" is proved to be better recognized by the proposed voice recognition system than Google voice recognition system. However, a short sentence of 3 "No it's not" is proved to be better recognized by Google system.

For 40 sentences, Google voice server is proved to be approximately 1.25% better than the proposed system.

5 Conclusion

Because Android based smart phone released in Korea is not equipped with built-in Korean voice engine thus it processes voice recognition via Google server, it takes a long time and internet needs to be activated. These are weaknesses. Therefore, this paper proposed Android based built-in Korean voice recognition system and implemented it and reduced processing time for voice recognition by connecting C code based HTK using JNI. The proposed Android based voice recognition system is proved to have better processing time with similar recognition performance compared to Google server. However, this paper didn't consider accents found at specific dialect from certain districts. Thus there might be some cases to deteriorate recognition rate when unclear pronunciation is inputted. Therefore, in order to enhance the performance of this system, it will be necessary to consider characteristics of people in specific districts. In addition, more experiments and various ranges of ages need to be considered to build more convenient and easy-to-use of interface for both normal and disabled people. Especially, more robust recognition system against noise by considering various environments needs to be implemented. Especially, this system is expected to become more efficient mean for voice interface when it is used for disabled people.

References

1. Mulder, A.: Hand gestures for HCI. Technical Report 96-1, vol. Simon Fraster University (1996)
2. Wu, Y., Huang, T.S.: Vision-Based Gesture Recognition: A Review. In: Braffort, A., Gibet, S., Teil, D., Gherbi, R., Richardson, J. (eds.) GW 1999. LNCS (LNAI), vol. 1739, p. 103. Springer, Heidelberg (2000)
3. Bau, O., Poupyrev, I., Israr, A., Harrison, C.: TeslaTouch: Electrovibration for Touch Surfaces. In: UIST (2010)
4. Rabiner, L.R.: A tutorial on hidden Markov models and selected applications in speech recognition. Proc. IEEE 77(2), 257–286 (1989)
5. Reynolds, D.A., Rose, R.C.: Robust text-independent speaker identification using gaussian mixture speaker models. IEEE Transactions on Speech and Audio Processing 3(1), 72–83 (1995)
6. Jurafsky, D., Martin, J.H.: Speech and Language Processing, 2nd edn. Prentice Hall (2008)
7. Rabiner, L.R., Juang, B.H.: Fundamentals of Speech Recognition. Prentice-Hall (1993)
8. Android NDK, `http://developer.android.com/sdk/ndk/index.html`
9. Google Speech API, `http://developer.android.com/sdk/index.html`

A Study on the Waste Volume Calculation for Efficient Monitoring of the Landfill Facility

Youngdae Lee[1], Seungyun Cho[1], and Jeongjin Kang[2]

[1] Dept. of Digital Media Engineering, Anyang University, Korea
[2] Dept.of Information and Communication, Dong-Seoul University, Korea
{Youngdae Lee,Seungyun Cho,Jeongjin Kang,youngday77}@daum.net

Abstract. For the enhancement of civilization of a city, the standard landfill facility is needed for the efficient, and computerized management. In this paper, we proposed the waste volume calculation method using the point cloud of the surface of three dimensional object based on stereo camera measurement. This computes the quantity of waste volume for continuous monitoring. It helps not only to predict the evaluation factor of the usable age of a landfill facility. Furthermore, it can be used for the basis of general algorithm of the three dimensional object.

Keywords: land-fill, volume calculation, stereo camera, calibration.

1 Introduction

This research is for to determine the reliability and accuracy of the information of the national waste volume management. At the moment, management of water, air and oil is been done well however systematic information management system of waste landfill is not yet constructed[1]. Environmentally related areas such as 'water', 'air', 'soil' etc are managed under the latest technology (Environment TMS). Whereas, on the other hand, waste landfill is not yet managed in a scientifically. The need for research and development of this technology are as follows.

Firstly, the reliability of the national waste landfill volume management and the accuracy of the capacity are required. Due to the difference of measurement units of the import waste weight (tons) and the landfill volume (m3) there are errors in statistics accuracy. There are problems where information show low reliability at areas such as landfill management where reclamation is possible. Monitoring for waste landfills in real-time operations management and follow-up management is required [2].

It is possible to determine the volume of daily incoming capacity of waste landfill through the import management information, however it is difficult to determine reclamation progress-related information such as landfill location, thickness, spreadly regulation, compression·hardness of the ground etc.

Especially reclamation progress-related information such as waste landfill capacity, residual capacity, waste landfill location is essential to estimate the post land use and waste stabilization of the situation, despite the fact that systematic management is not being made.

T.-h. Kim et al. (Eds.): EL/DTA/UNESST 2012, CCIS 352, pp. 158–169, 2012.

Especially, work information related to waste landfill and information of reclamation progress can become an appropriate landfill management data or can become a basic data if using the landfill post-lot. Therefore it is necessary to keep the information [3].

Figure 1 is a diagram showing the importance of research and development and the improvement direction and Figure 2 shows the objective of the research and development of this work.

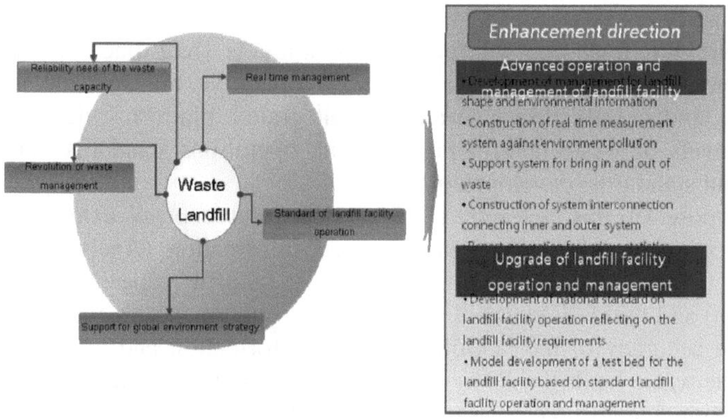

Fig. 1. The necessity and enhancement of research and development

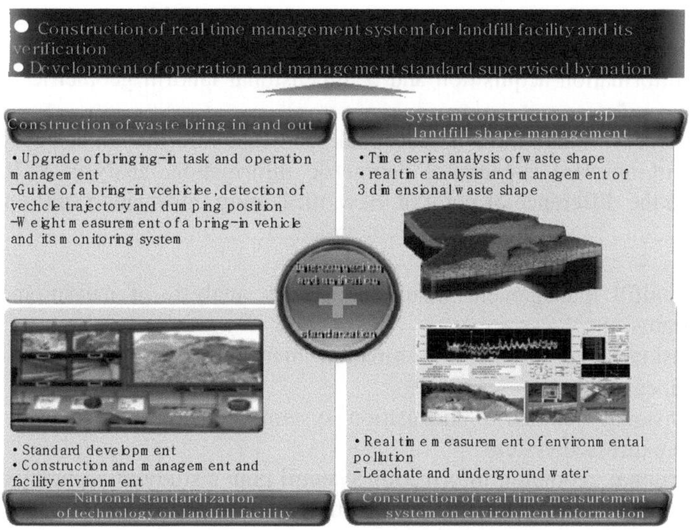

Fig. 2. The objective of research and development

The goals of the research and development of this project is as follows. This research is to advance and commercialize waste landfill operation/management technology of waste landfill and landfill environment measurement and management, which are relatively un-organized compared to the environment information and management (TMS) of air, water etc.

This research is to advance waste landfill operations management technology and to build 'landfill situational awareness integrated platform' by integrating landfill related information such as 'Standardized national waste landfills based technology' which defines waste landfill based technology, waste import and reclamation process, landfill geometry information and real-time measurement, analysis of environmental information (leachate, ground water, ect.), landfill history and management information etc.

Therefore, the final goal of the present study is [real-time landfill geometric management development and waste landfill operative management advancement technology(landfill situational awareness integrated platform) development] and [national levels of waste landfill management, operations standards (national waste management standards) development].

The purpose of this research is to produce and express external information (landfill geometric information) and internal information (Analysis of difference according to the change of point of view, landfill capacity and volumetric information) and build '3D landfill geometric information expression system'. Also to analyze the accuracy of the landfill geometric information and to meet the level of accuracy the waste landfill asks by conducting 'Research of maintaining management of 3-dimensional landfill geometric information accuracy'.

In this research, for the environmental monitoring of the project, it is necessary to measure the waste landfill quantity and to build a statistic of the waste reclamation and to research for the system which plans the amount of reclamation. 3 dimensional landfill geometric information systems is part of the landfill context-aware integrated platform field. Largely we can distinguish the technology between 3 dimensional geometric information acquisition and 3 dimensional landfill geometric information expression.

In other words, within the 3 dimensional geometric information category includes: expression of outward appearance geometric information, analysis of information according to the difference of point of view, measuring information of the volume[4]. Detailed execution information for research and development to achieve the goals in this study are as follows [4].

Waste landfill management status and survey analysis of measurement survey operation status.

3 dimensional measurement information management plan to optimize waste landfill business.

[3 dimensional geometric information system] construct 3D landfill geometry information expressed system.

[3 dimensional geometric information system] plan a study of accuracy analysis of 3 dimensional landfill geometry information and to maintain the accuracy of 3 dimensional landfill geometry information.

[standardized] Develop interlocking technology of landfill situational awareness integrating platform of the landfill geometric information expression system.

In this study, the core foundation of the three-dimensional waste landfill picture measurement and systematic calculation method are studied. Studies on the effects of the landfill environmental are carried out a lot however, there are hardly any research on the volume of landfill output. Therefore the waste landfill volume and volume calculation method presented in this research can be used as a standard model for the improvement of the waste landfill.

The study is constructed as follows: Firstly, chapter 2 discusses about development methods, chapter 3 mentions the presented volume calculation methods, chapter 3 discuss about the presented algorithms. In chapter 4 examines the performance of the presented algorithms through computer simulation tests. In chapter 5, review the accuracy of the volume calculation through actual experiments and in chapter 6 we explain the results.

2 Procedure of Waste Volume Calculation

2.1 Overall Procedure

In the study as a method for measuring waste landfill, we construct a computer vision system. For hardware, we made and used a stereo camera. Firstly, through camera calibration we fixed the distortion of the stereo camera system and then we got the 'cloud' of the points of waste surfaces of the landfill we want to measure. Then we convert these points into normal coordinates and then carry out a systemic calculation accordingly to the converted coordinates.

Before calculating the actual volume, we created a mathematical volumetric model and compared it to the given algorithm efficiency. Accordingly the presented algorithm value was almost the same value to the given reasonable grid size and number proving the presented method was reasonable. Figure 3 shows the installment of stereo camera on the top of control and monitoring tower on the boundary of the landfill area.

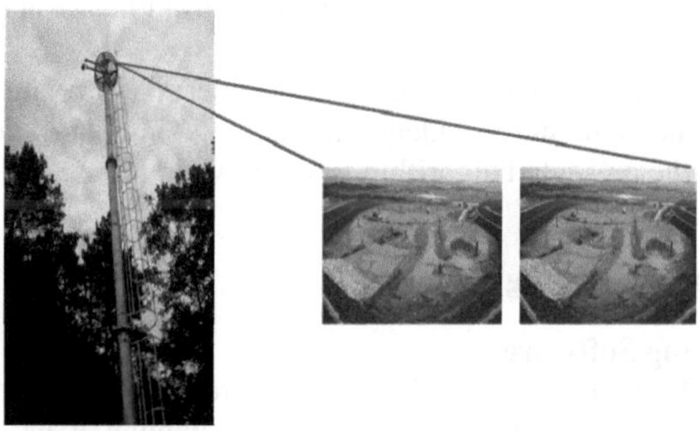

Fig. 3. The installment of stereo camera for monitoring the landfill task

For the development we used something called OpenCV, which is an open type computer vision library to rebuild the surface. For Visual C++ we used OpenCV and MS Visual C++ to create the overall algorithm. For this product, typically when you purchase a stereo camera the calibrated 3 dimensional data points are already produced. Therefore there is no need to calibrate a stereo camera. However as stereo cameras are expensive and do not have the specifications required for the remote measurements we decided to make and use the stereo camera ourselves.

We made a stereo camera to measure the waste landfill capacity and firstly calibrated the camera in order to fix the distorted values and then we got the 'point cloud' of the surfaces of the waste landfill. Then we convert these points into normal coordinates and then carried out a systemic calculation accordingly to the converted coordinates. Before calculating the actual volume, we created a mathematical volumetric model and compared it to the given algorithm efficiency. Accordingly the presented algorithm value was almost the same value to the given reasonable grid size and number proving the presented method was reasonable. Figure 4 shows the overall procedure of the proposed method.

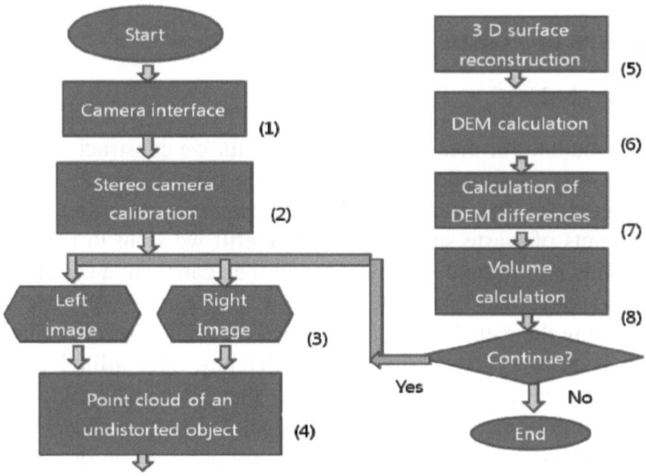

Fig. 4. The Flowchart of Computation for the Filling-Up of Rubbish in LandFill Facility

We constructed a stereo camera by using two cameras and fixing the two by a pole and obtained left and right stereo videos, this is the commonly known method. The entire overview of the presented algorithm is as shown in Figure 4.

2.2 Comparison of Existing Software

2.2.1 The Existing Software

As shown in Table 1. The only existing software to measure the waste landfill capacity is Kuraves-G2. As shown in Picture 4, although it has full functions of (1)~(8) it is an expensive commercial software. The Shapematrix and Photo Modeller[6] are also required to technical developments of (6)(7)(8), it is required to provide open API for it to be capable for systemic calculations. Pixelstruct[7] is a free software, however it requires technical developments in (3)(4)(5) also only provides source programs therefore program interpretation is difficult. Also requires technical developments of (1)(2)(6)(7)(8). CGAL[8]is and open software 3 dimensional surface reconstruction library and has sources applying to (4)(5), it still required technical developments in (1)(2)(3)(6)(7)(8).

Table 1. The software for surface reconstruction of an object

Item	*Site*	*Function*	*Merit*	*Demerit*	*Etc.*
Shape Matrix	3dsystems.co.kr	3D surface reconstruction etc.	accurate and multi functions It contains (1)~(5)	**No open API**	Commercial only
Photo Modeler	3dsystems.co.kr	3D surface reconstruction and 3D scanner	Multi functions It contains (1)~(5)	No open API	Commercial
Kuraves-G2	www.kurabo.co.jp/	3D surface reconstruction	Multi function It contains (1)~(8)	No open API	Commercial
CGAL	www.cgal.org	3D geometrical software and surface reconstruction	It contains (4)(5) Open source	(1)(2)(3)(6) (7)(8) is to be developed	Opened
Pixel Struct	http://da.vidr.cc/projects/pixelstruct/	3D surface construction	(1)(2)(6) Open source	(3)(4)(5)(7) (8)(9) to be developed	Opened
OpenGl_3D_1968561282006	sourceforge.net	3D surface reconstruction	(4)(5) open source	(1)(2)(3)(6) (7)(8), to be developed	Opened
Sufer	http://www.softpedia.com	Civil engineering and surface reconstruction	(4)(5)	No open API	commercial

2.2.2 Developed Method

In this research, firstly we constructed a stereo camera system by using Microsoft's Nikon cameras and used a tripod to mount the cameras. The interface between camera and the PC is usually linked by Camera-link of wired/wireless LAN. Table 1 shows Software related to surface rebuilding and systemic calculations of three dimensional objects. The constructed stereo camera and vision system setting drawing of the waste landfill are Figure 5 and 3 respectively. Our software not only has the functions of (1)~(5) but also it implements the volume calculation functions of (6)(7)(8) unlike the other methods.

3 The Volume Calculation Algorithm

3.1 Camera Calibration

We made and used a stereo camera to measure the waste landfill capacity and firstly calibrated the camera in order to fix the distorted values and then we gained the point cloud; of the surfaces of the waste landfill. Then we converted these pointes into normal coordinates and then carried out a systemic calculation accordingly to the converted coordinates. Before calculating the actual volume, we created a mathematical volumetric model and compared it to the given algorithm efficiency. Accordingly the presented algorithm value was almost the same value to the given reasonable grid size and number proving the presented method was reasonable. Figure 5 shows the extrinsic parameters obtained from the calibration procedure.

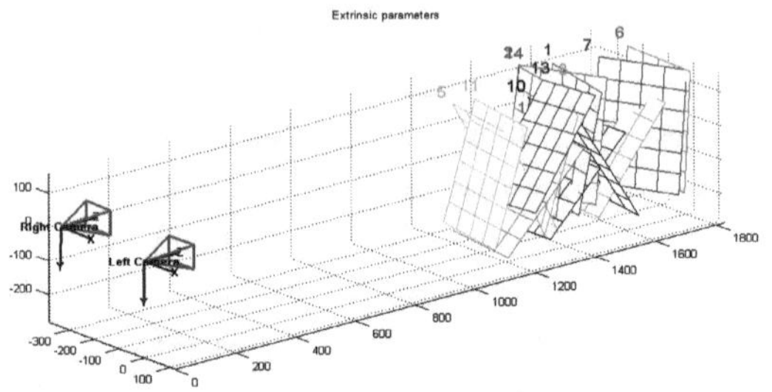

Fig. 5. The extrinsic parameters obtained from stereo camera calibration

3.2 The Suggested Algorithm Procedures

Stage 1: Camera interface: Use the device drive bundle software provided by the camera providers. Wireless interface of camera and a PC driver is used.

Stage 2: Stereo Calibration: Remodel the camera, calibrate parameters and remove any distortion and entirely calibrate. If in case of projection, measure the affine transformation and clairvoyance conversion and 3D pose.

Stage 3: Stereo image input: when the calibrated three dimensional surface points become and image on a surface obtain the image using the capture commands and save.

Stage 4: Image merging the three-dimensional point cloud: Calculate the corresponding points of the obtained three-dimensional surface cloud left and right calibrated image.

Stage 5: to obtain three dimensional system mashing use triangle meshes.

(a) As a calculation method use the red soil surface or the bottom as a flat surface to reference the plane.

(b) Display the selected grating on the surface of the criteria. For this purpose, calculate the average height for the center of each grid. When there are more TIN (triangular irregular network) calculate the total volume by multiplying the average height for the area of the standard plan.

4 Simulation

Figure 6 shows an example of the non-uniform triangular meshes to model the surface of an object. Using the systemic calculation algorithm according to the object surface and grid shape, performance comparison results are summarized as follows.

Gentle Slopes: $F_1 = x + y$ (1)

Concave Slopes: $F_2 = x^2 + y^2$ (2)

Un-even Slopes: $F_3 = 10 + 1.2^{(-1.5 * \sqrt{(X^2+Y^2)/5})} .* \cos(0.5 * Y) .* \sin(X)$ (3)

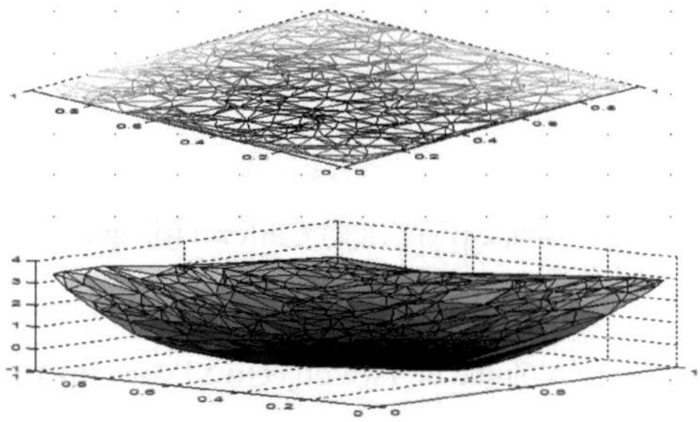

Fig. 6. The non-uniform triangular mesh and the objective function example

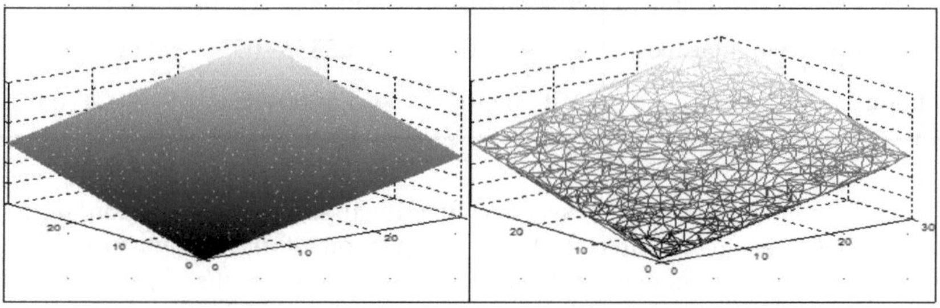

Fig. 7. The mesh model of slope shape:(left) Uniform triangular mesh model (right) Non-uniform triangular mesh model

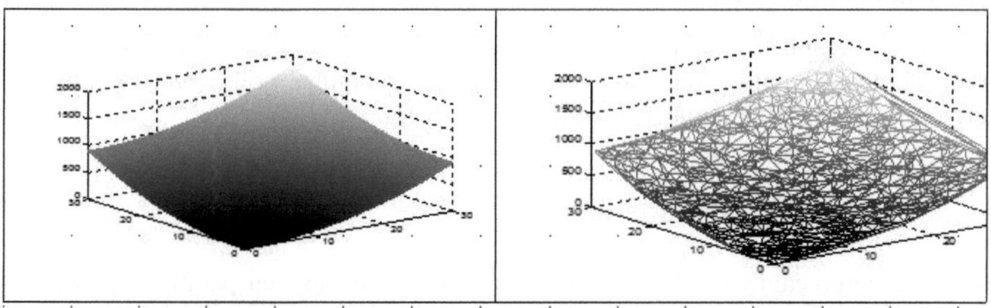

Fig. 8. The mesh model of convex shape (F_2) : (left) uniform triangular mesh model (right) non-uniform triangular mesh model

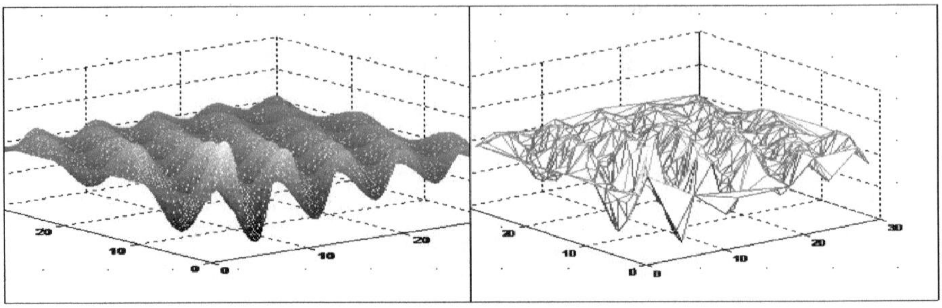

Fig. 9. The mesh model of wavy shape (F_3) : (left) Uniform triangular mesh model (right) Non-uniform triangular mesh model

Table 2. The Calculation of the Volume of Two objective Functions Using Uniform and Non-Uniform Triangular Mesh

mesh \ function	F_1	F_2	F_3
Uniform triangular mesh	2.7000e+04	5.4225+05	9.0005+03
Non-uniform triangular mesh	2.7397e+04	5.5338+05	9.0006+03
(solution)	2.7000e+04	5.5000+05	9.0000e+03

Figure 7,8, and 9 shows the respective functional surface shape according to the equations (1)(2) and (3). Table 2 shows comparison of the computational results between the uniform triangular mesh and non uniform one for the objective functions F_1, F_2 and F_3, respectively. From the Table 2, we can identify the fact that the volume by the presented method shows good performance for calculation of the volume of various functions.

[Simulation conditions]

Horizontal Length =30m, Horizontal sampling interval = 0.3m, Vertical length = 30m, Vertical sampling interval 0.2m, Irregular triangular grid = 900, number of horizontal grids = 100, number of vertical grids = 150.

5 Experiment and Review

Fixed the stereo camera and took stereo pictures of 2 rectangular parallelepiped boxes of which values are known and made a irregular triangular mesh model. Firstly, we compared whether it has bottom box or not. Figure 10 shows the stereo camera system made to experiment the volume calculation test in the lab.

Fig. 10. The stereo camera system for the test

Fig. 11. Two rectangular boxes for experiment

Fig. 12. The non-uniform triangular mesh model for two boxes

Figure 11 shows two stacked boxed which are photogrammetry targets. Figure 12 shows images taken of two stacked boxes and calculated the point clouds and made applied a non-uniform triangular mesh. In Figure 12 the vertical and horizontal lengths are measured from photogrammetry and the height is measured by taking away the bottom surface height from the top surface height and setting this value as the relative length. Systemic calculation algorithm was performed for each boxes.

Table 3. The Measurement comparison of two boxes with two methods

	Bog box			*Small box*		
	Measured by a scale	Measured by photogram	Error%	Measured by a scale	Measured by photogram	Error %
Left length (mm)	505	501	0.8	265	260	1.19
Width length(mm)	404	399	1.2	245	232	1.22
H eight(mm)	175	172	1.7	115	119	3.48
Volume(mm3)	35,791,875	34,382,628	3.9%	7,466,375	7,178,080	3.86%

In the Table 3, we can identify the calculation of the measured volume by the suggested method gives the very close results compared with the volume measured by a scale, which means our suggested method is correct and it can be valid way to measure the waste volume of a landfill facility.

Figure 13 is a specific view of the waste landfill of Ahn-sung city in Korea. Figure 14 shows the result of non-uniform triangular mesh model for the respective landfill. As currently the waste landfill progress has elapsed, the systemic calculation algorithm of the given point clouds proves that we can know the landfill volume at two points relatively, however it is difficult to know the absolute volume without the initial landfill photogrammetry. However we have the wastes landfills initial design drawings and measurement models therefore it is possible to estimate the absolute amount of the waste landfill at the surveyed time.

Fig. 13. The picture of the rubbish repository in anseong city in Korea

Fig. 14. Non-uniform trianglular mesh model of the landfill facility in anseong city in Korea

To do this, we need scaling between CAD drawings and photogrammetry point clouds. Also we need coordinate adjustment procedures. However these can be regarded as a separate study. When we make the surveying time and the photo measured time as the same time we can know the absolute value of the later measured waste landfill. However the absolute value of the waste landfill can be practically resolved if a stereo video is taken at early stages of the landfill construction, therefore does not change the validity of the method presented in the study.

6 Conclusion

Waste landfill required for a comfortable and safe environment, and to convert the toxic waste, produced by humans, by natural recycling back into harmless soil again. Therefore waste landfill capacity qualitative and quantitative monitoring evaluation is an important issue.

For this to happen, incessant observations and monitoring of the landfill environment by environmental sensors and vision sensors is required. There is a need to intelligently manage the environmental impact factors from the sensor measurements. This research presented an algorithm to calculate waste volume periodically for the advancement and standardization of waste landfill. After camera calibration, we can obtain point cloud data on the surface of the objects and this becomes the input of the presented volumetric calculation algorithm. Two volumetric calculation algorithms were presented based on the uniform and non-uniform triangular meshing method. The validity of the algorithm was verified through simulation and real experiments.

Acknowledgments. This work is supported by EI project - the real time measurement and analysis of - the institute of environment technology under ministry of environment of Korea.

References

1. Statistics of landfill facilities, Ministry of Environment (2010)
2. Research and field measurement of greenhouse gas emission from landfills, Korea Environment Corporation (2008)
3. Review of domestic applicability and case studies of domestic and foreign for verification National Greenhouse Gas Emission Factors (2011)
4. Waste landfill technologies-based research, SUDOKWON Landfill Site Management Corporation (2005)
5. A study on roadmap construction of maintenance project for sustainable landfill, Korea Environment Corporation (Korea Environment & Resources Corporation) (2009)
6. http://www.3dsystems.co.kr
7. http://da.vidr.cc/projects/pixelstruct/
8. http://www.cgal.org
9. http://www.sorceforge.net
10. http://www.kurabo.co.jp
11. http://www.opencv.org
12. Learning OpenCV: Computer Vision with OpenCV Library, Gary Bradski and Adrian Kaehler. O'Reilly

Design and Implementation of Program for Volumetric Measurement of Kidney

Young-Man Kwon[1], Young-Hwan Hwang[2], and Yong-Gyu Jung[1,*]

[1] Department of Medical IT and Marketing, Eulji University,
[2] Nephrology, Internal Medicine, Eulji General Hospital, Eulji Unversity,
553, Sanseong-daero, Sujeong-gu, Seongnam-si, Gyeonggi-do, 461-713, Korea
{ymkwon,ygjung}@eulji.ac.kr, ondahl@eulji.ac.kr

Abstract. In this paper, we designed and implemented the program, called ExACT. The main features and contributions of the program are as follows. First, we made the good abstraction for measuring the volume of the kidney. Thus we can implement the algorithm of program efficiently. Second, this program allows you to save the considerable time to calculate the volume of the kidney. Finally, we can get the more exact result than the manual segmentation.

Keywords: Computed Tomography, Kidney, Volumetric Measurement, DICOM, Graph Cuts, Minimum Cut, Maximum Flow.

1 Introduction

Recently, the technology of image segmentation is very important and is used in the analysis and diagnosis of numerous applications such as the study of anatomical structure, localization of pathology, treatment planning, and computer-integrated surgery [1]. Many computer-aided diagnostic systems have been developed for lung cancer, liver tumor, and breast disease [2]. However, relatively little research has been focused on kidney segmentation.

In this paper, we have focused the measurement of kidney volume because the kidney volume increases in patient with ADPKD(Autosomal Dominant Polycystic Kidney Disease). Thus the image segmentation is critical issue. To solve this, we use the solution of the maximum flow problem. This problem is one of the most fundamental problems in network flow theory and has investigated extensively [3, 4, 5]. This is also known as minimum cut problem. This can be solved by using augmenting path algorithm or preflow-push algorithm. We have used the latter and designed several objects to implement the calculation of kidney volume semi-automatically.

2 Related Works

Graph cuts approaches have been recently applied as global optimization methods to the problem of image segmentation [3]. The image is represented using an adjacency

* Corresponding author.

T.-h. Kim et al. (Eds.): EL/DTA/UNESST 2012, CCIS 352, pp. 170–176, 2012.

graph. Each vertex of graph represents image pixel, while the edge weight between two vertices represents the similarity between two corresponding pixels.

2.1 Object Segmentation Using Graph Cuts

Using the graph cut theory, we can compute the globally optimal partition of image by first transforming the image into an edge capacitated graph *G(V, E)* and then compute the minimum cut. One such transformation ia as follows. Each pixel within the image is mapped to a vertex $v \in V$. If two pixels are adjacent, there exists an undirected edge $(u, v) \in E$ between the corresponding vertices u and v. The edge weight $c(u, v)$ is assigned according to some measure of similarity between the two pixels; the higher the edge weight, the more similar they are. The minimum cut on the transformed edge capacitated graph will partition the graph into two parts with minimum capacity, i.e., the summation of the edge weights across the cut is minimized.

2.2 Multi-source Multi-sink Minimum Cut

The related theory of graph cut can be found in many text books. The minimum cut of interest in this paper is required to separate multiple source vertices $\{s_1, s_2, ..., s_n\}$ from multiple sink vertices $\{t_1, t_2, ..., t_m\}$ with the smallest capacity. This multi-source multi-sink problem can be converted to an ordinary single source single sink s-t minimum cut problem. One current method for such conversion is to first add two additional vertices, a super source vertex s and a super sink vertex t, then add a directed edge (s, s_i) with capacity $c(s, s_i) = \infty$ for each $i = 1, 2, ..., n$ and add a directed edge (t_j, t) with capacity $c(t_j, t) = \infty$ for each $j = 1, 2, ..., m$.

2.3 Overview of GCBAC Algorithm

The algorithm of the segmentation we used is the GCBAC [3] and look like Figure 1. After the image *I* is represented as an edge-capacitated adjacency graph *G* and an initial contour c_0 is given, the GCBAC algorithm consists of the following steps.

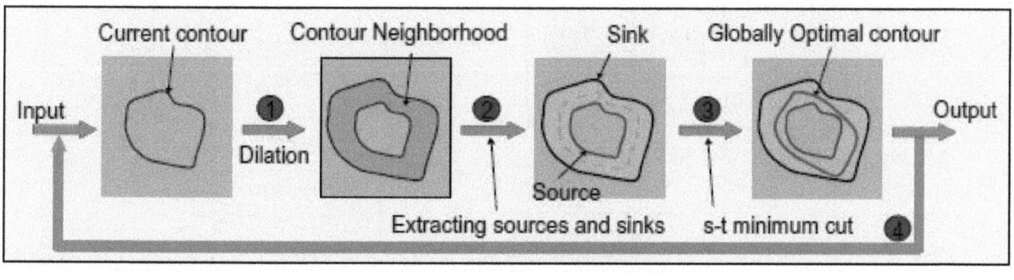

Fig. 1. A schematic of GCBAC algorithm

(0) Set the index of current step $i = 0$

(1) Dilate current contour c_i into its contour neighborhood $CN(c_i)$ with an inner contour IC_i and an outer contour OC_i.

(2) Identify all the vertices corresponding to the inner contour as a single source s_i and identify all the vertices corresponding to the outer contour as a single sink t_i to obtain a new graph G_i.

(3) Compute the *s-t* minimum cut $MC(G_i, s_i, t_i)$ to obtain a new contour $c_{i+1} = \arg\min_{c \in CN(c_i)} E(c)$, where $E(c) = capacity\ of\ MC(G_i, s_i, t_i)$.

(4) Terminate the algorithm if a resulting contour $\hat{c}$ reoccurs, otherwise set $i = i + 1$ and return step 1.

3 Design and Implementation

We designed and implemented the ExACT program, that means the EXamination of Abdominal CT(Computer Tomography) images. We can segment the kidney area from each slice automatically and modify it semi-automatically and finally calculate the volume of the kidney by using ExACT program.

3.1 Object Design

We designed several objects to implement the ExACT program. Major objects appears in Fig. 2. Roi(Region of interest) is the segmented area of kidney by program. The function of each object is as follows.

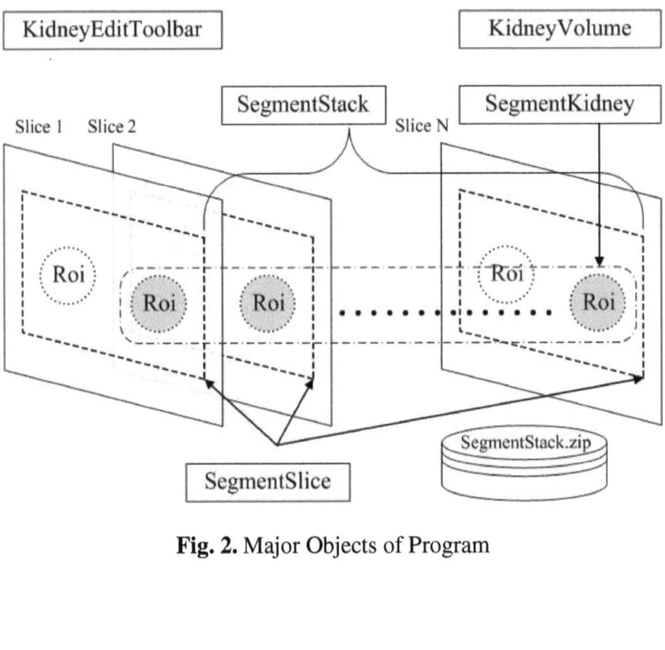

Fig. 2. Major Objects of Program

Table 1. The function of major objects

Object(Class) name	Functions
KidneyToolBar	User Interface
SegmentSlice	Have Left and Right ROI that is segmented kidney
SegmentStack	Have SegmentSlice object for all slice
SegmentStack.zip	Version of SegmentStack on the permanent storage
KidneyVolume	The object to calculate the volume of kidney
SegmentKidney	The object to combine left Rois or right Rois.

3.2 The Segmentation

We have to segment the region of kidney on each slice before we calculate the volume of kidney. The flow diagram to segment the region of kidney is as Fig. 3.

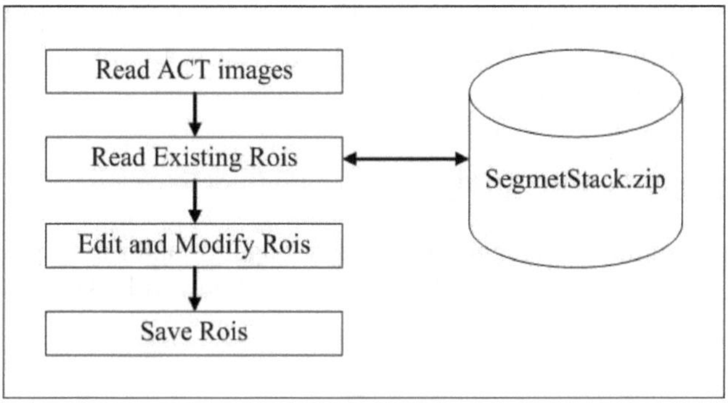

Fig. 3. The flow diagram to segment the region of kidney

As soon as you run the program, it read the abdominal CT images via dialog window and also read existing data of Rois if it exists. After that, users can edit and modify Rois by using the menu of program. The core is the GCBAC algorithm during this step. That is, we applied the preflow-push algorithm to solve the minimum cut problem. We reused the source code [4]. If the user finishes editing, he has to save Rois for next use. The related objects to segmentation are KidneyToolBar, SegmentSlice, SegmentStack.

3.3 The Volume Calculation

If the user finishes editing Rois, the next step is to calculate the volume of the kidney. The flow diagram to do this is as Fig. 4.

The first step is to check whether Rois are continuous. If it is no true, the program print the error message and stop. If it is true, the program finds the area of Rois by making Roi the binary image. Then the program calculates the volume of the kidney

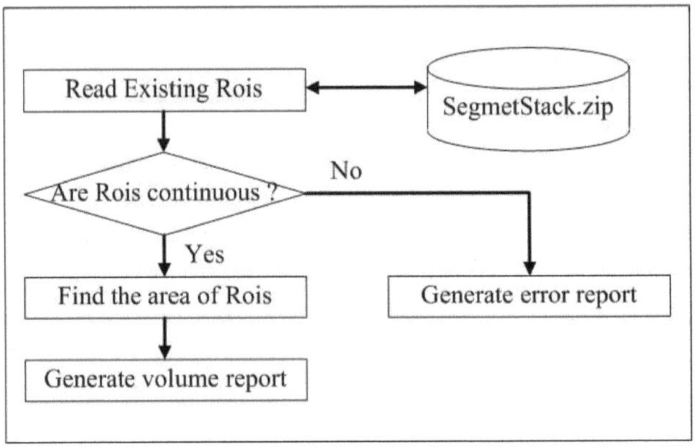

Fig. 4. The flow diagram to calculate the volume of the kidney

by the method of adding each volume of cylinder, that is the volume that multiply the height of slice by the area of Roi. The related objects to volume calculation are KideyVolume, SegmentKidney.

4 Experiments and Analysis

The ExACT program was implemented in Java language and run as plug-in program in ImageJ [6]. It can only read the DICOM file format now. It looks like Fig. 5.

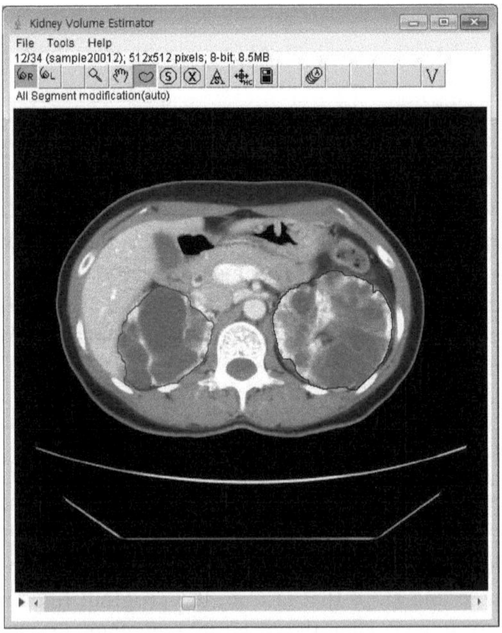

Fig. 5. The ExACT program

After the segmentation, the user can calculate the volume of the kidney. If you run the volume calculation and have no problem, it generates the report file. The report file looks like Fig. 6.

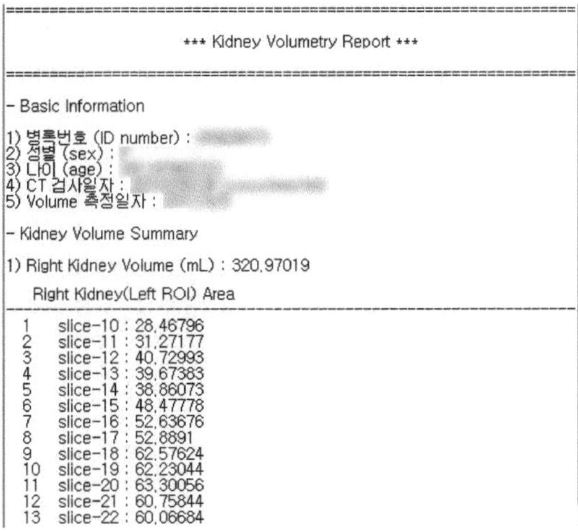

*** Kidney Volumetry Report ***

- Basic Information

1) 병록번호 (ID number) :
2) 성별 (sex) :
3) 나이 (age) :
4) CT 검사일자 :
5) Volume 측정일자 :

- Kidney Volume Summary

1) Right Kidney Volume (mL) : 320.97019

Right Kidney(Left ROI) Area

```
1   slice-10 : 28.46796
2   slice-11 : 31.27177
3   slice-12 : 40.72993
4   slice-13 : 39.67383
5   slice-14 : 38.86073
6   slice-15 : 48.47778
7   slice-16 : 52.63676
8   slice-17 : 52.8891
9   slice-18 : 62.57624
10  slice-19 : 62.23044
11  slice-20 : 63.30056
12  slice-21 : 60.75844
13  slice-22 : 60.06684
```

Fig. 6. The kidney volumetry report file

The above experiment use 34 slices of DICOM image. The size of the image is 512x512, the gap between slice is 5 mm, the number of pixel per mm is 0.683594. These information can be obtained from DICOM file. It took 10 minute to calculate the kidney volume from. Generally the calculation takes 30 minute per one person manually. So we can achieve our objective to reduce the time of volume calculation one third.

5 Conclusion

In this paper, we designed and implemented the program, called ExACT. We have achieved our objective for the time of the kidney volume measurement using ExACT program.

In the future, we have a plan to reduce the more time of measurement by developing the automatic segmentation algorithm after semi-automatic segmentation of only one slice. That is used for initial value for automatic segmentation. Also we have a plan to develop the analysis program for the cyst of kidney.

References

1. Withey, D.J., Koles, Z.J.: A Review of Medical Image Segmentation: Methods and Available Software. International Journal of Bioelectromagnetism 10(3), 125–148 (2008)
2. Lin, D.-T., Lei, C.-C., Hung, S.-W.: Computer-Aided Kidney Segmentation on Abdominal CT images. IEEE Transaction on Information Technology in Biomedicine 10(1), 59–65 (2006)

3. Xu, N., Ahuja, N., Bansal, R.: Object segmentation using graph cuts based active contours. Computer Vision and Image Understanding 107, 210–224 (2007)
4. Ahuja, R.K., Orlin, J.B.: A Fast and Simple Algorithm for the Maximum Flow Problem. Operations Research Society of America 37(5), 748–759 (1989)
5. Goldberg, A.V.: A New Approach to the Maximum-Flow Problem. Journal of the Association for Computing Machinery 35(4), 921–940 (1988)
6. Burger, W., Burge, M.J.: Digital Image Processing (An Algorithmic Introduction Using Java). Springer (2008)

Evaluation of Time Complexity Based on Triangle Height for K-Means Clustering

Shinwon Lee[1] and Wonhee Lee[2,*]

[1] Department of Computer System Engineering, Jungwon University, Chungbuk, Republic of Korea
[2] Department of Information Technology, Chonbuk University, Baekje-daero, deokjin-gu, Jeonju, Jeonbuk, 561-756, Republic of Korea
swlee@jwu.ac.kr, wony@jbnu.ac.kr

Abstract. K-means algorithm is an iterative algorithm. The main idea is to define k initial seeds, one for each cluster. At each loop, the reassignment step of documents into the nearest center's group is followed by the calculation step of the center of each cluster. No changes as a result of a loop mean the end of this algorithm. But, the different initial seeds cause different result. So, the better choice is to place them as far away as possible from each other. We propose a new method of selecting initial centers in K-Means clustering. This method uses triangle height for initial centers of clusters. After that, the centers are distributed evenly and that result is more accurate than initial cluster centers selected random. It is time-consuming, but can reduce total clustering time by minimizing the number of allocation and recalculation. We can reduce the time spent on total clustering.

Keywords: clustering, Time complexity, K-means, initial center.

1 Introduction

Cluster-based Information retrieval forms gather related documents into clusters and the search result of a highly related cluster of user query in all documents.

Clustering method which is the gathering of several clusters according to special value on a large data is divided into hierarchical clustering [1][5], partitioning clustering[4][6], graph theory clustering. Mass information of modern society is limited to process data using hierarchical clustering or graph theory clustering and is inefficient to time complexity.

In this paper, we deal with K-means algorithm which is one of the methods of partitioning clustering for mass data. It is easy to implement, if the time complexity is O(N) and the number of data is N. But it is too dependent on initial centers of clusters. Meaning, the result of clustering is different to the initial selected centers of cluster. Generally, when K-Means algorithm processes allocation and recalculation repeatedly, centers move into proper location. But if initial centers of cluster is selected and concentrated in a partial area that result is not proper or the time of allocation and

* Corresponding author.

T.-h. Kim et al. (Eds.): EL/DTA/UNESST 2012, CCIS 352, pp. 177–183, 2012.

recalculation is increased. So we improve the performance of K-Means to select initial centers of cluster with calculating rather than random selecting. This method uses the triangle height among initial centers of cluster. It is time-consuming, but reduces total clustering time by minimizing the count of allocation and recalculation.

In this paper, chapter 2 describes K-Means algorithm and the initial center refining method of previous study. Chapter 3 proposes the method using triangle height for initial center setting method. Chapter 4 evaluates time complexity on proposed clustering method. Chapter 5 experiments on time complexity. In chapter 6, we conclude.

2 K-Means Algorithm

The printing area is 122 mm × 193 mm. The text should be justified to occupy the full line width, so that the right margin is not ragged, with words hyphenated as appropriate. Please fill pages so that the length of the text is no less than 180 mm, if possible.

K-Means algorithm is partitioning clustering. The concept is to minimize the average Euclidean distance of each patterns with the center of the cluster [3][4]. The center of cluster is the mean of the pattern belonging to the cluster, and is defined as follows.

$$\vec{\mu}(\omega) = \frac{1}{|\omega|}\sum_{\vec{x}\in\omega}\vec{x} \tag{1}$$

In this expression, ω is a set of patterns belonging to the cluster, $\vec{x}$ is a particular pattern belonging to the cluster. The pattern is represented as a vector with real values.

Figure 1 is K-Means algorithm.

$K - Means(\{\vec{x}_1,\ldots,\vec{x}_N\}, K)$

1. $(\vec{s}_1, \vec{s}_2, \ldots \vec{s}_K)$ // $Select\ Random\ Seeds(\{\vec{x}_1,\ldots,\vec{x}_N\}, K)$
2. $for\ k \leftarrow 1\ to\ K$
3. $do\ \vec{\mu}_k \leftarrow \vec{s}_k$
4. $while\ stopping\ criterion\ has\ not\ been\ met$
5. $do\ for\ n \leftarrow 1\ to\ N$
6. $do\ j \leftarrow \arg\min_j |\vec{\mu}_j - \vec{x}_n|$
7. $\omega_j \leftarrow \omega_j \cup \{\vec{x}_n\}$ // vector reallocation
8. $for\ k \leftarrow 1\ to\ K$
9. $do\ \vec{\mu}_k \leftarrow \frac{1}{|\omega_k|}\sum_{\vec{x}\in\omega_k}\vec{x}$ // center recalcuration
10. $return\ \{\vec{\mu}_1,\ldots,\vec{\mu}_K\}$

Fig. 1. K-Means algorithm

3 Initial Center Setting Using Triangle Height

In this paper, we improve the K-Means algorithm using a new method on initial centers of cluster. This method uses triangle height to replace the initial center. When we know the three lengths of the triangle, we can calculate triangle height by Heron's formula. By doing so, the initial centers of cluster randomly selected will be biased in some areas, and this phenomenon can be prevented. And the clustering was used to improve speed and the accuracy of clustering. In the proposed K-Means algorithm, a set C of the initial centers of cluster is the following equation (3).

$$C = \max \sum_{i=1}^{k} \left\| c_{height} - c_i \right\| \qquad (2)$$

ci is ith center of cluster, cheight is triangle height from c1 to ck.

1. Select Random *K* centers
2. $for\ x \in X$

2.1 Select *Candidate Cluster* with the closest *x*

$candidate\ Cluster \leftarrow min\ dist_{i=0,\dots,k}(x, c_i)$

2.2 After replacing previous center by selected *candidate Cluster*, calculate new triangle height

$newHeight \leftarrow \sqrt{C^2 - \left((a^2 + c^2 - b^2)/2a\right)^2}$

$a = \overline{c_2, c_3}, b = \overline{x, c_3}, c = \overline{x, c_2}$

2.3 if $newHeight > oldHeight$ then $c_i \leftarrow x$

3. $return\ \{c_1, \dots, c_k\}$

Fig. 2. Initial center setting algorithm

Figure 3 describes setting of initial centers of cluster using two-dimensional data, when K is 3. There are c1, c2, c3 centers, and new data x1 will look for the closest center. Comparing the triangle height between h0, h1, we can confirm that the result is x1. Now, put x1 instead of c1, calculate the height {h0, h1} between each centers as follows.

$$newHeight \leftarrow \sqrt{C^2 - \left((a^2 + c^2 - b^2)/2a\right)^2}$$
$$a = \overline{c_2, c_3}, b = \overline{x_1, c_3}, c = \overline{x_1, c_2} \qquad (3)$$

$$oldHeight \leftarrow \sqrt{C^2 - \left((a^2 + c^2 - b^2)/2a\right)^2}$$
$$a = \overline{c_2, c_3}, b = \overline{c_1, c_3}, c = \overline{c_1, c_2} \qquad (4)$$

Each height can be compared with the distance between the existing centers. Comparing the two heights, newHeight value substituted x1 for c1 the larger value, so x1 is replaced by the new c1. (x1, c2, c3) is newHeight, and is then compared with x2. On the other hand in the case of x2, the height h2 of (x2, c2, c3) is the smaller than height h0 of c1,c2,c3, so x2 isn't replaced by the new c1. This process is repeated for the set X with xi.

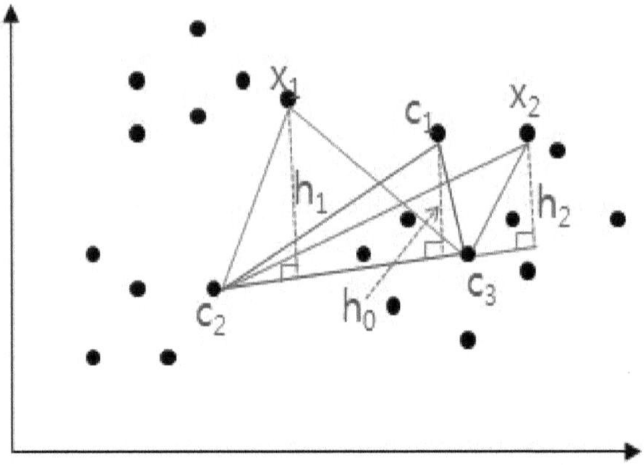

Fig. 3. Initial center shifting using triangle height

4 Evaluation of Time Complexity

Compared to existing methods of selecting initial centers, the method proposed in this paper requires the process of calculating the triangle height. The time required for clustering are as follows:

$$T(initial\ center\ setting)+T(allocation\text{-}recalculation) \tag{5}$$

This process takes time in addition.

K is the number of all clusters, k is the kth cluster, and N is data set, and $x \in N$. One repetition time is K*N.

In the algorithm shown in Figure 2, Step 2.1, it takes 1K time to select candidate Cluster with the closest x, Step 2.2, it takes 2K time to replace previous centers by x and calculate height value of centers, and 2K time to calculate the distance between height values of each centers. So the total amount of time is 4K. When time complexity of allocation-recalculation on previous K-Means algorithm is O(KN), time complexity of triangle height is as follows:

$$\fallingdotseq O(4KN) \tag{6}$$

The process of allocation and recalculation needs 1 unit time for allocating each document in cluster, 1 unit time for recalculating center with documents included in each cluster. The formula is as follows:

$$O(2iKN) \tag{7}$$

i is the repeated number until allocation and recalculation is finished.

So, the overall time of total clustering is as follows:

$$O(4KN)+O(2iKN)\approx O(N) \tag{8}$$

i and k are constant, so it is linear time N.

5 Experiment

For evaluation of clustering results we created with 300 pieces of data and tested this clustering performance. The number of data points was a small number of restrictions were used to make it easy to identify with the naked eye. Clustering experiments execute 10 repetitions around each initial cluster center setting method, checking the result.

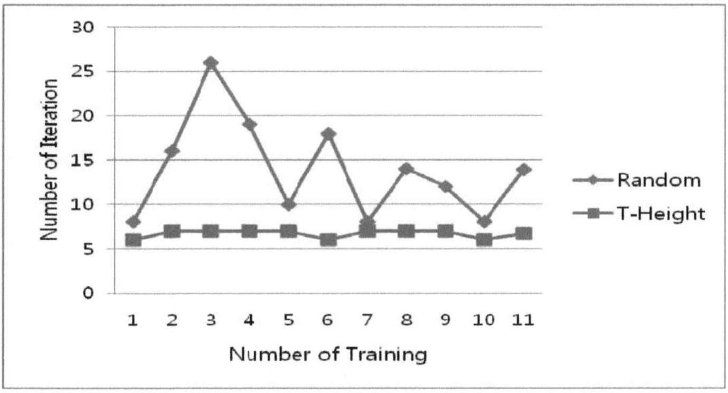

Fig. 4. The number of iteration, K=5

As shown in Figure 4, when using triangle height, we can see that the number of iteration is reduced to 6.7 then to 13.9 when using random.

Figure 5 displays the necessary time. Even though triangle height distance required modifying time, reducing the number of allocation and recalculation, the total necessary time could be reduced.

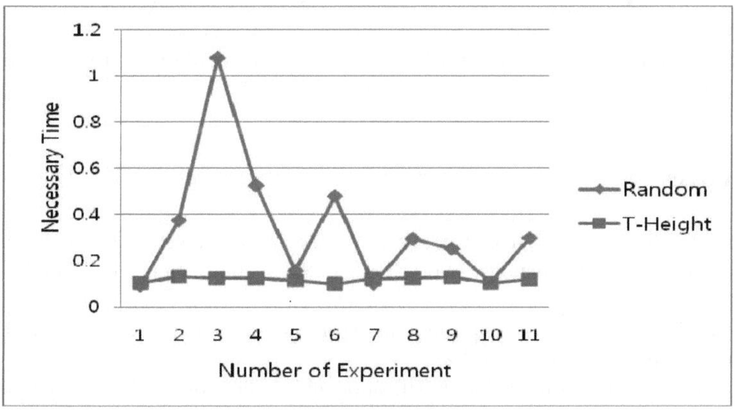

Fig. 5. Necessary Time, K=5

Figure 6 is necessary time, when each k value is 5 to 20, N=300. We can see the variation of triangle height is smaller than that of random clustering. The reason is that the initial centers are distributed more widely on the outer area of data. By doing so, the initial center of cluster is dependent on the performance of K-Means clustering. It can be concluded that there is an improvement of necessary time, the number of iteration.

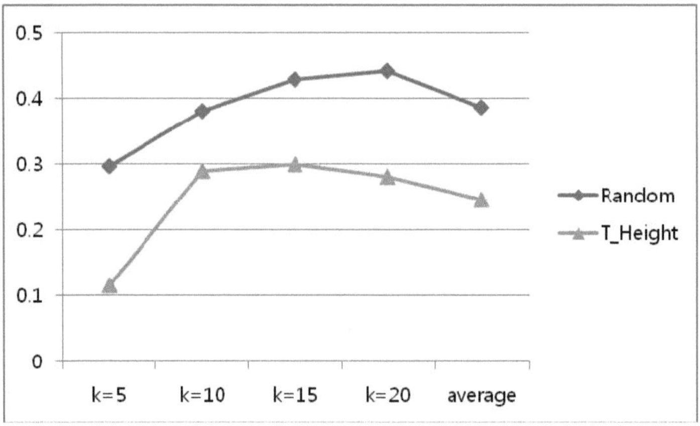

Fig. 6. N=300, Necessary time

6 Conclusion

In this paper, we proposed a method for selection of the initial center to improve the performance of K-Means algorithm which is one of partitioning algorithms mainly used in large amounts of data. K-Means is easy to implemented in general because time complexity is linear when the number of pattern is N. However, depending on whether or how to set the initial centers of cluster, the result of cluster is dependent on the initial centers of cluster.

We reduced the number of allocation and recalculation process to allocate documents to each cluster and to recalculate centers.

References

1. Adami, G., Avesani, P., Sona, D.: Clustering documents in a web directory. In: Proceedings of the 5th ACM International Workshop on Web Information and Data Management, pp. 66–73 (2003)
2. Lloyd, S.P.: Least squares quantization in PCM, Special issue on quantization. IEEE Trans. Inform. Theory 28, 129–137 (1982)
3. McQueen, J.: Some methods for classification and analysis of multivariate observations. In: Proceedings of the Fifth Berkeley Symposium on Mathematical Statistics and Probability, pp. 281–297 (1967)
4. Meedeniya, D.A., Perera, A.S.: Evaluation of Partition-Based Text Clustering Techniques to Categorize Indic Language Documents. In: IEEE International Advance Computing Conference(IACC 2009), pp. 1497–1500 (2009)

5. Sahoo, N., Callan, J., Krishnan, R., Duncan, G., Padman, R.: Incremental hierarchical clustering of text documents. In: Proceedings of the 15th ACM International Conference on Information and Knowledge Management, pp. 357–366 (2006)
6. Yu, Y., Bai, W.: Text clustering based on term weights automatic partition. In: 2010 The 2nd International Conference on Computer and Automation Engineering (ICCAE), pp. 373–377 (2010)
7. Cho, Y.-H., Lee, G.-S.: Prediction on Clusters by using Information Criterion and Multiple Seeds. The Journal of IWIT 10(6), 153–159 (2010)
8. Jeon, J.-H., Kim, M.-S.: A Study of Criterion for Efficient Clustering Estimation of Temporal Data. The Journal of IWIT 11(5), 139–144 (2011)

Improving Pitch Detection through Emphasized Harmonics in Time-Domain

Hyung-Woo Park[1], Myung-Sook Kim[2], and Myung-Jin Bae[1,*]

[1] School of Electronic Engineering, Soongsil University,
[2] Department of English Language and Literature, Soongsil University
Sangdo-ro 369, DongJak-Ku,Seoul, 156-743, Republic of Korea
{parkhyungwoo,kimm,mjbae}@ssu.ac.kr

Abstract. In speech signal processing, it is crucial to detect the accurate pitch period of voice in time domain. The concept of pitch period is being utilized in various fields, including systems for speech enhancement, automatic speech recognition, speaker classification, and even voice guiding for the visually impaired. The periodicity of a voice signal has been emphasized in order to detect the pitch period more accurately as we can see in the current techniques, such as 'peak and valley technique,' 'auto-correlation method,' or 'center-clipping and signal-square.' However, all of these methods present a problem in finding accurate pitch period due to noise as well as the transitional section between voiced and unvoiced sounds. This paper proposes an improved method for detecting pitch period in time domain more accurately by using emphasized harmonics through non-linear clipping and synthesis technique.

Keywords: Speech signal processing, Pitch detection, Pitch period, Emphasized harmonics, Non-linear clipping and synthesis.

1 Introduction

Speech signal processing is classified into two categories: synthesizing voice and the applications of voice analysis[1][2]. Results from synthesizing voice can be applied to various systems for making our everyday life more convenient, such as Text-To-Speech (TTS), Automatic-Response-System (ARS), or voice guiding systems for the visually impaired. In applying the voice analysis, the voice signals can be largely divided into voiced sounds and unvoiced sounds by speech generation models. In the voiced sounds, a pitch period is the basic vibration of vocal cords and shows the unique feature for each speaker. The more accurate pitch period detection is, the more accurate speaker recognition and speech enhancement can be made possible. Furthermore, the accurate pitch period can synthesize voices more naturally in the speech synthesis systems and can be used for modeling the efficient voice enhancement processing systems[1][2].

* Corresponding author.

T.-h. Kim et al. (Eds.): EL/DTA/UNESST 2012, CCIS 352, pp. 184–189, 2012.

However, it is difficult to measure a pitch period of the voice signal accurately and reliably for the following reasons[1]. Firstly, the excitation waveforms from vocal cords produce not a perfectly periodic signal but rather a quasi-periodic signal. Secondly, speech system responds to time with varying impulses along with changes in phonemes, or changes in meaningful sounds. Lastly, speech signal can be easily corrupted by additive elements in time domain, such as noise and channel convolutional distortion. Because of these reasons, we usually emphasize the original signal using any technique available to us when we measure the pitch. There are several methods currently available, such as 'peak and valley technique,' 'auto-correlation method,' 'clipping and square method,' and 'difference function of a signal.' Still, we cannot expect to get a clear pitch period when the sound is mixed with noise or other additive elements, causing a need for additional calculation.

This paper proposes a new method of emphasizing the periodicity of pitch by using non-linear clipping and synthesis technique. This method has a couple of advantages of having less distortion of the original signal and offering an easy calculation.

The paper is structured as follows. Chapter 2 explains the characteristics of continuous speech signals and discusses the current methods of emphasizing harmonics in pitch. Chapter 3 proposes a new technique for emphasizing harmonics using nonlinear clipping and synthesis. Chapter 4 is the results of the experiment for applying the new proposed method. Chapter 5 is the conclusion.

2 Speech System Model and Traditional Pitch Detection Methods

2.1 Linear Model of Voice Speech System

The linear model of voice speech system has been designed by first name Fant in 1950s. This model regards voice signals as a sound-source through the vocal track, and each component of vocal track and sound-source is independent from one another. The method uses quasi-periodic pulses for voiced sounds, white-Gaussian-noise for unvoiced sounds, and glottal sounds to complete the vocal cord model[1]. Figure 1 illustrates the block diagram of 'speech generation model.' Excitation sources use pulse trains and white sound for presenting the Voiced/Unvoiced signals by switching mode in time slot. In the Voiced section, the pitch period is the most important information regarding excitation source. The vocal track can be modeled as a resonance tube, or a formant frequency.

In this speech system model, there are two important parameters; pitch and formant. Pitch can be explained by voiced signals. A voiced sound is produced when the air is forced to push through openings between glottis (vocal cords)[1]. The tension of vocal cords controls the vibration. If the flow of air coming out through the vocal cords is closed periodically, the excitation source is vibrating quasi-periodically as it produces voiced sounds. The time from one opening of vocal cords to their next opening is denoted as fundamental period T_0, and the vibrating speed of vocal cords is denoted as fundamental frequency F_0.

Formant is defined as 'the spectral peaks in the sound spectrum[1]. In speech science and phonetics, formant is also used to represent an acoustic resonance of the human vocal tract[2]. It is often illustrated as an amplitude peak in the frequency spectrum of the sound, which can be measured by using a spectrogram or a spectrum analyzer. Although vowels are usually spoken with a high fundamental frequency, the frequency of the resonance may lie over the widely spread harmonics and hence no clear peak is visible.

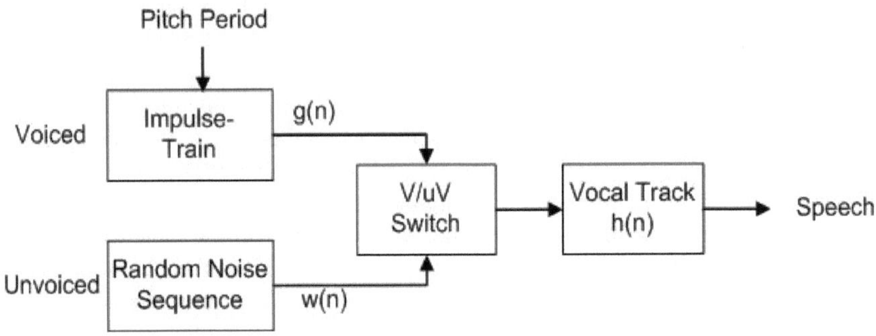

Fig. 1. Speech generation model

2.2 Traditional Pitch Detection Methods

A wide variety of pitch detection methods has been studied so far but they can be largely categorized into time-domain methods and frequency-domain methods[1]. The pitch detection method in time domain is shown in Figure 2. Given the speech signal, it first emphasizes the periodic element in time domain. Then, the pitch is detected using decision logic. There are several emphasizing methods in time domain, including Autocorrelation method (ACM), Average-Magnitude-Difference-Function (AMDF), and parallel processing method. For a large part of decision processing in time domain, we do not need to transform domains since pitch is detected only by emphasizing the periodic element. And what we need to do in this method is simple calculation, such as addition and subtraction, or simple comparison. When the pitch is interfered with noise or when the pitch is located in transitional section between phonemes, however, the decision logic becomes complicated and therefore produces improper calculations.

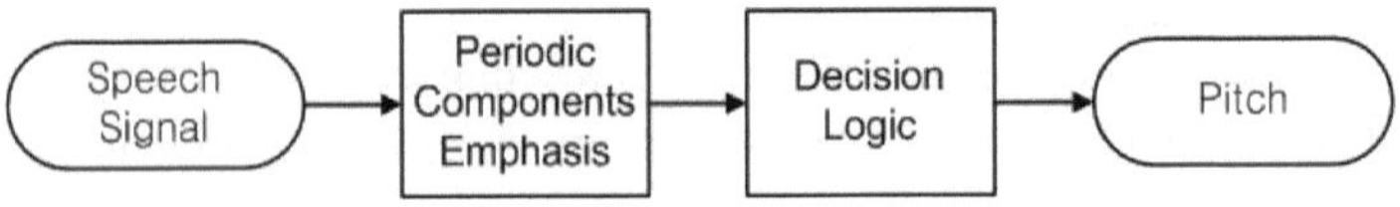

Fig. 2. Pitch detection method in time domain

The pitch detection method in frequency domain is shown in Figure 3. When speech signal is given, time domain signals are first converted into frequency domain, providing input for spectrum calculation. After the harmonics are emphasized in the second step, the decision logic detects the pitch. In this method, harmonics are highlighted as we can see in Frequency Lifter method and Comb-filtering method. In general, a spectrum frame is obtained in each unit of 20 ~ 40ms, and therefore can be less influenced by the transitional section or additive background noise than the time domain method as previously mentioned. However, converting time domain signals into frequency domain is complex and processing time can be much longer if we increase the resolution when finding fundamental frequency.

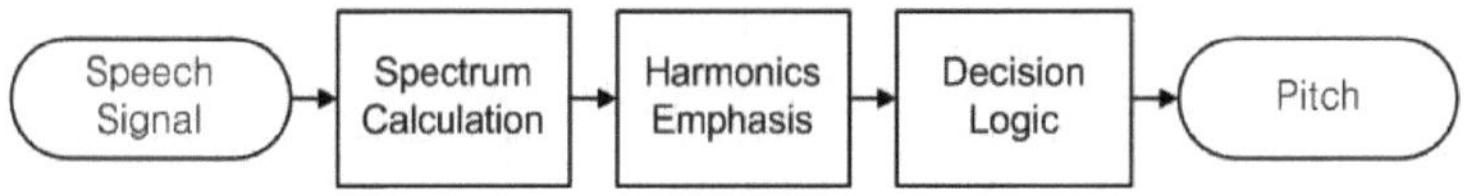

Fig. 3. Pitch detection method in frequency-domain

2.3 Traditional Pitch Harmonics Enhancing Methods

As explained in section 2.2, all of pitch detection algorithms emphasize the period of speech signals before detecting the pitch. The 'correlation method' in time and frequency domain, is one of the most popular techniques in pitch detection. This method emphasizes peaks and valleys, and reduces the noise interference automatically. The 'center-clipping method' enhances periodic components in signal less than in the 'correlation' method, but it reduces calculation in time domain. The AMDF is simple in calculating the period, but its performance is low. And many other studies for enhancing the pitch period have suggested various pitch detection systems.

3 Pitch Detection Using Emphasized Harmonics in Time Domain

A speech signal is time variant and can be approached from several perspectives including pitch, formant, and energy. In short time analysis, the signal is quasi-periodic with respect to pitch, and formant is enveloped in a group of energy. Pitch is a crucial element to be applied in various fields as previously mentioned. But it is difficult to find an exact pitch period when a signal is corrupted by noise, located in between starting and ending sections of speech, or located in transitional parts of the voice signals. Due to these problems, in order to find the pitch period, harmonics, or periodic components of speech, should be emphasized.

This paper proposes a new method for enhancing periodic signals by using non-linear clipping and synthesis. When we have discontinuous signals, 'non-linear clipping' can be applied to frequency response, which will work similar to high-pass filtering. By repeating the clipping in every discontinuous section, harmonics in high component are emphasized. Then, the highlighted signal will be synthesized with the original signal and thus pitch can be detected more clearly.

Figure 4 below is a block diagram for the proposed algorithm. Input signals are separated in short time frames, and nonlinear clipped signals are created for emphasis.

After clippings, the original signals are clipped and synthesized. This will naturally enhance the quality of signals by emphasizing harmonics. The signal periodicity of pitch will be highlighted for detecting the pitch, and eventually improving the overall performance of pitch detection.

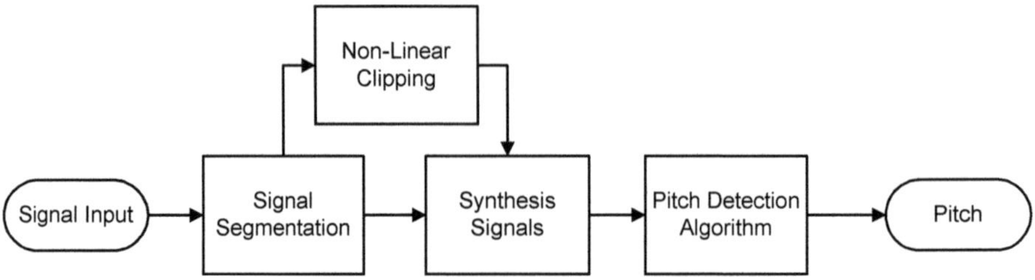

Fig. 4. Block diagram of proposed method

4 Experiment and Results

To verify the performance of the proposed method, we conducted an experiment for recorded speech signals in a lab environment. Various data of signal-to-noise ratio(SNR) were prepared for comparison of the results of the experiment between processed and non-processed values. The speech signals were recorded by five male and five female adults repeatedly reading 'National Charter of Education.' The data were sampled at 8 kHz and the number of bits per sample was 16. And 32ms window was taken for short time analysis.

Non-linear clipping and synthesis were processed to strengthen the periodicity of pitch and emphasize harmonics. For pitch detection, the frequency-correlation method was used. Pitch was originally inspected at intervals between 80 ~ 500 Hz and the one detected in the range of zero value was ignored .

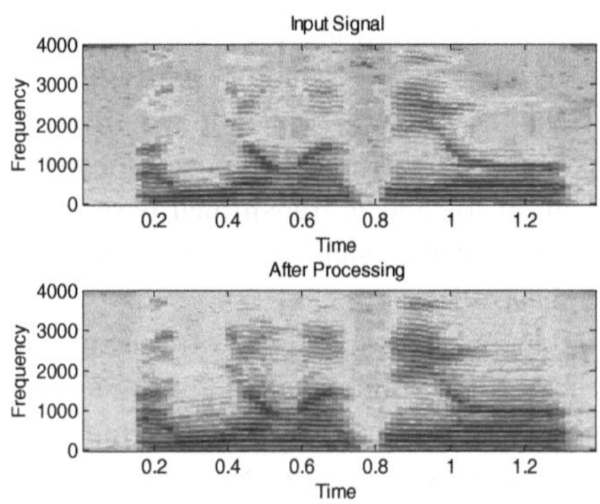

Fig. 5. Experiment result of 30dB SNR signal

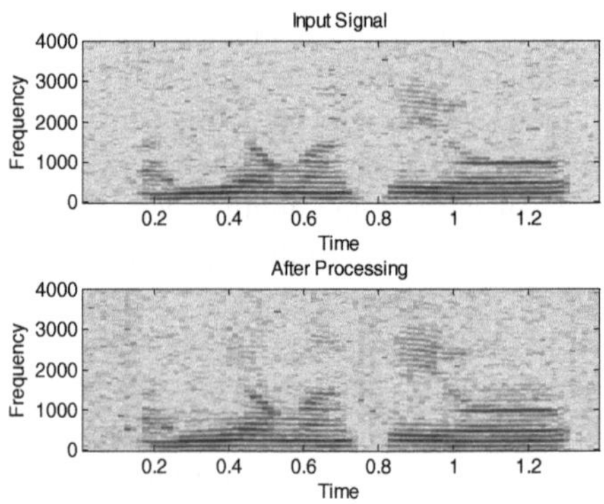

Fig. 6. Experiment result of 0dB SNR signal

Figure 5 and Figure 6 illustrate the results of the experiment before and after processing the proposed method. The figures in the upper part are the original data and the ones in the lower part are the processed data. The result of Figure 5 shows 30 dB SNR signal and Figure 6 shows 0dB SNR signal. From the upper Figure 5, we can get emphasized harmonics of the proposed method. From 1000Hz to 2000Hz at 1.2 second, we can find enhanced harmonics and in all data, we confirmed that signal quality was enhanced and improved. In the lower Figure 6, we also find more harmonics in higher frequency, which was less influenced by noise in silence section.

5 Conclusion

The pitch of the voice is being used in a variety of speech signal processing systems. It is an important factor in improving the naturalness of a speech synthesizer, increasing the recognition rate of speech recognizer, and examining the characteristics of speech signals. However, when signals are corrupted by noise or located in transitional section of speech or between starting and ending points of voice, the pitch detector makes some errors. If the errors are accumulated, we may have more serious problems in speech processing. Therefore, the performance of pitch detection should be improved so that more precise pitch period can be used in various fields of speech signal processing.

In this paper, we proposed a new method to emphasize the periodicity in order to improve the accuracy of pitch detection. The proposed new techniques are non-liner clipping and synthesis. Calculation during the process is not much complicated doing only clipping and synthesizing. As shown in the experiment results, we can confirm the proposed method produce more enhanced and emphasized harmonics. In the future research, we will discuss in more details the way of enhancing parameters of non-liner clipping and its performance.

References

1. Bae, M.J., Lee, S.H.: Digital Voice Signal Analysis. Books Publishing Dong Young (1998)
2. Rabiner, L.R., Schafer, R.W.: Introduction to Digital Speech Processing. The Essence of Knowledge (2007)
3. Park, H.-W., Khil, A.-R., Bae, M.-J.: Pitch Detection Based on Signal-to-Noise-Ratio Estimation and Compensation for Continuous Speech Signal. In: Lee, G., Howard, D., Ślęzak, D., Hong, Y.S. (eds.) ICHIT 2012. CCIS, vol. 310, pp. 767–774. Springer, Heidelberg (2012)
4. Song, Y.H., Ahn, J.H., Bae, M.J.: On the noise detection from correlation of near pitch waveforms. GESTS Society, GESTS Int'l Trans. Computer Science and Engineering 44(1), 45–54 (2008)
5. Yang, W.Y., Jo, Y.S.: Digital Signal Processing and MATLAB. Brain Korea (2001)
6. Oh, Y.W.: Voice Information Processing. Hong-Reung Press (1998)
7. Ji-Soo, O., Kang, J.-J., Lim, M.-J., Lee, K.-Y.: Design and Implementation of an Emotion Recognition System using Physiological Signal. IWIT 10(1), 57–62 (2010)
8. Lee, Y.-S., Park, Y.B.: An acoustic study of feeling information extracting method. IWIT 10(1), 51–55 (2010)

Enhanced Secure Authentication for Mobile RFID Healthcare System in Wireless Sensor Networks

Jung Tae Kim

Dept. of Electronic Engineering, Mokwon University,
800, Doan-dong, Seo-Ku, Daejeon, 302-729, Korea
jtkim3050@mokwon.ac.kr

Abstract. As telecommunication technologies in telemedicine services are developed, the expeditious development of wireless and mobile networks has stimulated wide applications of mobile electronic healthcare systems. However, security is an essential system requirement since many patients have privacy concerns when it comes to releasing their personal information over the open wireless channels. Due to the invisible feature of mobile signals, hackers have easier access to hospital networks than wired network systems. This may result in several security incidents unless security protocols are well prepared. In this paper, we analyzed authentication for healthcare system architecture to apply secure mobile health systems in the hospital environment. From the analyses, we can estimate optimal requirements to implement topology of system and its vulnerabilities.

Keywords: Mobile health system, U-health System, EMR database, Wireless network, Security, Authentication .

1 Introduction

As information technologies are rapidly developed with fusion of a variety of technology such as nano-technology, IT (Information Technology), bio-technology. This technology leads to great breakthrough industry. E-healthcare system has been realized with hospitals independently. Their main purpose is to communicate information in hospital with electrically. Recently the trend of healthcare system has moved to healthcare system based on mobile device with limited resources and low power. For the past few years, healthcare organizations over the world have also had a blueprint to adopt the Health Information System (HIS) based on the wireless network infrastructure. As a part of the wireless network, a mobile device has been employed in a large scale of hospitals due to its outstanding mobility. For instance, immediate access to the Electronic Medical Record (EMR) database offered through the mobile device may reduce the processing time to access and update EMR. The owner of personal information will also suffer from hackers due to personal information being used maliciously [1]. For this reason, the Department of Health and Human Services (HHS) in the United States has recently issued “an interim final rule regulating when and how patients should be notified if their healthcare information has been exposed

T.-h. Kim et al. (Eds.): EL/DTA/UNESST 2012, CCIS 352, pp. 190–197, 2012.

in a security breach by hospitals, physician offices and other healthcare organizations." [2]. In order to improve medical service quality in hospitals and enhancement of safety control for patients, integrating RFID technologies into medical industries has progressively become a trend on these days. To effectively incorporate RFID techniques with the existing HIS (Hospital Information Systems) is gradually developed. In healthcare, RFID systems are usually combined with other technologies such as bluetooth, mobile devices, and sensors for different purposes. Passive RFID tags are primary used for patient identification and drug authentication while active RFID tags are mainly used for the tracking purpose [3]. Mobile networks not only provide mobility to patients, but also allow physicians so they can access patients' data anytime and anywhere. This brings important benefits to both patient and medical service provider. During the process of constructing an m-healthcare system, wireless sensors act as personal digital assistants that monitor the state of a patient, while also working for physicians by sending or receiving instant messages, either to hospitals to query about the patient's information, or to the patient to remind him or her about necessary medication or examinations. Recently the trend of healthcare system has moved to healthcare system based on mobile device with limited resources and low power. In general, radio frequency identification (RFID) is an automated data-capture technology that uses low-power radio waves to communicate between readers and tags with mobile agents. Adoption of RFID in healthcare can not only reduce cost and improve efficiency by tracking asset and patient's location, but also reduce medical errors to improve patient safety. In ubiquitous sensor network, the security demand for the sensor is very lightweight due to limited memory allocation such as power, memory, bandwidth, computational capabilities [4]. In this paper, we analyzed security mechanism and protocols to prevent any security threats and vulnerabilities under the mobile health environment. At the beginning of this paper, related studies with E-health security mechanism will be introduced to compose secure mobile health architecture. Secondly, identity authentication procedures on each network and application layer of the mobile health service will be focused as the main point of this paper. Lastly, a security assessment will be conducted to prove the improvements of proposed security mechanism and future works relevant to the healthcare system will also be addressed to reinforce the mobile health system.

2 Related Works

In the real world, information related with healthcare service is very confidential and sensitive; divided security mechanism is required for mutual security. Telemedicine system often consists of the combination of communication infrastructure, physiology monitoring subsystem and care management subsystem. Mobile healthcare system based on RFID was proposed. They present a mobile healthcare service (MHS) platform that uses the RFID technology and mobile devices for identifying and positioning persons and objects both for inside and outside hospital. They also demonstrate how it can be obtained patient's location and bio-information for hospital and government to make real time reaction based on the application for SARS infection control precautions [5]. On top of authentication, the system determines a set of actions performed by the user which is called authorization. Due to specific requirements regarding security and usability standard mechanisms for enabling terminal and application mobility are not acceptable for health care information systems. Jelena Mirkovic proposed a service architecture framework (the CONNECT framework) that enables content adaptation and session management for ubiquitous patient support systems and addresses requirements specific for healthcare systems [6]. Most ubiquitous or mobile health systems are lacking a system that combines both network security and QoS (Quality of Service). Cheng-ChanHung, et.at have presented on the study of a ubiquitous healthcare network with security and QoS. He investigated the possible security and QoS methods of a ubiquitous healthcare network platform in OSI (Open System Interconnections) layers. This network platform is based on the Wireless Overlay Networks (WON) Bluetooth, 802.11 and 802.16 over IPv6 Network, and provides a secure and stable U-healthcare platform by including the application of healthcare sensors with RFID, U-healthcare PDA, VoIPv6, falling detection, and patient orientation [7]. Pardeep Kumar, et al, have analysed a user authentication for healthcare application using wireless medical sensor networks between medical sensor attached human and hospital staffs [8]. His proposed scheme include a novel two-factor professionals authentication (user authentication), where the healthcare professionals are authenticated before access the patient's body data; a secure session key is establish between the patient sensor node and the professional at the end of user authentication. To improve the processing performance and help to control the workload, the idea of bucket index has been implemented in the system based on mobile agents. Consequently, our task in this paper is building a secure and efficient wireless data access architecture using various mechanisms and protocols as a step to the U-health system.

3 Enhanced Security Mechanism

The security design of the protocol should not impede normal operations, and should prevent a malicious adversary from getting any information. As mentioned in the background section, mobile health may bring unlimited convenience to customers and staffs in hospitals. However, security vulnerabilities can be found and would be used by hackers in terms of Information Technology. Security breaches may result in a loss of data or leakage of personal information unless hospital information systems are designed with security features. However, it is easy to commit a mistake that many organizations neglect security parts as security features do not generate any visual profit for them. To summarize, it is an obvious fact that well-organized security plan can prevent the expected problems in advance before they happen. It also means they can save money, time and man-power for a recovery after security incidents. Therefore, security parts in organizations should be valued high priority. EHR systems have two main security concerns: transmission and access. Transmission security refers to the healthcare delivery organization's ability to ensure that transmitted data is safe from potential security threats an route, and access security refers to the healthcare delivery organization's ability to ensure that system access is granted only to appropriate individuals. Transmission security concerns typically arise during wireless network implementation. The Wired Equivalent Privacy (WEP) protocol was designed to provide the same level of privacy as a wired network, but due to security concerns over the WEP standard, experts continue to debate whether WEP alone is sufficient for HIPAA transmission security. Consequently, the healthcare delivery organization should use a combination of WEP and other security protocols for wireless networks. Authentication and privacy protection In order to avoid such potential security breaches, the existing HealthAgents architecture should tackle some generic security requirements. In this section, we will discuss and propose authentication methods based on network and application respectively. Also, database security measures will be proposed in order to establish a secure mobile health environment.

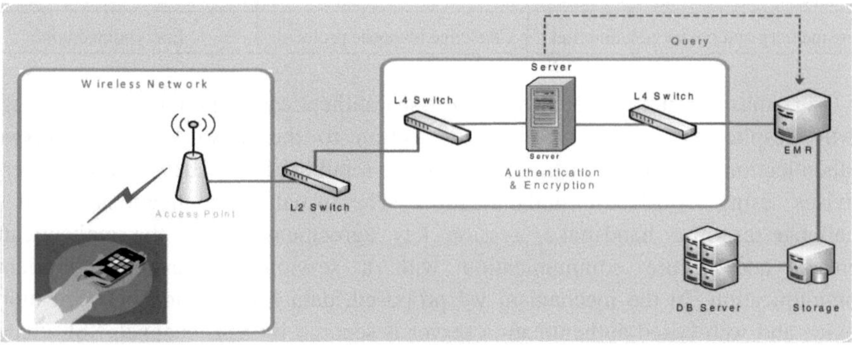

Fig. 1. Topology of Mobile Healthcare System with Mobile Device

Weider D. Yu, et al proposed a web-based wireless mobile system design of security and privacy framework for u-Healthcare. He developed a framework for u-Healthcare which is centered on the security and privacy of the electronic health records. The framework provides the user with an enriching experience and by providing features like security levels, federated identity, SSL the data is made secure in the ubiquitous environment [9]. Table 1 has shown the list of characteristics differences between e-Healthcare and u-Healthcare. Vulnerabilities to patient EHR information in u-healthcare service environment should be considered to protect it. Vulnerabilities are activity carried by users, weak usernames and passwords, unreasonable permissions, dissimilation, ports and services, unencrypted data transfer and buffer overrun

Table 1. Characteristics and differences between e-healthcare and u-healthcare [9]

e-healthcare	Mobile healthcare
Any time service	Anytime, Anywhere service
Mobile and Web interfaces	Mobile and Peripheral device interfaces
Online mode	On-line and Offline mode
Geographically constrained	Geographically distributed
No location tracking	Location aware solution
Single security agent	Collaborating security agents
Single domain security infrastructure	Multi domain security infrastructure

Table 2 shows structure of secure layer and its characteristics.

Table 2. Structure of secure layer and its characteristics

Mobile Device	Network	Database
RFID, NFC security issues	Two way authentication	Private data protection
Privacy, light weight protocol	Digital certification, IPSec., Encryption engine	EMR data security
Limited hardware resources and memory	SSL channel	Authentication mechanism
Low memory and power consumption	Challenge response protocol	Encryption engine

Users must be authenticated by web-based authentication system for accessing to EMR despite the user establishes connection to the network through network authentication [10, 11]. The Security Guidance republished by HIPAA in USA, report advises using two-factor authentication. The usual authentications based on challenge-response handshake, session key agreement during the authentication process and secure communication with a session key enable confidential communication. In the mechanism we proposed, data transmission between mobile device and web-based authentication server is secured by SSL channel. SSL channel automatically generates and exchanges keys [11]. Symmetric cryptography supported by OpenSSL is chosen for cryptographic control because that public key scheme decrypts at speeds more than the maximum 100 times slower than symmetric key scheme. Fig 2 shows authentication between mobile device and secured database.

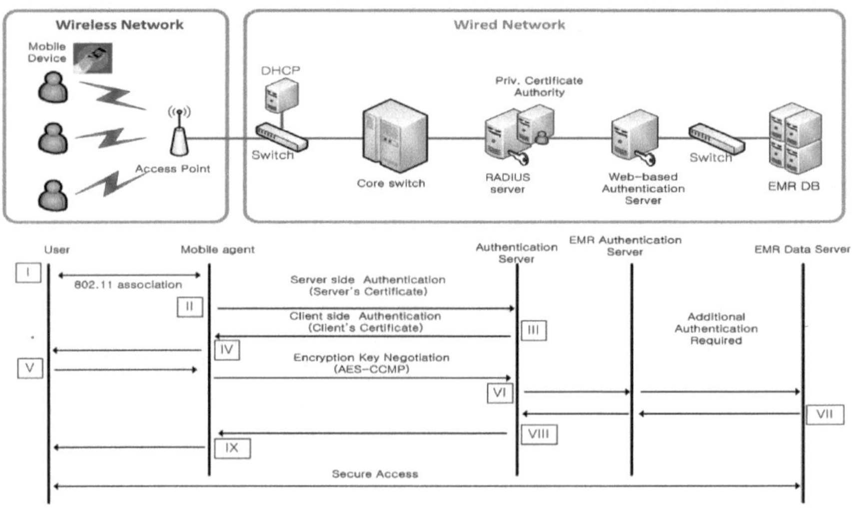

Fig. 2. Authentication process between mobile and EMR server

Table 3. Defined Parameters

Mobile device	Mobile device
S	Web based authentication server
D	Database
C(x)	Cipher-text
q	Query for response request
r	Response for query
k	Key
n	New key(Random number)
R(x)	Result of request
H(x)	Hash functioned with x
En(x,k)	Encryption of x by key
De(x,k)	Decryption of x by key

To understand the scheme in authentication based on application, user authentication scenario is presented in Figure 2. Here, we describe in detail the application based authorization procedure. To prevent unauthorized user access, user verification and identification are required.

I *User verification by pass code*

II $M : C(id) = En(H(id), k)$

$M : C(pw) = En(H(pw), k)$

$M -> S : [C(id), C(pw)]$

III $S : H(id) = De(C(id), k)$

H(id)*is used to check the session for user.*

Session Confirm : Fail

$S : H(pw) = De(C(pw), k)$

Authentication Confirm: Success (stat2)

Generate new key: n

Create session for 10 minutes

$S : C(n) = En(n, k+1)$

$S -> M : [R(stat2), C(n)]$

IV $M : n = De(C(n), k+1)$

Store : n (new key)

V $M : C(id) = En(H(id), n)$

$M : C(q) = En(q, n)$

	$M->S:[C(id),C(q)]$
VI	$S:H(id)=De(C(id),k)$
	Session confirmation : Created
	$S:q=De(C(q),n)$
	$S->D:[H(id),q]$

VII	*Check the requestor's security level*
	by H(id) *and search response the query*
	$D->S:[H(id),r]$
VIII	$S:C(r)=En(r,n+1)$
	The requestor of the respond will be determined by H(id)
	$S->M:[R(staB),C(r)]$
IX	$S:q=De(C(r),n+1)$

As mentioned above, the authorization scheme that based reasonable encryption algorithm and minimum workload oriented design supports the HIS requirement such as a confidentiality and privacy with rapid process. However, more defensive methods should be applied to the HIS against malicious attacks.

4 Security Analyses

As a last step, proposed multi-layer security mechanism is assessed by comparison to fragile security mechanism which can often be used in real industries. The contents are categorized as below. In terms of mutual security, the use of ID and password for access to EMR database can be vulnerable. While, authentication using the digital certificate will prevent illegal access even if hackers obtain the user's ID and password in the proposed mechanism. Also, each individual or group will be assigned different authorization for access to DB based on their role. In addition, the proposed mechanism employs multiple encryption methods to protect data securely. To disclosure data, hackers need to know all different encryption methods and their keys. Next, DB performance in our model satisfies two key factors which include security and speed. Encryption makes data confidential and the bucket index improves the DB speed. On the other hand, the proposed security model has an issue with compatibility. The latest wireless devices may be required because some of old devices cannot support WPA2, but it could be worth to invest in new devices because it may provide mutual security to the wireless hospital system.

5 Conclusion

The use of the mobile device in the hospital environment offers an opportunity to deliver better services for patients and staffs. In this paper, we proposed the security mechanism focused on the multi-layer authentication with sensible information management in the hospital. It was also implemented with consideration the characteristics of the hospital in the real world, so that optimized security protocols and mechanisms are employed for the high performance and security. Finally, a challenge in the near future will be the integration of Ubiquitous Sensor Network with security protocols to the hospital environment.

Acknowledgments. This research was supported by Basic Science Research Program through the National Research Foundation of Korea (NRF) funded by the Ministry of Education, Science and Technology (grant number: 2012-0007896)

References

1. Vajda, I., Buttyan, L.: Lightweight Authentication Protocols for Low Cost RFID Tags. In: Proc. 2nd Workshop on Security in Ubiquitous Computer, pp. 76–82 (2007)
2. Acharya, D., et al.: Security in Pervasive Healthcare Networks: Current R&D and Future Challenges. In: 11th International Conference on Mobile Data Management, pp. 305–306 (2011)
3. Yao, W., Chu, C.-H., Li, Z.: The Use of RFID in Healthcare: Benefits and Barriers". In: IEEE International Conference on RFID Technology and Applications, pp. 128–1342 (2010)
4. Boukerche, A., et al.: A Secure Mobile Health System Using Trust-Based Multicast Scheme. IEEE J. on Selected Areas in Communications 27(4), 387–399 (2009)
5. Li, C.-J., et al.: Mobile Healthcare Service System Using WID. In: IEEE, International Conference on Networking, Sensing and Control, pp. 1014–1019 (2004)
6. Mirkovic, J., et al.: A framework for the Development of Ubiquitous Patient Support Systems. In: 2012 6th International Conference on Pervasive Computing Technologies for Healthcare (PervasiveHealth) and Workshops, pp. 81–88 (2012)
7. Hung, C.-C., Huang, S.-Y.: On the Study of a Ubiquitous Healthcare Network with Security and QoS. In: IET 2010, pp. 139–144 (2010)
8. Kumar, P., et al.: A User Authentication for Healthcare Application Using Wireless Medical Sensor Networks. In: 2011 IEEE International Conference on High Performance Computing and Communications, pp. 647–652 (2011)
9. Yu, W.D., et al.: A Web-Based Wireless Mobile System Design of Security and Privacy Framework for u-Healthcare. In: 2008 10th IEEE Intl. Conf. on e-Health Networking, Applications and Service, pp. 96–101 (2008)
10. Kim, J., Sahama, T.: A Study on the Encryption Model for Numerical Data. Journal of Information and Communication Convergence Engineering (JICCE) 7(1), 31–34 (2009)
11. Kwon, S.-H., Park, D.-W.: Hacking and Security of Encrypted Access Points in Wireless Network. Journal of Information and Communication Convergence Engineering (JICCE) 10(2), 156–161 (2012)

A Study of Remote Control for Home Appliances Based on M2M

YouHyeong Moon[1], DoHyeon Kim[2], WonGyu Jang[2], and SungHyup Lee[2]

[1] Dept. of Computer Engineering, Jeju National University, Jeju, Korea
{kimdh,myh21}@jejunu.ac.kr
[2] Dept. of Convergence Promotion, Korea Communications Agency, Seoul, Korea
{jwg0619,shlee}@kca.kr

Abstract. Recently, products are appeared with functional components for smart home by supporting the efficient information providing service and a variety of remote controlling electric products through smart information devices such as smart phone. Thus, this paper proposes the architecture and service scenario for remote control and information provision service of home appliance using M2M(Machine-to-Machine)-based remote control function. Also, this paper implements Open API(Application Program Interface) to support the remote control home appliance service using WCF(Windows Communication Foundation) technology of .NET.

Keywords: M2M, Home Appliance, Remote Control Service, Smart Home.

1 Introduction

Recently, wireless and mobile communications technologies including WiFi, 3G, LTE, WiMax are broadly used for information communication with spreading smart devices such as smart phone [1]. Also, emerging technology, M2M(Machine-to-Machine) is popular for convergence services based on smart phone [2][3]. Hence, in this paper, we propose the architecture and service scenario for remote control of appliances by communicating between smart device and home appliances as method for communication between machines. And we implement the WCF(Windows Communication Foundation)-based API to remotely control door, air conditioner, window, etc in home and define the WCF-based home appliance control concept.

The remainder of this paper is organized as follows. Section 2 presents architecture and service scenario using API(Application Program Interface) is explained in detail. A service is described an implementation environments and a detail process of service in section 3. And some final conclusions are given in section 4.

2 Proposed M2M Architecture for Remote Control in Home

We present the architecture and service scenario for communication between machines. This architecture supports to remote control of appliances by communicating between

T.-h. Kim et al. (Eds.): EL/DTA/UNESST 2012, CCIS 352, pp. 198–203, 2012.

smart device and home appliances in figure 1. Then, home appliance with communication capabilities acts like an M2M devices with wireless network capabilities, interface and user interface into the M2M network. This M2M device can be operated by the remote control user via wireless network and it can be directly connected to the wireless network or can be connected via the M2M gateway to the wireless network. M2M service capability provider for remote control of home appliance supports M2M communication services to the M2M application entities, and provides specific functional capabilities which assist in communicating for remote control of home appliances with communication capabilities by remote controlling user. M2M application entity for remote control of home appliance creates to bundle together, and treat as a single system element, stakeholders above the M2M scope. And, this M2M application entity sends and receives a command of remote control, that sends and receives the result of remote control and that displays the result of remote control. The remote controlling user is an individual, who have authorization to remotely control his/her home appliances with his/her devices.

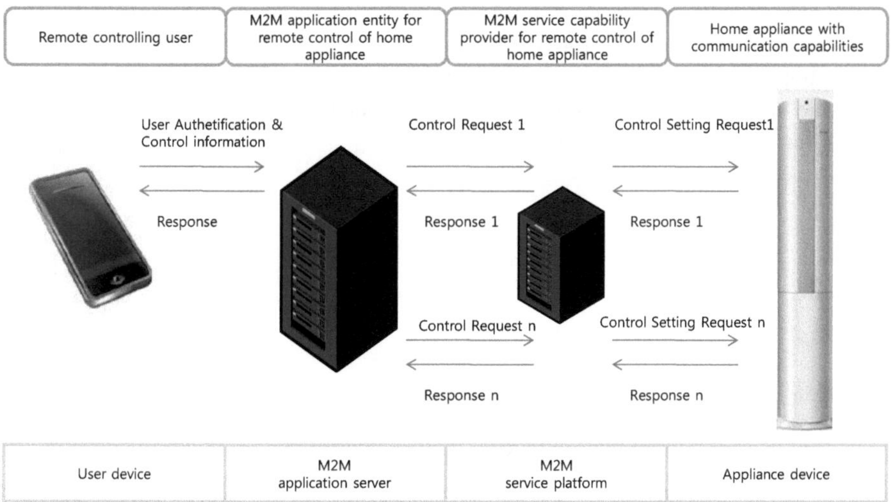

Fig. 1. Architecture and service scenario for remote control of home appliances

The home appliances with the M2M device capabilities are directly attaching to the wireless network and perform registration in the M2M system. Or they setup the connection with the M2M gateway. Registration includes the capability to maintain information describing the home appliances with the M2M device capabilities (e.g. the type of home appliances, etc.). The remote control user using the handset or the PC sends a request to turn on or turn off the home appliance remotely. The result of the requested operation is returned to the remote control user from the home appliance with M2M capabilities via wireless network [4].

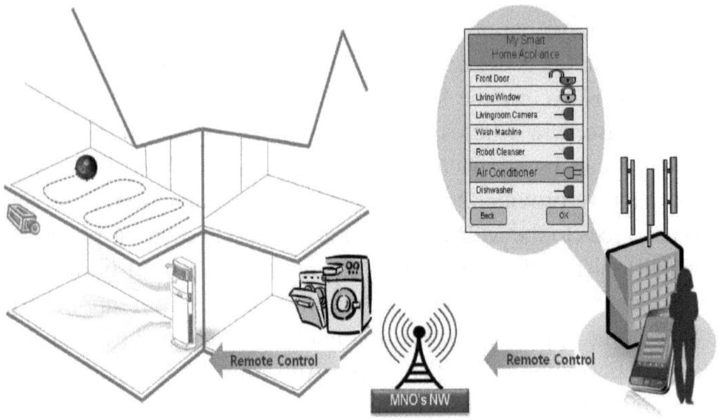

Fig. 2. Remote control service for home appliances [4]

We design API of remote control service for home appliances. API's function provides open API function for remote control service for home appliance database. For example, when user want to turn on an air conditioner before user arrives in home, he turns on a heating system to configure database by API call in connecting a system for working by smart phone.

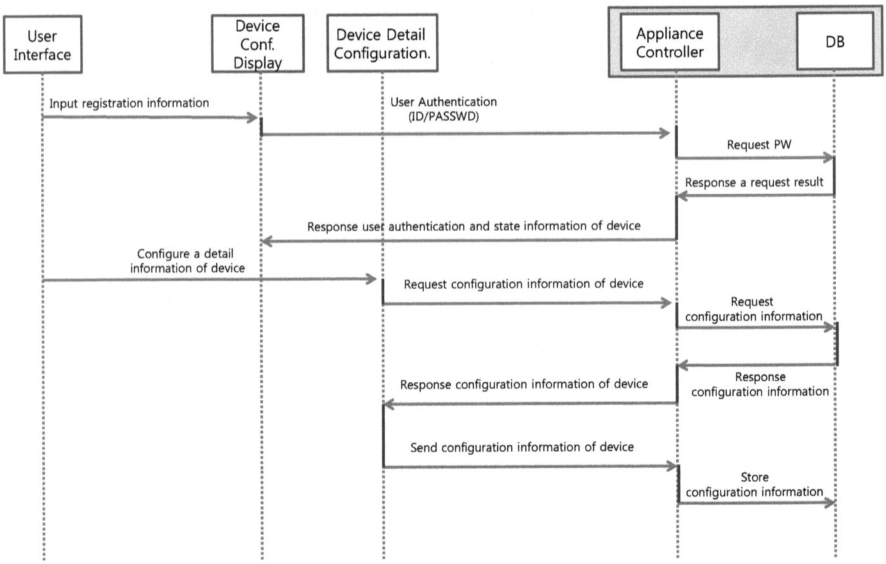

Fig. 3. Sequence diagram of remote service for home appliances

The API of remote control service for home appliances provides a configuration function of device using smart devices or Web browser by supporting each functional API. In figure 3, ID/PASSWD is used for user authentication via API. Then each device sequentially calls API for configuring and controls a device configuration.

3 Development of Remote Control Service for Home Appliances

3.1 Implementation Environments for Remote Control Service

We implement the remote control service for home appliances in server-client system and OS is MS Window XP SP2, use IIS Server. And we use for developing a database using MS-SQL and use program language, C#.net and WCF [5].

3.2 Database for Home Appliances

Database system sends the requested information by server. A user_info is shown user_id as PK, each user distinguishes with PK. Device is controlled as user account by user information connecting to database system using user_id. The configuration information of device indicates Appliance_Data and the specific information of each device is distinguished by FK user_id and PK appliance_type. Also, a reservation information of AirCon_Reservation is managed by user_id. Figure 4 shows the database structure of remote control service for home appliances.

Fig. 4. Database structure of remote control service for home appliances

3.3 API for Remote Control Service

We developed the configuration information interface for client to connect API and set interface configuration. Each client call an API of remote control service for home appliances and interface, class for interface is implemented in client system. Figure 10 shows an example for user authentication process. 'bool loginByIDAndPass' work for user authentication and 'GetAppliance_info_frontdoor' checks power configuration information of device. 'SetAirConOn performs power configuration information of device. The remain functions are defined to API and they are implemented to set by parameters. Figure 5 shows an approach and set the API configuration address using WCF.

```
public interface
IRemoteControlApplianceServer
{

[System.ServiceModel.OperationContra
ctAttribute(Action="http://tempuri.org/
IRemoteControlApplianceServer/LoginB
yIDAndPass",
ReplyAction="http://tempuri.org/IRem
oteControlApplianceServer/LoginByIDA
ndPassResponse")]
    bool LoginByIDAndPass(string
PersonCode, string PassWord);

}
```

Fig. 5. Configuration information of API

3.4 Results

Figure 6 shows the connecting process between server and client using WCF. User is authorized to call 'LoginByIDAndPass API' described as figure 6. After user authorization, display screen converts to figure 7 and device's information shows by API to index from DB. User can particularly configure a control plane such as figure 7. Also, user is able to configure a home appliance (example : air conditioner) with specific parameters for remote control.

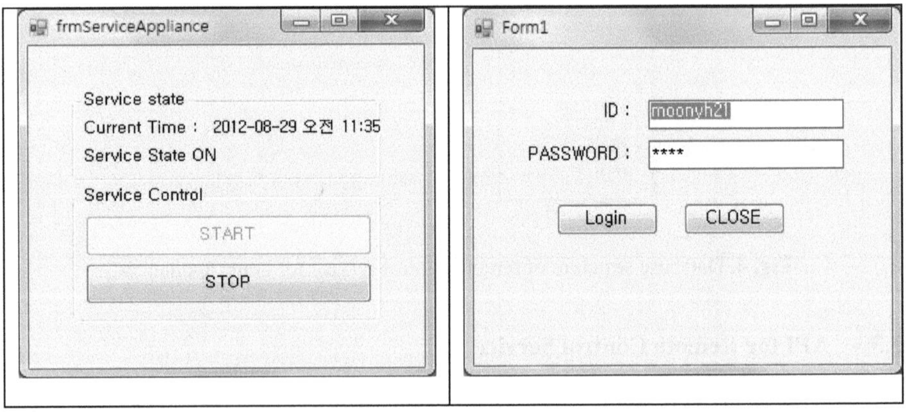

Fig. 6. Service configuration(left) and user authentication(right)

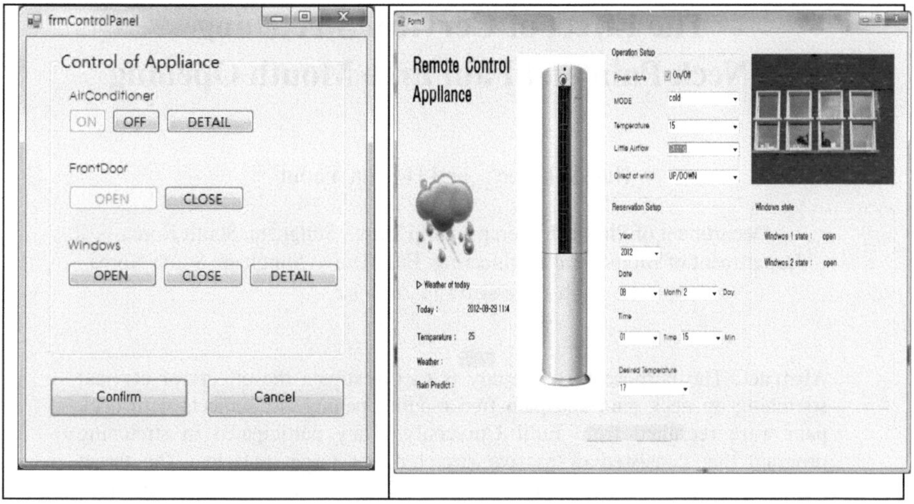

Fig. 7. Power configuration (left) and Detail information of device (right)

4 Conclusions

Since a rapid development of mobile communication technology and an appearance of emerging technology such as M2M, researchers deeply interesting in new convergence service such as smart home. Thus, this paper proposes the method for remote control and information provision service of home appliance using M2M-based remote control function. Also, this paper implements Open API to support the remote control home appliance service using WCF technology of .NET. Finally, we confirm the implementation system and show the implementation results.

Acknowledgments. This research was supported by the ICT Standardization program of KCC(Korea Communications Commission). Corresponding author; DoHyeun Kim (e-mail: kimdh@jejunu.ac.kr.).

References

1. Kayastha, N., Niyato, D., Wang, P., Hossain, E.: Applications, Architectures, and Protocol Design Issues for Mobile Social Networks: A Survey. Proc. of the IEEE 99, 2130–2158 (2011)
2. Chang, K., Soong, A., Tseng, M., Xiang, Z.: Global Wireless Machine-to-Machine Standardization. IEEE Internet Computing Magazine, 64–69 (2011)
3. WCF(Windows Communication Foundation), http://www.microsoft.com
4. ETSI TR 102 857 V0.3.0 (June 2010), http://www.etsi.org
5. Net, Windows OS, MS-SGL, http://www.microsoft.com

The Effect of Cervical Stretching on Neck Pain and Pain Free Mouth Opening

Han Suk Lee[1,*] and Ho Jun Yeom[2]

[1] Department of Physical Therapy, Eulji Univ., Sungnam, South Korea
[2] Department of Biomedical Engineering, Eulji Univ., Sungnam, South Korea
hyeom@eulji.ac.kr

Abstract. The purpose of this study is to investigate the effects of cervical stretching on neck pain and pain free mouth opening. 12 subjects with neck pain were recruited from Eulji University. They participated in stretching program that consisted of passive stretching of target muscles. The target muscles were the upper trapezius, SCM, Scalenes, Lavator scapulae, suboccipitalis. The stretching for each muscle was accoplished in pain free range and applied 3 thines per week for 4 weeks. In order to determine the effect of stretching, pressure pain threshold, NDI, and active pain-free mouth opening were measured at pre and post intervention. NDI score was decreased and PPTs were significantly difference in bilateral thapezius, Levetor, Scapula, suboccipitalis and left scaleneus except right scaleneus and bilateral SCM. Active pain-free mouth opening was increased after cervical stretching. Patients with chronic neck pain treated stretching exercise directed at the cervical spine might be beneficial in decreasing neck pain and increasing pain-free mouth opening. We can consider the stretching exercise chronic neck patients as well as TMJ patients as self-management instruction within pain-free range.

Keywords: Cervical stretching, neck pain, pain free, mouth opening.

1 Introduction

Neck pain has been considering a significant health care problem and reported that the life time and point prevalence of neck pain is almost as high as the prevalence of low back pain [1]. It can be severely disabling and costly and aggravated by neck movement or sustained neck postures. Therefore, physical therapist has been treating neck pain patient with massage, heat application, active exercise, stretching, mobilization, and so on [2]. Particularly, neck cannot move with just one muscle, physical therapist has to focus on 5 muscles (upper trapezius, SCM, suboccipitalis, scalenues, Levetor, Scapula) that can affect neck movement [3].

TMJ (Temporo mandibular joint) usually moves from 1500 to 2000 repetition to close and open a mouth in a day for functional activities like breathing, chewing, speaking. TMJ will deform muscle, bone and cartilage with time and this deformity cause an adaptation of body with a decreasing pain and anxiety and change from normal posture to abnormal posture [4]. 75% of man may suffer with TMJ problem at

[*] Corresponding author.

T.-h. Kim et al. (Eds.): EL/DTA/UNESST 2012, CCIS 352, pp. 204–210, 2012.

least once in a lifetime and one-third suffers more than one symptom [5]. In case of TMJ patient, they cannot close a mouth or suffer from symptoms like headache, neck and shoulder pain, head forward posture and so on. Sometimes, those symptoms affect the quality of life and activity of daily living of people and it became a social issue [6][7]. The treatment of TMJ has been changed various like injection, use of modality to control a pain, massage, joint mobilization, postural education, relaxation of stress, cognitive education and so on [5][7][8].

Some of treatment directly applys on TMJ and others accomplish on cervical with mobilization and muscle reeducation. Particularly, head forward posture is induced by compensation of imbalanced muscles which move TMJ. Finally, upper trapezius, splenius, Levetor, Scapula got more problems [9]. Eriksson[10] found the movement of head precede the movement of mandibular and motions of cervical, atlato-occipital and temporo-mandibular occur at the same time and this motion activate the muscles of neck and TMJ and mouth opening was accomplished by head-neck extension and mouth closing was accomplished by head-neck flexion.Reduced activation of deep cervical muscle leads to augment the activation of SCM(sternocleidomastoid muscle) and AS(anterior scalene) and decrease the relaxation of cervical muscle. It makes some problems of control at cervical spine and pain and dysfunction of cervical. This means patient with TMD (temporomandibulardisorder) has cervical-associated disorder [6]. Catnazariti [3] emphasized the pathophysiological relationship between the cervical spine and masticatory system and suggested to identify masticatory dysfunction among causes of neck pain. La Touche [8] investigated the effect of joint mobilization and exercise at cervical spine for 19 patients with TMD during 5 weeks and found decreasing facial pain, increasing PPT (pressure pain threshold)s over the masticatory muscle and increasing pain-free mouth opening after intervention.

We have to consider intimate associations between head and cervical posture and movement of TMJ during treatment but the evidence is unclear [11]. Furthermore, it can be hypothesized that treatment targeted to the cervical spine may also have an effect on TMJ movement. The purpose of this study was to investigate the effects of pain and TMJ movement for neck pain patient if we apply stretching exercise protocol targeting the cervical muscle and find the correlation between the improvement of neck pain and jaw movement.

2 Methods and Experimental Setup

12 subjects with neck pain as primary complaint in the last 6 months aged twenty, were recruited from the University of Eulji and Neck Disability Index(NDI) score to assess disability was from 5 to 14. A NDI showed good psychometric properties to assess self-rated disability in neck pain [1]

Participants were excluded if they presented with any of the following :(1) sign or symptoms of neurological or orthopedic problems (2) history of neck surgery in 1 month of the study (3) diagnosis of systemic disease(rheumatoid arthritis) (4) diagnosis of fibromyalgia syndrome. Chronic neck pain was defined as generalized neck pain provoked by neck postures, neck movement or palpation of the neck muscle. All subjects read and signed an informed consent form before their inclusion. The intervention applied 3 times per week for 4 weeks and other co-interventions were discouraged. In order to determine whether reduction in pain is accompanied by changes in muscles, two measures were recorded. Current neck disability index was accomplished and local pain sensitivity was measured using the pressure algometer. In addition, active pain-free mouth opening was recorded to measure the change of jaw movement after intervention. These measures were taken during 2 periods: a pretreatment period prior to (pre) and post-treatment period following passive stretching of the target muscles. The target muscles were the upper trapezius, SCM, Scalenes, Levator, Scapula, suboccipitalis. The stretching for each muscle was accomplished in pain free range and repeated 3 times and hold for 15 sec at one session.

Active Pain-free Mouth Opening

In a sitting position without cervical movement, subjects were asked to open the mouth as wide as possible without causing pain. At the end postion of pain -free mouth openning, the distance between upper-lower central incisors was measured . The intra-tester reliability of this procedure was found to be high (ICC=0.9-0.98)(Goulet et al 1998).

Pressure Pain Threshold(PPT)

Minimal amount of pressure needed for the pressure sensation to first change to pain with an analogical pressure algometer (Commander TM algometer JTech Medial. Patients were instructed to say "stop" when the sensation changed from pressure to pain. The mean of 3 trials was calculated over each point and used for the main analysis. A 30-second resting period was allowed between each trial. The reliability of pressure algometry has been found to be high (intra-class correlation coefficient 0.91; 95% confidence interval [12]. PPT was assessed over the upper trapezius (middle of the front edge of the upper trapezius fibers), SCM, Scalenes, Levetor, Scapula, suboccipitalis.

Statistical Analysis

Data were analyzed with the SPSS package version 12.0(SPSS Inc, Chicago, IL). Paired t-test was used to compare pre and post hold relax technique at PPT and mouth opening. The statistical analysis was conducted at a 95% confidence level, and a P value less than .05 was considered as statistically significant.

3 Results

A total of 12 patients, mean age 21.08 years old participated. None of the patients started drug therapy during the time of the study. In this sample of patients with cervical, the average NDI was 6.75(Table 1). Paired t -tests were performed on the NDI, pressure algometer data and active mouth opening. Increases in pressure algometer values indicate that a greater force was required to elicit threshold pain from the trigger points, reflecting decreased trigger point sensitivity.

Table 1. Characteristics of subjects

Variables	Mean ± SD
Age(year)	21.08 ± 1.67
Weight(kg)	52.95 ± 4.91
Height(cm)	161.87 ± 4.43
NDI(score)	6.75 ± 1.71
Mouth Opening(cm)	3.91 ± 0.50

Pressure Pain Threshold and NDI Score

The NDI score taken prior to (pre) and following (post) the stretch showed a reliable pre to post reduction in neck disability. Comparing the pre to post algometer values yielded highly reliable increases in threshold values following the stretch in all of cervical muscles and significant difference was identified in bilateral trapezius, Levetor, Scapula, suboccipitalis and left scalenes ($p<0.05$). However, no significant difference was identified over right scalenes and bilateral SCM(Table 2).

Table 2. Changes in pressure pain thresholds (kg cm^2) over the cervical muscle muscles

		Pain threshold			
		Pre stretching	Post-stretching	T	P
Trapezius	RT	28.34± 6.50	37.91±7.54	-4.0	0.002
	LF	30.43± 5.86	38.09±6.50	-3.432	0.006
Levator	RT	30.85± 4.86	38.50±6.71	-4.33	0.001
	LF	31.04± 6.52	36.84±7.13	-2.578	0.026
Scaleneus	RT	26.45± 2.85	27.09±4.79	-0.46	0.652
	LF	25.45± 2.51	28.10±2.80	-2.476	0.031
Suboccipitali 3	RT	17.40± 2.67	19.21±2.75	-2.36	0.037
	LF	18.86± 3.05	21.81±2.34	-4.070	0.002
SCM	RT	18.76± 1.67	19.20±1.55	-0.816	0.432
	LF	18.80± 2.54	19.31±2.62	-0.503	6.625
NDI		6.75	5.91	3.079	0.010

RT: right, LT:Left

Active pain -free mouth opening

Active pain-free mouth opening was increased from 3.91cm to 4.48 after stretching and there was significant difference ($p<0.05$)(Table 3).

Table 3. Changes in active pain -free mouth opening(cm)

	Pre-stretching	Post-stretching	T	P
Mouth opening(cm)	3.91±0.05	4.48±0.74	-2.87	0.015

4 Discussions

The results of this study showed that subjects with chronic non-severe neck pain had at reduced pain on neck and improved the ability to mouth opening after stretching exercise.

Passive stretches have some benefit. it makes muscle relax and pain release even though it could be harmful Marshell [13] suggested passive stretching increases hamstring extensibility and decreases passive stiffness, with no change in stretch tolerance defined by pain intensity as well as strength. But, Parmer [14] and Marangoni [9] suggested passive manual stretching decreased pain. In addition, Ylinen [15] found manual therapy and stretching exercise on neck pain and disability considerably decreased neck pain and disability in women with non-specific neck pain. Even though, Manual therapy was more effective option than stretching, he recommend stretching may be considered as a first choice because it is easy to perform and inexpensive to introduce. In our study, the subjects with stretching directed at neck experienced an increased PPT over all of cervical muscle, which was similar with the results of Ylinen [15] investigating decreased neck pain after stretching exercise.

One possible explanation for the improvement in decreased neck pain may be mediate via the Sherrington's law of reciprocal innervation because stretching results in improved strength of inhibited antagonistic muscle and this cause a decreasing muscle tension and an increasing circulation and it may related with in decreased neck pain. In addition, we try to do stretching in pain -free range. Therefore stretching did not damage the fiber.

We also found an increase of 6mm in pain-free mouth opening after stretching of the neck, which was slightly better to the results of Blanco [16] study investigating changes in active mouth opening after the treatment of masseter muscle. According to recently studies, manipulation on upper cervical and exercise directed at the cervical spine can increase in active mouth opening [8][17].

As the application of an indirect approach directed to the cervical spine induced similar improvements in mouth opening when compared with treatment of TMJ, perhaps cervical techniques might be used as a complementary approach to manage pain in patients with TMD. One possible explanation for the improvement in pain-free mouth opening may be related to reposition of cervical spine induced muscle relaxation by stretching. Some studies have reported neck muscle is related with movement of jaw [3][18] . Other studies have demonstrated that range of motion of the mouth is influenced by position of cervical spine [10][11]. Therefore, it is possible that the stretching applied in the neck can improve the biomechanical adaptation of the cervical spine with relation to the temporomandibular joint, increasing pain-free mouth opening. The other possible explanation is also plausible that the reduction in pain in the neck region will also increase pain-free mouth opening.

Our study had several limitations. First, generalization might be difficult because the sample size was small. Second, we did not control the psychological factors like stress that can affect to muscle tension. Furthermore, we did not include a control group, so we could not consider the effect of time after the interventions directed at the cervical spine because the improvements of subjects may be related to the passage of time.

Future randomized controlled trials with a large number of subjects and including a control group which did not receive the treatment or received other treatment for neck should be conducted in order to further explain the effectiveness various interventions directed at the cervical spine for patients. In addition, Future randomized studies have to consider the effect of time including the follow up periods.

5 Conclusions

The results of our study demonstrated that patients with chronic neck pain treated stretching exercise directed at the cervical spine might be beneficial in decreasing neck pain and disability, increasing PPTs over the neck muscles and increasing pain-free mouth opening. Therefore, we can recommend the stretching exercise chronic neck patients as well as TMJ patients as self-management instructions.

Future randomized studies should investigate the cause that the cervical treatment affects the TMJ movement.

Acknowledgments. "This work (Grant No. sm124566) was supported by Medium Business Administration in 2011."

References

1. Vernon, H.: The Neck Disability Index: state-of-the-art, 1991-2008. J. Manipulative Physiol. Ther. 31, 491–502 (2008)
2. Hoving, J.L., Koes, B.W., de Vet, H.C.W., et al.: Manual therapy, physical therapy or continued care by a general practitioner for patients with neck pain. Annals of Internal Medicine 136(10), 713–722 (2002)
3. Catanzariti, J.F., Debuse, T., Duquesnoy, B.: Chronic neck pain and masticatory dysfunction. Joint, Bone, Spine: Revue Du Rhumatisme 72(6), 515–519 (2005)
4. Saito, E.T., Akashi, P.M.H., Sacco, I.C.N.: Global body posture evaluation in patients with temporomandibular joint disorders. Clinical Science 64(1), 35–39 (2009)

5. Wright, E.F., North, S.L.: Managemnet and treatment of temporomandibular disorder: A clinical perspective. The Journal of Manual and Manipulative Therapy 17(4), 247–254 (2009)
6. Armijo-Olivo, S., Silvestre, R., Fuentes, J., Da Costa, B.R., Gadotti, I.C., Warren, S., Major, P.W., Thie, N.M.R., Magee, D.J.: Electromyographic activity of the cervical flexor muscle in patients with temporalmandibular disorders while performing the craniocervical flexion test: A cross-sectional study. Physical Therapy 91(8), 1184–1197 (2011)
7. McNeely, M.L., Armijo Olivo, S., Magee, D.J.: A systematic review of the effectiveness of physical therapy interventions for temporaomandibular disorders. Physical Therapy 86(5), 710–725 (2006)
8. La Touche, R., Fernandex-de-las-penas, C., Fernandez-carnero, J., Escalante, K., Angulo-diaz-parrendo, S., Paris-Alemany, A., Cleland, J.A.: The effects of manual therapy and exercise directed at the cervical spine on pain and pressure pain sensitivity in patients with myofascial temporaomandibular disorders. Journal of Oral Rehabilitation 36, 644–652 (2009)
9. Marangoni, A.H.: Effects of intermittent stretching exercises at work on musculoskeletal pain associated with the use of a personal computer and the influence of media on outcomes. Work 36(1), 27–37 (2010)
10. Eriksson, P.O., Henrikson, H., Nordh, E., Zafar, H.: Co-oridinated Mandibular and Head Neck Movements during Rhythmic jaw activities in man. Journal of Pental Research 79(6), 1378–1384 (2009)
11. Olivo, S.A., Bravo, J., Magee, D.J., Thie, N.M., Major, P.W., Flores-Mir, C.: The association between head and cervical posture and temporomandibular disorders: a systematic review. Journal of Orofacial Pain 20(1), 9–23 (2006)
12. Chesterton, L., Sim, J., Wright, C., Foster, N.: Interrater reliabilityof algometry in measuring pressure pain thresholds inhealthy humans, using multiple raters. Clin. J. Pain 23, 760–766 (2007)
13. Marshell, P.W., Cashman, A., Cheema, B.S.: A randomized controlled trial for the effect of passive stretching on measures of hamstring extensibility, passive stiffness, strength and stretch tolerance. J. Sci. Med. Sport 14(6), 535–540 (2011)
14. Parmar, S., Shyam, A., Sabnis, S., Sancheti, P.: The effect of isolytic contraction and passive manual stretching on pain and knee range of motion after hip surgery: A prospective, double-blinded, randomized study. HongKong PhysiotherapyJournal 29(1), 25–30 (2011)
15. Ylinen Jari, J., Takala, E.-P., Nyknen, M., Hkkinen, A., Mlki, E., Pohjolainen, T., Karppi, S.L., Kautiainen, H., Airaksinen, O.: Active neck muscle training in the treatment of chronic neck pain in women, a randomized controlled trial. JAMA 21 289(19), 2509–2515 (2003)
16. Rodríguez-Blanco, C., Fernández-de-las-Peñas, C., Hernández-Xumet, J.E., Peña-Algaba, C., Fernández-Rabadán, M., Lillo-de-la-Quintana, M.C.: Changes in active mouth opening following a single treatment of latent myofascial trigger points in the masseter muscle involving post-isometric relaxation or strain/counter-strain. J. Bodyw. Mov. Ther. 10, 197–205 (2006)
17. Mansilla-Ferragut, P., Fernández-de-las-Penãs, C., Alburquerque-Sendín, F., Cleland, J.A., Boscá-Gandíá, J.J.: The immediate effects of atlanto-occipital joint manipulation on active mouth opening and pressure pain sensitivity in women with mechanical neck pain. J. Man Physiol. Ther. 32, 101–106 (2009)
18. Komiyama, O., Arai, M., Kawara, M., Kobayashi, K., De Laat, A.: Pain patterns and mandibular dysfunction following experimental trapezius muscle pain. J. Orofac Pain 19(2), 119–126 (2005)

A Performance Evaluation of AIS-based Ad-hoc Routing (AAR) Protocol for Data Communications at Sea

Seong Mi Mun and Joo Young Son*

Department of Computer Engineering, Korea Maritime University,
727 Taejong-ro, Yongdo-Gu, Busan, Korea
mmlab@hhu.ac.kr

Abstract. Future ships at sea would need broad and stable data communication system like that on land. Current satellite and RF media do not satisfy the needs of communications due to high costs and low bandwidth respectively. In this paper, we introduce an AIS (Automatic Identification System)-based ad-hoc network model and an AIS-based ad-hoc routing protocol (AAR) which can enhance ship-to-ship and ship-to-shore data communications environments remarkably. We also show through simulated results by QualNet that AAR offers better performance in terms of throughput, end-to-end delay and packet loss ratio than the conventional ad-hoc routing protocols such as AODV and LAR.

Keywords: Ad-hoc Network, AIS-based Maritime Data Communication Network, AIS-based Ad-hoc Routing Protocol.

1 Introduction

Ships at sea communicate with other ships and nodes on land using satellite and/or RF networks. These carriers have constraints on cost, bandwidth, and transmission range. Ships at sea may be equipped with one or more media such as AIS, VHF, HF, MF, International Maritime Satellite Fleet Broadband (Inmarsat FB), and 3/4G mobile cellular media of W-CDMA or LTE. Increasing data traffic on shore and use of analog voice channels on VHF can cause the networks to be jammed seriously [1]. Digital data communication methods using VHF have been studied, which can be positively applied as alternative digital communication channels at sea in the near future [2, 3, 4, 5, 6, and 7].

AIS is an automatic supply system which provides ships in transmission range with navigation information, such as maritime mobile service identity (MMSI), heading (HDG), speed of ground (SOG), course of ground (COG), and so on. IMO introduced the system in 2002 as an international standard to enhance the safety and security of ships [8]. AIS makes it possible for ships at sea to identify and locate each other in advance, aiding in the prevention of collisions.

---

* Corresponding author.

T.-h. Kim et al. (Eds.): EL/DTA/UNESST 2012, CCIS 352, pp. 211–218, 2012.

We have introduced an AIS-based ad-hoc network model and an AIS-based ad-hoc routing protocol (AAR), which enlarge transmission ranges and cover shadow areas [9]. Performance of AAR in terms of throughput, end-to-end delay and packet loss ratio are evaluated by QualNet simulator. In this paper, the results of the simulation are shown and compared with those of AODV and LAR. This paper is organized as follows: in section 2, we describe AAR protocol shortly. The simulation results are presented in section 3. Finally, conclusions are stated in section 4.

2 AAR Routing Protocol

2.1 Packet Format

AAR packets are enclosed in the AIS message type 6 to send data and control messages. In other words, AAR packets are placed in the Binary Data field in the AIS message type 6 (see Table 1).

Table 1. Message Format of the AIS Message Type 6

Parameter	Number of bits	Description
Message ID	6	always 6
Repeat indicator	2	to indicate how many times a message has been repeated
Source ID	30	MMSI of source station
Sequence number	2	0-3
Destination ID	30	MMSI of destination station
Retransmit flag	1	0 = no retransmission = default; 1 = retransmitted
Spare	1	Not used.
Binary Data	936 (Max.)	Appl. ID = 16bit; Data = 920bits

Six types of packets are defined in AAR. Three bit-wide message type (msgType) field classifies the functionalities of messages: 000 and 001 are Destination Location Discovery Request (DLD_Req) and DLD Reply (DLD_Rep). 010 and 011 are Route Discovery Request (RD_Req) and RD Reply (RD_Rep). Finally 100 and 110 are Data Sending and Acknowledgement. Fig. 1 shows AAR packet format [9].

30bit	30bit	3bit	30bit	30bit	Max 857bit
HSMMSI	HDMMSI	msgType	PSMMSI	PDMMSI	data

Fig. 1. AAR Packet Format

HSMMSI and HDMMSI are source and destination MMSI (Maritime Mobile Service Identity) specified in the header of AIS message type 6, which are addresses used to forward a packet to a next neighbor node by link-by-link basis. PSMMSI and

PDMMSI denote source and destination MMSI, which specify the original source and final destination addresses of a packet.

Table 2. Tables in each node

Table Name	Field
Base Station Table (BT)	Base Station ID (BID), Longitude, Latitude
Routing Table (RT)	DMMSI, NMMSI
Neighbor Node Table (NT)	MMSI, Longitude, Latitude, HDG, SOG, COG
Far Node Table (FT)	MMSI, Longitude, Latitude, HDG, SOG, COG

AAR needs four types of tables to route packets (Table 2) [9]. Base station table (BT) stores BS's MMSI (BID) and its location information. As BSs are located at fixed places onshore and the locations are well known by ships, BT has fixed values. Routing table (RT) has routing information. Destination MMSI (DMMSI) denotes final destination, and next MMSI (NMMSI) is next node's MMSI to reach the final destination. Neighbor node table (NT) stores information of nodes that can be reached in one hop. Regular AIS messages are collected and retained in NT by each node. Finally, far node table (FT) stores node information gathered through the VNS (Vessel Naming Service) and relaying packets. HDG, SOG and COG in NT and FT show the mobility of nodes.

2.2 AAR Routing Algorithm

AAR is based on AIS-based ad-hoc network model depicted in Fig. 2.

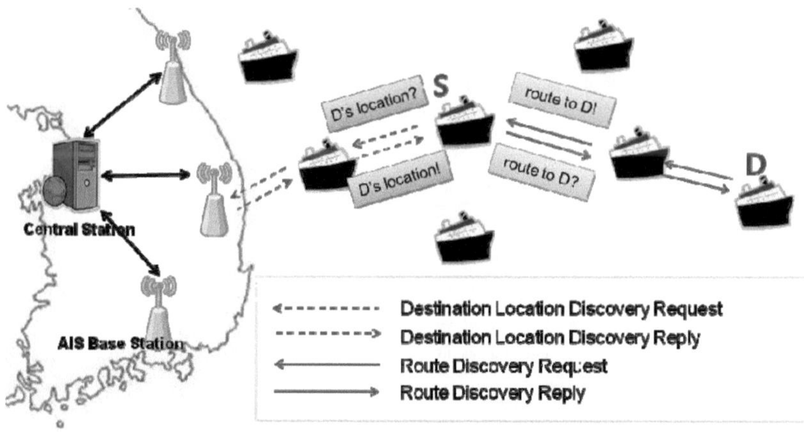

Fig. 2. An AIS-based Ad-hoc Network Model

Ships in this network model are assumed to be equipped with AIS. Ships are identified by their MMSIs defined in AIS. Base stations (BS) on shore collect AIS information of vessels not only in transmission range but reached by the multi-hop ad-hoc manner. The center station (CS) collects information from the BSs, so it has full knowledge about almost vessels with AIS at sea. CS shares the information to the BSs through the Internet on land. Then BSs can provide the vessels in transmission range with the location and navigation information of vessels, which can also be propagated to vessels out of range by the multi-hop ad-hoc method. This model uses in the Vessel Naming Service (VNS) of the BS which is very similar to DNS of the Internet. In VNS, when a vessel wants to know location of another vessel (A), it sends a query named Destination Location Discovery Request with MMSI of the vessel (A) to the closest BS. Then the BS replies with the location HDG, SOG and COG of the MMSI.

In AAR, A source node (S) performs destination location discovery (DLD) and route discovery (RD) to get an optimal route to a destination node (D) as follows:

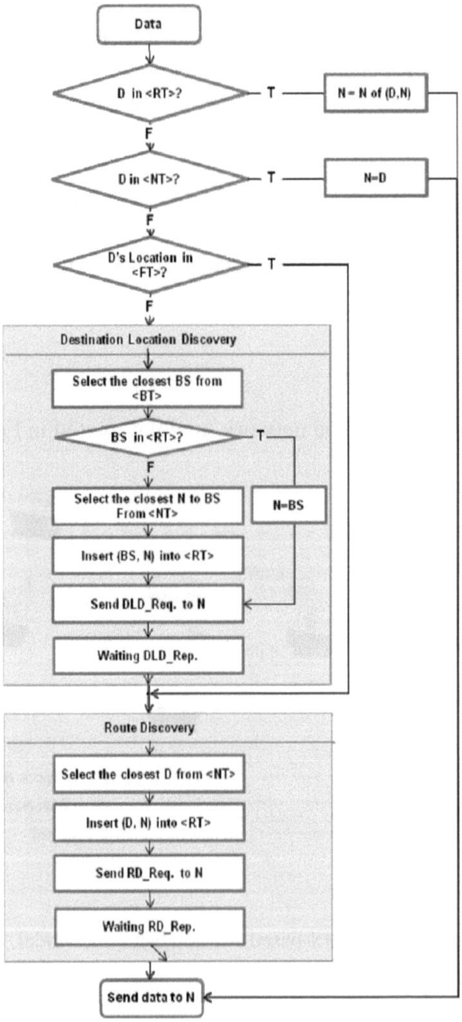

Fig. 3. Flowchart of AAR algorithm

First of all, S looks up its own RT to find out the route cache to D. If RT already has D's route, which means pair of (DMMSI, NMMSI) exists in RT where DMMSI is D's MMSI and NMMSI is next node's MMSI to reach D, then the message is immediately sent to NMMSI. Otherwise, no route to D has been known to S yet. Then S should perform route discovery (RD).

Firstly, S should check out NT or FT has D's location information. If no cache exists, S performs DLD before RD step. The VNS by BS are used in DLD. S gets the closest BS's location from BT. S requests DLD to the BS sending a 'DLD_Req' packet with MMSI of D. A 'DLD_Rep' packet from the BS with D's location is replied to S. Then S goes to RD step in which S selects a closest node to D among neighborhood nodes in NT as a next node to reach D. S inserts a pair of the node's MMSI (NMMSI) and DMMSI into RT. S sends an 'RD_Req' packet to the next node which relays the packet recursively just like S to reach D. The sequence of nodes contributing to relaying the 'RD_Req' packet to reach D is the route from S to D. The RD step is successfully finished when an 'RD_Rep' packet is returned to S from D through the reverse route found in above. Then S finally sends a message data to D through the route. Figure 3 shows a flowchart of AAR algorithm.

3 Simulation Results

3.1 Simulation Environment

We have evaluated the performance of AAR using QualNet 5.0 network simulator. Table 3 shows detailed simulation parameters.

Table 3. Simulation parameters

Parameter	Value
Number of Node	20, 40, 60(ea)
Simulation time	5000(s)
Items to send	200, 400, 600
Item Size	256, 512(bytes)
Sending Interval	5, 10, 15, 20, 25(s)
Start Time	1(s)
End Time	3000(s)
Physical/Mac Layer	802.11b
Routing Protocol	AAR, AODV, LAR1
Applications	CBR
Number of Applications	1, 3, 5

Five simulation scenarios have been performed with 20 nodes, 200 packets, 512 bytes, one of CBR and five different packet sending intervals. Each scenario was tested 100 times with seven randomly chosen seeds. The final results shown in this paper are the average of the simulated values. Fig. 4 shows one of scenarios simulated by QualNet. Node 1 is BS. Node 11 and 15 are source and destination, respectively.

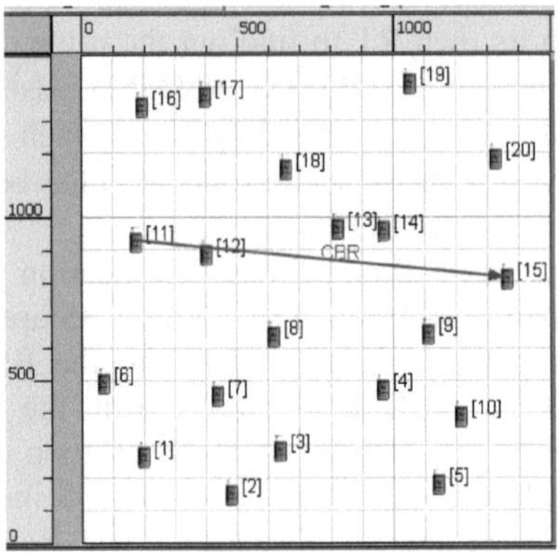

Fig. 4. A deployment model

3.2 Simulation Results

AODV and LAR are also evaluated and compared with AAR. Figure 5, 6 and 7 depict their performance in terms of end-to-end delay, packet loss rate, and throughput, respectively.

In case of AODV, source nodes flood 'RouteRequest' packets to the network until reaching destination nodes which cause heavy control overheads. Therefore AODV has the lowest performance relatively.

In LAR1, source nodes use location information and calculate 'request zone' to minimize immediate nodes. In conclusion, source nodes flood just within the request zone to discover routes to destination nodes. As LAR1 tries to make control overheads lower thought 'request zone' concept, it shows higher performance than AODV. In AAR, nodes send packets to a nearest next node to reach destination node, so the control overheads can be minimized. AAR shows higher performance than two well-known protocols in not only lightly but also heavily loaded network environments. The end-to-end delay is got better as 53% of LAR1 and 8% of ADOV on average. The packet loss ratio is improved as 39% of LAR1 and 4% of AODV. The throughput of AAR is slightly better than that of LAR1, but becomes much better than AODV (14%).

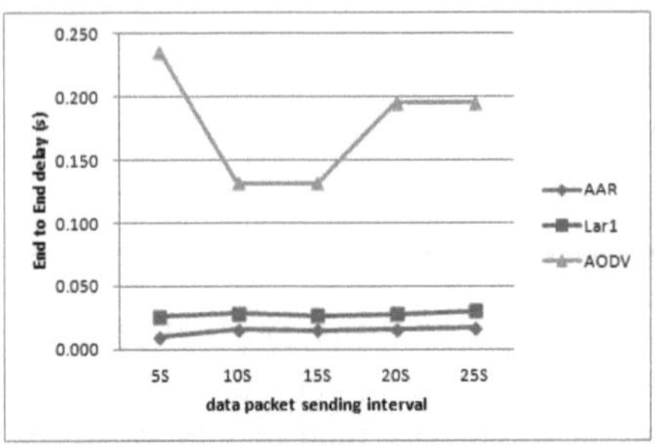

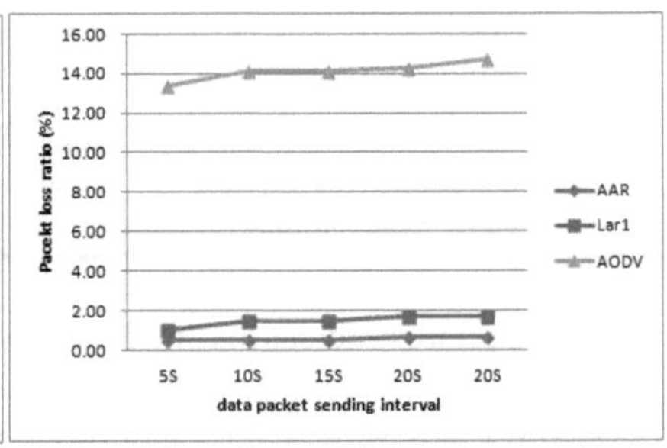

Fig. 5. End to End Delay

Fig. 6. Packet loss ratio

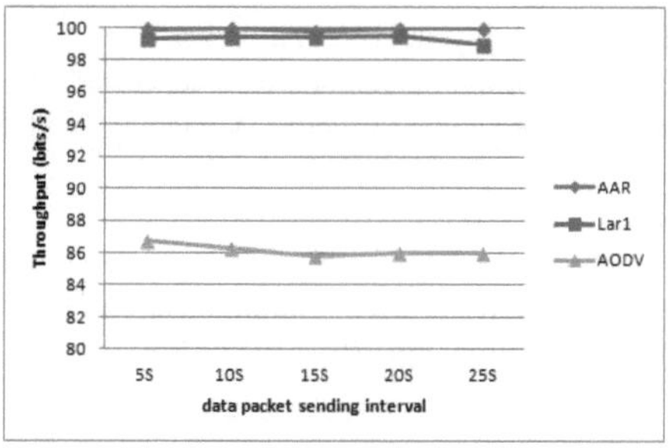

Fig. 7. Throughput

4 Conclusion

We have proposed an AIS-based ad-hoc network model and AAR routing protocol for vessels based on the network model [9]. In this model, a novel VNS service by BS is defined and used in AAR protocol. AAR protocol basically adopts the AIS systems. Thanks to ad-hoc manner, the communication range can be significantly enlarged proportional to the number of hops. In this paper, we have presented the simulated results by QualNet which show that AAR gives higher throughput and also sends packets with much lower end-to-end delay and packet loss ratio than AODV and LAR1.

References

1. Mun, S.M., Jang, W.S., Yang, G.S., Son, J.Y.: Development of A 4S Multiple Media Switching Server and An Information Exchange System. In: Proceedings of the International Symposium on Marine Engineering & Technology, Busan, Korea, October 25-28, pp. 307–308 (2011)
2. Jung, J.S., Kim, S.Y.: A Design of Communication Network Architecture for E-Navigation Services. Journal of Navigation and Port Research 32(1), 37–45 (2008)
3. Mun, S.M., Son, J.Y., Jo, W.R., Lee, W.B.: An Implementation of AIS-based Ad hoc Routing(AAR) Protocol for Maritime Data Communication Networks. In: The 2012 8th International Conference on Natural Computation, Chongqing, China, May 29-31, pp. 1014–1017 (2012)
4. Son, J.Y., Mun, S.M.: Max-Win based Routing (MWR) Protocol for Maritime Communication Networks with Multiple Wireless Media. Journal of the Korean Society of Marine Engineering 34(8), 1159–1164 (2010)
5. Son, J.Y.: A Routing Scheme by Normalized Transmission Characteristics (NTCR) for Multi-Carrier MANETs at Sea. Journal of the Korean Society of Marine Engineering 35(8), 1092–1097 (2010)
6. Son, J.Y.: A Carrier Preference-based Routing Scheme (CPR) for Multi-Layered Maritime Data Communications Networks. Journal of the Korean Society of Marine Engineering 35(8), 1098–1104 (2011)

7. Ta, T.D., Tran, T.D., Do, D.D., Nguyen, H.V., Vu, Y.V., Tran, N.X.: GPS-based Wireless Ad-hoc Network for Marine Monitoring, Search and Rescue(MSnR). In: Proceeding of IEEE 2nd International Conference on Intelligent Systems, Modelling, and Simulation, pp. 350–354 (2011)
8. IMO SOLAS Ch.V, Reg.19.2.4 (2009)
9. Mun, S.M., Son, J.Y., Jo, W.R., Lee, W.B.: An Implementation of AIS-based Ad hoc Routing(AAR) Protocol for Maritime Data Communication Network. In: 8th International Conference on Natural Computation, pp. 1014–1017 (2012)

Multimodal Biometric Systems and Its Application in Smart TV

Yeong Gon Kim[1], Kwang Yong Shin[1], Won Oh Lee[1], Kang Ryoung Park[1,*], Eui Chul Lee[2], CheonIn Oh[3], and HanKyu Lee[3]

[1] Division of Electronics and Electrical Engineering, Dongguk University, Seoul, Republic of Korea
csokyg@gmail.com, skyandla@dongguk.edu, 215p8@daum.net, parkgr@dongguk.edu

[2] Division of Computer Science, Sangmyung University, Seoul, Republic of Korea
eclee@smu.ac.kr

[3] Electronics and Telecommunications Research Institute (ETRI), Daejeon, Republic of Korea
{cioh,hkl}@etri.re.kr

Abstract. Biometrics has become as one of the most promising technologies over the last few decades. This technique uses a person's physiological or behavioral characteristics (such as fingerprint, face, iris or voice) to identify an individual. Many researches show that multimodal biometric techniques which combine more than two biometric technologies provides better performance than unimodal one since they use two or more physiological or behavioral characteristics. Therefore, the multimodal biometrics has vividly researched recently. In this paper, we provide a review of multimodal biometric techniques. In addition, we discuss fusion of biometrics and various fusion scenarios that are feasible in multimodal biometric systems. Experimental results showed that the multimodal biometric system based on face and both irises outperformed compared to the unimodal biometric system. Finally, we discuss about some applications for smart TV environment based on multimodal biometric technologies.

Keywords: Multimodal biometrics, Fusion of biometrics, Smart TV.

1 Introduction

Biometrics is a technique for identification of an individual by his or her physiological or behavioral characteristics such as face, fingerprint, iris, voice, vein, ear and gait recognition, etc. Most unimodal biometric systems have a variety of problems such as noisy data, intra-class variations, non-universality or spoof attacks [1]. As a typical example of biometrics, face recognition is a technique which identifies individuals based on their unique facial characteristics. Unlike many other recognition methods such as fingerprint, palm print and finger-vein recognition, they do not need to require an individual to directly contact with the sensor in order for recognition. Therefore, it can

* Corresponding author.

T.-h. Kim et al. (Eds.): EL/DTA/UNESST 2012, CCIS 352, pp. 219–226, 2012.

easily facilitate the use of face recognition in surveillance or automatic recognition with high convenience. However, a face needs to be well lighted by controlled light sources in face recognition system. In addition, various facial poses and expressions should be also considered because these factors cause performance degradation of face recognition. Although iris recognition is regarded as the most accurate and reliable biometric system, it is more expensive than some other biometric systems and conventional authentication systems such as password, smart card. In addition, iris recognition is susceptible to poor image quality which is affected by dense eyelash, eyelid occlusion, large specular reflections on glasses surface, or defocusing. One of the methods to overcome these limitations is to utilize multimodal biometrics, which combines two or more human physiological or behavioral traits. Many studies have been presented that multimodal biometric systems can provide better performance compared to unimodal biometric systems [2, 3]. Therefore, multimodal biometrics has been indispensable in the future trend of biometric technology. In this paper, we provide a review of multimodal biometric techniques. In addition, we discuss fusion of biometrics and various fusion scenarios that are feasible in multimodal biometric systems. We aim at representing the latest advances that resolve common problems associated with unimodal biometrics. In addition, we discuss about some applications for smart TV environment based on multimodal biometric technologies. The remainder of the paper is organized as follows. Section 2 explains the fusion of multimodal biometrics. Section 3 introduces previous researches on multimodal biometrics. In addition, conventional multimodal biometric systems are introduced in section 4. Some applications in smart TV based on multimodal biometrics are explained in section 5. Finally, section 6 gives conclusions.

2 Multimodal Biometric Fusion

There are many possible multimodal biometric systems (face with fingerprint, fingerprint with iris, iris with fingervein, etc) depending on the number of traits, sensors, and feature sets. In general, multimodal biometric systems can be designed by four ways [3].

(1) Single biometric trait, multiple sensors: the same trait can be obtained from different sensors (e.g. visible and infrared faces), and combined or fused to improve the performance. This can reduce the problem of noisy data, but there are still other potential problems of unimodal biometric systems.

(2) Single biometric trait, multiple representations: the same trait is obtained by a single sensor. Depending on feature extraction and matching methods, the obtained data are combined to improve the performance (appearance and shape based methods).

(3) Single biometric trait, multiple units: different units in the same trait are used to improve the performance (e.g. left and right irises). In case of fingerprint, it is possible to integrate information presented by two or more fingers of the same person. A multimodal biometric system based on this scheme can detect live and fake biometric traits by asking a user to randomly provide a subset of biometric measurements (e.g. left middle finger after right ring finger).

(4) Multiple biometric traits: multiple biometric traits of an individual can be obtained and fused to improve the performance (e.g. face and iris).

Since the above three cases (1), (2), and (3) uses single biometric trait (although left and right irises can be regarded as different trait [12]), they have some problems of unimodal biometric systems. On the other hand, a multimodal biometric system based on multiple traits is expected to be more robust to noise, solve the problem of non-universality, improve the overall accuracy, and prevent from spoof attacks [4]. For this reason, many researchers have employed this scheme. In this paper, we mainly discuss multimodal biometrics on the basis of multiple biometric traits.

The important problem of multimodal biometrics is how to fuse multiple features from each sensor to achieve high accuracy. Many algorithms and researches have been studied related to multimodal biometric fusion. Generally, the fusion of information can be performed at different levels: feature level, matching score level and decision level [2].

- Fusion at the feature extraction level: Feature sets are obtained from each sensor in which each feature set is used as a vector. Then the vectors are fused or combined to form a unique feature vector. By using this combined feature vector, matching and final decision are done.
- Fusion at the matching score level: Matching score which indicates the similarities between the feature vector and template vector. It is used for combining matching scores generated by each sensor and final decision is done.
- Fusion at the decision level: The resulting feature vectors obtained from each sensor are used for matching, and two results (accept or reject) of each sensor are combined. A final decision is determined by conventional rules (AND, OR rules).

Fusion at the feature extraction level is expected to provide better performance since the feature set contains more key information about the input biometrics data than the final decision of a matcher. However, fusion at this level has difficulties to apply in practice due to the following reasons. The feature sets of each modality may be incompatible (e.g. real values of eigen-coefficients of face, and binary codes of iris). Most commercial biometric systems do not provide the feature sets which are used in their systems publicly. Therefore, among the above mentioned techniques, fusion at the matching score level is preferred because of the ease in accessing and combining the scores by different matchers such as face and iris recognition systems [2].

In a multimodal biometric system, a variety of schemes can be used according to methods of acquiring traits, features extraction and classification. Since the matching scores obtained from each modality can be calculated by different methods, score normalization is required to change these scores into those of common domain before fusion or combination. There are many methods to normalize the matching scores such as Min-max, Z-score, decimal scaling, median and MAD, tanh-estimators, etc [3].

In a multimodal biometric system, the normalized scores are combined and final decision is made, which is done by comparing the fused final score with a predetermined threshold. If the final score as similarity is greater than the threshold, a user is accepted as genuine. If not, he is rejected as imposter. Thus, since the final decision is made by the final score, fusion technique is also important. There have been many studies related to fusion schemes to combine the scores generated by different matchers. These include MIN, MAX, SUM, Weighted SUM, PRODUCT, k-NN classifiers, support vector machines (SVMs), decision trees, and Bayesian methods, etc [2], [4].

3 Previous Researches on Multimodal Biometrics

In this section, we introduce previous multimodal biometrics researches. The methodologies of multimodal biometrics are reviewed. A person authentication system using two features, fingerprint and finger vein, is presented by Nguyen *et al.* [5]. They proposed a capturing device which acquires fingerprint and finger vein images simultaneously. The matching scores of the fingerprint and finger vein recognition are combined based on a SVM. The experimental results show that the overall accuracy of the proposed system is 99.5% and its usability is comparable to that of the fingerprint and finger vein sensors. Wang *et al.* proposed a multimodal biometric system using face and iris features [6]. The face and iris features are extracted respectively, and fused in feature level. The extracted features are normalized using z-score model and combined by feature level fusion based on series rule. They performed experiments on CASIA iris database and two face database (ORL database and Yale database). The experimental results show that the proposed algorithm outperforms fusions by sum rule and weighted sum rule.

Liau and Isa proposed a face-iris multimodal biometric system based on fusion at the matching score level using SVM [7]. To improve the performance of individual face recognition and iris recognition, a feature selection method is suggested by removing the redundant and irrelevant information which are included in each feature. The results show that an optimal subset of feature sufficiently describes iris and face images by removing redundant and irrelevant features with improving the performance. Darwish *et al.* describe a multimodal biometric authentication based on the face and ear recognition [8]. The proposed system used the extracted face and ear images to form the respective feature spaces based on PCA algorithm. The experimental results show better results than individual face or ear recognition. The proposed system obtained an accuracy of 92.24% with FAR of 10% and FRR of 6.1%. Raghavendra *et al.* proposed a multimodal biometric system comprised of face and palmprint recognition [9]. They used different fusion schemes at matching score level and feature level. This scheme showed to be more efficient compared with other fusion schemes. The experimental results show the performance improvement of 6%. A multimodal biometric system using iris and periocular information is presented by Woodard *et al.* [10]. The proposed system combined iris and periocular texture. The periocular texture is extracted from the region of the skin surrounding the eye. The experimental results demonstrate that valuable information is contained in the periocular region and it can be fused with iris texture to improve the accuracy. Tong *et al.* developed score-level multimodal fusion algorithms based on predictive quality metrics and employed them for the fusion of face and fingerprint recognition [11].

They modeled the relation in context of fusion scenario by Bayesian Networks. The decision for recognition is done by probabilistic inference. The experimental results show that the proposed methods provide better performance than that of face or fingerprint recognition. In addition, the fusion scheme with both quality of face and fingerprint image achieves better performance and outperforms other fusion methods.

To overcome the limitation of single biometric system, Kim *et al.* proposed multimodal biometric system based on the face and both irises' recognition by using a SVM [13]. The experimental results showed that the multimodal biometric system outperformed compared to unimodal biometric systems as shown in Table 1.

Table 1. Accuracy of the unimodal and multimodal biometric systems (unit: [%]) [13]

	Face	Left iris	Right iris	Face and both irises
EER	4.527	3.965	3.289	0.131

4 Conventional Multimodal Biometric Systems

Many of multimodal biometric systems are currently available. This section lists the latest multimodal biometric systems that are used in many applications [14-19]. IrisAccess 7000 provides a multi-factor verification solution based on the iris, and smart card or PIN [14]. D-station produced by Suprema is a multimodal biometric system which is on the basis of the fusion of face recognition and fingerprint recognition. D-station, equipped with two fingerprint sensors and a camera for face recognition, offers various recognition modes according to user's setting. [15]. HIIDE Series 4 is the world's first hand-held tri-biometric system that is a portable multimodal biometric system integrating face, iris and fingerprint [16]. Guardian R Jump Kit provides compact and accurate mobile solution for capturing and transmitting forensic-quality digital fingerprints, images of face and iris [17]. This system is optimized for usage in harsh, remote or hostile environments. A multimodal biometric system combined the face, iris, and fingerprint, SEEK II is designed for rugged field use, making it easy and quick for military, border control to identify subjects and verify their identities in the field [17]. DSVII-PA is a handheld device designed to provide ID verification and passport authentication based on facial, fingerprint, and iris biometrics [18]. BioTRAC is also a hand-held type of multimodal biometric system on the basis of face, iris, fingerprints, voice, and signature [19].

5 Applications in Smart TV

With the rapid development of intelligent TV, Smart TV can provide the various functionalities such as TV broadcasting, web-surfing, social network service (SNS), teleconference, video-on-demand (VOD), television-commerce (T-commerce), and T-banking, etc. Recently, with the interest of Smart TV, the application of Smart TV has been diversified for users' convenience. Many commercialized Smart TVs includes a built-in camera to provide intelligent services and higher convenience to users.

Especially, user identification on Smart TV is required for the service of T-commerce and T-banking. Recently, in order to prevent young children from watching the TV for long time, the monitoring system based on user identification is used in the smart TV. In addition, in order to measure the effect of advertisement on TV, automatic user identification and gaze detection based on the camera are considered instead of the conventional device of people meter which should be manually operated. There are some researches using face recognition in TV environment [20-22]. In the researches [20, 21], they use the face recognition for providing the user adaptive service. Ernst *et al.* use the techniques of recognitions of face, expression, gender and head pose in order to measure the effect of the advertisement on TV [22].

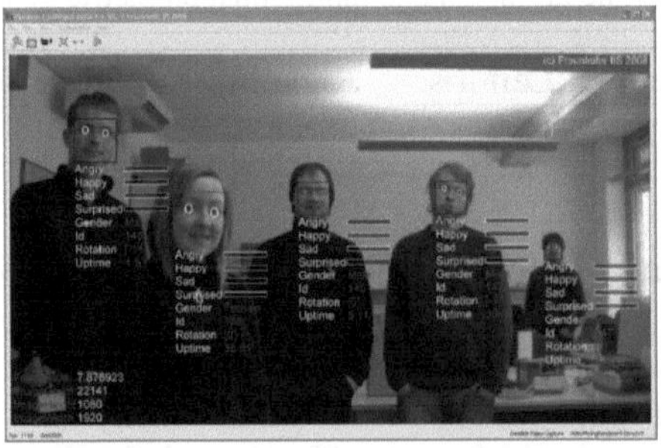

Fig. 1. Example of recognition of facial expression, gender, user ID, and head pose [22]

However, there are the limitations in their systems to be applied to higher security applications (e.g. T-commerce and T-banking, etc) in the TV environment. That is because a user can have various facial pose and expression, and illumination variations can happen on the user's face while watching TV as shown in Fig. 2. And, the performance of face recognition is inevitably degraded by these factors.

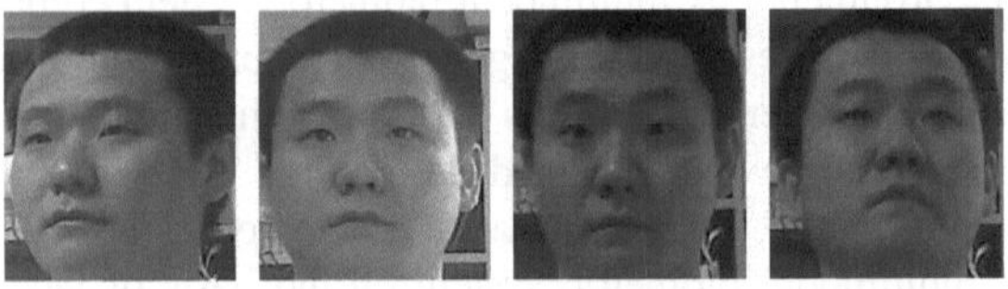

Fig. 2. Examples of captured face images by the camera in Smart TV environment

To overcome these problems, multimodal biometrics combining face and iris recognition can be considered. However, it has the difficulty to be used in TV watching environment because of its size and cost as shown in Fig. 3 [23, 24].

(a) (b)

Fig. 3. Examples of conventional iris recognition systems at a distance. a) InSight^{TM} VM [23]. b) Iris on the Move [24].

So, other techniques can be considered for the multimodal biometric system by using the remote controller which includes a fingerprint, finger-vein scanner or microphone. Based on them, fingerprint (or finger-vein) and speaker recognition can be combined with the face recognition by the camera of TV. However, there are still the issues of reducing the size of fingerprint (or finger-vein) sensor in order to apply them to the conventional remote controller. In case of the speaker recognition, the problem of reducing the environment noises should be also solved in noisy TV environment as future work.

6 Conclusions

Multimodal biometric systems have more advantages than unimodal biometric systems. Existing problems of unimodal biometrics like noisy data, non-universality or spoofing attack can be solved effectively in the multimodal biometric systems. Furthermore, efficient fusion and normalization methods are helpful to further enhance the accuracy of multimodal biometric systems. Although multimodal biometric systems have also some disadvantages such as cost, complexity and processing time, it is expected that multimodal biometrics would be one of the future trend of biometric technology. In addition, it can be used in Smart TV for the application of high security.

Acknowledgments. This research was supported by the Korea Communications Commission (KCC), Korea, under the title of "Development of Beyond Smart TV Technology"(11921-03001).

References

1. Jain, A.K., Ross, A.: Multibiometric systems. Commun. ACM 47, 34–40 (2004)
2. Ross, A., Jain, A.K.: Information fusion in biometrics. Pattern Recognit. Lett. 24, 2115–2125 (2003)
3. Ross, A., Jain, A.K.: Multimodal biometrics: an overview. In: Proceedings of Proc. XII European Signal Processing Conference, pp. 1221–1224 (September 2004)

4. Jain, A.K., Nandakumar, K., Ross, A.: Score normalization in multimodal biometric systems. Pattern Recogn. 38, 2270–2285 (2005)
5. Nguyen, D.T., Park, Y.H., Lee, H.C., Shin, K.Y., Kang, B.J., Park, K.R.: Adv. Sci. Lett. 5, 85–95 (January 2012)
6. Wang, Z., Wang, E., Wang, S., Ding, Q.: Multimodal biometric system using face-iris fusion feature. J. Comput. 6, 931–938 (2011)
7. Liau, H.F., Isa, D.: Feature selection for support vector machine-based face-iris multimodal biometric system. Expert Syst. Appls. 38, 11105–11111 (2011)
8. Darwish, A.A., Abd Elghafar, R., Fawzi Ali, A.: Multimodal face and ear images. J. Comput. Sci. 5, 374–379 (2009)
9. Raghavendra, R., Dorizzi, B., Rao, A., Kumar, G.H.: Designing efficient fusion schemes for multimodal biometric systems using face and palmprint. Pattern Recognit. 44, 1076–1088 (2011)
10. Woodard, D.L., Pundlik, S., Miller, P., Jillela, R., Ross, A.: On the fusion of periocular and iris biometrics in non-ideal imagery. In: Proceedings of the International Conference on Pattern Recognition, pp. 201–204 (August 2010)
11. Tong, Y., Wheeler, F.W., Liu, X.: Improving biometric identification through quality-based face and fingerprint biometric fusion. In: Proceedings of IEEE Computer Society Conference on Computer Vision and Pattern Recognition Workshops, pp. 53–60 (June 2010)
12. Daugman, J.: How iris recognition works. IEEE Trans. Circuits Syst. Video Technol. 14, 21–30 (2004)
13. Kim, Y.G., Shin, K.Y., Lee, E.C., Park, K.R.: Multimodal biometric system based on the recognition of face and both irises. Int. J. Adv. Robot. Syst. 9, 65–70 (2012)
14. IrisAccess 7000, http://irisid.com/irisaccess7000
15. D-station, http://www.supremainc.com/eng/bbs/bbs/download.php?bbs_code=10022&bbs_cate=1&filename=D-Station Brochure(e)_100712.pdf&file_no=340
16. HIIDE Series 4, http://l1id.com/files/224-HIIDE_0908_final.pdf
17. Guardian R jump kit and SEEK II, http://www.crossmatch.com
18. DSVII-PA, http://www.datastripsystems.com/images/b_new/sell_sheets/Sell_Sheet_DSVIIPA.pdf
19. BioTRAC, http://www.is.northropgrumman.com/products/biotrac/assets/BioTRAC.pdf
20. An, K.H., Chung, M.J.: Cognitive face analysis system for future interactive TV. IEEE Trans. Consumer Electron. 55(4), 2271–2279 (2009)
21. Hwang, M.-C., Ha, L.T., Kim, N.-H., Park, C.-S.: Person identification system for future digital TV with intelligence. IEEE Trans. Consumer Electron 53(1), 218–226 (2007)
22. Ernst, A., Ruf, T., Kueblbeck, C.: A modular framework to detect and analyze faces for audience measurement systems. In: Proceedings of the 2nd Workshop on Pervasive Advertising, Lubeck, Germany (2009)
23. InSight^{TM} VM, http://www.aoptix.com/assets/docs/resources/AO_InSight_VM.pdf
24. Matey, J., Hanna, K., Kolcyznski, R., LoIacono, D., Mangru, S., Naroditsky, O., Tinker, M., Zappia, T., Zhao, W.-Y.: Iris on the Move: Acquisition of Images for Iris Recognition in Less Constrained Environments. Proc. IEEE 94, 1936–1947 (2006)

Selective Removal of Impulse Noise Preserving Edge Information

Young-Man Kwon and Myung-jae Lim*

Department of Medical IT and Marketing, Eulji University,
553, Sanseong-daero, Sujeong-gu, Seongnam-si, Gyeonggi-do, 461-713, Korea
{ymkwon,lk04}@eulji.ac.kr

Abstract. In this paper, we proposed the efficient method of removing impulse noise preserving edge information. This method do its job for the pixel which is identified as impulse noise using mean shift segmentation instead of all pixel of image by the existing method. We found that impulse noise was cleaned efficiently by the proposed algorithm and the quality of image was improved by measuring PSNR in result image.

Keywords: Impulse noise, Median filter, Mean shift, Clustering, Edge Information, Segmentation.

1 Introduction

Impulse noise can be caused by sharp, sudden disturbances in the image signal. Its appearance is randomly scattered white or black (or both) pixels over image. this noise is also called shot noise, or binary noise, salt and pepper noise.

Median filter is a nonlinear filtering technique widely used for removal impulse noise. Despite its effectiveness in smoothing noise, the median filter tends to remove fine details when it is applied to an image uniformly [1, 2]. So as to overcome this drawback, several methods have attempted [3, 4, 5].

In this paper, we proposed the new algorithm to remove the impulse noise. But it preserves the detail edge information so that the image looks like the original image with a little noise. We applied the median filter on the identified pixels that are corrupted. That is, we did decision-based median filtering. We used the mean shift segmentation algorithm for decision.

2 Related Works

There are many methods such as low pass filtering, median filtering, rank order filtering, outlier removal filtering, and morphological filtering to get rid of impulse noise.

* Corresponding author.

T.-h. Kim et al. (Eds.): EL/DTA/UNESST 2012, CCIS 352, pp. 227–232, 2012.

2.1 Median Filter

A number of modified median filtering have been proposed, minimum-maximum exclusive mean(MMEM) filter, pre-scanned minmax center-weighted(PMCW) filter, decision-based median filters, conditional signal-adaptive median(CSAM) filter [4].

In the MMEM method, pixels that have values close to the maximum and minimum in a filter window are discarded, and the average e_w of remaining pixels in the window are computed. If the difference between the center pixel and e_w exceeds a threshold, the center pixel is replaced by e_w; Otherwise, unchanged.

In the decision-based filtering, image pixels are first classified as corrupted and uncorrupted, and then passed through the median and identity filters, respectively. The main issue of the decision-based filter lies in building a decision rule, or a noise measure, that can discriminate the uncorrupted pixels from the corrupted ones as precisely as possible.

2.2 Overview of Mean Shift

Mean shift avoid estimation of the probability density function. In image processing, the feature space consists of quantitative image properties, which are mapped into a point in a multi-dimensional space of image description parameters. Once the mapping of all image points is completed, the feature space is more densely populated in locations corresponding to the significant image features. These denser regions of the multi-dimensional feature space form clusters. In the image segmentation context, this may correspond to the individual image object and background [6, 7].

The only free parameters of mean shift are the size and shape of the region of interest. More precisely speaking, this is the identification of multivariate density kernel estimator. In this paper, we have used the Epanechnikov kernel. It is defined as follows.

$$K_E(x) = \begin{cases} c\left(1 - \|x\|^2\right) & if \|x\| \le 1 \\ 0 & otherwise \end{cases}$$

The kernel profile $K_E(x)$ of which is given by

$$K_E(x) = \begin{cases} 1 - x & for\, 0 \le x \le 1 \\ 0 & for\, x > 1 \end{cases}$$

The guaranteed convergence of the mean shift to the local maximum of a probability density function is density mode. It is obtained due to the adaptive magnitude of the mean shift vector (the mean shift vector magnitude converges to zero). Mean shift mode detection algorithm is as follows.

(1) Using multiple initializations covering the entire feature space, employ the mean shift procedure to identify the stationary points of $\hat{f}_{h,K}$

(2) Prune these points to only retain the local maxima corresponding to the density modes.

The mean shift image segmentation consists of 2 main steps - discontinuity preserving filtering and mean shift clustering. Let pixels in the original d-dimensional image be denoted by x_i and pixels of the filtered image by z_i, these pixels being represented in the joint spatial-range domain.). Mean shift discontinuity preserving filtering algorithm is as follows.

(1) For each image pixel x_i, initialize step $j = 1 \, and \; y_{i,1} = x_i$

(2) Compute $y_{i,j+1}$ as the successive locations of the kernel *G* until convergence $y_{i,con}$.

(3) The filtered pixel values are defined as $z_i = \left(x_i^s, y_{i,con}^r\right)$, i.e., the value of the filtered pixel at the location x_i^s is assigned the image value of the pixel of convergence $y_{i,con}$.

And Mean shift image segmentation algorithm is as follows.

(1) Employ the mean shift discontinuity preserving filtering and store all information about the d-dimensional convergence points $y_{i,con}$.

(2) Determine the clusters $\{C_p\}_{p=1,\ldots,m}$ by grouping all z_i, which are closer than h_s in the spatial domain and h_r in the range domain. In other words, merge the basins of attraction of these convergence points.

(3) Assign $L_i = \{p \mid z_i \in C_p\}$ for each pixel $i = 1,\ldots,n$.

(4) If desired, eliminate regions smaller than P pixels as small image region.

3 The Proposed Algorithm

In this paper, we proposed the algorithm such as Fig. 1. The first step is to do mean shift discontinuity preserving filtering. The second step is to determine clusters based on the result of the first step. We call these steps mean shift segmentation, which cluster image pixels so as to preserve the detail edge.

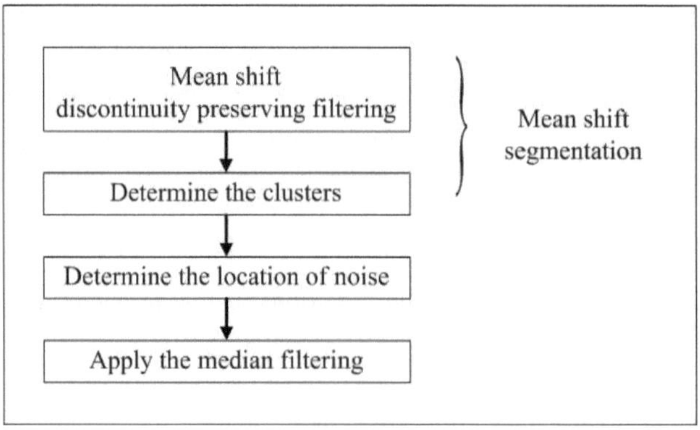

Fig. 1. The proposed algorithm

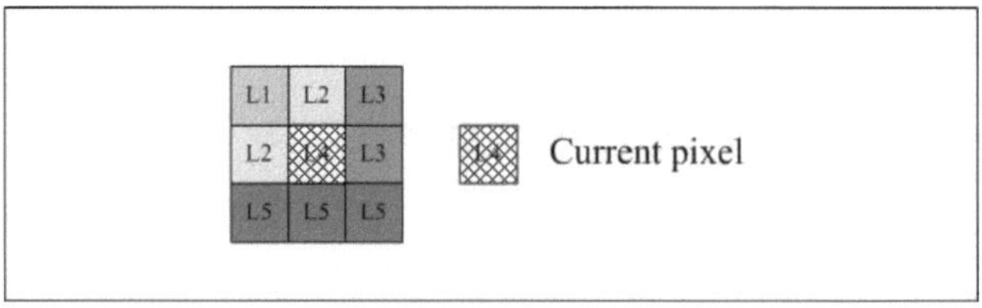

Fig. 2. The current pixel and its neighborhoods

The third step is to determine the location of impulse noise. For this, consider the 3x3 neighborhoods of the current pixel in Fig. 2. Each pixel has labels which is the result of step 2. If pixels belong to same cluster, they have the same label. We decide the current pixel as the location of the impulse noise if current pixel is isolated from 4-neighbor. That means 4-neighbor pixels of the current pixel must have different labels from the current pixel such as Fig. 2.

The 4-th step is very simple. We can apply the median filter for the location of the impulse noise.

4 Experiments and Analysis

The median filtering has done for all the pixel of image but the proposed algorithm has done for the location identified as impulse noise. For example, the original image and the 10 % impulse noise image appears in Fig. 3.

Fig. 3. The original image and 10% impulse noise image

The location of impulse noise by the proposed algorithm appears in Fig. 4.

Fig. 4. The location of impulse noise during 1-pass and 2-pass

The result of median filtering appears in Fig. 5.

Fig. 5. The result of median filtering during 1-pass and 2-pass

The result of proposed algorithm appears in Fig. 6.

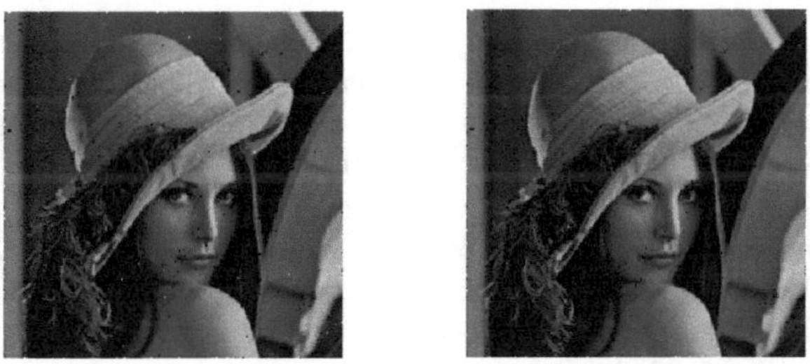

Fig. 6. The result of median filtering during 1-pass and 2-pass

Table 1. PSNR of result to degree of noise level

Noise Applied method		2 %	5 %	10 %	20 %
Median Filtering	1-pass	38.27 dB	37.92 dB	37.31 dB	36.50 dB
	2-pass	37.40 dB	37.20 dB	36.74 dB	36.20 dB
The proposed Algorithm	1-pass	47.06 dB	43.48 dB	40.59 dB	37.76 dB
	2-pass	46.62 dB	43.39 dB	40.54 dB	37.96 dB

We experimented the proposed algorithm for the image of 256x256 size to remove the impulse noise and compared the result with the result of pure median filtering algorithm. Experiments have been done for the case of 2%, 5%, 10%, 20% impulse noise and the result appears in Table 1. As performance measures, we used the peak signal-to-noise ratio (PSNR) defined as follows.

$$PSNR = 10\log_{10}\left(\frac{\sum_{n=1}^{N^2} 255^2}{\sum_{n=1}^{N^2} (\hat{p} - p)^2}\right)$$

Where N^2 is the total number of pixels in an image. In the case of all, we can find easily the proposed algorithm outperforms the median filters.

5 Conclusion

In this paper, we proposed the efficient algorithm of removing impulse noise by using the mean shift segmentation information. The result image preserved the edge information of original image than the result of median filtering. We confirmed this facts by calculating the square of error.

In the future, we have a plan to reduce the more noise still preserving the edge information of the image by analyzing the relationship with impulse noise and segmentation information. So as to achieve this goal, the more research is needed.

References

1. Gonzalez, W.: Digital Image Processing Using Matlab. Prentice Hall (2004)
2. McAndrew, A.: Introduction To Digital Image Processing with Matlab. Thomson (2004)
3. Hwang, H., Hadded, R.A.: Adaptive median filter: New algorithm and results. IEEE Transactions on Image Processing 35(4), 499–502 (1995)
4. Pok, G., Liu, J.-C., Nair, A.S.: Selectiev Removal of Impulse Noise Based on Homogeneity Level Information. IEEE Transactions on Image Processing 12(1), 85–92 (2003)
5. Chan, R.H., Ho, C.-W., Nikolova, M.: Salt-and-Pepper Noise Removal by Median-Type Noise Detectors and Detail-Preserving Regularization. IEEE Transactions on Image Processing 14(10), 85–92 (2005)
6. Comaniciu, D., Meer, P.: Mean Shift: A Robust Approach Toward Feature Space Analysis. IEEE Transactions on Pattern Analysis and Machine Intelligence 24(5), 603–619 (2002)
7. Sonka, M., Hlavac, V., Boyle, R.: Image processing, Analysis and Machine Vision. Thomson (2008)

High Speed LDPC Encoder Architecture for Digital Video Broadcasting Systems

Ji Won Jung and Gun Yeol Park

Department of Radio Communication Engineering, Korea Maritime University
727 Taejong-ro, Yeongdo-Gu, Busan 606-791, Korea
jwjung@hhu.ac.kr

Abstract. In this paper, we proposed high speed LDPC encoder architecture for DVB-S2 standard. The proposed LDPC encoding architecture is based on a parallel 360 bits-wise operations. The key issues for realizing high speed are using the two kinds of index addresses and make use of memories efficiently. We implemented a half rate LDPC encoder on an FPGA, and confirmed its maximum throughput is up to 10 Gbps on 100MHz clock.

1 Introduction

Low density parity check codes, first introduced by R.G Gallager[1] decades ago and rediscovered by Spielman, Mackay and many others, can achieve very good performance when decoded with the belief-propagation or the sum-product algorithm. The remarkable performance of LDPC codes has positioned them as strong candidates for forward-error-correction codes in many emerging digital communication system, such as DVB-S2 and IEEE 802.11n. In this paper, we focused on LDPC codes in DVB-S2 standards.

DVB-S2 is the first digital video broadcast standard in which LDPC codes are adopted as forward error correcting codes. In this standard, 21 variations of LDPC codes are defined by structured parity check matrices, of code length 16200 or 64800, and the code rate varies from 1/4 to 9/10. Some researchers have already reported their LDPC decoder for DVB-S2[2][3]. One of them also implemented an LDPC encoder. However, no mention is made about their hardware encoder architecture.

However, implementing LDPC codes in hardware is by no means a trivial task, even from the point of view of today's VLSI technology. Many authors have addressed this issue for both encoding and decoding of LDPC codes, e.g. structured LDPC is proposed to facilitate the hardware implementation with just subtle sacrifice of performance[5]. An efficient encoding method of DVB-S2 LDPC codes is presented in this paper. We show that encoding of DVB-S2 LDPC codes is very simple owing to the special property of the parity check matrices. It is done without reference to the code generation matrices. The memory requirement is only the length of the codewords and some addresses of index. In this paper, we discuss encoding architecture which achieves high speed, and easy operation.

T.-h. Kim et al. (Eds.): EL/DTA/UNESST 2012, CCIS 352, pp. 233–238, 2012.

2 Encoder Architecture

All codes are defined by structured parity check matrices which can be partitioned into two parts, such as information part and parity part. Parity part has staircase structure and information part has new column pattern which appears in every 360 columns. The following 359 columns are cyclic shifts of first column by q. Given a parity check matrix H, the goal of encoding is to computing the systematic codeword c from the input sequence k. Denote the input information sequence as $k = [k_0, k_1, \ldots k_{k_b-1}]$, and codeword sequence as

$N = [k_0, k_1, \ldots k_{k_b-1}, p_o, p_1, \ldots, p_{n_b-k_b-1}]$. Where, k_b, n_b are input bit length and coded bit length, respectively.

Information sequences are divided into q groups, i.e

$$k = [k_0, k_1, \ldots, k_{q-1}]. \tag{1}$$

Where, each element of k is a vector of length 360, i.e. $k_i = [k_{i,0}, k_{i,1}, \ldots, k_{i,359}]$.

The method presented above suggests an efficient circuit implementation, which is roughly described in Fig. 1.

The circular shift operation can be done with register, and messages, $k = [k_0, k_1, \ldots, k_{q-1}]$, shown in eqn. (1) are fed into the registers in sequentially and 360 bits parallel form. The register requirement is 360 bits for message.

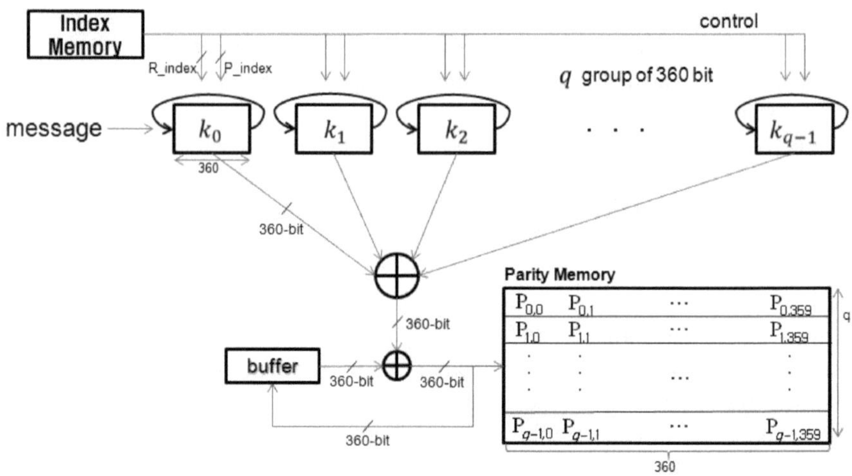

Fig. 1. Proposed encoder structure for DVB-S2 LDPC codes

Two kinds of address index are necessary for 360 bits parallel processing. *R_index* indicates d_c registers among the q registers and *P_index* indicates initial position within register. d_c means number of row weight. Fig. 2 shows index memory of half rate LDPC encoder. The depth of memory is q.

26	27	30	36	74
10	10	20	37	41
4	16	27	38	51
		⋮		
0	19	32	35	43

(a) *R_index* memory

60	101	293	0	179
310	299	74	0	206
329	346	42	0	222
		⋮		
62	144	2	0	199

(b) *P_index* memory

Fig. 2. Index memory structure

For example, we can see the values of the first row in *R_index* memory are " 26 27 30 36 74 " and *P_index* are " 60 101 293 0 179 ". It means that from the *26-th* to the *74-th* registers are read at the same time among the *q* group of register as shown Fig. 2, and from the *60-th* to the *179-th* are initial read points of each register of *R_index* memory. 360 bits operations are done in one cycle.

The parities are expressed by eqn.(2) and (3).

$$\sum_{i=0}^{359}\sum_{j=0}^{(dc-2)-1} \mathrm{K}_{R\_index[0,j],(P\_index[0,j]+i)\%360} = \mathrm{P}_{0,i} \qquad (0\text{-}th \text{ row}) \tag{2}$$

$$\sum_{i=0}^{359}\sum_{j=0}^{(dc-2)-1} \mathrm{K}_{R\_index[x,j],(P\_index[x,j]+i)\%360} \oplus \mathrm{P}_{x-1,i} = \mathrm{P}_{x,i} \qquad (X \neq 0\ th \text{ row}) \tag{3}$$

Index terms [*x*,*j*] denote *x-th* register pointer of among the *q* register and *j-th* position within *x-th* register.

As shown in eqn.(2) and eqn.(3), the 360 parities are can be solved simultaneously, and store those on parity memory with size of $q * 360$ bits.

After finishing the processing of eqn.(2) and eqn.(3), parities are stored on parity memory, last operations are must be done shown in eqn.(4).

$$P_{i,j} = P_{i,j} \oplus P_{i-1,j} (i = 1,\ldots,\ q-1,\ \ j = 0,\ldots,359) \tag{4}$$

However, in order to obtain the eqn.(4), required clocks are m_b clocks ($m_b = n_b - k_b$). The eqn.(4) terms are bottle neck point for implementing the high speed LDPC encoder. Therefore we proposed the other approach scheme for high speed LDPC encoder. As shown in parity memory of Fig. 2, in aspect to the last address of parity memory, $p_{q-1,0}, p_{q-1,1},\ldots, p_{q-1,359}$ can be easily obtained from eqn. (5)

$$P_{q-1,j} = p_{q-1,j} \quad if\, p_{q-1,j-1} == 0$$
$$P_{q-1,j} = p_{q-1,j} \quad else\ for\ j = 1\ to\ 359 \tag{5}$$

If $p_{q-1,0}$ equals 0, next parities $p_{i,1}(i = 0\ to\ q\text{-}1)$ are the same as existence memory value, however If $p_{q-1,0}$ equals 1, next parities $p_{i,1}(i = 0\ to\ q\text{-}1)$ are inverse the existence memory value. Therefore, expanding the above equation, the following equation hold:

$$\mathrm{P}_{q-1,k} = \mathrm{P}_{q-1,k} \oplus \mathrm{P}_{q-1,k-1},\ (k = 1 \sim 359) \tag{6}$$

Fig. 3 shows the operations of last address of parity memory as shown in eqn.(5). It needs 359 clocks for processing the eqn.(6)

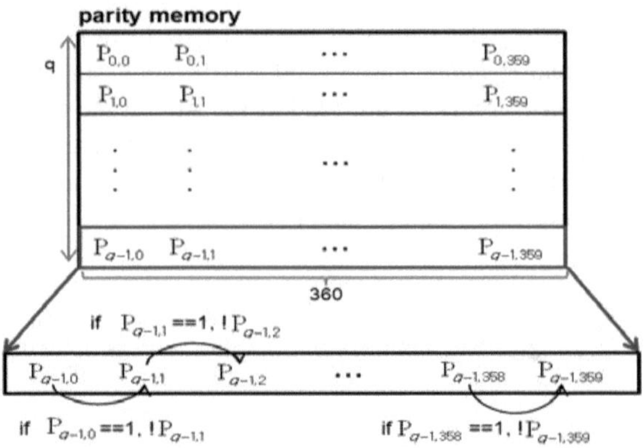

Fig. 3. The operations of last address of parity memory

After finishing operations of eqn.(5), we should recalculate the parities buffered in the first address to the *(q-2) th* address based on parities of last address. Eqn. (7) shows the last operations of LDPC encoder as shown in Fig. 4.

$$\mathrm{P}_{i,j} = \mathrm{P}_{i,j} \oplus \mathrm{P}_{q-1,j} \quad i = 0 \sim q-2,\ j = 1 \sim 359 \tag{7}$$

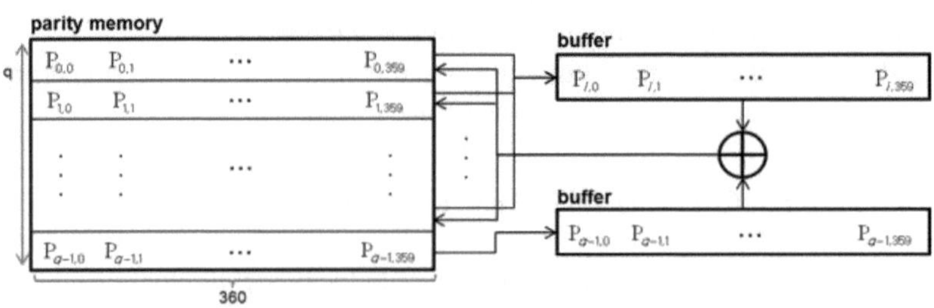

Fig. 4. The operations of the last encoding processing

3 Complexity

The memory requirement is $q * 360$ bits for message and another 360 bits for buffering the previous values. The complexity of the proposed LDPC encoder for DVB-S2 codes is summarized in Table 1.

Table 1. Complexity of the proposed LDPC encoder

Number of EXORs	1081
Number of registers with 360 bits	$q+1$
Number of memory	Parity memory : $q*360$ *R_index* memory : $q*35$ *P_index* memory : $q*45$

Two 360 bits EXORs operations are needed as shown in Fig. 1, and another two 360 bits EXORs operations are needed shown in Fig.4 and Fig. 5. The registers are used for pipelined data of 360 bits. We implemented this encoder circuit on an FPGA, Xilinx Vertex5-LX155T. The total delays are $(3q + 360 + \alpha)$ clocks and α is delay for memory read/write and minor operations.

4 Conclusions

In this paper, we proposed high speed LDPC encoder architecture for DVB-S2 standard. And the fact that the proposed encoder works on a single clock, and provides a parallel 360 bits-wise operations. We implemented half rate encoder circuit for DVB-S2 codes on an FPGA. The synthesis result shows that it occupies 36801 flip-flops and 90 register blocks with 360 bits and two RAMs for index memory, and works on 100MHz clock. We confirmed its maximum throughput is up to 10 Gbps.

Acknowledgments. This research was supported by the MKE(The Ministry of Knowledge Economy), Korea, under the ITRC(Information Technology Research Center) support program supervised by the NIPA(National IT Industry Promotion Agency)(NIPA-2012-H0301-12-2005).

References

1. Gallager, R.G.: Low-Density Parity-Check Codes. IRE Trans. Infom. Theory IT-8, 21–28 (1962)
2. Eroz, M., Sun, F.W., Lee, L.N.: DVB-S2 low density parity check codes with near Shannon limit performance. Int. J. Satell. Commun. Network 22(3), 269–279 (2004)
3. Urad, P., Yeo, E., Paumier, L., Georgelin, P., Michel, T., Lebars, V., Yeo, E., Gupta, B.: A 135Mb/s DVB-S2 Compliant CODEC based on 64800b LDPC and BCH Codes. In: Proc. ISSCC 2005, San Francisco, USA, pp. 446–447 (February 2005)

4. Kienle, F., Brack, T., Wehn, N.: A synthesizable IP core for DVB-S2 LDPC code decoding. In: Proc. Design, Automation and Test in Europe 2005, vol. 3, pp. 100–105 (March 2005)
5. Yokokawa, T., Nakane, M., Kan, M.: A Low Complexity and Programmable Encoder Architecture of the LDPC codes for DVB-S2. In: 3rd Turbo Coding Conference, Munich, Germany, (April 2006)

Estimation of the Vestibular-CNS Based on the Static Posture Balance: Vestibular-Central Nervous System

Jeong-lae Kim[1] and Kyu-sung Hwang[2,*]

[1] Department of Biomedical Engineering Eulji University, Seoul, Korea
[2] Department of Funeral Science Eulji University, Seoul, Korea
{jlkim,hks}@eulji.ac.kr

Abstract. To estimate vestibular-CNS system for vestibular nuclei that can stand a static state of body for a posture balance. It was necessary to develop physical parameters in the static posture and this system was considered of relation on the vestibular-CNS system and acquired of the body sway change. And there was based on the static position, thereby considered a vestibular mechanism. And then, there was a slight change in Vestibular and CNS. This showed a difference smaller at the exercising after than before in the vestibular. And, there presented a diminutive difference smaller at the exercising after than before in the CNS. In the future, this system will be express to an assessment for body balance in dynamic condition. We hope to a management a body movement and to control the sensory system.

Keywords: Vestibular-CNS system, Estimation, vestibular nuclei, body standing.

1 Introduction

As in the human ability to maintain balance depends on information from several body systems, interactions among which are controlled in the cerebellum. These systems include vestibular input[1]. Maintaining and controlling posture balance in static state requires correctly detecting the condition through peripheral sensory system, that is used the information provided by the vestibular system[2]. The afferent information must be processed and interpreted correctly by the central nervous system(CNS) through spinal and brainstem reflexes and higher order structures[3, 4]. For controlling human posture, one should know how well an intended motion has finally been achieved. A desired body state directs a controller within the CNS to generate motor commands that drive related functions in the body[5]. To control body postural balance, accelerations due to motion should be perceived. Eye and body movements, subjective vertical orientation, and motion sickness all depend on the way the human CNS deals with the gravito-inertial force resolution problem [6] .

In this study, co-relation of the vestibular-CNS system for vestibular nuclei based physical system was estimated to a physical signal in the static state. Physical

* Corresponding author.

T.-h. Kim et al. (Eds.): EL/DTA/UNESST 2012, CCIS 352, pp. 239–245, 2012.

parameters have body condition for the eye open and close. This system was used to establish the stability for the evaluation, prevention and treatment of the biomechanical information and to control data processing system.

2 Related Works

2.1 Basic Physical Condition

Static state from the body posture is decided a physical signal when there is movement of the center of weight to produce on each side of a on the balance plate. Balance was the center of mass to maintain over the base of support and to control the vestibular condition from physical condition. Limits of stability refers to the maximum angle from vertical that can be tolerated without a loss of balance[7]. The postural balance system consists of subsystems such as included the vestibular and CNS[8]. The parameter relies on vestibular condition of body balance relationships to measure physical condition. Physical compound flowchart collects to static state of the body and to experiment on the parameter as shown Figure 1.

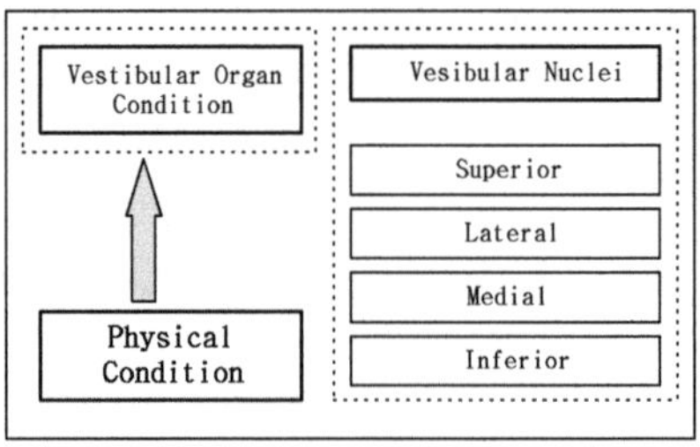

Fig. 1. Structure of Physical and Vestibular condition

2.2 Component of Vestibular Mechanism and Body Balance

The vestibular system relies on force of gravity and inertia. Within the vestibular are membranous sacs: utricle and saccule. Both saces are surrounded by perilymph and contain another fluid. The saccule is slightly smaller than the utricle. The end organ for balance within the utricle is located at the bottom. Arising from the utricle are the superior, lateral and posterior semicircular canals, which are membranous. In this way the fluids of vestibule are set into motion, which stimulates the vestibular mechanism[1]. Data analysis takes an account of a posture balance, and has the vestibular and central nervous condition from the static physical condition as shown Figure 2.

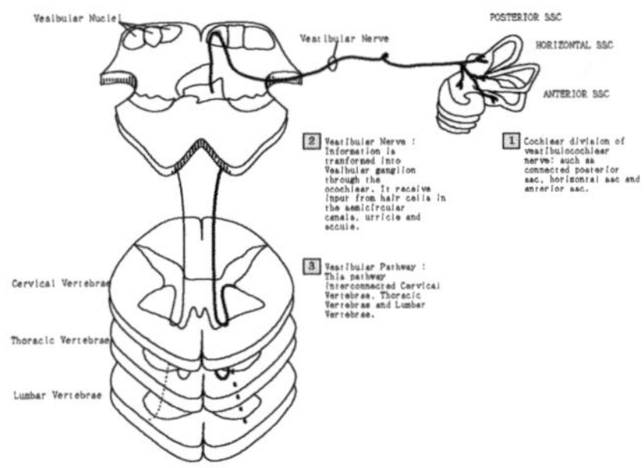

Fig. 2. Parameter of pathway vestibular mechanism for balance

3 System Design: Physical Control System

3.1 Preprocessing

The proposed physical control system mainly present the monitoring subjects that had a body sway and posture balance. There are normally showed the body condition is stable, while were assistance of body condition when the physiological condition becomes normal and stable.

3.2 System of Physical Control System

The architecture of the proposed system was depicted in Fig 3. System architecture of a Vestibular-CNS system presented physical signal for static state by the force platform. Data sheets acquired a data control system signal processing. The equipment was designed as data acquisition system(PXI-6251 DAQ) and Signal processing system(PXI-1409, NI., USA). Signal processing was used computer analysis from acquiring signal[9][10][11].

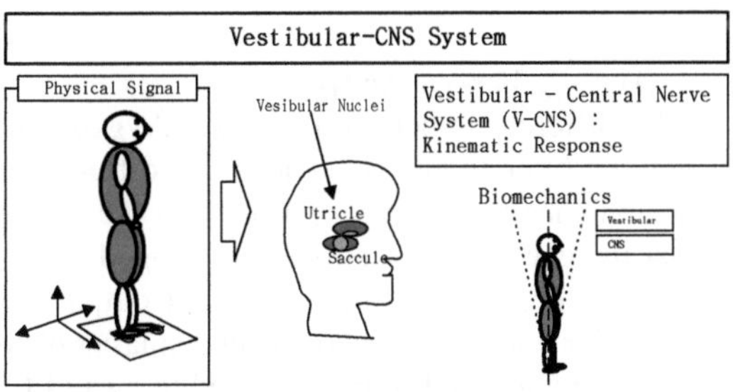

Fig. 3. System architecture of a Vestibular-CNS system presented physical signal for static state by the force platform. Data sheets acquired a data control system signal processing or etc.

4 Experimental Results

4.1 Experimental Results

The subsection gives a analysis for our proposed system, these parameters and condition are dependent on each other. In order to further understand how to use these parameters to design each parameter. Several data are performed and results are explained as follows.

Comparison of Ves-$_{ASP}$ Avg$_{BNO}$, Ves-$_{ASP}$ Avg$_{BNC}$

The more average of the differences between Ves-$_{ASP}$ Avg$_{BNO}$ and Ves-$_{ASP}$ Avg$_{BNC}$ observed with body moving before(Figure 4). The many differences of the vestibular parameter confirmed the balance for standing position on the eye open and eye close. The outcome shows that the eye close situation has changed more than the eye open situation of body moving before. The average different output Avg$_{BNO}$ and Avg$_{BNC}$ was 2.84±0.61. The vestibular condition was presented smaller different EC condition than EO condition. The vestibular condition confirmed to sway EC condition of body moving before. The vestibular function sustained to balance for the static state that identified the stability of body sway on the eye open.

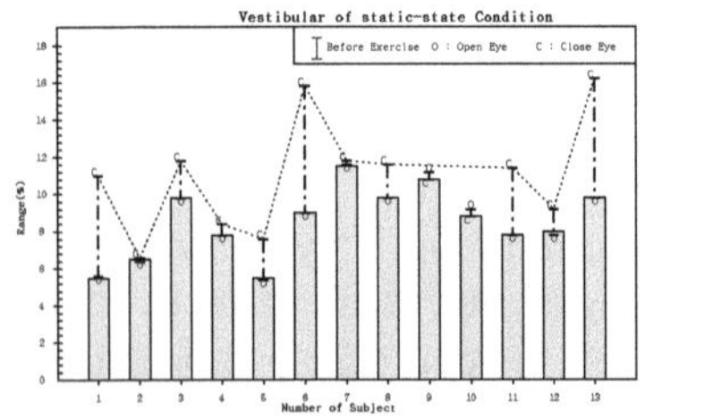

Fig. 4. Signal data of the static-state condition in the before movement (Vestibular condition of Stat-O & Stat-C)

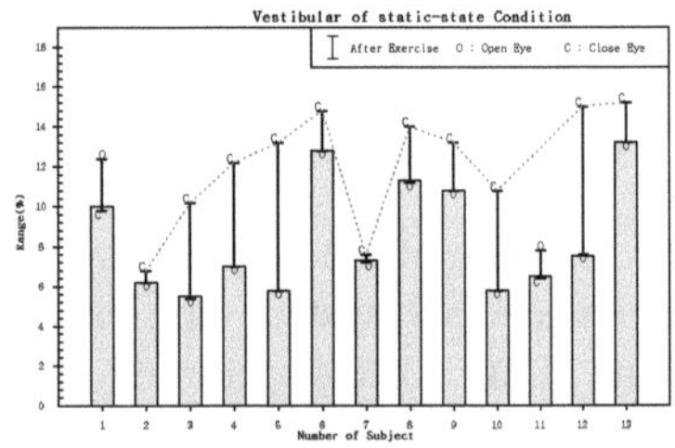

Fig. 5. Signal data of static-state condition in the after movement (Vestibular condition of Stat-O & Stat-C)

Comparison of Ves-$_{ASP}$ Avg$_{ANO}$, Ves-$_{ASP}$ Avg$_{ANC}$

The more average of the differences between Ves-$_{ASP}$ Avg$_{ANO}$ and Ves-$_{ASP}$ Avg$_{ANC}$ observed with body moving after(Figure 5). The many differences of the vestibular parameter confirmed the balance for standing position on the eye open and eye close. The outcome shows that the eye close situation has changed more than the eye open situation of body moving before. The average different output Avg$_{ANO}$ and Avg$_{ANC}$ was 1.88±0.18. The vestibular condition was presented smaller different EC condition than EO condition. The vestibular condition confirmed to sway EC condition of body moving before. The vestibular function sustained to balance for the static state that identified the stability of body sway on the eye open.

Comparison of CNS-$_{ASP}$ Avg$_{BNO}$, CNS-$_{ASP}$ Avg$_{BNC}$

The slightly smaller average of the differences between CNS-$_{ASP}$ Avg$_{BNO}$ and CNS-$_{ASP}$ Avg$_{BNC}$ observed with body moving before(Figure 6). The slightly smaller differences of the CNS parameter confirmed the balance for standing position on the eye open and eye close. The outcome shows that the eye close situation has changed more than the eye open situation of body moving before. The average different output Avg_{BNO} and Avg_{BNC} was 0.12±0.03. The CNS condition was presented slightly smaller different EC condition than EO condition. The CNS condition confirmed to sway EC condition of body moving before. The CNS function sustained to balance for the static state that identified the stability of body sway on the eye open.

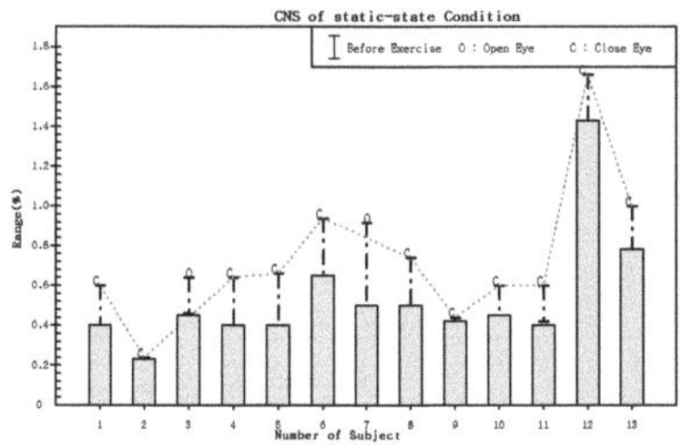

Fig. 6. Signal data of the static-state condition in the before movement (CNS condition of Stat-O & Stat-C)

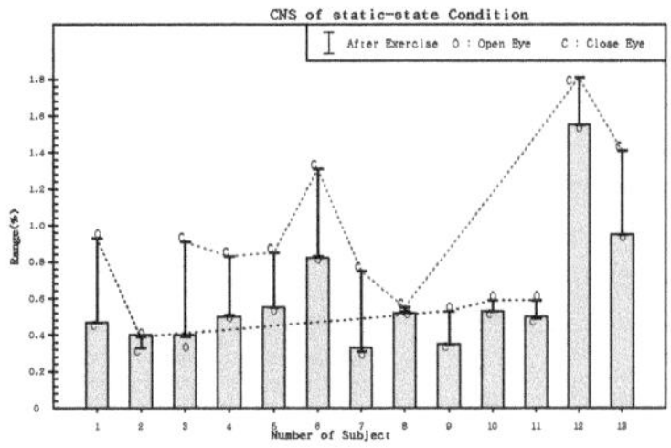

Fig. 7. Signal data of the static-state condition in the after movement (CNS condition of Stat-O & Stat-C)

Table 1. Average data for static posture balance : Vestibular($Ves\text{-}_{ASP}$), CNS($CNS\text{-}_{ASP}$). Presentation of body moving of before with eye open(NO) and after with eye close(NC) : Avg_{BNO} , Avg_{ANC}

Average	Avg_{BNO}	Avg_{BNC}	Avg_{ANO}	Avg_{ANC}
$Ves\text{-}_{ASP}$	8.2±2.21	11.04±2.82	9.51±3.36	11.39±3.18
$CNS\text{-}_{ASP}$	0.57±0.32	0.69±0.35	0.66±0.33	0.81±0.46

Comparison of $CNS\text{-}_{ASP}$ Avg_{ANO}, $CNS\text{-}_{ASP}$ Avg_{ANC}

The diminutive average of the differences between $CNS\text{-}_{ASP}$ Avg_{ANO} and $CNS\text{-}_{ASP}$ Avg_{ANC} observed with body moving after(Figure 7). The diminutive differences of the CNS parameter confirmed the balance for standing position on the eye open and eye close. The outcome shows that the eye close situation has changed more than the eye open situation of body moving after. The average different output Avg_{BNO} and Avg_{BNC} was 0.15±0.13. The CNS condition was presented tiny smaller different EC condition than EO condition. The CNS condition confirmed to sway EC condition of body moving after. The CNS function sustained to balance for the static state that identified the stability of body sway on the eye open.

4.2 Performance Evaluations

As shown in Fig. 8, the stability estimation presented a result of the static state by the eye open and eye close. On the posture balance showed a difference to the body condition such as moving after and before. The average difference resulted less on EC condition for body moving of after that was presented stable state. This shows stability part become small stable while closing the eyes. This result was a small change in moving after and before (Table 2).

Table 2. Average data of stability for static posture (Stab-$_{ASP}$) . Presentation of body moving of before with eye open(NO) and after with eye close(NC).(Average of Avg_{BNO}, Avg_{BNC}, Avg_{ANO}, Avg_{ANC})

Average	Avg_{BNO}	Avg_{BNC}	Avg_{ANO}	Avg_{ANC}
Stab-$_{ASP}$	18.08±10.61	23.95±13.15	20.63±12.42	19.93±12.42

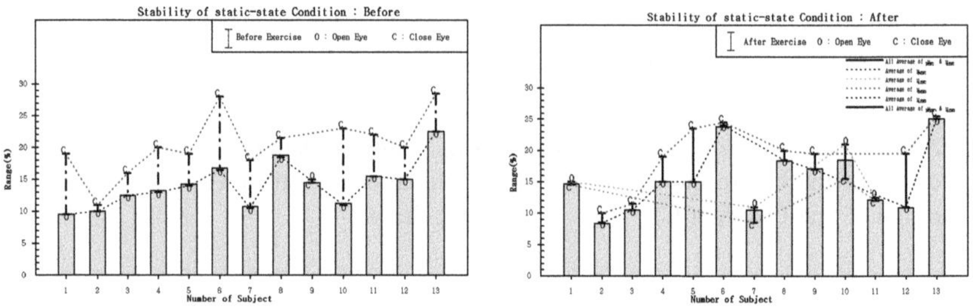

Fig. 8. Signal data of stability in the static posture (Stab-$_{ASP}$, Avg_{BNO}, Avg_{BNC}, Avg_{ANO}, Avg_{ANC})

5 Conclusion

We was defined an estimate model of vestibular-CNS system on the basis of the static state in the standing body. This model was confirmed posture balance with vestibular and CNS that evaluated a stability relations based on parameters. Experimental result analyzed balance of posture status.

In conclusion, this method for evaluating static posture state in a standing body obtained reliable and stable data. This system was considered of relation on the vestibular-CNS system and acquired of the body sway change. And there was based on the static position, thereby considered a vestibular mechanism.

Observation for the relation of vestibular-CNS system presented a changed parameter from body sway in posture balance. This showed a difference smaller at the exercising after than before in the vestibular. And, there presented a diminutive difference smaller at the exercising after than before in the CNS. The vestibular condition and CNS system was an equivalent different of body movement on the after and before. Also, this condition of the average difference was presented for body moving on the EC and EO.

Furthermore, in case the signal data managed the body variation condition of brain nervous system. In the future, this system will be express to an assessment for body balance in dynamic condition. We hope to a management a body movement and to control the sensory system.

References

1. Martin, F.N., Clark, J.G.: Introduction to Audiology, vol. 8, pp. 274–312. Pearson Edu. Inc. (2003)
2. Massion, J.: Movement, posture and equilibrium: interation and coordination. Prog. Neurobiol. 38, 35–56 (1992)
3. Winter, D.A., Patla, A.E., Rietdyk, S., Ishac, M.G.: Ankle muscle stiffness in the control of balance during quit standing. J. Neurophysiol. 85, 2630–2633 (2001)
4. Beloozerova, I.N., Sirota, M.G., Orlovsky, G.N., Deliagina, T.G.: Activity of pyramidal tract neurons in the cat during postural correction. J. Neurophysiol. 93, 1831–1844 (2005)
5. Bos, J.E., Bles, W.: Theoretical consideration on canal-otolith interation and an observer model. Biol. Cyber. 86, 191–207 (2002)
6. Mergner, T., Rosemeier, T.: Interaction of vestibular, somatosensory and visual signals for postural control and motion perception under terrestrial and microgravity conditions-a conceptual model. Brain Res. Rev. 28, 118–135 (1998)
7. Lai, C.C., Lee, R.G., Hsiao, C.C., Liu, H.S., Chen, C.C.: A H-QoS-demand personalized home physiological monitoring system over a wireless multi-hop relay network for mobile home healthcare applications. J. of Network and Computer Applications 32, 1229–1241 (2009)
8. O'Sullivan, S.O.: Assessment of motor function. In: O'Sullivan, S.B., Schmitz, T.J. (eds.) Physical Rehabilitation: Assessment and Treatment, 4th edn., pp. 501–532. FA Davis, Philadelphia (2001)
9. J.S., Lee, M.H., Lim, M.J., Lee, K.Y.: A Study of the Health Monitoring System for u-Healthcare. The Journal of IWIT 9(4), 9–15 (2009)
10. Lee, K.J., Park, S.W.: Patient Classification Scheme for Patient Information Management in Hospital U-Healthcare System. The Journal of IWIT 10(3), 131–137 (2010)
11. Lee, S.H., Lim, M.J.: Implementation of U-Healthcare Environment for Patient Recognition Applied Algorithms of Extracting Face Feature Points. The Journal of IWIT 9(4), 53–57 (2009)

A Study on a New Non-uniform Speech Coding Using the Components of Separated by Harmonics and Formants Frequencies

Seonggeon Bae and Myungjin Bae*

Information and Telecommunication Department,
Soongsil University, 1-1 Sangdo 5 dong DongJak-Ku,
Seoul, 156-743, Republic of Korea
sgbae123@empal.com, mjbae@ssu.ac.kr

Abstract. In speech processing, coding may be define as a digital representation of speech sound that provides efficient storage, transmission, recovery, and perceptually faithful reconstruction of the original speech. In the coding methods, the waveform coding method can maintain the high quality and personality, but the major drawback to this method is large amount of data required. Therefore, we suggest a waveform coding method using the nonuniform sampling and separated bandwidth of speech signals. Results show that this algorithm is robust in noisy environments, and we can get the average compression ratios of 5.67 and the gains of 3dB in our algorithm for original speech.

Keywords: Non-uniform sampling, Quantization, Peak and valley.

1 Introduction

Speech encoding method for storing or transmitting in signal processing can largely be classified into waveform coding method, source coding method, hybrid encoding method, etc., and to maintain intelligibility and naturalness, waveform coding method is mainly used. This coding process is the method of storing and synthesizing after removing repeated, unnecessary remaining components, and The waveform coding methods until now have been researched as PCM, ADM, DPCM, ADPCM, etc. However, it has the disadvantage that large amount of memory is required due to enormous quantity of data. Main point of speech coding is to process it by considering, especially, transmission and compression rate of data, speech quality of playback, and processing velocity among the information transmitted. In general, unnecessary remaining component which is existed in the voiced signal is known to be derived from relatively high correlation between samples. Therefore, to reduce data quantity or transmission rate for storing or transmission of speech, the remaining ingredient which is existed in the uniform sampling, i.e., the sample which has high correlation between samples and gives lesser influence from the viewpoint of recognition shall be removed. In general, for speech signal, problem can be generated

* Corresponding author.

T.-h. Kim et al. (Eds.): EL/DTA/UNESST 2012, CCIS 352, pp. 246–251, 2012.

for the recognition when voice is reconstructed in accordance with the characteristic of input signal for speech signal. Therefore, to maintain intelligibility and naturalness of speech, work to improve speech shall be carried out. Due to the improvement of calculation time of computing, various calculation methods have been presented. One of these methods is the waveform method in which improvement work is performed at time domain, and it is known to be excellent in terms of intelligibility and naturalness characteristic. In addition, there is the frequency method which is the parameter method to have improvement by detecting characteristic frame of speech, and this has the disadvantage that calculation quantity is too much to be applied to various speech. It is the hybrid method which is made by taking advantages of waveform and frequency method, and improvements have been made for this owing to the development of computing. In this study, to use this hybrid method, the method with non-uniform sampling in speech signal obtained from time domain will be used. Especially, in the case of voiced signal, as it is concentrated in the voiced signal with large amplitude, the improvement method which is searching and using peak and valley which are characteristics of voiced signal for synthesizing to emphasize linearity is to be presented. At chapter II, existing method which is to search recognizable characteristic of voiced signal, and at chapter III, signal method to use the proposed non-uniform sampling method will be described, and at chapter IV, conclusion and study direction in the future will be presented.

2 Existing Method

According to the study which considers recognizable characteristic of voice signal, it can be understood that in the case of the signal made by differentiating and clipping original voice wave from the recognition test of Licklider and Pollack, almost no deterioration is generated when comparing to 99% of recognition level of original signal as its value of recognition level is 97%. The coding method to use peak and valley of sound by utilizing this characteristic has been presented, and this has been used by considering the recognizable aspect. Therefore, this recognizable aspect of voice signal will be affected by the peak and valley which are appeared in the standardization and quantization. By utilizing this characteristic, numerous applications for synthesizing or coding section are possible, and especially for jamming environment, great support have been conducted for searching important factors of recognition signal by re-constituting filter and considering characteristics of peak and valley. As shown in the figures, the first one shows typical characteristics of peak and valley, and the second one displays properties of peak and valley. Final figure indicates influences which appear from clipping of sound and overload.

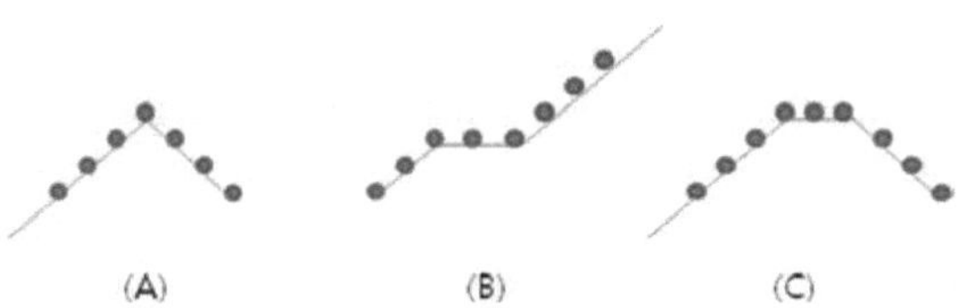

Fig. 1. Quantization influence signal Typical peak (b) Peak, valley simultaneously (c) Overload

In these 1 cases, as the last one is appeared by the influence for overload, it can give the most influence to the recognizable characteristic of sound. In here, overload is the phenomenon which is appeared in the clipping environment of sound, and great influence will be affected to the recognizable section when deteriorated signal is reconstituted at this section. Therefore, in this study, the improvement method applying to clipping signal will be used by considering only the section which is generated by the influence of overload and by using this kind of important recognition signal.

Waveform reconstruction is performed by using cosine interpolation method based on such parameters as the magnitudes and the intervals of the peak and the valley. The reconstructed waveform, $S_k(n)$, obtained by cosine interpolation method is represented as follows;

$$S_k(n) = [\frac{M(k-1) - M(k)}{2}\cos(\frac{\pi n}{I(k)}) + \frac{M(k-1) + M(k)}{2}], \qquad 1 \le n \le I(k) \tag{1}$$

where, $M(.)$ is the magnitude of non-uniformly sampled data and $I(.)$ is the interval of them.

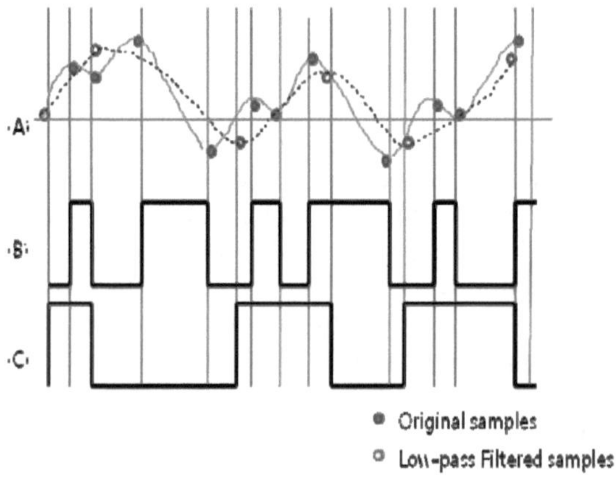

Fig. 2. Examples of non-uniform coding (A) peaks and valleys (B) original nonuniform coding (C) nonuniform coding using Low pass filter signal

3 Proposed Method

According to the speech production mechanism, since higher frequency band is related to the sound produced from the constriction structure than from the resonance structure, the 3rd and 4th formants have higher frequencies. The 1st and the 2nd formant frequencies of most phonemes of speech are less than 2.5 kHz. Also, the formants higher than this cutoff frequency have quite broad bandwidths. Therefore, non-uniform sampling can be only applied to the signal component of the original waveform less than 2.5 kHz without terrible loss of intelligibility. Fig. 4 shows the encode and the decode block diagram of the method proposed in this paper. In the encode block diagram, S(n) is speech signal digitized uniformly by A/D converter and sampler, and $S_L(n)$ is the law-pass filtered signal at 2.65 kHz as cutoff frequency. The conventional non-uniform sampling is applied to this low-pass filtered signal and such parameters as the magnitudes, M(.). and the intervals, I(.), of the peak and the valley points are Quantized by the scalar quantizer to interval I, and index of gain. At the same time, LPFed speech component $S_L'(n)$, is reconstructed by the inverse quantizer, the non-uniform sampling, and the cosine Interpolation technique. Then, the residual signal, $S_H(n)$, between the original signal and the reconstructed low pass filtered signal is obtained.

$$s_L(n) = \frac{1}{N}\sum_{k=0}^{N-1} s(n+k), 1 \le N \le filter\_coefficien\ t \tag{2}$$

$$s_H(n) = S(n) - S_L'(n) \tag{3}$$

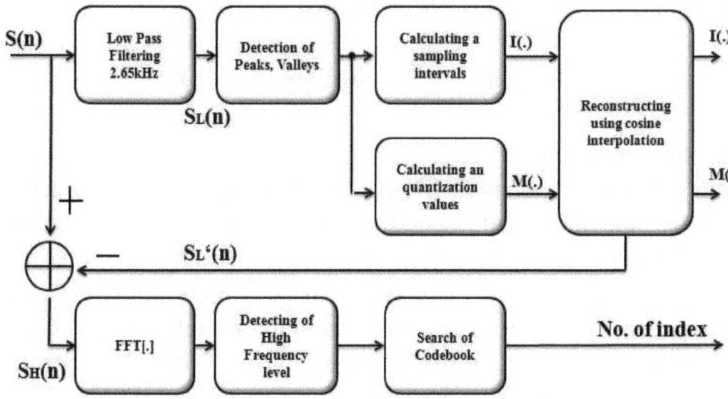

Fig. 3. A new speech encoder scheme proposed in this paper

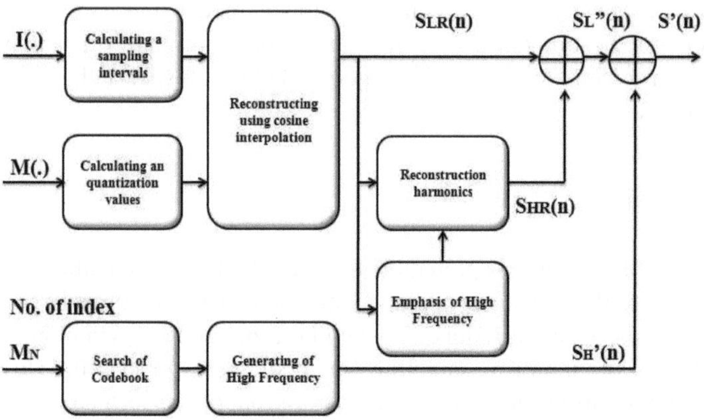

Fig. 4. A New speech decoder scheme proposed

Fig. 3, 4 shows the encoding and the decoding block diagram of the method proposed in this paper. In this block diagram, S(n) is speech signal digitized uniformly by A/D converter and sampler, and $S_{LP}(n)$ is the law-pass filtered signal at 2.67 kHz as cutoff frequency. The conventional non-uniform sampling as like (1) equation is applied to this low-pass filtered signal and such parameters as the magnitudes, M(.) and the intervals, I(.), of the peak and the valley points are Quantized by the scalar quantizer to interval I, and gain, M. At the same time, LPFed speech component $S_{LP}(n)$, is reconstructed by the inverse quantizer, the non-uniform sampling, and the cosine Interpolation technique. Also, to improve high frequencies the harmonic signals, $S_H(n)$, using the post filter as the positive clipping and the weighted filter is obtained.

$$s_L''(n) = S_{LR}(n) + S_{HR}(n) \tag{4}$$

$$s'(n) = S_L''(n) + S_H'(n) \tag{5}$$

To improve the harmonic signal, $S_{LR}(n)$ is added to $S_{HR}(n)$. where 0.3 is a compensation value of magnitude in speech signal.

$$s_{HR}(n) = 0.3 * absolute\ (S_{LR}(n)) \tag{6}$$

where n is the number of samples.

Major components of the residual signal consist of the 3rd and upper formants of speech. Generally, the magnitude spectrums of the higher formants have a more bandwidth than that of 1st or 2nd formant and the positions of the formants are assigned to a little important information to speech intelligibility. To preserve the naturalness of speech by the 3rd and upper formants, pseudo random Gaussian noise is added to the waveform reconstructed roughly with the nonuniform sampling parameters. Generally, since the characteristic of the residual signal between the original and the reconstructed low-band waveform is rather a pseudo colored than a white noise, we can roughly approximate the residual signal to one of eight colored Gaussian noise. The encode procedure can much reduce the data rate to achieve higher compression ratio than that of the conventional non-uniform sampling even in the noisy environment and also get a good quality of speech by reconstructed harmonics signal.

4 Conclusion

Generally, waveform coding is preferable to obtain high speech quality. However, the major drawback of the waveform coding technique is that it requires large amounts of data because of the inherent redundancy as like a nonuniform sampling. To remove the redundancy of uniform sampling method were proposed. However, the conventional nonuniform sampling method is improper to speech signal since speech is nonstationary especially when speech signal changes rapidly.

In this paper, we proposed new nonuniform sampling method using the components of separated by harmonics and formants frequencies. The proposed nonuniform sampling technique is applied to the low-pass filtered speech signal to reduce the effect of 3th and 4th formants information. To preserve the naturalness, the higher formants as 3th and 4th component are compensated by adding the white Gaussian noise. To keep to the intelligibility, the harmonics as fundamental frequencies are emphasized by adding the rectifying negative signals in speech signal

We proposed new nonuniform coding and decoding methods, so the proposed method in speech signal can be compressed 3 times and improved 3dB gains higher than the conventional non-uniform sampling method.

References

1. Bae, S.-G., You, K.-B., Bae, M.-J.: A Study on Enhancement of Speech Signal Using Separated Bandwidth and Non-uniform Sampling. In: Lee, G., Howard, D., Kang, J.J., Ślęzak, D. (eds.) ICHIT 2012. LNCS, vol. 7425, pp. 723–729. Springer, Heidelberg (2012)
2. Sohn, J., Kim, N.S., Sung, W.: A statistical model-based voice activity detector. IEEE Signal Processing Lett. 6(1), 1–3 (1999)
3. Accardi, A.J., Cox, R.V.: A modular approach to speech enhancement with an application to speech coding. J. Acout. Soc. Am. 10(3), 1245 (2001)
4. Jeong, C.-J., Bae M.-J.: Analysis regarding vocalizations of teuroteu singers. The Institute of Electronics Engineers of Korea, Summer Scholarship Contest of 2009, pp. 1090–1091 (2009)
5. Bae, M.J., Lee, S.H.: Digital Voice Signal Analysis, ch. 3, 6. Books Publishing Dong Young (1998)
6. Agarwal, T., Kabal, P.: Pre-processing of noisy speech for voice coders. In: Proc. IEEE Workshop on Speech Coding, Tsukaba, Japan, pp. 169–171 (October 2002)

A Development of Authoring Tool for Online 3D GIS Service Using LoD and Multi-mapping

Ran Choi, Seoung-soo Bae, Hyeon-Choel Kim, and Chang-Suk Cho

Div. of Information and Telecom., Hanshin Univ.,
411 Yangsan-dong, Osan-si, Gyeonggi-do, 447-791 Korea
cscho@hs.ac.kr

Abstract. We propose an authoring tool for online 3D GIS system in which LoD and multi-level mapping technique were introduced. A new LoD technique is proposed here to join the polygons on the boundaries between the two parts with different sampling rates. To provide 3D GIS information with high definition in online, optimization strategy is indispensible for controlling CPU sharing process and memory effectively. Semaphore algorithm for controlling threads is introduced to prevent from deadlock of process. The proposed system was designed to use as an authoring tool, so that this system assembles the terrain data and image as the standardized squared blocks. Hence any other area can be transformed to 3D GIS system easily if the terrain data and images of the area are divided as the squared blocks with the determined order and criteria of the blocks. The determined order and criteria of the blocks can be stored by user as a text file. JAVA and JWS was selected to implement this system instead of C language for online service to exclude Active-X control.

Keywords: 3D GIS, LoD, multi-mapping, semaphore, authoring tool.

1 Introduction

Google, Naver and Daum are providing online map services in their web environment. In recent they start to provide 3D map service for some special area but their services are restricted to mainly 2D map services now. Commonly online 3D GIS service needs too large memory including huge digital terrain data in comparison with PC environment, since the 3D service should have a reality for user to feel like looking around its area. From such reason it is the important technique to deal memory effectively when implementing 3D GIS system on online. As another important point, most of the online 3D GIS system depends on custom-built process when it is built. Hence an authoring tool is indispensible to make 3D GIS system easily.

For providing 3D GIS service on online, web-based 3D GIS system using DEM and VRML were reported [1] and [2], and XML web was also introduced to develop GIS system [3]. Shin reported LoD (Level of detail) technique to make terrain automatically [4]. Also some reports suggested LoD technique to use memory effectively [5] and [6]. But those have limitations to provide reality and also didn't suggest authoring tool for 3D GIS system.

T.-h. Kim et al. (Eds.): EL/DTA/UNESST 2012, CCIS 352, pp. 252–257, 2012.

We propose an authoring tool for online 3D GIS system encoded in JAVA, in which LoD and multi-level mapping technique were introduced. JAVA was selected instead of C language for online service to exclude Active-X control. To execute the system directly in web pages JWS (JAVA Web Start) is used also. Here a new technique to use LoD was introduced to implement 3D terrain, so that the far area from the view point has fewer polygons than close area. Moreover it would be an important merit in business that our system can be used as an authoring tool to build 3D GIS system. The 3D GIS system can be easily built only to upload simply DEM data and aerial photos.

2 Implementation and Algorithms

2.1 Aerial Photos and DEM Data

To build 3D map we used aerial photos and DEM data whose area includes the river Gyeongan-Cheon flowing through Yongin-si, The reduced ratio of the aerial photos is 1:6000 and the size is 1.3G (18432 24676), and the size of height map extracted from DEM is about 67M. In height map of fig. 1 the brightness shows elevation of terrain. Its bright part represents high elevation.

(a) Aerial photo (b) Height map

Fig. 1. Aerial photo and height map of the area including the river Gyeongan-cheon

The original data is used after pre-processing since its size is too large to be handled in PC environment. To show the entire area the aerial photos are reduced as two stages in pre-processing. All the photos are reduced and combined as one image having 1024*1024 pixels in the first stage. In the first stage the image has low definition. The image pre-processed in the first stage is used to show entire 3D map of Gyeongan-Cheon. In the second stage, all the photos are combined and divided to squared blocks having 1024*1024 pixels, whose definitions are very high. In the first and second stage the height map also are combined and divided according to the same process and block size as photos. The height map is reformatted to polygon base. Fig. 2 shows the mapping process with the height map and the photo.

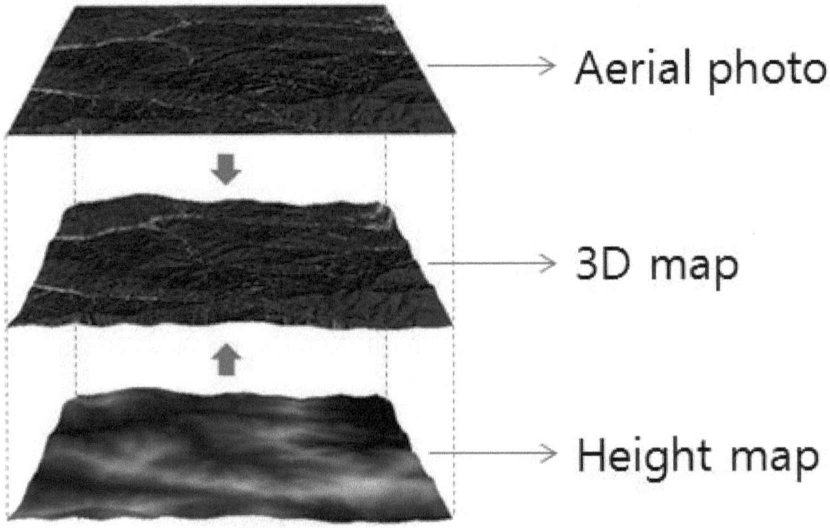

Fig. 2. 3D map with the image pre-processed from the aerial photo and the height map

2.2 Implementation of 3D GIS System

All the pre-processed terrain data including images and heights need 1.4 GB memories and have ten thousands of polygons. If we try to present ten thousands of polygons for entire area, then we can see a realistic landscape for the area. But it takes too long time to upload and present it in online. Furthermore many polygons are overlapped in narrow area such as the area far from view point. For effective use of memory LoD technique is applied in order that the area near view point are shown as very high definition and the other area done as low definition. Therefore the terrain model is specified as two parts. In the area far from view point, the number of points to be rendered are reduced by sampling and mapped by the terrain image having low definition. Whereas in the area near to view point, the number of point is not reduced with no sampling and mapped by the divided squared block map (as described in section 2.1) having original definition. Fig. 3 shows the boundary between the two part of 3D terrain map to which LoD is applied.

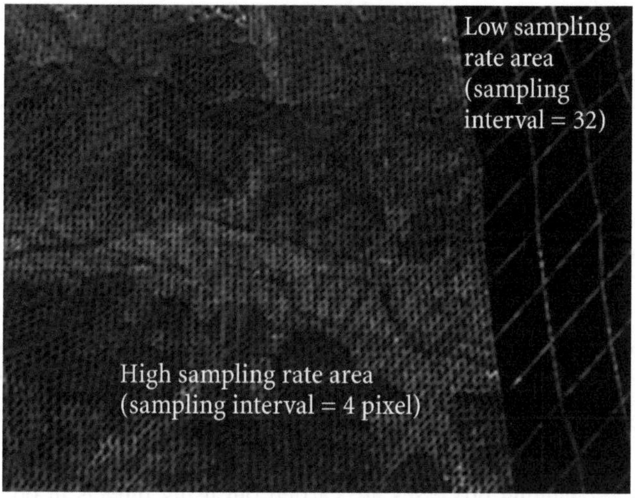

Fig. 3. The boundary between the two parts of 3D terrain map to which LoD is applied

One of the problems to apply LoD is occurred to join the polygons on the boundaries between the two parts with different sampling rates, since the part far from a view point have lower sampling rate (same as larger interval) than the closer area to view point. To join the parts having different sampling rates equation 1 is used here.

$$z_n = z_k + \frac{n}{N}(z_{k+1} - z_k)$$
$$n = (0,1 \ldots N),\ N = S_L / S_H . \quad (1)$$

Here z_n means height z value of the terrain with high sampling rate and z_k z value having low sampling rate. S_L means high sample rate (same as small interval), S_R low sample rate. Fig. 3 shows the joined result of the two parts having different sampling rate using equation 1.

Another problem to apply LoD is to change the terrain height data and images having different definitions. When the terrain data near to view point is changed with the terrain having high sampling rate, the image of the terrain should be changed with the image having high definition. To change it the view point position picked by mouse is inputted to the equation 2. In equation 2, M(x,y) means index of the squared terrain block (as described in section 2.1) and p(x,y) the point picked by mouse. S_{map} is the side size of the squared terrain block.

$$M(x,y) = \frac{P(x,y)}{S_{map}} . \quad (2)$$

Fig. 4 shows the changing process using LoD technique. In the procedure, firstly the entire terrain with the related image having low definition is loaded. After doing it, the terrain near the view point (same as camera point) is changed with the terrain and image having high sampling rate and definition.

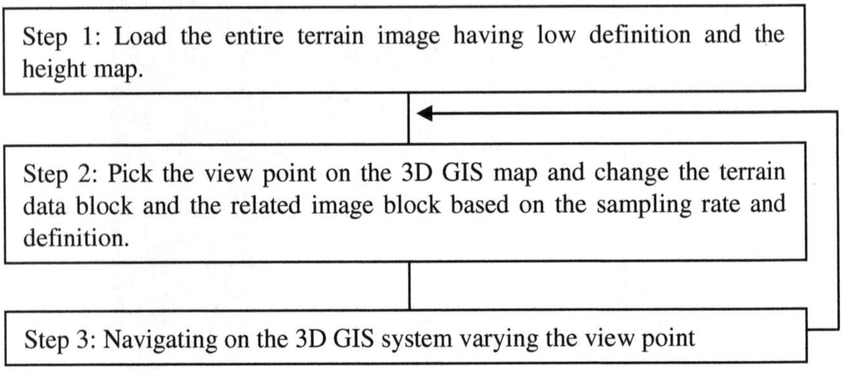

Fig. 4. Changing procedure of the terrain and the image

In step 2 the changing processes are carried out using threads in order to control the limited CPU resource effectively. The semaphore also is used to control the threads to prevent deadlock [7]. To provide 3D GIS system as online tour, UI (User Interface) including camera controls and other geographical information were implemented.

2.3 Implementation of Authoring Tool for 3D GIS System

The proposed system was designed to use as an authoring tool, so that this system assembles the terrain data and image as the standardized squared blocks. Hence another area can be transformed to 3D GIS system easily if the terrain data and images of the area are divided as the squared blocks with the determined order and criteria of the blocks. The determined order and criteria of the blocks can be stored by user as a text file.

Geographic information as well can be inputted easily using the pop-up window of this system. Fig. 5 shows the pop-up window to input the geographic information. The pop-up window will be turned up in administrator account when a point on the map is clicked by mouse, and the administrator can input the information about the position. After being done by administrator user can see the information to click the spot images appearing on UI.

3 Result

An authoring tool for implementing 3D GIS system in online is presented here. This system provides the 3D GIS service with high definition using LoD and multi mapping. To provide information with such high definition in online, optimization strategy is indispensible for controlling CPU sharing process and memory effectively. Semaphore for controlling threads is introduced to prevent from deadlock of process.

(a) (b)

Fig. 5. (a) Pop-up window for inputting geographic information on a point. (b) The window shows the name and spot image on the point after inputting it.

All the terrain data and images were divided into standardized squared blocks, so that any other area can be loaded and implemented to 3D GIS system easily. Also this system provides the input function for geographic information as the pop-up window to administrator. This system was implemented to the river Gyeongan-cheon as the first object area. However it was developed as an authoring tool to implement 3D GIS system easily for any other places, so that will be expected to be used widely for the 3D GIS system.

References

1. Araya, S., Jin, H., Araya, R.: An Effective Terrain Model for Web-Based 3D Geographic Information Systems. Electronics & Communications, 43–52 (2002)
2. Huang, B., Lin, H.: GeoVR: a web-based tool for virtual reality presentation from 2D GIS data. Computers & Geosciences 25, 1167–1175 (1999)
3. Chang, Y.-S., Park, H.-D.: XML Web Service-based development model for Internet GIS applications. International Journal of Geographical Information Science 20, 371–399 (2006)
4. Shin, J.-E., Cho, C.-S.: An Implementation of terrain manufacturing system using LOD algorithm. In: 2002 Autumn Conference of Korea Multimedia Society, pp. 511–515. Korea Multimedia Society (2002)
5. Zhang, Z.: Interactive Visualisation of 3D City Models Based on Adaptive Streaming of 3D-GIS Data. Information Assurance and Security 2, 417–420 (2009)
6. Cellier, F., Gandoin, P.-M., Chaine, R., Barbier-Accary, A., Akkouche, S.: Simplification and streaming of GIS terrain for web clients. In: Web3D 2012 Proceedings of the 17th International Conference on 3D Web Technology, pp. 73–81. ACM, New York (2012)
7. Silberschatz, A., Galvin, P.B., Gagne, G.: Operating System Concepts, 6th edn., pp. 201–206. John Wiley & Sons, Inc. (2003)

Electric Vehicle Charging Control System Hardware-In-the-Loop Simulation(HILS) with a Smartphone

Kyung-Jung Lee, Sunny Ro, and Hyun-Sik Ahn

Department of Electronics Engineering, Kookmin University, Seoul, Korea
ahs@kookmin.ac.kr

Abstract. This paper presents EV(Electric Vehicle) charging control system HILS with a smartphone. The charging control system is consisted of an EV, an EVSE(Electric Vehicle Supply Equipment), a smartphone and EV-to-environment communication mechanism, where the mechanism is based on a smartphone core and on the Bluetooth. We implement a Bluetooth-CAN gateway in an EV for the interconnection between a smartphone and an EVSE. The system focuses to combine information technology and to provide convenience of drivers for EV charging. It is shown by using the charging control system HILS that EV charging process can be easily controlled and monitored via a smartphone.

Keywords: Electric vehicle, Wireless communication, CAN(Controller Area Network), Bluetooth.

1 Introduction

Recently, the requirements of government are increasing to replace fossil fuels and reduce gas emissions since economic and environmental reasons. For this reason, research on an EV has been going on last decade. Also, EV infrastructure is developed rapidly to provide efficient EV charging and charge management in recent years [1-4].

EV infrastructure requires intelligent interconnection using communication networks among a driver's smartphone, an EV and an EVSE for EV charging. The great amount of wires in a vehicle makes the cost of wiring very high, increasing the weight of the vehicle too. Decades ago the communications moved from direct connections to busses, actually widely used are CAN bus for control communications and EV charging will benefit from data analysis and remote interaction. Mobile applications are a raising business area in Computer Science, with the widespread utilization of a smartphone, and the increasing availability of Bluetooth wireless communications[5].

In this paper, we present EV charging control system HILS with a smartphone. An EV driver receives charging status data from an EVSE in real time such as the available driving distance, charging time and price. This information can be retrieved from an EVSE offering a smartphone via Bluetooth to request the charging status and

T.-h. Kim et al. (Eds.): EL/DTA/UNESST 2012, CCIS 352, pp. 258–264, 2012.

to influence the charging process from communication area. EV charging application based a smartphone is implemented and aimed at increasing convenience of EV drivers with Bluetooth wireless network. Also, Bluetooth-CAN gateway in an EV is implemented to exchange charging data and charging control command between an EVSE and a smartphone. Finally, the experiment is conducted to verify the performance of proposed EV charging control system HILS.

2 System Overview

The construction of EV charging system with a smartphone is as shown in Fig. 1. It is consisted of several different components such as an EVSE, an EV and a smartphone. These modules use different communication technologies in order to increasing mobility of the system[6].

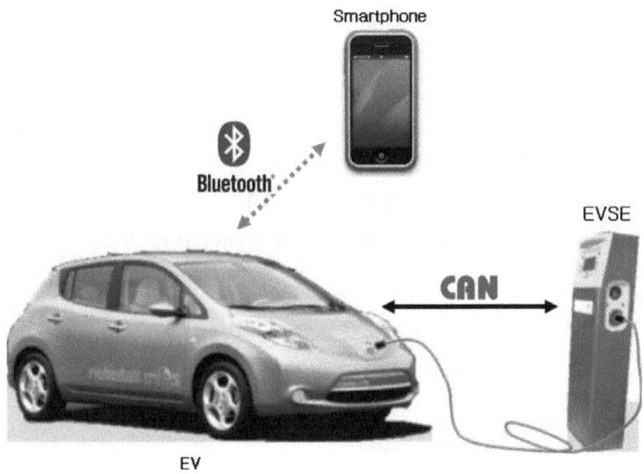

Fig. 1. The construction of EV charging control system with a smartphone

2.1 EV Charging Control System with a Smartphone

An EV has a wired plug-in connection with an EVSE and a wireless Bluetooth connection with a driver's smartphone to share information on the charging process. The charging controller of the vehicle monitors the current state of charge, the predicted end of charge, the capacity of the charge, the actual charging speed and other information inside the car.

An EVSE enables interoperability with all types of electrical vehicles, establishes a secure connection with the vehicle and a driver's smartphone using Bluetooth, verifies the authentication of the user before delivering energy, provides to the user information on the cost and maximum suppliable power, provides methods for automatic payment and billing systems, gives additional internet-based services, exchanges information with the power grid on the power request and power availability, exchanges information with a database of the central management service.

A Driver's smartphone is the instrument that identifies the driver to the other agents. The driver controls the charging process through a smartphone using a Bluetooth connection. A smartphone performs a secure authentication of the driver itself with charging station, enabling the billing process. The driver defines the amount of charging required and the recharging speed on the basis of the actual charge status of the battery, of the time the user have at disposal, of the cost that depends on the charging station, the charging power required, the energy at disposal of the power grid company in that moment. The driver receives in a smartphone additional services through Wifi, UMTS, and GPS connections for example: information on the status of the account for paying the recharge and other services, location and price of the nearest charging stations.

2.2 Network Configuration for EV Charging Control System

A driver can interact with charging station manually or with other wireless technologies, but actually a driver's smartphone interacts with the EV charging control system only using Bluetooth. Recent applications use a gateway between CAN and Bluetooth protocols for the maintenance and the monitoring of the status of the car. EV charging control system for design at lower levels of the Bluetooth and CAN network inside the EV charging control system has been developed. The network architecture of the EV charging control system is as shown in Fig.2.

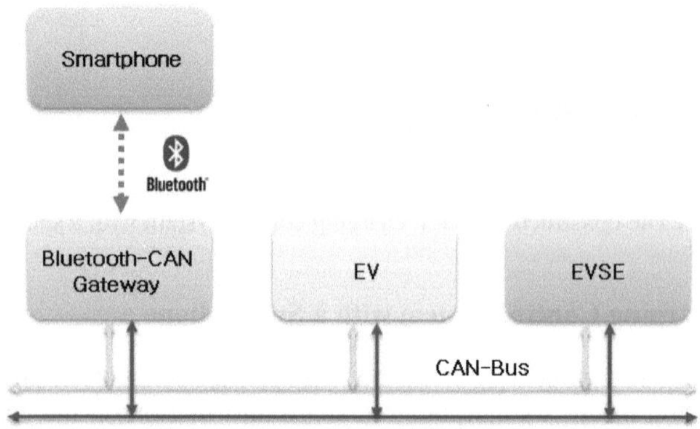

Fig. 2. Network architecture of the EV charging control system with Bluetooth and CAN networks

Especially, The Bluetooth-CAN gateway is connected between the CAN bus and the Bluetooth channel. Besides all of the above specifications, one of the main requirements for EV charging control system is the compactness of the electronic board. Description of Bluetooth-CAN Gateway is as shown in Fig. 3.

To this focus, the electronic system has been designed according to a modular approach. Bluetooth-CAN Gateway is consisted of three modules: Bluetooth module board, 2287M MCU(Micro Controller Unit) and CAN transceiver board. In particular, the embedded electronic system includes the following components.

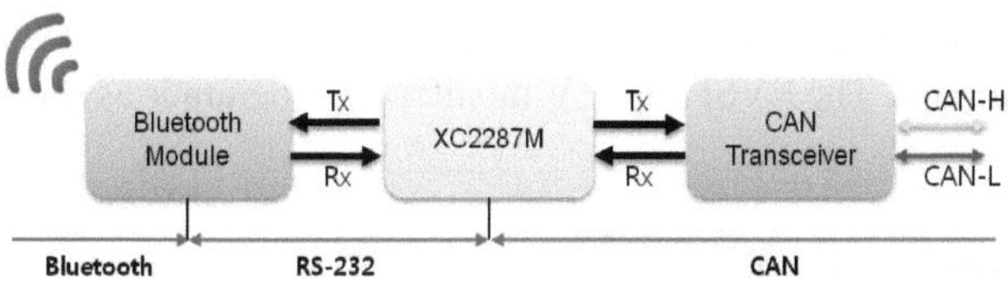

Fig. 3. Description of Bluetooth-CAN Gateway

- A CAN controller set with appropriate baud rate.
- A Infineon 16bit-microcontroller XC2287M MCU to implement the primary functionalities for EV charging control and the Bluetooth-CAN gateway.

3 The Structure of EV Charging Control System HILS

An EVSE has an EVCU (Electric Vehicle Control Unit) for charging management, AC-DC converter for converting AC power into DC power and monitoring system for monitoring of EV charging status. An EVSE delivers power information to an EV using the CAN protocol.

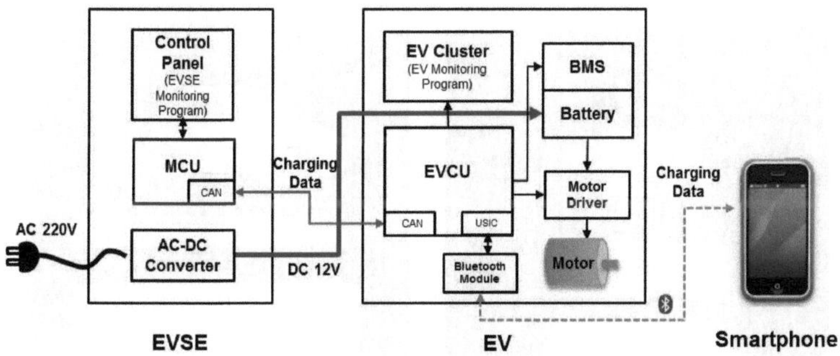

Fig. 4. The Structure of HILS for EV charging system

An EV is consisted of main core an EVCU for the control of an EV, BMS for battery information management and control, Battery, DC motor driver and DC motor for driving an EV and monitoring system for check the charging status. Bluetooth-CAN gateway in an EV is implemented to exchange charging data and charging control command between an EVSE and a smartphone. The Structure of EV charging control system HILS is as shown in Fig. 4.

4 Implementation and Experimental Results

Both the EVSE and EV monitoring programs are implemented to confirm EV charging data. These software programmed by JAVA display EV charging status on the PC through serial port, it can also be shown as a waveform. In addition, The EV monitoring program can send charging control command to an EVSE via CAN for EV charging control. The EVSE and EV monitoring program is as shown Fig. 5.

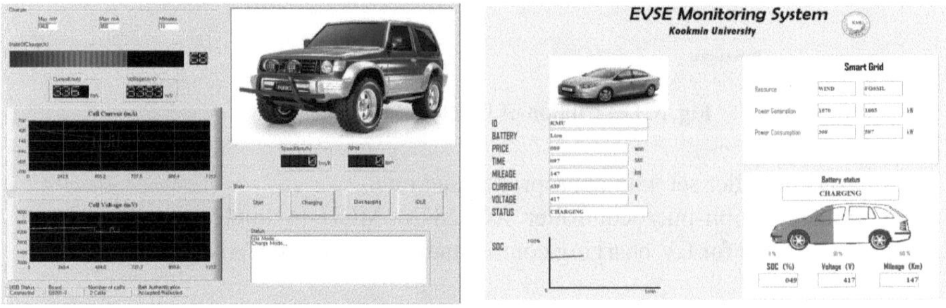

Fig. 5. The EV and EVSE monitoring program

Also, the smartphone application is implemented by Android OS for EV charging status monitoring and control. It can send charging certification, EV charging start and stop. Also, it displays charging status such as SOC(State Of Charge), charging time, available mileage distance and price. The application is as shown Fig. 6.

Fig. 6. The Smartphone application for EV charging control

The two main critical aspects of the EV charging system are the charging interaction and the throughput of the gateway. The throughput has been experimentally evaluated as the minimum both the CAN bus the Bluetooth of the EV charging system[7,8]. The Bluetooth channel has represented the bottleneck of the system since it is loaded by EV charging data. For this reason, Channel usage in the EV charging system network must be under maximum network usage of Bluetooth to avoid bottleneck. Maximum network usage in gateway of EV charging control system HILS is as shown in Table 1.

Table 1. Maximum Network usage in gateway of EV charging control system HILS

Network	Network Baud rate [bit/s]	System throughput [bit/s]	Usage [%]
CAN	500000	19000	3.8
Bluetooth	9600	9600	100

And measurement results of network usage using implemented EV charging control system HILS is as shown in Table 2. CAN network usage is 2.62% and Bluetooth network usage is 68.75%. In this result, Gateway in EV charging control system HILS is confirmed no data loss because measured network usages are under maximum network usage. Accordingly, data transmission reliability of implemented gateway is valid.

Table 2. Experimental results of Network usage in gateway of EV charging control system HILS

Network	Network Baud rate [bit/s]	System throughput [bit/s]	Usage [%]
CAN	500000	13100	2.62
Bluetooth	9600	6600	68.75

5 Conclusions

This paper presented EV charging system with a smartphone. The EV charging system was consisted of an EVSE, an EV and the smartphone application. An EVSE was connected with an EV via CAN and a smartphone was connected with an EV via Bluetooth. Bluetooth-CAN gateway was implemented for communication between a smartphone and an EVSE. The validity of this system was tested using EV charging control system HILS. By the experimental result, it is verified that the reliability of transmission data was tested in communication between an EVSE and a smartphone with a Bluetooth-CAN gateway.

Acknowledgments. This research was supported by the MKE(The Ministry of Knowledge Economy), Korea, under the ITRC(Information Technology Research Center) support program (NIPA-2012-H0301-12-2007) and CITRC(Convergence Information Technology Research Center) support program (NIPA-2012-H0401-12-2003) supervised by the NIPA(National IT Industry Promotion Agency).

References

1. Markel, T., Kuss, M., Denholm, P.: Communication and Control of Electric Drive Vehicles Supporting Renewables. In: The 2009 IEEE Vehicle Power and Propulsion Systems Conference, pp. 27–34. IEEE Press, Dearborn (2009)
2. Chen, Y., Oudalov, A., Wang, J.S.: Integration of Electric Vehicle Charging System into Distribution Network. In: The 8th International Conference on Power Electronics, pp. 593–598. IEEE Press, Jeju (2011)
3. Markel, T.: Plug-in Electric Vehicle Infrastructure: A Foundation for Electrified Transportation. In: The MIT Energy Initiative Transportation Electrification Sysmposium, Cambridge (2010)
4. Ferreira, J.C., Monteiro, V., Afonso, J.L., Silva, A.: Smart Electric Vehicle Charging System. In: 2011 IEEE Intelligent Vehicle Symposium(IV), pp. 758–763. IEEE Press, Baden-Baden (2011)
5. Fredriksson, L.-B.: Bluetooth in Automotive Applications. In: The Bluetooth 1999 Conference, London (1999)
6. Conti, M.: B4V2G: Bluetooth for Electric Vehicle to Smart Grid Connection. In: Proceeding of Intelligent Solutions in Embedded Systems (WISES), pp. 13–18. IEEE, Rogensburg (2011)
7. Spelta, C., Manzoni, V., Corti, A., Goggi, A., Savaresi, S.M.: Smartphone-Based Vehicle-to-Driver/Environment Interaction System for Motorcycles. IEEE Embedded Systems Letters 2, 39–42 (2010)
8. Magnus, P., Fredrik, G.: A Bluetooth-CAN Gateway. Electrical Engineering Students at Chalmers University of Technology for Sigma System AB (2001)

Construction of Korean Semantic Annotated Corpus

Hye-Jeong Song[1,3], Chan-Young Park[1,3], Jung-Kuk Lee[2,3], Min-Ji Lee[4], Yoon-Jeong Lee[4], Jong-Dae Kim[1,3], and Yu-Seop Kim[1,3,*]

[1] Dept. of Ubiquitous Computing, Hallym University, 1 Hallymdaehak-gil, Chuncheon, Gangwon-do, 200-702 Korea
{cypark,kimjd,hjsong,yskim01}@hallym.ac.kr
[2] Dept. of Computer Engineering, Hallym University, 1 Hallymdaehak-gil, Chuncheon, Gangwon-do, 200-702 Korea
percussive@gmail.com
[3] Bio-IT Research Center, Hallym University, 1 Hallymdaehak-gil, Chuncheon, Gangwon-do, 200-702 Korea
[4] Dept. of Ubiquitous Game Engineering, Hallym University, 1 Hallymdaehak-gil, Chuncheon, Gangwon-do, 200-702 Korea
Kshel2000@hallym.ac.kr, yjlee2612@gmail.com

Abstract. Semantic role labeling is to determine semantic relationships between a predicate and its arguments in a sentence. Although semantic annotated corpus should be necessary to do the labeling, unfortunately, Korean language is lack of the corpus data. In this paper, we construct Korean Proposition Bank (PropBank) corpus and Sejong case frame annotated corpus. Semantic annotation means a task which gives a semantic tag to an argument word in consideration of the dependency relationship between a predicate and the argument. And semantic annotated corpus is used in semantic role labeling based on machine learning methods. We annotate the syntactic annotated corpus built by Korea Electronics and Telecommunication Research Institute. We use frame files for Korean PropBank and Sejong case frame dictionary for Sejong case frame annotated corpus.

Keywords: Korean PropBank, Semantic Role Labeling, Semantic Tagged Corpus, Sejong Case Frame Annotated Corpus.

1 Introduction

For semantic role labeling, a large semantic annotated corpus is required. Proposition Bank (PropBank) [1] has been widely spread to be used in semantic analysis of a given sentence. PropBank has its English and Chinese [2] version of relatively enough size and Hindi [3] and Arabic [4] version are now being constructed and utilized in semantic analysis researches. However, because Korean does not have enough appropriate training data for the semantic analysis, it fails to show an acceptable recall and precision value. To make matters worse, many researches related to semantic

* Corresponding author.

T.-h. Kim et al. (Eds.): EL/DTA/UNESST 2012, CCIS 352, pp. 265–271, 2012.

analysis in Korean could not try to begin. Consequently, the lack of related corpus data is a main obstacle in semantic analysis in Korean.

Originally, University of Pennsylvania built the Korean PropBank[1]. However, because the corpus uses English tag system, it's hard to adapt it to Korean language. Especially, as concern in Korean language has become decreased in U.S. society, modification and update of the existing corpus is delayed without any plan. To solve this problem, we begin constructing Korean PropBank corpus and Sejong case frame annotated corpus. Sejong project[2] has built many kinds of annotated corpus including raw corpus, syntactic annotated corpus and many other linguistic resources. Sejong corpus is the most widely used linguistic data in Korea. Semantic annotation task is to give a proper semantic tag to syntactically annotated corpus. We use the syntactic annotated corpus built by Korea Electronics and Telecommunication Research Institute[3].

Section 2 describes the whole process of semantic tagging work and section 3 explains tagging results. Conclusion and future works are explained in section 4.

2 Annotation Process

2.1 Annotation Targets

Semantic role is the underlying relationship that a participant has with the main verb in a clause[4]. Argument is a sentential constituent having direct dependency relationship with the verb (predicate). In building Korean PropBank, we annotate all argument directly related to the predicate, such as case suffix, attaching suffix, state adverb, aspect adverb, and etc. In building Sejong semantic corpus, we annotate only arguments with a case suffces because of lack of defined semantic roles in Sejong project.

Table 1 shows dependency structure of Korean sentence "결국 텐트속에서 사람들이 호흡장애를 일으켰다". The dependency is explained with two index numbers. The first index means the order of the argument shown in the sentence. The second one indicates a sentential constituent on which the argument directly depends. For PropBank annotation, we try to tag all arguments whose second indices are 5. However, for Sejong annotation, among the arguments, we select only arguments having their case suffices whose first indices are 2, 3, and 4.

2.2 Semantic Roles

Annotators should find the underlying relationship between a predicate and an argument and give a proper semantic role tag to the argument with consideration of PropBank frame files and Sejong case frame predicate dictionary.

---

[1] http://www.ldc.upenn.edu
[2] http://www.sejong.or.kr
[3] http://www.etri.re.kr
[4] http://www.sil.org/linguistics/GlossaryOfLinguisticTerms/WhatIsASemanticRole.htm

Table 1. This table shows the dependency structure of a sentence "결국 텐트속에서 사람들이 호흡장애를 일으켰다". This structure is from ETRI syntactic annotated corpus.

1	5	결국[용언불가능보통명사]
2	5	텐트_속[용언불가능보통명사]+에서[부사격조사]
3	5	사람_들[용언불가능보통명사]+이[주격조사]
4	5	호흡_장애[용언불가능보통명사]+를[목적격조사]
5	0	일으키[일반동사]+었[관과거시제선어말어미]+다[평사형종결어미] +[문미기호]

Table 2. Semantic Roles defined in PropBank and Sejong case frame dictionary

PropBank Semantic Roles			Sejong Semantic Roles		
ARG0	ARG1	ARG2	AGT	THM	EXP
ARG3	M-ADV	M-CAU	MAG	EFF	COM
M-CND	M-DIR	M-DIS	LOC	DIR	GOL
M-EXT	M-INS	M-LOC	FNS	SRC	INS
M-MNR	M-NEG	M-PRD	CNT	CRT	PUR
M-PRP	M-TMP		Npr		

Table 2 shows semantic roles defined in PropBank and Sejong case frame dictionary. In PropBank, arg0 means an agent of the given predicate. Arg1 means a patient and arg2 means an instrument, benefactive thing and attribute of the predicate. Arg3 shows that the argument is a starting point/benefactive/attribute and arg4 indicates the argument to be en ending point of the predicate. ArgM is tagged to other modifiers of the predicate. ArgM includes MNR (a manner), LOC (locative), TMP (temporal) and others.

In Sejong roles, AGT means an agent like Arg0 in PropBank. And THM for a patient, LOC for the time and space, FNS for resulting state of the predicate, and others are defined and used.

2.3 PropBank Annotation Task

A predicate '일으키다' in Table 1 has a PropBank frame structure shown in Figure 1. The predicate '일으키다' has three necessary arguments. An argument of 'creator' sense is ARG0, an argument of 'thing created' is ARG1, and an argument of 'patient' is ARG2. In view of syntactic structure, a subjective argument is ARG0, an objective argument is ARG1, and a complementary argument is ARG2. When mapping this information to the Table 1, a subjective word '사람들' is to be tagged with ARG0 and an objective word '호흡 장애' is tagged with ARG1. However, because arguments '텐트 속에서' and '결국' could not be decided to be complemented arguments or to be 'patients' of the predicate word, we should select most proper roles from other ARGM roles, instead of deciding to be ARG2.

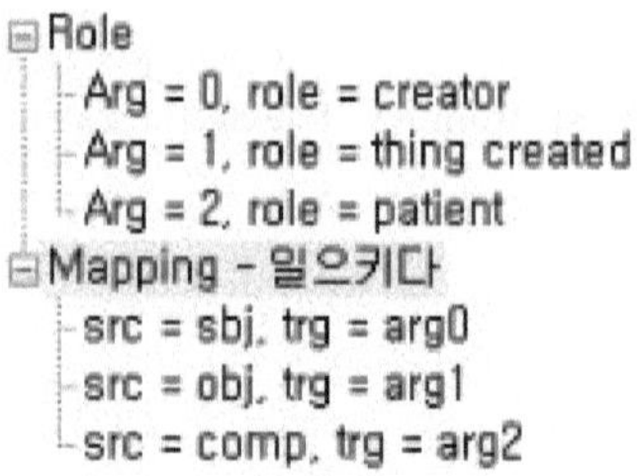

Fig. 1. Frame information of '일으키다' in PropBank frame files

When the appropriate semantic role is not suggested in the frame files, we retrieve proper annotated examples from example sentences in the frame files. An argument '결국' has been tagged with CAU and DIS in the frame files. Among these, we annotate it to be DIS by considering the context of the given sentence. However, '텐트 속에서' is not shown in the frame files examples. In this case, annotators should select the most proper role intuitively. In the case of Table 1, we give LOC to '텐트 속에서' because the argument means the location of the predicate.

2.4 Sejong Annotation Task

In Sejong annotation, only arguments with case suffices are to be annotated. Firstly, we retrieve the predicate in the Sejong case frame dictionary. Figure 2 shows all senses of the predicate '일으키다'. Annotators should find out the most similar sense to that of the given sentence and use the case frame structure of the selected sense.

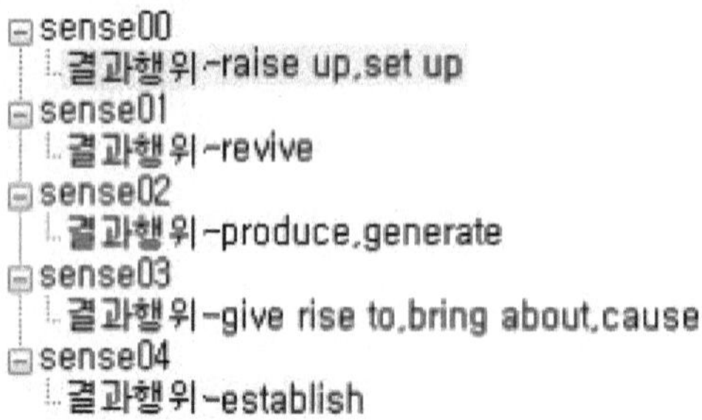

Fig. 2. Meanings of '일으키다'in Sejong case frame dictionary

Because the predicate '일으키다' in Table 1 has most similar sense to that of the sense02, we use the case frame structure information of that sense. The case frame structure of the sense02 is shown in Figure 3.

When the predicate '일으키다' is used with the sense of sense02, it has two necessary arguments, X and Y. In this case X should be tagged with EFF and Y to be THM. With this information, annotators can give the proper tag to each argument very easily. In table 1, '사람들이' of a subjective word could be EFF and '호흡 장애를' of an objective word to be THM. However, a semantic role of another argument with case suffix '텐트 속에서' is not defined in the case frame dictionary. Annotators decide its proper role with their intuition. In this case, because '텐트 속에서' means location of the predicate, annotators give LOC for time and space to the argument.

[격틀]
X=N0-이 Y=N1-를 V

[선택제약]
X - EFF / 인간|구체물
Y - THM / 기체|물리학적대상|현상|(먼지)

Fig. 3. Case frame structure of sense02 of '일으키다'

3 Annotation Results

Table 3 shows the dependency structure of the given whole sentence and Table 4 shows its annotation results. In this sentence, we found 4 predicates, '지나가다', '움직이다', '미끄러지다', and '사라지다'. Annotators try to give the proper roles to the arguments related to the 4 predicates separately. In table 4, the file name means the file including the original sentence and its dependency structure. The number next to the file name means the index of the predicate in the sentence. The first number next to dashed line is the index of the argument and the second number next to a colon (:) is the depth of its modifiers. If the number is 1, then the argument doesn't have any modifiers. If the number is 3, then the modifier has its own another modifiers. The PropBank role is shown outside the parenthesis, and Sejong role is inside the parenthesis.

Until now, we annotate more than three thousand sentences and their ten thousand predicates. On average, one sentence has 3.3 predicates and 7.2 arguments.

Table 3. Dependency Structure of the sentence "하슬람은 정신착란을 정의하기 위해서 제대로 말을 못 하고, 입이 비뚤어지고, 팔과 다리가 마음대로 놀며, 기억을 제대로 못하는 환자와 의식이 불분명한 환자를 비교했다."

```
1 2 몇_분[용언불가능보통명사]+ 이[주격조사]
2 12 지나가[일반동사] + 았[과거시제선어말어미] +
     고[대등 연결어미]+,[컴마기호]
3 4 그런[지시관형사]
4 12 다음[용언불가능보통명사]
5 6 이[지시관형사]
6 12 은빛_생물체[용언불가능보통명사] + 는[일반보조사] (주격)
7 8 전혀[부정부사]
8 9 움직이[일반동사] + 는_것_같[기타보조용언] + 지_않[기타보조용언] +
  게[종속연결어미]
9 12 미끄러지[일반동사] + 듯[종속연결어미]
10 11 바다_속[용언불가능보통명사] + 의[관형격조사]
11 12 어둠_저편[용언불가능보통명사] + 으로[부사격조사]
12 0 사라지[일반동사] + 어_가[기타보조용언] + 았[과거시제선어말어미]
    + 어요[평서형종결어미] + .[문미기호]
```

Table 4. Annotation Results of the sentence in Table 3

```
etri#doc_2242.txt 2 지나가다 --- 1:1-ARG1(THM) 2:0-rel
etri#doc_2242.txt 8 움직이다 --- 7:1-ARGM-EXT() 8:0-rel
etri#doc_2242.txt 9 미끄러지다 --- 8:2-ARGM-MNR() 9:0-rel
etri#doc_2242.txt 12 사라지다 --- 2:2-ARGM-DIS() 4:2-ARGM-TMP() 6:2-
ARG1(THM) 9:3-ARGM-MNR() 11:2-ARG2(GOL) 12:0-rel
```

4 Conclusion

This paper explains the semantic annotation task. For the task, we use syntactic annotated corpus with dependency structures and give proper semantic roles to the arguments of the given predicate. We try to build the Korean PropBank and Sejong case frame annotated corpus concurrently.

The semantic annotated corpus built in this research will be used as the training corpus data for the semantic role labeling in many of machine learning based approaches. And in the future, we will build much bigger Korean PropBank and Sejong semantic corpus by continuing annotation work.

Acknowledgments. This research was supported by Basic Science Research Program through the National Research Foundation(NRF) funded by the Ministry of Education, Science and Technology(2010-0010612).

References

1. Palmer, M., Gildea, D., Kingsbury, P.: The Proposition Bank: An Annotated Corpus of Semantic Roles. Computational Linguistics 31(1), 71–105 (2005)
2. Xue, N., Palmer, M.: Automatic Semantic Role Labeling for Chinese Verbs. In: Procs. of the 19th International Joint Conference on Artificial Intelligence (2005)
3. Hwang, J., Bhatia, A., Bonial, C., Mansouri, A., Vaidya, A., Xue, N., Palmer, M.: PropBank Annotation of Multilingual Light Verb Constructions. In: Procs. of the Fourth Linguistic Annotation Worlshop, pp. 82–90 (2010)
4. Palmer, M., Badko-Malaya, O., Bies, A., Diab, M., Maamouri, M., Mansouri, A., Saghouani, W.: A Pilot Arabic Propbank. In: Procs. of the International Conference on Language Resources and Evaluation (2008)

Web Based File Transmission System for Delivery of E-Training Contents

Yu-Doo Kim[1,*], Mohan Kim[2], and Il-Young Moon[1]

[1] Department of Computer Science Engineering, KoreaTech, Korea
{kydman,iymoon}@koreatech.ac.kr
[2] Department of Aviation and Technology, San Jose State University, USA
Mohan.Kim@sjsu.edu

Abstract. The rapid growth of telecommunication technology has led to the development of many smart devices. In particular, the smartphone market has been growing rapidly following the development of third-generation telecommunication technology. As a result, most people are expected to use a smartphone within a few years. Furthermore, the market for smart devices such as tablets and smart TVs are growing rapidly. Therefore, most people are expected to own various smart devices within a few years. Especially, education systems using smart devices will very useful. So we are implementing a car mechanics e-training system using smart devices. But it is not support real time contents updating. In this paper, we implement web based file transmission system for delivery of e-training contents.

Keywords: File Transmission, E-Training, CDN, Web, HTML5.

1 Introduction

Current IT(Information Technology) systems are focusing on smart devices. Especially e-learning is changing the smart learning system as supporting various smart devices such as smart phone, tablet and smart TV.

In the past project, we had implemented car mechanic e-training system for desktop and we will develop e-training system supporting various smart devices[1]. But current system is not supporting real time contents updating Therefore we study about contents delivery technology. As a result, web technology is suitable for this system because it is support various platform. Especially, HTML5 is hot issue on the web technologies[2][3]. For supporting various platforms, it must use web technology. So we studies HTML5 technology for file transmission. Through web socket and File API of HTML5, we had implemented it.

In this paper, we subscribe about HTML5 technology. Especially, web socket and File API technology are very useful for file transmission. Next it design web based file system architecture and implement it using various web technology. And then, we analyze performance of this system and compare with mobile and desktop system. Finally, we conclude this paper.

* Corresponding author.

T.-h. Kim et al. (Eds.): EL/DTA/UNESST 2012, CCIS 352, pp. 272–276, 2012.

2 HTML5

HTML5 is a markup language for structuring and presenting content for the World Wide Web, and is a core technology of the Internet originally proposed by Opera Software. It is the fifth revision of the HTML standard and, as of September 2012, is still under development. Its core aims have been to improve the language with support for the latest multimedia while keeping it easily readable by humans and consistently understood by computers and device. HTML5 is intended to subsume not only HTML 4, but XHTML 1 and DOM Level 2 HTML as well[4].

HTML5 is not software that has to be installed but rather a new version of the language HTML. Web browsers must support this new version of HTML in order to correctly display web pages using HTML5 functions. It is upon the developers of browsers to update their software to use HTML5 users simply must allow these updates to be done on their computers, but do not have to install additional software.

Especially, HTML5 is support web socket API and File API[5][6]. Web socket is web based communication API. Through it, we will send the contents to other devices. File API is support accessing local file systems. So we can implement file transmission application based on web.

2.1 File API

The HTML 5 specification offers File API for manipulating both binary and text files on client side. Your imagination is the only limitation for the capabilities of this technology. Remember, the files are saved to a sandbox area, not in real file system.

2.2 Web Sockets API

HTML5 offers a new interface called Web Sockets API, that allows you to open a socket to the webserver and remain opened until server or you close it and provides you a two-way communication. This saves a lot of time, when you have to save time. Because XHR requests just closes after the response is received, so a great time is saved when you do not have to re-open a TCP connection. Web Sockets offer both binary and text transfer. One disadvantage, a single message cannot exceed 32KB, or I cannot, Chrome throws an error that frame size is too big. So it will show lower speed than traditional sockets such as TCP and UDP.

3 Web Based File Transmission

This system's architecture is very simple. It had composed by two methods.

First is file sender part using web socket. It acts to find a file using File API and transfer the contents to other devices. Next is receiver part, it is receiving the contents from sender using web socket too. After that, it will store file to the receiver devices. Figure 1 shows architecture of this system.

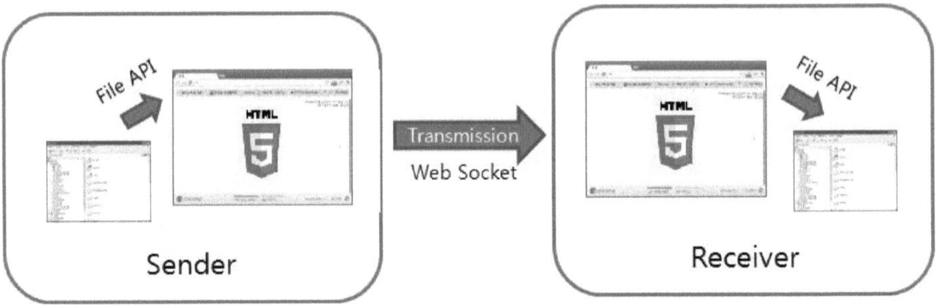

Fig. 1. System Architecture

In this system, we use famous web based FTP file transmission library. There are many web based FTP library as open source project. Among them, we consider two open source libraries. First is wsftp and next is wftp[7][8].

In the two libraries, we decide that using wftp because it is supporting easy UI(User Interface) and various function. Figure 2 shows a screenshot about FTP system on the desktop and figure 3 shows mobile FTP system. These systems are same because it developed by web technology.

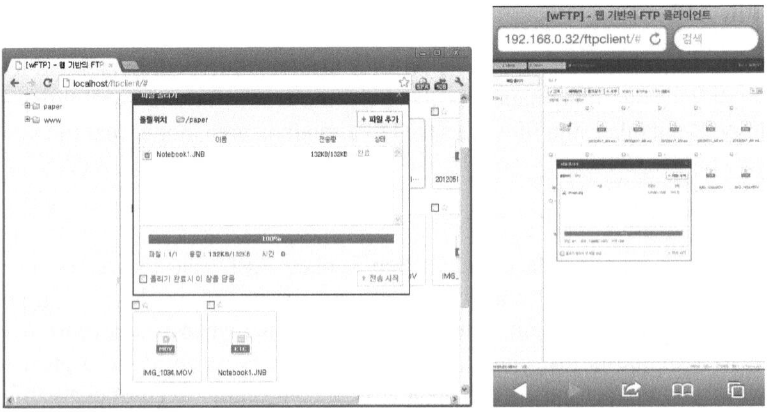

(a) Desktop (b) Mobile

Fig. 2. Screenshot of FTP system

4 Performance Analysis

In this paper, we analyze the speed of the two platforms. First is file transmission time on the desktop. Next is analysis same method on the mobile device. Through this method, we compare speed between desktop and mobile device based web file transmission application. We check a download and upload speed on the four times. In this experiment, we expect that upload speed is show lower speed than speed because it use HTTP protocol when download contents. It is using Web Socket if it upload a contents. In these results, we expect Web Socket is lower than traditional network technology yet. Nevertheless, we can recommend using web based file transmission system because it is support various platform. Current users use various devices and it need contents sharing between devices. Therefore smart users can use contents transmission easily through web based file transmission application.

It is running on iPhone4 mobile device and Quad Core desktop PC. It shows on Table 1. Research results can show Figure 3. We were experiment three times. First is 10Mb file transmission. Next is 20Mb, 30Mb and 40Mb transmission.

Table 1. Test Environment

System	Hardware and OS	Network
Mobile	iPhone 4 iOS 6	WiFi
Desktop	Quad 2.5Ghz Windows XP	WiFi

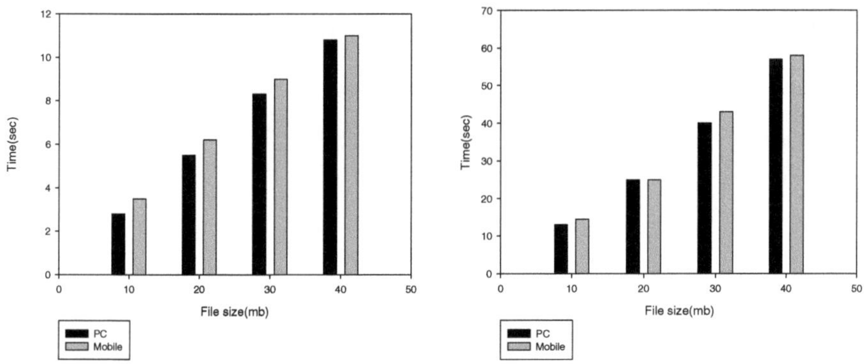

(a) Download Speed (b) Upload Speed

Fig. 3. Download and Upload Speed

5 Conclusion

In this paper, we design web based contents transmission for E-Training system and performance analysis the speed of the two methods. First is file upload time and download time on the desktop and mobile platforms. Through this method, we compare speed between desktop and mobile device based web file transmission application. Next is compare with traditional TCP file transmission and Web Socket file transmission. In this experiment, we expect that web socket is show lower speed than TCP. But web based system is supporting various platform easily. So we recommend using web based file transmission system and expect that Web Socket will be advanced.

Acknowledgments. This research was supported by a grant from the R&D Program(Industrial Strategic Technology Development) funded by the Ministry of Knowledge Economy(MKE), Republic of Korea. Also, The authors are deeply thankful to all interested persons of MKE and KEIT(Korea Evaluation Institute of Industrial Technology).

References

1. Kim, Y.D., Lee, S.U., Moon, I.Y.: A Study on Mobile Virtual Training System using Augmented Reality. The Journal of Korea Navigation Institute 15, 1047–1052 (2011)
2. HTML5 Reference, http://dev.w3.org/html5/html-author/
3. Tournski, E.: Cloud-based collaborative creation and simulation of courses of action: Creation of a prototype web application using new HTML5 features. In: Computational Intelligence for Security and Defence Applications, pp. 1–6 (2012)
4. HTML5 Differences from HTML4, Working Draft, World Wide Web Consortium, April 5 (2011)
5. File API W3C, http://www.w3.org/TR/FileAPI/
6. The WebSocket API Editor's Draft, http://dev.w3.org/html5/websockets/
7. wsFTP Project, https://github.com/mustafaakin/wsftp
8. wFTP Project, https://github.com/seogi1004/wftp

A Study on Judgment of Intoxication State Using Speech

Geumran Baek and Myungjin Bae*

Information and Telecommunication Department, Soongsil University,
369 Sangdo-ro DongJak-Gu, Seoul, 156-743, Republic of Korea
judybaek@hanmail.net, mjbae@ssu.ac.kr

Abstract. Nowadays, the various forms of studies are under progress to identify the individuals such as using fingerprints, iris, voice, etc. And among them, the unique voice parameters of individual are being applied in diverse fields such as security, communication services, biorhythm checks, criminal investigation data, etc. In this study the research on the extraction of parameters to judge the intoxication by comparing the speech before and after the drinking using speech analysis. To do that, the physical changes and changes in the vocal cord and area of vocal tract of a person after drinking and the influence of alcohol on the phonation were observed. In addition, a study to find the parameters, which enable to judge the intoxication, by studying the differences of the phonation in the domain of time and the frequency before and after the drinking from various speakers was conducted.

Keywords: vocal cord, vocal tract, intoxication.

1 Introduction

The moderate intake of alcohol provides the help in various ways to the people, but excessive drinking is harmful for the health. In addition, driving after drinking may take away many lives by causing serious accident. The Government is making various efforts to prevent not only the car accidents, but also maritime and aerial accidents by drunken operation. As a part of those efforts, in the case of ships, blood alcohol level is measured before and after the sail, but it is difficult to measure during the sailing. Obviously, the coast guards measure it through the direct contact in the sea, but this method is very dangerous because of the difficulties in docking the ships or possibility of fleeing. Therefore, an indirect and objective method to judge the intoxication during long distance sailing is needed. Mostly the intoxication is determined indirectly through the communication with the operator, however if the operator may deny the alcohol consumption, it is hard to determine whether the operator may consume it or not[5,6]. Therefore, in this study, the research on the algorithm to determine the intoxication through the speech analysis was conducted. In Section 2, the physical and phonation changes after drinking were examined, and in Section 3, the characteristics after drinking in the domain of time and frequency were extracted. In Section 4, the experiment and results were explained, and in Section 5, the conclusion was made.

* Corresponding author.

T.-h. Kim et al. (Eds.): EL/DTA/UNESST 2012, CCIS 352, pp. 277–282, 2012.

2 Changes of Voice after Drinking

When people consume the alcohol, several different physical changes occur according to the concentration of alcohol in blood. Since alcohol deteriorates the activities of the central nervous system, and even a small amount of alcohol deteriorate some functions of the brain. If an adequate amount of alcohol is taken in the body, the heartbeat becomes faster, the blood vessels are expanded, and the blood pressure can be lowered a little bit. In addition, it can increase the appetite, stimulate the gastric secretion and makes to urinate often. Ethanol, which is one of the main ingredients of alcohol, is rapidly absorbed in the stomach and the small intestine, and becomes the energy source by being decomposed into the water and carbon dioxide by the alcohol dehydrogenase of the liver, but part of it is released without being changed when breathing or excreted through the urethra. Also, there is a tendency to speak louder during drinking. This is because alcohol(ethanol) works in the central nervous system, and acts as a substance that restricts the nervous action of the brain. In other words, drinking alcohol causes the motor skill deterioration, rational judgment deterioration, deterioration of control, deterioration of cognition and concentration ability, deterioration of situational judgment ability, etc[1].

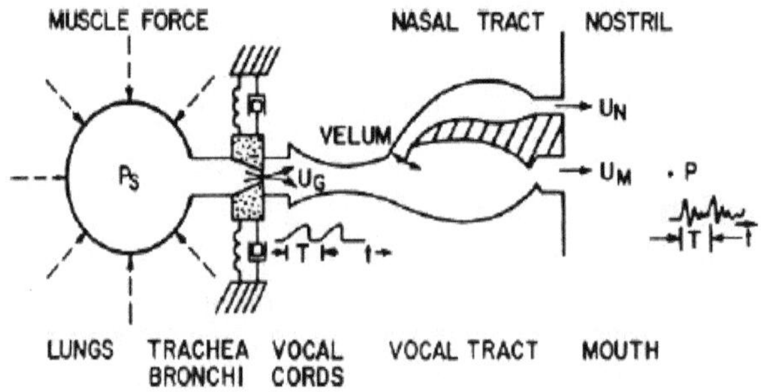

Fig. 1. Voice Generation Model

Fig. 1 is shown the lower glottis system consisted of the lungs, respiratory tract and respiratory organs, and is the source of energy to generate the voice. The voice is the acoustic wave form emitted from this system when air is released from the lungs and disturbed by the stricture point in the vocal tract. The voice can be divided into 3 parts according to the excitation; sonant, fricative and plosive sounds. These 3 sounds are produced and changed by vocal cord, vocal tract and quasi periodic pulse of the air. In this instance, the force of the air can be changed depending on the respiration volume of the lungs. Since the lung capacity is increased after drinking, the duration time of the voice is changed by lowering the speed of lung's movement, and changing the vocal cords and pulse of the air, etc[2,3]. Also, since alcohol has a diuretic effect, it may cause the dehydration in the mucous membrane of larynx, cause the change in voice by working on the vocal cord, and reduce the flexibility and elasticity of the mucous membrane of the vocal cord. And the complete opening and closing of vocal cord may not occur when the sub-glottal pressure is applied. As a result, the increase of viscosity in the vocal muscles and incomplete opening and closing of the glottis increase the minimum pressure required for phonation and the long capacity of the speaker.

In the aspect of the signal processing, the White Noise is generated from the lung, and as it passes the vocal tract, the resonance is generated in the frequency corresponded to that characteristics, and the rests are vanished by offset. The resonant frequency generated at this moment referred to as the formant frequency or simply as the formant. The specific speech signals can be represented by several specific formants. Therefore, the formant is working as important element in the speech signal modeling. The parameter working as important element in the speech signal together with the formant is the pitch. The pitch means the peaks represented widely along the axis of time generated by the periodic vibrations of the vocal cords, and generally, referred to as the Fundamental Frequency [2,3].

3 Extraction of Voice Characteristic after Drinking

Table 1. is shown the maximum amplitude, average energy and dynamic range, investigated before and after drinking. Although the average value of the maximum amplitude and the average energy were increase, they do not represent any significance because the magnitude was of less than 1dB. In fact, the cases that the maximum amplitude was decreased, were 30%, and the cases that the average energy was decreased were 46%.

Table 1. Changes in the maximum amplitude, average energy and dynamic range after drinking [unit: dB]

	20s	30s	40s	50s	Average
Maximum amplitude	1.3	-0.4	0.3	1.0	0.5
Average Energy	0.1	-0.5	0.0	1.8	0.4
Dynamic Range	2.9	2.7	3.8	2.3	2.9

On the other hand, in the average change in dynamic range, the significant results of 2.9dB were obtained. The case that it was decreased was represented from only person, corresponded to 3%. The Fig 3 is shown the distribution of the average evergy on the sound source that particularly represent such characteristics. this graph shows the relative occupation rate of the overall amplitude energy, and the characteristics of the phonation energy of individual speaker. Fig. 2-(1) is the graph before drinking, and while the peak difference between the small phonation and big phonation was represented as 3.5dB, in the Fig. 2(2), which is corresponded to after drinking, it was represented as 5.5dB as being increased by 2dB. In addition, it is observed that the envelope curve became considerably gentle when the small phonation was made. Similar results were obtained from the other sound sources, too.

Through these results, two characteristics can be drawn. First characteristic is that the deviation in the volume of the voice after drinking gets bigger after drinking. This is consistent with the general phenomenon that when being drunken, the voice becomes too louder or too smaller without maintaining the appropriate sound volume constantly. And the second characteristic is that, when watching the waveform after drinking, it is observed that the proportion of waveform distributed over high energy level is increase than that over low energy level. This is deemed to be a phenomenon that since the hearing functions are decreased after drinking, the speaker talks louder voice opening the mouth wider, and as such, the lung capacity is increased.

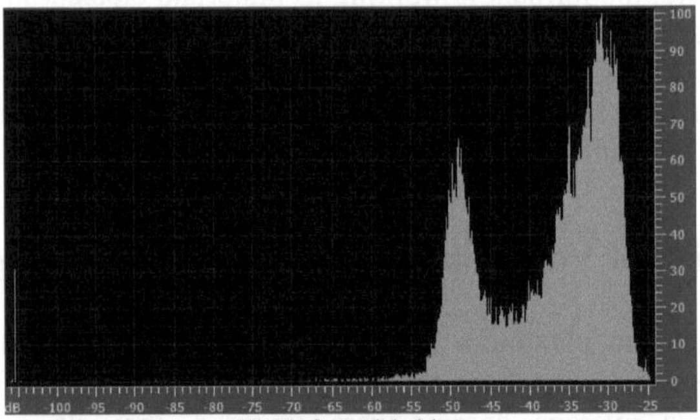

(1) Before drinking

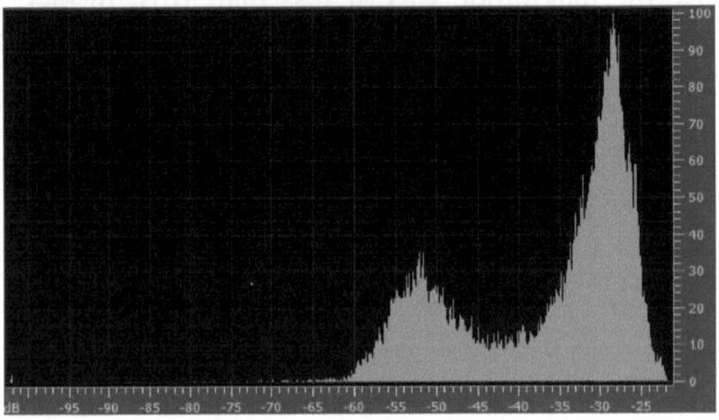

(2) After drinking

Fig. 2. Energy Distribution Chart before and after Drinking

As shown in Fig. 3, for the parameters generally used in synthesis, coding and voice recognition or speaker identification, the formant information is widely used in case of analyzing on the frequency. It is because the basic analysis on the sound is possible as this analyzes the characteristics of the individual on the frequency. Therefore, existing method estimates the drinker using the changes in the formant. However, although the judgment by the extraction of parameters through the domain of frequency can be used as the personalized information because it is good, in case that the variation of the sound is severe, new parameters are required to determine if the extraction of exact characteristics on the changes in the vocal tract is possible. Therefore, this article needs the factor to define not only the unique feature of the sound but also clearness and tone getting away from such fundamental parameters[3,4,7].

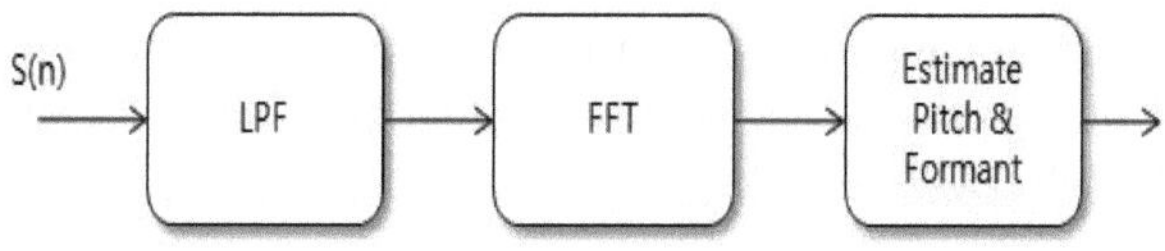

Fig. 3. Extraction method of common parameter

It is observed that in case of drinkers, generally the sound distinguished by unit syllable in the natural sound connected with the vowel and consonant changes considerably. This is corresponded to drop the accuracy in the vowel, which connect the consonant with consonant, and final consonant, and it is deemed to happen as what pronounced by unit syllable is damaged in the vocal tract, the muscular organ. It was observed that these characteristics clearly appeared when the voices of the various drinkers were examined. The first and most outstanding characteristic was the changes of the pitch comparing the voices before and after drinking. The second characteristic was that the change of inclination in the formant, and it is observed that the inclination of the formant after drinking was increased comparing with before drinking. And for last, it was observed that the fluctuation rates of the 3rd formant and the 4th formant has increased in the voices after drinking.

4 Experiment and Results

The voices before and after drinking were recorded from total 36 persons composed of each 5~8 persons of 20's, 30's, 40's and 50's, and analyzed. Each person drank the alcohol more than 20% of their drinking capacity, and for the sound sources, the experimental texts combine with 5 basic vowels, numbers, and declarative sentences, etc with duration of 1 minute 30 seconds to 2 minutes were used. As the interface for the voice signal input and output, AD/DA converter was used, and the data was entered in 16 nit with 10kHz of sampling.

First, in the domain of time, as mentioned in previous Section, the average and variance of the energy per frame were obtained and the distribution of the energy values existed above the threshold obtained from experiment, the distribution was calculated. As a result, it was observed that the distribution of voice energy after drinking was represented higher than before drinking. The energy distribution obtained from these characteristics was used as parameter to determine the voice after drinking.

The second parameter used was made using the fluctuation rate in the 3rd formant and 4th formant. Fig. 4 is shown the judgment diagram using the process of building DB of the proposed method and the proposed comparison method. A database is built by converting the input signals to the frequency domain and using the comparison method for two LPF. Generally, the LPF using 4kHz is defined to have voice signal without loss. However, since in the signal filtered in 2.75kHz, the 3rd formant 3 and 4th formant are removed, it has only low-frequency signal formant. The signals maintaining the characteristics of the 3rd and 4th formants can be made by calculating the difference between the two signals filtered as such. Although these signals are ignored in existing researches, now, they have cognitive information as very important parameter. Here, they are used by measuring the band with at -35 dB based on the maximum gain (0 dB) and building database. Although the sound signals typically have been used under the premise that there are not important parameter above than 4kHz, since it is as same as the unique clearness of the voice is deleted, in the actual experiment, the signal was measure by amplifying the bandwidth up to 8kHz.

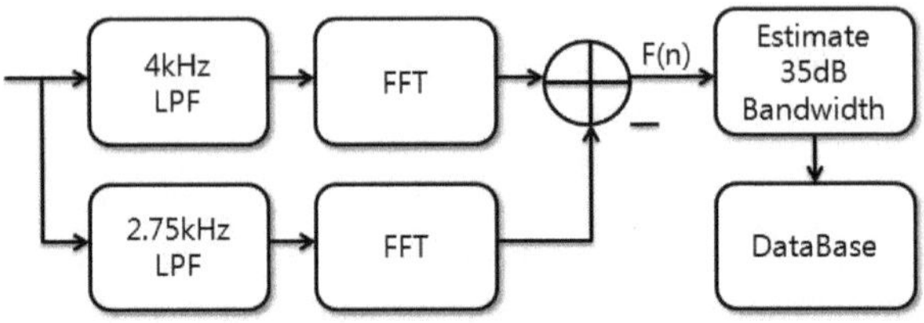

Fig. 4. Method to build a database for the proposed method

In the test results applying two parameters having the highest accuracy out of the various characteristics introduced in previous Section, the voices after drinking were compared with the voices before drinking stored in database and more than 85% of accuracy was obtained.

5 Conclusion and Future Research

In this study, as a parameter to identify the drinker, the changes in the higher harmonics which is corresponded to the energy distribution and high frequency were used. This method considers the hearing ability and the change in phonation after drinking, and uses the fact that the 3rd and 4th formants have more influences in the changes after drinking. As a result, 85% of accuracy of identifying the voices after drinking comparing with the voices before drinking was obtained .

In future, it is necessary to conduct the research in order to be able to identify the drinking in the continuous signal without having database, that is, speaker's drinking independently from database using these data. In addition this can become the standard to detect the important changes in the speaker's information, and can be expanded as much important parameter by examining the variation in recognizing the speaker.

References

1. Murata, K., Kawashima, M., Inaba, R.: Auditory threshold reduction on alcohol ingestion. Psychopharmacology 157, 188–192 (2001), doi:10.1007/s002130100782
2. Han, J.-S.: Speech signal processing. Osungmedia 12, 60–61 (2003)
3. Rabiner, L.R., Schafer, R.W.: Digital processing of Speech Signal, pp. 38–115 (1978)
4. Bae, M.-J.: Digital speech synthesis. Dongyoung, pp.225-227
5. Yi, E.–Y., Park, H.-W., Bae, M.-J.: A Study on the Duration Change in Drunk. In: Acoustical Society of Korea and Signal Processing Conference, vol. 29(1) (2012)
6. Kyon, D.-H., Bae, M.-J.: Analysis of Voice Energy after Drinking. In: Acoustical Society of Korea and Signal Processing Conference, vol. 29(1), pp. 105–106 (2012)
7. Bae, S.-G., Park, H.-W., Baek, G.-R., Bae, M.-J.: A Study on a Drinking Judgement Method of Speech Signal using the Ratio of Harmonic Deviation. In: Acoustical Society of Korea and Signal Processing Conference, vol. 29(1) (2012)

Research of Color Affordance Concept and Applying to Design

Pakr Sung-euk

Jungwon University, Dongbu-ri 5, Goesan-eup, Goesan-gun, Chungcheongbuk-do, South Korea 367-805
pse@jwu.ac.kr

Abstract. Color Affordance is a very useful term in the fact that it is a new approach method that applies various environments and human relationship as well as various psychology researchers' opinion in an overall systematic theory. Color Affordance has its basic principle in using color in a certain field to directly and indirectly induce human action. However, there has never been a systematic case study regarding specific color affordance concept. Although the above mentioned color marketing, color dynamics, color therapy, are all affordance theory based on human psychology and remembrance to color and physiological phenomena, this broad affordance concept has insufficient aspects in regards to various human environment or specific situations.

Keywords: Color, Affordance, Color Affordance, Design.

1 Introduction

Color Affordance is interpreted in a broader term than the concept of color and it is actively applied in the fields of human cognitive behavior and design to systemize the concept of affordance of human reaction to color. Thus, a certain situation or form is combined with color to induce the feelings and specific behavior of users. Color does not show a meaning or affordance concept by itself. Moreover, the application of general psychology, remembrance, emotion, etc. of color adjustment in coloration is a broad activity and it is when it comes to application to specific situations or subtle design. So, the use of Color Affordance in design has the property to reduce confusion to users and induce them towards a clearer goal.

1.1 Concept and Design Application of Affordance

Affordance means to induce a certain behavior and thus, it is called so. The root word 'Afford' originally means various things such as 'to have enough to get ~, to be able to ~, to provide ~, to calculate' but, there is a definition unavailable in general dictionaries in the field of human-computer interaction, cognitive psychology, industrial design, interaction design, environmental psychology, and artificial intelligence that means 'something that connects different concepts'. In other words, it means the connecting functionality of uses, actions, and functions that are presentable according to a particular relationship between object and organism (usually people).

T.-h. Kim et al. (Eds.): EL/DTA/UNESST 2012, CCIS 352, pp. 283–288, 2012.

Naoto Fukasawa understood this term as a central element of design and emphasized the importance of discovery in regards to conscious behavior dissolved in environment through the expressions of 'design contained in the environment', and 'design within behavior.' Therefore, he mentioned that there is intentional behavior as well as unconscious behavior, and among these two conscious behavior and instinctive behavior the latter, which is instinctive and subconscious behavior, has a much larger domain than we realize, and it is such unconscious behavior where designing hints can be obtained from. This expression is not clearly laid out but such behavior is induced by the latent information (affordance) contained within the environment, and design by behavior is said to be the discovery and balance of value (affordance) within the environment.

The computer, which carries out very complex functions, provided an easier environment to users through the appearance of GUI(Graphic User Interface) while the automatic function in cars brought about the demand of female drivers and various automatized appliances made all operation possible with a button. This caused a trend of design research and application in consideration of human psychology and molding not only in industrial design but also in various other fields such as architecture, computer, user interface, etc.[1]

1.2 The Role of Design and Color

The human history with color originates form the primitive times. Through the many color information of nature, we were able to survive by the basic knowledge of distinguishing between the poisonous and safe. In the modern society, not only the place where humans live in but also the things we wear, the things we eat all have a close relation to color. Much of the information in a human's daily life is dependent on sight with the highest dependency of over 80% among the five senses of human beings, which are taste, feel, sight, smell, and hearing. Color not only greatly affects our feelings and emotions but also plays a large role in fundamental communication between human beings.

The concept of beauty and ugliness cannot exist in a single independent color. Many people are interested and researching the psychological effects of color since long back. Unstable emotions, unpleasant feelings, and other neurotic mental illnesses can occur from environments with the wrong color environment while good feelings, fresh and joyful emotions can be formed from a wondrous color environment. The change in color has a great effect on homes, workplaces, services, etc. through artists, craftsmen, manufacturers, suppliers, sellers, and computers. Moreover, color goes beyond the simple concept of color to deeply affect not only our emotions and feelings but also applied in the field of communication, creating an outstanding visual effect that can substitute language. [2]

In such a viewpoint, many companies nowadays are increasing their sales through the sales strategy of color by using the emotional reaction of color. Various methods are used, such as color marketing to directly link to customer purchasing behavior, human emotions to color for working environment, equipment facilities, instruments etc. by choosing color combination that gives people pleasure or colors that control certain behavior by affecting psychological feelings, and also application of color dynamics to induce safe behavior. Furthermore, health treatment called color therapy that uses colors for psychological and emotional treatment and stabilization are also widely used and in search of.

2 Concept of Color Affordance

Designers, planners, engineers who make certain products, services, system are considered to have succeeded in a convenient design if the user can guess the use of the product by taking an intuitive look at it. Here, if affordance is put into good use, the user can figure out the use of it through previous experience. In this case, the product is used in the method that the designer had intended and is considered a good condition of design. Moreover, the use of color in design has the property to reduce confusion to users and induce them towards a clearer goal.

Color Affordance is interpreted in a broader term than the concept of color and it is actively applied in the fields of human cognitive behavior and design to systemize the concept of affordance of human reaction to color. Thus, a certain situation or form is combined with color to induce the feelings and specific behavior of users. Color does not show a meaning or affordance concept by itself. Moreover, the application of general psychology, remembrance, emotion, etc. of color adjustment in coloration is a broad activity and it is when it comes to application to specific situations or subtle design.[3]

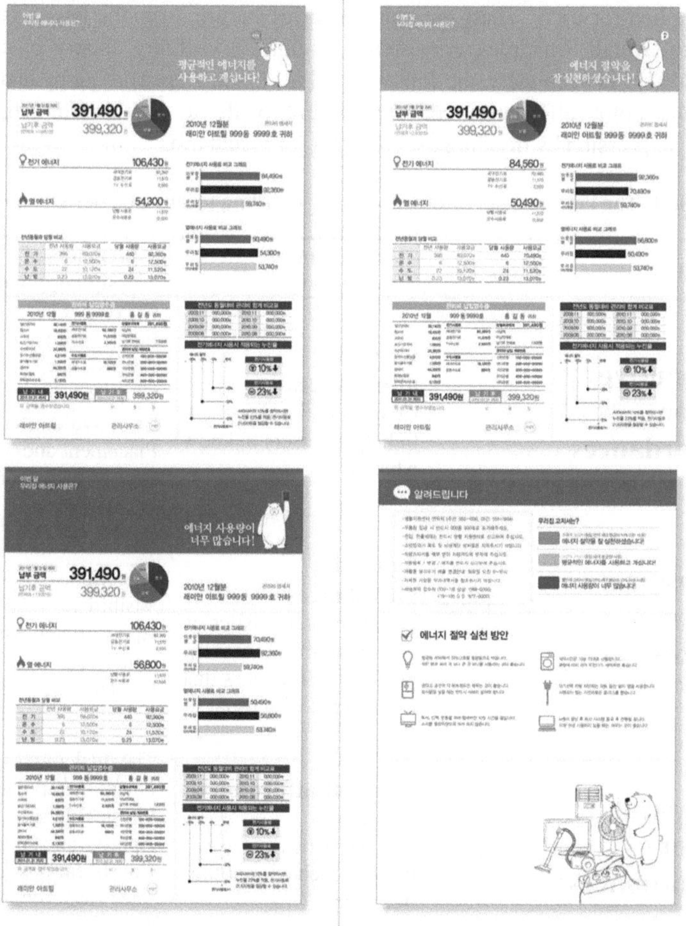

For example, from January to March of 2011, the Ministry of Knowledge Economy and Korea Energy Management Corporation carried out an experimental issuance of a maintenance bill in 600 complexes of the Seoul Bangbaedong Sanmsung Raemian Apartment Hill for the design and color adjustment (figure1. source: Institute of Design Promotion). This bill shown was divided into three colors of green, yellow and red according to the user energy consumption. This resulted in an average 10.7% reduction of energy consumption per household. If this were calculated on nationwide houses, a 336 billion won worth of energy would be saved per year. This is a good example of the application of color affordance to induce users to reduce the consumption of energy.(*Remark 1.)*

2.1 Characteristics of Color Affordance

As shown above, the concept of Color Affordance is interpreted more broadly than color and is actively utilized in areas of human cognition and design to systemize the concept of affordance in regards to human reaction to color. Color affordance is not simply the combination of the theory to color. There are many theories that are considered when design is applied for users. There are many theories starting from the basic visual design principles to Gestalt Principles, consistency, legibility, visibility, theory of constraints, etc. of form. [4] In such view, the following tables 1 and 2 are laid out by understanding and applying color affordance concept more broadly to meaningful situation and information expression by dividing the elements for visual test.

Table 1. The kind of color affordances and according to situation design applied

Kind	Situation	Affordances situation	Elements of design applied
Cognitive color affordances	Cognitive situation	**Cognitive affordances-** Characteristics designed to help the users to know what is	Clarity, Accuracy, Predictability, Consistency, Compatibility, Error avoidance, Placement and Group Relevance, Persuasiveness
Sensuous color affordances	Cognitive situation	**Sensuous affordances-** Design characteristics of cognitive affordances or physical affordances that make you feel sensual	Attention, Visibility, AppropriatenessLay out, Readability,
Physical color affordances	Cognitive situation	**Physical affordances-** The design characteristics of the physical behavior at the interface	The difficulties of object manipulation, Physical fatigue, Appropriate size, Consistent position, The effectiveness of actions

Table 2. Visual verification element of color affordances

Kind	Shape perception	Color Perception
Color Perception	Shape, Position, Orientation, size, Intuitive, Remember Information, Concentrate	Emotional information, Brightness, color, Texture, Emotional feeling, Mood, Comfort
Apply design theory	Gestalt Gestalt psychology, Recognition memory, Consolidation and memory, Constancy, consistency, Theory of constraints, Depth of visual design Principles, Information processing, By careless over the space, The foreground and background, Mapping, readability	Color perception, Interference effects, Automatically, Homeostasis, Consistent, and Color, reminiscent of Coloration effects, Colors of emotions (visibility, attention, advances temperature sense, circa Almanac)

3 Visual Verification Element of Color Affordances

Table 3. Visual verification element of color affordances

Example	Situation	Color Affordances
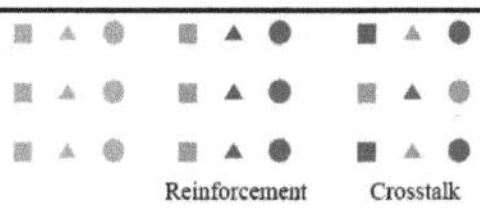	If combine colors and shapes Gestalt laws of similarity - interpreted differently	Cognitive Sensuous
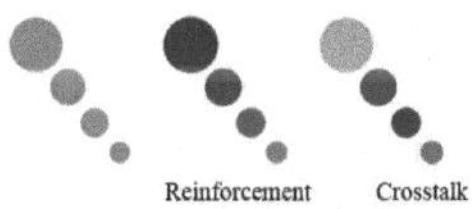	If combine colors change The laws of visual design(increase laws) - interpreted differently	Sensuous Physical
	If combine colors in certain circumstances(form) Cognitive (behavioral) reactions yield different results ex) **Red:** Fire, pizza house, the house of blood donation **Green**: shelter, eco house	Cognitive Physical
	If combine colors in certain circumstances(form) Cognitive (behavioral) reactions yield different results ex) intersection, hospitals, Red Cross	Cognitive Sensuous

Table 3. (*continued*)

	According to changes in color tone - categorization / grouping	Cognitive Sensuous Physical
	If combine colors in certain circumstances(form) Behavior induced or constrained	Cognitive Sensuous Physical
	If combine colors and shapes Stroop interference effect- Interfere with information processing of stimuli(color)	Cognitive Sensuous Physical

4 Design Application Possibility of Color Affordance

The visual cognition of form is intuitive and rational while color has an individual and emotional tendency. Among a lot of visual information around us, it is true that the information from color is especially influential to human psychology and the following actions to it. Color Affordance is a very useful term in the fact that it is a new approach method that applies various environments and human relationship as well as various psychology researchers' opinion in an overall systematic theory.

Color Affordance has its basic principle in using color in a certain field to directly and indirectly induce human action. However, there has never been a systematic case study regarding specific color affordance concept. Although the above mentioned color marketing, color dynamics, color therapy, are all affordance theory based on human psychology and remembrance to color and physiological phenomena, this broad affordance concept has insufficient aspects in regards to various human environment or specific situations.

Through various combination of information, Color Affordance is a necessary field to a designer that has to provide their best. What is important is not how a design situation and problem is expressed but how the users react to the expressed design and how they behaved. The modern society is rapidly changing in environment and creating many new design situations that did not exist in the past. In such a situation, the active use of color affordance in the beginning planning of design will be needed for taking a more active measure.

References

1. Kim, L.A.: `http://blog.naver.com/lionel_kim?Redirect=Log&logNo=140106707741/`
2. Choe, Y.Y.: Coloration Education Study through the Psychological Approach of Color. Ph.D. Thesis (2008)
3. `http://ko.wikipedia.org/wiki/affordance`
4. Park, H.J.: A development of affordances design strategy for improvement of pedagogical usability on e-learning contents user interfaces. P40. Ph.D. Thesis (2012)
5. (Remark 1.) form Korea design Center

An ANFIS Model for Environmental Performance Measurement of Transportation

Sang-Hyun Lee[1], Jong-Han Lim[2], and Kyung-Il Moon[3]

[1] Dept. of Cultural Industry Management, Honam University, Korea
[2] Dept. of Mechanical and Automotive Engineering, Gachon University, Korea
[3] Dept. of Computer Engineering, Honam University
{leesang64,kimoon}@honam.ac.kr,
kkjong@gachon.ac.kr

Abstract. Fuzzy logic has also been applied to life cycle assessment (LCA) mainly to assess uncertain values or to use on individuals' judgments as input data in LCA studies. This paper presents an environmental performance measurement using an adaptive neuro-fuzzy inference system (ANFIS) in an LCA model for comparing alternative transportation fuels. The most promising fuels include compressed natural gas (CNG) and biodiesel. The potential environmental benefits of these alternative fuels can be measured using LCA methodology. The methodology allows quantitative information on the material and energy flows to be integrated with qualitative information reflecting such aspects as the social acceptability of different types of environmental damage. The proposed ANFIS model is used to represent uncertainties in the data so that the model can predict both the magnitude of the environmental impacts of the alternative fuels and the corresponding desirable levels of these estimates. Results of a case study show biodiesel to be superior to both CNG and diesel in terms of overall environmental impact.

Keywords: Aggregation, ANFIS, LCA, Transportation fuels.

1 Introduction

This Life Cycle Assessment (LCA) is a methodology that considers a vehicle's entire life cycle, from material and vehicle production through its lifetime on the road to the end-of-life disposal, as well as the life cycle of its fuel sources. Current regulations in discussion around the world are focused on measurement of tailpipe emissions only, which is a reflection of the lifetime on the road. However, it is not just vehicle use that generates greenhouse gas (GHG) emissions, but all of its life cycle stages. Emphasis on the road lifetime alone may have the unintended consequence of increasing GHG emissions during the vehicle life.

An LCA approach assists automakers in evaluating and reducing the total energy and lifetime GHG emissions of their products. Some manufacturers are using LCA to evaluate the contribution of materials and design decisions to total vehicle lifetime emissions. Their objective is to assess possible driving phase improvements against

T.-h. Kim et al. (Eds.): EL/DTA/UNESST 2012, CCIS 352, pp. 289–297, 2012.

manufacturing phase and end-of-life disadvantages associated with GHG-intensive materials. The LCA approach to quantifying environmental burden is formalized by the International Organization for Standardization (ISO) 14040 series. Notable documents in this series are ISO 14040:2006 - Principles and Framework (ISO 2006a) and ISO 14044:2006 - Requirements and Guidelines (ISO 2006b), which together outline many fundamental concepts relevant to develop and conduct an LCA study. ISO breaks the LCA framework into four stages: goal and scope definition, inventory analysis, impact assessment, and interpretation. More information regarding the details of each stage can be found in the ISO documents, which are an essential resource for any LCA practitioner. One key finding of the LCA study is that vehicle size is as important a determinate of emission impact as fuel/technology type - the results show that vehicle size is strongly correlated to overall environmental impact as quantified by the Cleaner Drive rating system. Moving down one FISITA passenger car category typically reduces the Total Cleaner Drive rating by 6-8 points [1]. For a medium sized passenger car, this equates to a reduction in the total life cycle environmental impact of around 12%-16%. For all fuels/technologies, the difference between the rating of the smallest and largest car categories is around a factor of 2.5 [1].

LCA provides a framework for quantifying natural resource usage, air emissions release and the resultant environmental impacts per unit of transportation service delivered. In particular, such information provides warranty policy-makers with an adequate warranty assessment of potential environmental benefits of alternative fuels, which will aid in making subsequent cost-benefit analyses and planning. LCA models simulate the environmental flows and impacts of transportation systems in a virtual environment, thus allowing their behavior to be studied before they are actually built or implemented. The process of development of such models requires reconciling two potentially conflicting considerations.

This paper presents the application of fuzzy multiple attribute decision-making in an LCA model for comparing alternative transportation fuels.

2 Modeling Framework

The printing area is 122 mm × 193 mm. The text should be justified to occupy the full line width, so that the right margin is not ragged, with words hyphenated as appropriate. Please fill pages so that the length of the text is no less than 180 mm, if possible. A schematic diagram of a generic life cycle system for fuels and vehicles is illustrated in Figure 1. In this study, focus is placed only on the fuel cycle, since prior studies have shown it to be the dominant contributor to total environmental impact [5]. Also, we use the decision hierarchy model regarding the application of fuzzy multiple attribute decision-making [2]. The three alternatives used in their paper are diesel, biodiesel and CNG. Biodiesel is assumed to be coconut oil methyl ester, which is produced by transesterification of coconut oil with methanol derived from NG [3].

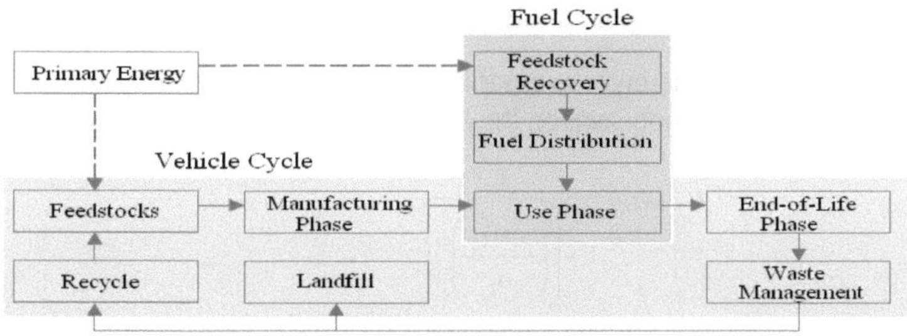

Fig. 1. Vehicle and Fuel Cycles

Ratings for each attribute can be computed using a previously developed fuzzy LCA model [4], which in turn is based on GREET 1.5a [5] augmented with impact assessment capability using the EDIP method [6]. This form of uncertainty is fuzzy nature and is best dealt with using fuzzy mathematics. Imprecise quantities can be represented using fuzzy numbers.

3 ANFIS Structure and Aggregation Process

In this paper, we use a modified ANFIS structure and aggregation process. The suggested approach uses the gaussian functions for fuzzy sets and the generalized bell function for the rule outputs. The initial parameters of the network are the mean and standard deviation of the membership functions (antecedent parameters) and the coefficients of the output function (consequent parameters). The ANFIS learning algorithm is then used to obtain these parameters. This learning algorithm is a hybrid algorithm consisting of the gradient descent and the least-squares estimate. Using this hybrid algorithm, the rule parameters are recursively updated until an acceptable error is reached.

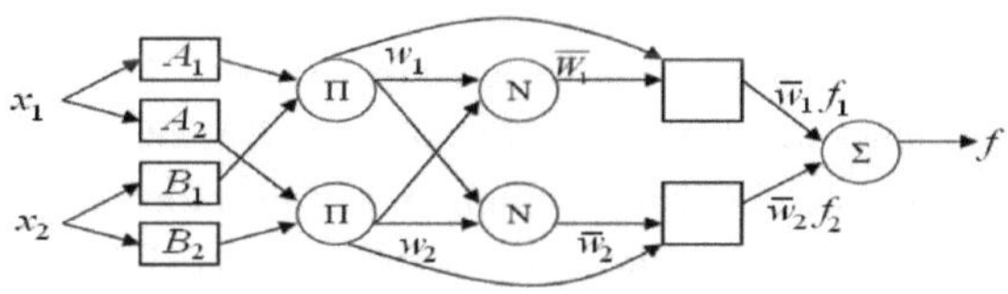

Fig. 2. ANFIS Structure

As illustrated in Figure 2, the reasoning mechanism can be implemented using a supervised learning system. In Figure 3, the square nodes represent adaptive nodes with parameters and circle nodes represent fixed nodes without parameters. As a Type III Fuzzy Control System, ANFIS has the following layers as represented in Fig. 3. The brief explanation of these layers and functions used within each layer is as follows;

Layer 0: It consists of plain input variable set.

Layer 1: Every node in this layer is a parametric node represented by a square node in Figure 3, with a node function seen on the following equation (1)

$$\mu_{A_i}(x) = \frac{1}{1 + \left[\left(\frac{x - c_i}{a_i} \right)^2 \right]^{b_i}} \tag{1}$$

Here, A is a generalized bell fuzzy set defined by the parameters {a, b, c}, where *c* is the middle point, *b* the slope and *a* is the deviation.

Layer 2: Every node in this layer is a fixed node which processes incoming signals and sends the product out. The function is a T-norm operator that performs the firing strength of the rule, e.g., fuzzy AND, and OR. The simplest implementation just calculates the product of all incoming signals.

Layer 3: Every node in this layer is fixed and determines a normalized firing strength. It calculates the ratio of the *j* th rule's firing strength to the sum of all rules firing strength.

Layer 4: The nodes in this layer are adaptive and are connected with the input nodes (of layer 0) and the preceding node of layer 3. The result is the multiplication of normalized firing strengths with the corresponding rule as seen on $w_i f_i = w_i(p_i x + q_i y + r_i)$ (p, q, r are the consequent parameters).

Layer 5: This layer consists of one single node which computes the overall output as the summation of all incoming signals using the overall output

$$\sum_i \overline{w}_i f_i = \frac{\sum_i w_i f_i}{\sum_i w_i} \tag{2}$$

Fig. 3 shows, the model used in this research for environmental performance. As mentioned before, according to the environmental criteria, 8 inputs are fed into ANFIS model and one variable output is obtained at the end. The last node (rightmost one) calculates the summation of all outputs.

Takagi and Sugeno's fuzzy if-then rules are used in the model. The output of each rule is a linear combination of input variables and a constant term. The final output is the weighted average of each rule's output. The basic learning rule of the proposed network is based on the gradient descent and the chain rule. In the designing of ANFIS model, the number of membership functions, the number of fuzzy rules, and the number of training epochs are important factors to be considered. If they were not selected appropriately, the system will over-fit the data or will not be able to fit the data. Adjusting mechanism works using a hybrid algorithm combining the least squares method and the gradient descent method with a mean square error method. The aim of the training process is to minimize the training error between the ANFIS output and the actual objective. This allows a fuzzy system to train its features from the data it observes, and implements these features in the system rules.

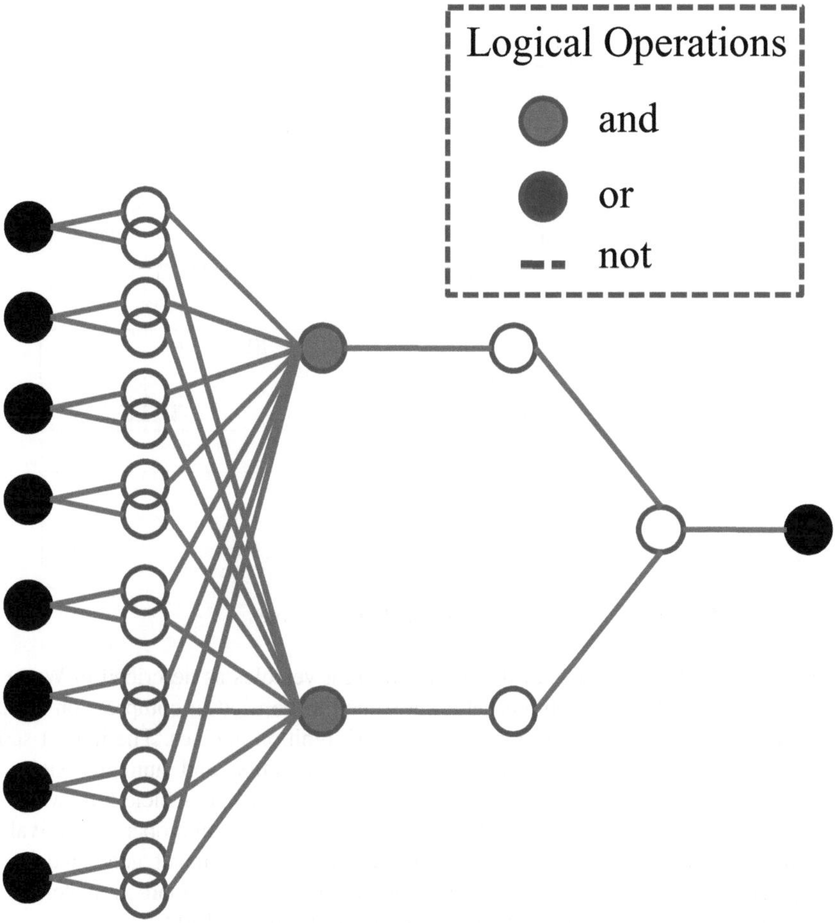

Fig. 3. ANFIS Model of Fuzzy Inference

4 Results

Results of the use of ANFIS model for the comparative LCA of three different fuels are discussed. In the results it should be noted that lower impact scores are considered as more desirable. The environmental impact scores of diesel, biodiesel and CNG, prior to aggregation by the suggested model, are shown in figure 4.

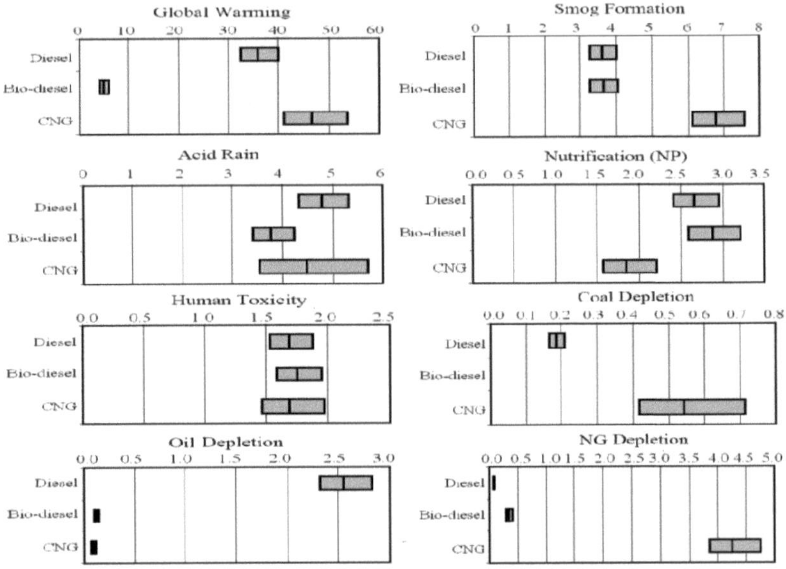

Fig. 4. Environmental impact scores

These are results for the use of these fuels in light vehicles as described in Wang [5] and Tan et al. [4]. Diesel and biodiesel are assumed to be used in compression-ignition engines while CNG is assumed to be used in spark-ignition engines. The impact scores for global warming, acid rain, smog formation, nitrification and human toxicity are normalized and expressed in microperson-year equivalents per vehicle-km, while the impact scores for depletion of oil, coal and NG are expressed in microperson equivalents per vehicle-km. A person-year equivalent is the quantity of impact generated by the average person in the world in 1990; for resource depletion, a person-equivalent is the average quantity of resource available in the world per person in 1990.

Normalization to these units is common practice in LCA; details can be found in Wenzel et al. [6] and Tan et al. [4]. The results are fuzzy, with the length of the bars signifying the spread or uncertainty of the fuzzy distributions. These uncertainties arise from the cumulative effect of variability in each part of the fuel cycle [6]; in this case they result from factors such as: vehicle age, type and fuel economy; driving conditions; and energy consumption during fuel production, distribution and storage. It is notable that the variability for CNG tends to be much greater than that of the other two fuels. Two contributing factors include the uncertainty with regard to engine type (e.g., purpose-built CNG or converted from gasoline) and uncertainties about the CNG production and distribution infrastructure, as discussed below. It is notable that biodiesel has very low impact with respect to global warming. This property is inherent in all bio-fuels, which are largely C_{O2}-neutral; on a life-cycle basis the C_{O2} uptake from photosynthesis during fuel raw material production offsets the C_{O2} emissions from the downstream combustion of the bio-fuel.

Human toxicity effects are about the same for all three fuels. As expected, diesel and CNG exhibit high oil and NG depletion potentials, respectively. The use of a life cycle framework in assessing environmental impacts gives some surprising results.

These impacts represent those generated not just by the vehicles themselves, but also those resulting from the fuel cycle, as shown in Figure 4.

Table 1 shows the weights assigned to the eight environmental criteria for two scenarios. This table is the same scenarios as described in Raymond and Alvin [13]. We use this table for comparing the fuzzy multiple attribute decision method and the suggested ANFIS approach.

Table 1. Motor Specifications

Environmental Criterion	Scenario 1	Scenario 2
Global Warming	Moderate	Very high
Acid Rain	Moderate	High
Smog Formation	Moderate	High
Nitrification	Moderate	Moderate
Human Toxicity	Moderate	Very high
Oil Depletion	Moderate	High
Coal Depletion	Moderate	Low
NG Depletion	Moderate	Moderate

In Scenario 1, the crisp (non-fuzzy) impact scores of biodiesel, diesel and CNG are 0.91, 1.52 and 1.86, respectively. From these results alone it is not immediately apparent that diesel is only weakly superior to CNG. So, the fuzzy distributions must be displayed as in Figure 5. Figure 5 shows the aggregate environmental impacts of the three alternatives when all environmental criteria are equally considered to be moderately important (Scenario I). Biodiesel has the lowest overall environmental impact, followed by diesel and then by CNG. Some overlap is evident in the scores. The parameters of the generalized bell function about bio-diesel, diesel and CNG are estimated by (0.26, 1.32, 0.91), (0.39, 1.41, 1.52) and (0.32, 1.21, 1.86), respectively. The degrees of indifference are 0.58 between biodiesel and diesel, 0.21 between biodiesel and CNG, and 0.89 between diesel and CNG. The corresponding degrees of dominance for the pair comparisons are thus 0.42, 0.79 and 0.12, respectively.

Compared with the result by the fuzzy multiple attribute decision method, the degree of indifference is lower than that between bio-diesel and CNG. Thus, the dominance degrees for the pair comparisons are more reasonable than simple additive weighting method.

In Scenario 2, the crisp impact scores of biodiesel, diesel and CNG are 1.26, 2.25 and 2.52, respectively. From these results alone it is not immediately apparent that diesel is only weakly superior to CNG. Similarly, the fuzzy distributions are required. Figure 6 shows the results for Scenario 2. The parameters of the generalized bell function about bio-diesel, diesel and CNG are estimated by (0.10, 1.20, 1.26), (0.23, 1.07, 2.25) and (0.34, 1.20, 2.52), respectively. The degrees of indifference are 0.09 between biodiesel and diesel, 0.07 between biodiesel and CNG, and 0.82 between diesel and CNG. The corresponding degrees of dominance for the pair comparisons are thus 0.91, 0.93 and 0.18, respectively. Compared with the result by the simple additive weighting method, the indifference degrees are very low except that between diesel and CNG. Although the ranking of the alternatives remains the same in case of the simple additive weighting method, the degrees of indifference are mostly high. Thus, ANFIS has a pretty good means to determine the degrees of indifference. In conclusion, the degree to which biodiesel is superior to the other two fuels, taking into account uncertainty in the data, is increased. The change can be attributed mainly by the increased weight given to global warming, a criterion in which biodiesel outperforms diesel and CNG significantly. ANFIS approach can represent more explicitly the results by the simple additive weighting method.

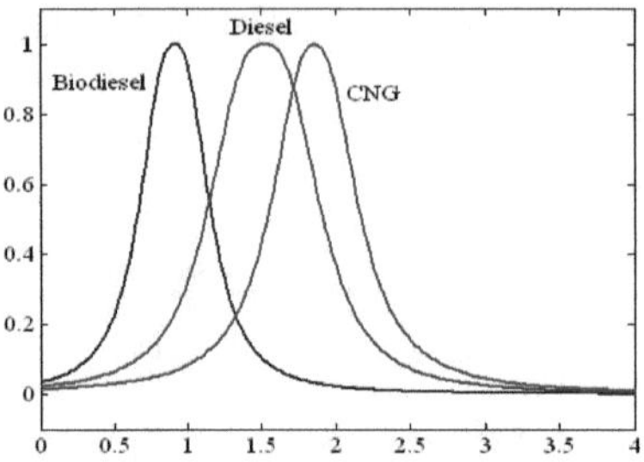

Fig. 5. Fuzzy Aggregate Environmental Impacts for Scenario I

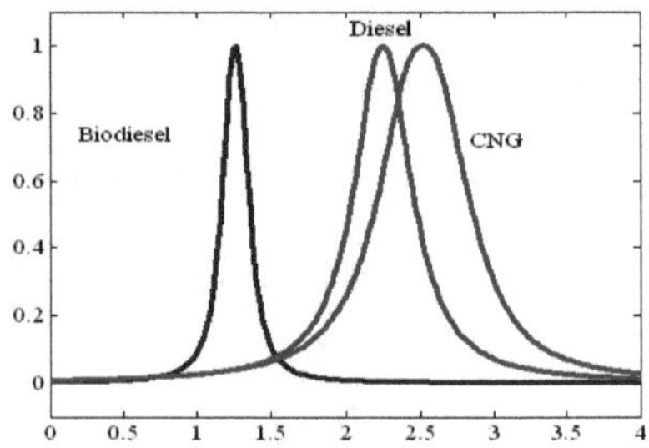

Fig. 6. Fuzzy Aggregate Environmental Impacts for Scenario II

Table 2 shows typical interpretations. Thus it becomes possible to translate numerical results from the model into linguistic statements which can be understood more easily for purposes of policy development and decision support. Thus, the degree of dominance is desirable to exceed 0.5 for the difference in environmental impact between two alternatives to be considered significant. In both scenarios, the degree to which biodiesel dominates the other two fuels will be judged to be desirable. On the other hand, although the aggregate impact of diesel is lower than that of CNG, the difference in performance is insignificant. The results of the case can be interpreted as: biodiesel is environmentally superior to diesel and CNG, while the latter two fuels do not differ significantly from each other.

Table 2. Interpretation of Dominance Degree

Value	Linguistic Interpretation
0.00	None
0.25	Weak
0.50	Normal
0.75	Strong
1.00	Very strong

It is also evident from the geometry of the fuzzy numbers that degree of dominance is determined not just by the distance between the middle points of the generalized bell functions, but also by the slope and the deviation of the fuzzy distributions. It becomes more difficult to establish definitive superiority when there is a high degree of uncertainty in the data - as will often happen when new or unproven technologies are being assessed. The method described here thus gives an effective framework for comparative assessment of alternative fuels for transportation, including those (such as hydrogen) which are not yet technologically mature.

5 Conclusion

A decision support model for comparing alternative motor vehicle has been developed based on ANFIS and LCA principles. The model predicts environmental impacts measured on a life cycle basis and incorporates data uncertainty. The fuzziness of the environmental impact estimates allows alternatives to be ranked in order of preference without losing information regarding the degrees of superiority or dominance among the competing technologies. This feature is essential in effective decision making systems to prevent misinterpretation of the model outputs by human users. The methodology also allows quantitative information on the transportation systems' material and energy flows to be integrated with qualitative information reflecting such aspects as the social acceptability of different types of environmental damage. The model is demonstrated through a comparison of diesel, biodiesel and CNG. For the specified weights used in the decision scenarios, biodiesel was predicted to be superior to the other two fuels in terms of environmental considerations. This is the same result as described in Raymond and Alvin [2]. But, the degree of dominance is more apparent since it is determined not just by the distance between the middle points, but also by the slope and deviation of the fuzzy distributions. Because a person-year equivalent is the quantity of impact generated by the average person, and for resource depletion, a person-equivalent is the average quantity of resource available in the world per person, the simple additive weighting can be more or less inaccurate. The suggested ANFIS model can be expanded to provide comprehensive decision support for a wider range of fuels, vehicle types and transport modes. The work includes refining of the database to improve accuracy of predictions, and development of an upgraded system. Ultimately, non-environmental considerations, including economic and social aspects, should also be integrated into this ANFIS framework.

References

[1] Camden: Life Cycle Assessment of Vehicle Fuels and Technologies Report. London Borough of Camden, London, UK (2006)

[2] Raymond, T., Alvin, C.: A fuzzy decision support model for the selection of environment-friendly fuels for road vehicles. Journal of the Eastern Asia Society for Transportation Studies 6, 3264–3275 (2005)

[3] Tan, R.R., Culaba, A.B., Purvis, M.R.I.: Application of possibility theory in the life cycle inventory assessment of biofuels. International Journal of Energy Research 26(8), 737–745 (2002)

[4] Tan, R.R., Culaba, A.B., Purvis, M.R.I.: Possibilistic uncertainty propagation and compromise programming in the life cycle analysis of alternative motor vehicle fuels. Journal of Advanced Computational Intelligence and Intelligent Informatics 8(1), 23–28 (2004)

[5] Wang, M.: GREET 1.5 - transportation fuel cycle model. Report ANL/ESD-39, Argonne National Laboratory, Chicago (1999)

[6] Wenzel, H., Hauschildand, M., Alting, L.: Environmental Assessment of Products. Methodology, Tools and Case Studies in Product Development, vol. 1. Chapman and Hall, London (1997)

Imaging Processing Based a Wireless Charging System with a Mobile Robot

Jae-O Kim, Sunny Rho, Chan-Woo Moon, and Hyun-Sik Ahn

Department of Electronics Engineering, Kookmin University, Seoul, Korea

Abstract. A vision based automatic recharging system for a mobile robot with wireless power transmission is presented. To obtain the maximum efficiency of power transmission, position of charging antenna is controlled with a vision data. To search for objective and recognize the antenna, Hough transform followed by SURF algorithm is applied. This sequential processing enlarges searching range. The information of pose from the image data is used to control the mobile robot.

Keywords: SURF, HT, Wireless Charging.

1 Introduction

A typical mobile robot has actuators which are operated by battery. As the robot moves for a long time, the battery is exhausted, and recharging is needed. Currently, automatic recharging is general trend for an intelligent robot. And usually, contact type of recharging with a guide mechanism is widely used. But in a circumstance on which guide mechanism is unavailable, for example, recharging between different type of robots, recharging outdoor and recharging when a robot is still moving, a wireless power transmission can be considered.

In this paper, wireless power transmission method for a mobile robot is investigated. To obtain the maximum efficiency of power transmission, vision based position control of a transmission antenna is implemented. To recognize the antenna, Hough Transform and SURF(Speeded-Up Robust Features) methods are used. The information of pose of antenna is used to control the mobile robot.

2 Background of Research

The pose of the wireless charging antenna is searched for and recognized with Hough Transform (HT) and SURF algorithm. The followings are brief review of the wireless power transmission, HT and SURF algorithm.

2.1 Wireless Power Transmission

Wireless Power Transmission is classfied into direct induction method and electromagnetic radiation method. In this research, near range direct induction method

T.-h. Kim et al. (Eds.): EL/DTA/UNESST 2012, CCIS 352, pp. 298–301, 2012.

is used. The whole system consists of transmission coil and receiver coil, and these two coils form a magnetic coupled circuit. Current of transmission coil induces voltage on coil receiver, and this voltage is used for charging. The efficiency of the wireless transmission is dependent on Q factor and coefficient of coupling K which is determined by inductor and ratio of size of two antenna [1].

2.2 HT (Hough Transform)

Hough Transform is widely used for searching a figure such as line and circle in an image pixel data. Eq. (1) denotes a basic equation of line and eq. (2) is another formulation of line which is represented in the parameter space. If a line becomes vertical, the slope becomes infinity, then, eq. (3) is used alternatively[2][3].

$$y_i = ax_i + b \tag{1}$$

$$b = -x_i a + y_i \tag{2}$$

$$x \cos\theta + y \sin\theta = \rho \tag{3}$$

2.3 SURF(Speeded-Up Robust Features)

SURF has similar function to SIFT, but SURF has less computational time than SIFT, and additional learning is easily implemented. SURF is relatively robust to image rotation, change of illumination and affine transform. To reduce the computational time, SURF uses approximated difference of Gaussian and convolution, and carries out scale calculation at each point with mask operation. To extract key point from the input image data, Hessian Matrix of eq. (4) is used.

$$H(\boldsymbol{x},\sigma) = \begin{bmatrix} L_{xx}(\boldsymbol{x},\sigma) & L_{xy}(\boldsymbol{x},\sigma) \\ L_{xy}(\boldsymbol{x},\sigma) & L_{yy}(\boldsymbol{x},\sigma) \end{bmatrix} \tag{4}$$

To extract feature point, SURF uses Haar filter on the sampled points in the divided blocks, and sets 4x4x4=64 feature vector as a key point feature.[4]

3 The Structure of Experimental System

Figure 1 shows the flow chart of the antenna position and orientation recognition process. The recognition process consists of two tasks. In the first task, the mobile robot finds the pose of the antenna candidate using Hough transform and in the second task it decides whether the detected feature is the antenna with the cropped image data and SURF algorithm. And also the second task determines the exact position and pose of the antenna and these data are used for the mobile robot motion control.

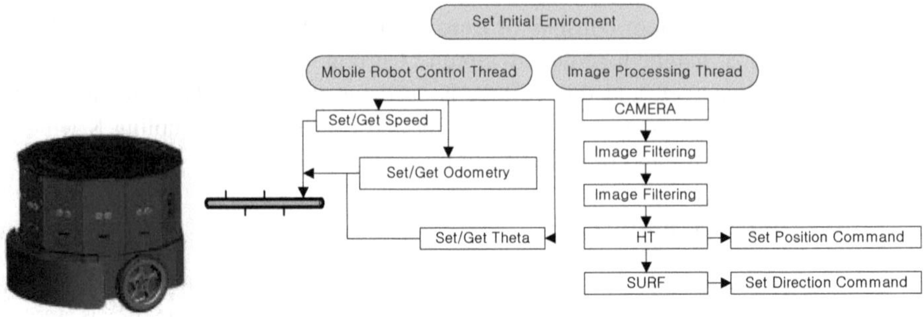

Fig. 1. Block diagram

4 Experimental Results

Figure 2 shows the implemented experimental set which consists of a wireless charging system, a camera and a mobile robot[5]. The charging system is BQ series wireless power transmission test kit of Texas Instruments[6][7]. Figure 2 shows the main control program which is running on the PC. This main program analyzes the camera image and controls motions of the mobile robot.

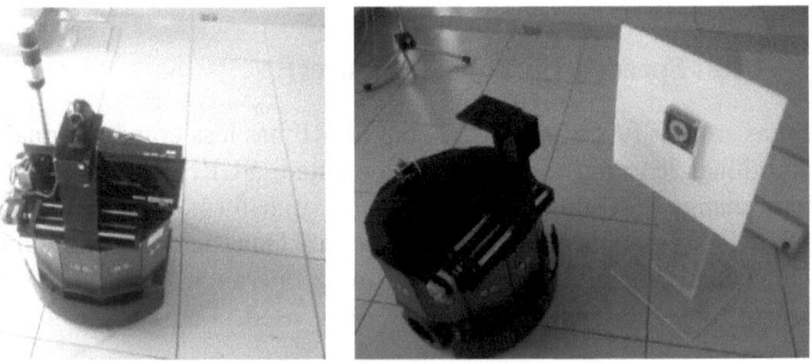

Fig. 2. Mobile Robot and the wireless power system

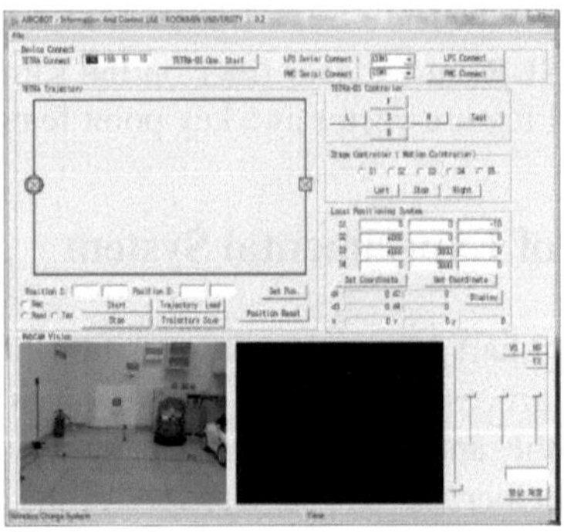

Fig. 3. Main Control Program

Figure 4 shows the experimental results. The right side is an image after processing. By Hough transform, region of interest is setup, and by SURF, the distance from the target and the inclination of the target is obtained.

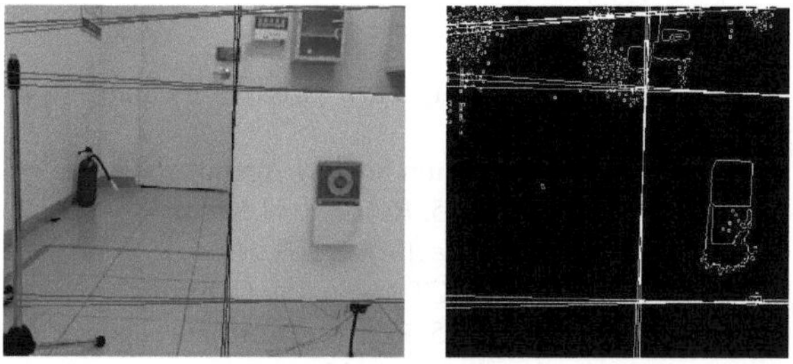

Fig. 4. The detected image

5 Conclusion

In this paper, a wireless charging antenna detection was studied. Two cascading image processing was conducted to extract the feature of the object. By Hough transform, boundary of the object was determined and a region of interest was set. In the following SURF processing, the feature of the object was obtained. This cascading method increases the range of search, but processing time is rather slow, so further improvement of algorithm is necessary.

Acknowledgments. This research was supported by the MKE(The Ministry of Knowledge Economy), Korea, under the ITRC(Information Technology Research Center) support program (NIPA-2012-H0301-12-2007) supervised by the NIPA(National IT Industry Promotion Agency).

References

1. Wireless Power Consortium, `http://www.wirelesspowerconsortium.com`
2. Hough, P.V.C.: Methods and Means for Recognizing Complex Patterns, U.S. Patent 3,069,654 (1962)
3. Duda, R.O., Hart, P.E., Use, C.: of the Hough Transformation to Detect Lines and Curves in Pictures. Comm. ACM 15, 11–15 (1972)
4. Bay, H., Ess, A., Tuytelaars, T., Luc van Gool, C.: SURF: Speeded Up Robust Features. Computer Vision and Image Understanding (CVIU) 110(3), 346–359 (2008)
5. TETRA-DS DasaRobot, DasaRobot (2009)
6. BQ25046EVM-687 EvaluationModule, Texas Instruments
7. BQ500110EVM-688 EvaluationModule, Texas Instruments

An Exploratory Study of the Positive Effect of Anger on Decision-Making in Business Contexts

Jung Woo Lee[1], Jin Young Park[2], and Kun Chang Lee[3,*]

[1] National Information Society Agency (NIA)
Seoul 100-775, Republic of Korea
ljw.bread@gmail.com
[2] SK Networks ICT Marketing Company
Seoul 100-845, Republic of Korea
jypjyr@gmail.com
[3] SKK Business School,
Department of Interaction Science
Sungkyunkwan University
Seoul 110-745, Republic of Korea
kunchanglee@gmail.com

Abstract. Current studies have shown the significance of emotions in decision-making. The basic emotion of anger has been an especially interesting area of research in the field of neuro-economics. In this paper we pose the question of how anger may affect decision outcomes in a business organization. Enterprises are conducted in time-limited, risk-taking and crisis-laden environments. Decision makers in such organizations must make important decisions in these environments, and thus may easily experience stress which leads to anger. In this paper, we hypothesize that anger is associated with positive outcomes by leading to increased motivation and affirming positive beliefs. To examine our hypothesis, we conducted in-depth interviews with organizational decision makers who have experienced anger while making decisions under time-limited, risk-taking and crisis-laden situations. Results from our qualitative research show that angry decision makers tend to obtain positive decision outcomes by positive motivation or beliefs derived from anger.

Keywords: emotion, anger, decision making, decision outcome, motivation, positive belief.

1 Introduction

Numerous studies have emphasized the importance of emotions in decision-making [4],[12]. A neurobiological approach also shows that emotions affect human decision-making. Damasio [4] has shown this connection between decision-making and emotion by pointing out that people who have brain damage in the regions associated with emotion cannot make simple decisions.

* Corresponding author.

T.-h. Kim et al. (Eds.): EL/DTA/UNESST 2012, CCIS 352, pp. 302–309, 2012.

The influence of emotions on decision-making has been a topic of active debate; many studies have focused on determining whether positive or negative emotions lead to better outcomes. Many researchers have argued that positive emotions are more closely related to optimistic decision-making and negative emotions to pessimistic choices [9].

Here, we concentrated on negative emotions. From a variety of negative emotions (e.g., anger, fear, aggression, sadness, etc.), we especially focused on anger. Anger is present in both everyday life and work settings [3]; thus it can be found among individuals in business organizations. Anger can be identified easily by people's facial expressions, gestures, and language [7]. Finally, anger is a basic emotion that many people experience frequently in business settings, where they are more exposed to time pressure, risk, and uncertainty than in everyday life. Because of such stressful environments, people are more prone to anger, an emotion that can interfere with the decision-making process, thereby affecting decision outcomes as well. Currently, there is a lack of research on whether negative emotions have positive effects on decision outcomes in an organization, especially in the business context. Here, we study the outcomes of anger: specifically, judgment and decision-making outcomes. Admittedly, this is a unique approach. The most frequently studied outcome of anger is aggression [2], but here we are concerned with how anger influences perceptions, beliefs, ideas, reasoning, and ultimately, choices [25]. Hence, our objective in this paper is to explore the role of negative emotions on positive decision effectiveness in an organization and to propose promising areas for future research. To do so, we focus on the positive aspects of anger: motivation and positive beliefs.

To discuss our research question, we conducted qualitative research on multiple cases: software NPD (New product development) in a small venture company, competitive bidding in a large SI (System Integrating) company and in a small software auditing company. In these cases, decision makers actively try to optimize decision outcomes by, for example, making good decisions to launch new products and to win contracts with a good margin.

2 Theoretical Background

For over two decades, research has supported the intuition that a pervasive atmosphere of negative emotions such as anger fosters relatively pessimistic expectations, whereas a globally positive mood can bring about relatively optimistic expectations (for a review, see [11]). The majority of laboratory experiments have found that good moods stimulate better performance on creative tasks [18], [19]. One study in a hospital setting done by Estrada et al. [8] shows that positive affect can facilitate the thorough, efficient, and flexible use of new information, which increases decision effectiveness [1].

Anger does not follow many of the typical patterns associated with negative emotions. Anger tends to trigger optimism rather than pessimism [22], [24], [23]. For example, angry decision makers tend to hold optimistic expectations about the future, because they believe it likely that they will succeed in a variety of life domains [10], [22], [24], [23]. This optimism is caused by the comparative activeness of manifestations of anger.

Anger tends to trigger actions and active self-defensiveness rather than pessimistic self-criticism. Thus, anger results in optimism that comes from a sense of certainty, predictability, and control over life outcomes [23]. Most importantly, the optimistic energy from anger affects one's reflections about the future.

From this point of view, we argue that decision makers in an organization under time pressure, laden with crisis, and full of uncertainty tend to be optimistic about their decision-making, which leads to improved outcomes. Current studies emphasize that anger has either positive or negative effects on decision-making. But current studies do not determine which effect of anger is more dominant, the positive or negative. We propose that anger is associated with positive decision-making outcomes.

3 Methods

We investigate the research question in the software NPD project and a highly competitive bidding, which are crisis-laden, pressured for time, and uncertain business field settings. We took several steps to answer the question: (1) data gathering from an initial interview to find decision maker's past episodes; (2) qualitative analysis of audio transcripts of the decision-maker making decisions in the field.

3.1 Data Collection

Our review of the decision-process literature suggested that people are most likely to engage in intuitive decision-making when they have higher decision-making authority, when there is time pressure, and in crisis-laden, complex, or uncertain situations [5], [29]: firefighters confronting fires, soldiers in combat situations, police officers in the field, chefs in the kitchen, CEOs and high officials in crisis situations, among others. Firefighters and soldiers have been subjects under the requirements (e.g., [20]). Further, Coget et al. [3] investigated the effect of anger and fear on decision-making effectiveness in the crisis-laden, time-pressured, risky field setting of movie directors making decisions on set and showed that angry movie directors drew upon their professional expertise and emotional experiences about a given situation to make an intuitive decision, and direct their movies effectively.

We gathered data from an initial interview to investigate Korean decision-makers' past experiences: two CEOs of new ventures in the field of software (navigation for a smartphone) and NFC (Near Field Communication). Also, we interviewed two sales representatives from an SI (system integration) and an ICT auditing company. This interview allowed us to identify what types of situations might elicit strong anger. On average, initial interviews lasted 1.5 hours per each interviewee. After gathering all the data, qualitative analyses were made of audio transcripts of these decision-makers in the field.

After the initial interviews, we excluded the case of the venture company that makes NFC solution. This company has a history of more than 10 years in the business, with multiple references on process. Also, the CEO delegated key decision-making to high-level managers and was mainly concerned with financial issues. We tried to contact the high-level mangers of this company, but due to internal security issues, no further interviews were authorized.

Interviewees' averaged 12 years of service in each business domain. The interviewee from the venture company is CEO and founder of the company, and mid-level managers from the SI company and the ICT auditing company were sales representatives for each company.

Table 1. Demographics of participants

Interviewees	Venture CEO	SI Sales Manager	ICT Audit Sales Manager
Position	Top Decision Maker	Mid-level Decision Maker	Mid-level Decision Maker
Arousal of Anger	Yes	Yes	Yes
Main Cause of Anger	Distrust from employees	Misjudgment by his Boss	
Effect of Anger	Positive Motivation	Positive Self-belief	Positive Self-belief
Decision Outcome	Positive (Launched Application)	Positive (Won Bidding)	Positive (Won Bidding)

4 Results

This study aimed to answer the following research question: Is anger associated with positive decision outcomes in an organization? To answer the question, we hypothesized that anger is associated with positive decision outcomes and identifies the outcomes of decision-making. In the case of S/W NPD, CEOs judged the decision outcome in terms of whether or not they launched a new product. And in the case of bidding, the sales representatives naturally considered winning a contract as the decision outcome. In summary, when engaged in the NPD, the angry CEOs emphasized motivation to "GO" to launch a new product. Also, the angry sales representatives engaged in bidding stressed positive beliefs to win a contract.

4.1 Motivation through Anger

- *H1.1. Anger is associated with motivation in a crisis-laden, risk-taking, and time-pressured organization.*

To address our first hypothesis, we found that before and after S/W NPD Venture was established, the CEO felt anger constantly because of the skeptical opinions about the venture from both inside and outside the company. Before initiating the venture, the CEO had strong beliefs about his idea, but few people affirmed his decision. During the stages of progress on the NPD, the final stage, just before launch of the navigation application, was when the CEO felt the greatest anger. Because he already had Plan B in progress, he could have dropped the development of the navigation application under the risky, crisis-laden situation. The market climate for car navigation systems was poor because of current competitors in dominant positions; thus, success was uncertain. Before making the final decision, the CEO had a meeting with his employees, during which he was angered by the debate, but felt optimism at the same time.

We argued fiercely in the conference room, and I even offered my employees a big drink together trying to convince them, but they would not listen. But what's so funny was that I felt even more confident in our navigation application when our employees said 'no.' I can say, all these oppositions made me stronger. Actually I should say thank you to all those people who said no. Those oppositions somehow motivated me to launch my innovative application to prove that we can do it.

Finally I made a decision. I announced to all our employees that we will close the Plan B project and only focus on the Main Project, which clarified there is no turning back. At the same time, I tried to focus on the navigation itself, mainly on customer's point of view. UI, algorithm, Speed was the main theme. The big competitor came up with Ver. 2.0 upgrade, so we had to hurry. I had weekly meeting with all the engineers, and daily meeting with board members to convince them and to generate more ideas. They kept trying to convince me to change my mind, but I was so sure.

The CEO insisted that anger can motivate an improvement in the decision-making process and outcome. After being angry, he developed strong confidence and willingness to succeed.

4.2 Positive Beliefs through Anger

- *H1.2. Anger is associated with positive beliefs in a crisis-laden, risk-taking, and time-pressured organization.*

With respect to our second hypothesis, we examined the case of highly competitive bidding, in which high-level managers should make decisions designed to win contracts. Regarding H1.2, we investigated a sales representative in an ICT audit company because its size is relatively small compared to general SI company, and whether to win bidding or not is very critical to the company.

Participation in bidding for ICT audit businesses starts from the sales representative's analysis of the contract. Before bidding, sales representatives should analyze whether or not his company can meet the customer's demand, and if the bidding price will cover the costs and make a profit. Decision-making should be done in a short period of time before the bidding closes. ICT audit businesses in Korea are normally low-margin businesses. It is usual that firms do not allocate enough budget for ICT audit because they consider it as a cost, not profit. Therefore, its market volume is quite limited. Thus, many ICT audit companies are challenged to maintain or expand their market share. While winning the market share, they must consider profit and winning ratio as well. Unlike other competitive bidding, winning a bid in the ICT audit sector is uncertain and unpredictable because technically there exist no big differences between competitors. Bidding price is therefore very important especially for the ICT companies.

Normally, customers tend to keep using their current ICT audit company in order to avoid system changes. But in this case, the new firm was looking for a new auditor which did not require a complicated technology. Losing this bid might damage personal and organizational reputations, which could have negative effects on future biddings on other firms. In addition, bidding was going to close in a few days. So, the sales representative had to make risky decisions to expedite the process.

For this case, the sales representative was going for a low bidding price to ensure winning, but the CEO objected to the sales representative's opinion. The CEO desired to win a bid with a big margin to invest in other fields. According to the interviewee, the CEO of the ICT audit company is usually very friendly with the sales representative, but when his opinion is not accepted, he often gets upset and expresses his anger. The sales representative was familiar with the CEO's character, but considering the importance of winning the contract, he was angry as well. The interviewee also insisted that normally he does not oppose the CEO's personal opinion. But at that time, the sales representative was even angrier than the CEO, and his anger strengthened his belief that he could win the contract at a lower price.

As usual CEO yelled at me saying he is more professional than I am. This is as I said, very usual situation. But this bidding was different. We hired too many auditors last year, and we had to worry about their salary in the first half of this year. I was angry because I thought my CEO was only obsessed with expanding investment, not caring about employees. I was 100% certain that bidding for higher price will definitely cause our loss. I was worried about a yearly projection. Some of my teammates were surprised to see me being angry and resisting. I did not step back, and convinced CEO for an hour, accomplishing my idea. Final result of this competitive bidding was exactly what I have expected. Four participants' service evaluation results were almost the same. Our price was the lowest, and we won the contract.

5 Concluding Remarks

This study aimed to examine the relationship between anger and decision outcomes. While previous research has proposed that anger can have positive effects [25], the relationship between anger and decision-making has not been fully examined, particularly in the business environment. In a qualitative study of an organizational unit charged with developing creative designs, George and Zhou [14] found that negative, rather than positive moods, facilitated on-the-job creativity in the unit they studied.

Our research is based only on qualitative research with a very small sample. Furthermore, we assumed that each interviewee felt anger, based on how they remembered the situations. Further experiments using modern technology like Functional Magnetic Resonance Imaging (fMRI) may objectify and clarify the emotions felt by the interviewees. Coget et al. [3] pointed out that the majority of studies on the role of affect in decision-making have been laboratory experiments, where time pressure and stakes are low, personal investment in decisions is imaginary, and the decision-making processes and outcomes studied are simple. However, we argue that our study can be compared with an experiment and contrasted with other negative emotions (e.g., sadness, aggression, and frustration, etc.). Modern functional brain-imaging methods can provide another perspective on the dynamics of anger on decision-making outcomes.

Acknowledgment. This research was supported by WCU(World Class University) program through the National Research Foundation of Korea funded by the Ministry of Education, Science and Technology (Grant No. R31-2008-000-10062-0).

References

1. Barsade, S.G., Gibson, D.E.: Why does Affect Matter in Organizations? Academy of Management Perspectives 21, 36–59 (2007)
2. Berkowitz, L.: Aggression: Its causes, consequences, and control. McGraw-Hill, New York (1993)
3. Coget, J., Haag, C., Gibson, D.E.: Anger and Fear in Decision-Making: The Case of Film Directors on Set. European Management Journal 29, 476–490 (2011)
4. Damasio, A.R.: Descartes' error: Emotion, reason, and the human brain. Bard/Avon Books, New York (1998)
5. Dane, E., Pratt, M.G.: Exploring Intuition and its Role in Managerial Decision Making. The Academy of Management Review 32, 33–54 (2007)
6. Edgett, S., Shipley, D., Forbes, G.: Japanese and British Companies Compared: Contributing Factors to Success and Failure in NPD. Journal of Product Innovation Management 9, 3–10 (1992)
7. Ekman, P.: Strong Evidence for Universals in Facial Expressions: A Reply to Russell's Mistaken Critique. Psychological Bulletin 115, 268–287 (1994)
8. Estrada, C.A., Isen, A.M., Young, M.J.: Positive Affect Facilitates Integration of Information and Decreases Anchoring in Reasoning among Physicians. Organizational Behavior and Human Decision Processes 72, 117–135 (1997)
9. Fenton-O'Creevy, M., Soane, E., Nicholson, N., et al.: Thinking, Feeling and Deciding: The Influence of Emotions on the Decision Making and Performance of Traders. Journal of Organizational Behavior 32, 1044–1061 (2011)
10. Fischhoff, B., Gonzalez, R.M., Lerner, J.S., et al.: Evolving Judgments of Terror Risks: Foresight, Hindsight, and Emotion. Journal of Experimental Psychology: Applied 11, 124–139 (2005)
11. Forgas, J.P.: Affective influences on attitudes and judgments. In: Davidson, R.J., Scherer, K.R., Goldsmith, H.H. (eds.), pp. 596–618. Oxford University Press, New York (2003)
12. Forgas, J.P.: Mood and Judgment: The Affect Infusion Model (AIM). Psychological Bulletin 117, 39–66 (1995)
13. Frijda, N.H., Kuipers, P., ter Schure, E.: Relations among Emotion, Appraisal, and Emotional Action Readiness. Journal of Personality and Social Psychology 57, 212–228 (1989)
14. George, J.M., Zhou, J.: Understanding when Bad Moods Foster Creativity and Good Ones Don't: The Role of Context and Clarity of Feelings. Journal of Applied Psychology 87, 687–697 (2002)
15. Goldberg, J.H., Lerner, J.S., Tetlock, P.E.: Rage and Reason: The Psychology of the Intuitive Prosecutor. European Journal of Social Psychology 29, 781–795 (1999)
16. Harmon-Jones, E., Sigelman, J., Bohlig, A., et al.: Anger, Coping, and Frontal Cortical Activity: The Effect of Coping Potential on Anger-Induced Left Frontal Activity. Cognition & Emotion 17, 1–24 (2003)
17. Hemenover, S., Zhang, S.: Anger, Personality, and Optimistic Stress Appraisals. Cognition & Emotion 18, 363–382 (2004)
18. Isen, A.M., Daubman, K.A., Nowicki, G.P.: Positive Affect Facilitates Creative Problem Solving. Journal of Personality and Social Psychology 52, 1122–1131 (1987)

19. Isen, A.M., Johnson, M.M., Mertz, E., et al.: The Influence of Positive Affect on the Unusualness of Word Associations. Journal of Personality and Social Psychology 48, 1413–1426 (1985)
20. Kaempf, G.L., Klein, G., Thordsen, M.L., et al.: Decision Making in Complex Naval Command-and-Control Environments. Human Factors: The Journal of the Human Factors and Ergonomics Society 38, 220–231 (1996)
21. Lerner, J.S., Dahl, R.E., Hariri, A.R., et al.: Facial Expressions of Emotion Reveal Neuroendocrine and Cardiovascular Stress Responses. Biological Psychiatry 61, 253–260 (2007)
22. Lerner, J.S., Gonzalez, R.M., Small, D.A., et al.: Effects of Fear and Anger on Perceived Risks of Terrorism. Psychological Science 14, 144–150 (2003)
23. Lerner, J.S., Keltner, D.: Fear, Anger, and Risk. Journal of Personality and Social Psychology 81, 146–159 (2001)
24. Lerner, J.S., Keltner, D.: Beyond Valence: Toward a Model of Emotion-Specific Influences on Judgement and Choice. Cognition & Emotion 14, 473–493 (2000)
25. Lerner, J.S., Tiedens, L.Z.: Portrait of the Angry Decision Maker: How Appraisal Tendencies Shape Anger's Influence on Cognition. Journal of Behavioral Decision Making 19, 115–137 (2006)
26. Moreno, K., Kida, T., Smith, J.F.: The Impact of Affective Reactions on Risky Decision Making in Accounting Contexts. Journal of Accounting Research 40, 1331–1349 (2002)
27. Reifen Tagar, M., Federico, C.M., Halperin, E.: The Positive Effect of Negative Emotions in Protracted Conflict: The Case of Anger. Journal of Experimental Social Psychology 47, 157–164 (2011)
28. Shaver, P., Schwartz, J., Kirson, D., et al.: Emotion Knowledge: Further Exploration of a Prototype Approach. Journal of Personality and Social Psychology 52, 1061–1086 (1987)
29. Sinclair, M., Ashkanasy, N.M.: Intuition. Management Learning 36, 353–370 (2005)
30. Tiedens, L.Z., Linton, S.: Judgment Under Emotional Certainty and Uncertainty: The Effects of Specific Emotions on Information Processing. Journal of Personality and Social Psychology 81, 973–988 (2001)

Integrating a General Bayesian Network with Multi-Agent Simulation to Optimize Supply Chain Management

Seung Chang Seong[1] and Kun Chang Lee[2,*]

[1] SKK Business School
Sungkyunkwan University
Seoul 110-745, Republic of Korea
[2] SKK Business School,
Department of Interaction Science
Sungkyunkwan University, Seoul 110-745, Republic of Korea
{seongsc,kunchanglee}@gmail.com

Abstract. In most manufacturing companies, supply chain management (SCM) has been successfully utilized to reduce costs, reduce risk, and improve customer satisfaction. Typical SCM approaches are the cost-focused just-in-time (JIT) approach and the risk-focused just-in-sequence (JIS) approach. Despite some successes, these two SCM approaches have suffered from ad hoc mismanagement and frequent failure due to high costs and uncontrolled risks. This paper proposes a new SCM approach, decentralized SCM, which incorporates multi-core tiers and platform commonization. To prove its validity, we have implemented a multi-agent simulation (MAS) platform named MASSOP (Multi-Agent Simulation-based SCM Optimization Platform) in which a general Bayesian network (GBN) is used to build an intelligent inference mechanism to predict sales and then feed this information back into the MAS engine to optimize SCM by reducing risk and cost. Using a data set compiled over the course of 40 years by an automobile manufacturing company as the basis for preparing the initial parameters for the MAS, MASSOP was built using Repast Simphony and then tested. The results were promising, robust, and statistically valid when compared with JIT and JIS.

Keywords: Multi-Agent Simulation, General Bayesian Network, Supply Chain Management, JIT, JIS.

1 Introduction

The usefulness of supply chain management (SCM) has been proven in numerous manufacturing companies, including automobile manufacturing companies, where it has been considered critical to their success in the hypercompetitive worldwide market. In an automotive company, SCM encompasses a seamless combination of

* Corresponding author.

T.-h. Kim et al. (Eds.): EL/DTA/UNESST 2012, CCIS 352, pp. 310–317, 2012.

participating partners, such as auto parts production companies, assembly lines, logistics, and marketing dealers. These typical components of SCM can often be troublesome [5].

SCM is primarily concerned with two major issues: (1) reducing risk and (2) controlling cost. The usefulness of SCM depends on how these two issues are resolved. Two traditional approaches to resolving these SCM issues are the cost-focused approach known as just-in-time (JIT) and the risk-focused approach known as just-in-sequence (JIS). JIT was advocated by numerous companies around the world for several decades. The advantages of JIT [1, 2, 3, 9, 10, 11] were significantly challenged by a series of natural disasters in Japan, including the Great Hanshin earthquake of 1995 and the Tohoku earthquake and tsunami of 2011. Whenever unexpected events occur that negatively affect the efficiency of JIT, some fundamental aspects of JIT that are usually taken for granted suddenly take on grave importance, such as the need for material logistics to work perfectly and for assembly lines to operate continuously without unexpected disruptions. To accommodate the drawbacks of JIT management, another type of SCM was proposed: JIS. While JIT focuses on saving time, JIS instead focuses on securing auto parts and components in the correct order to enable efficient assembly. JIS puts more emphasis on risk minimization, sacrificing some cost savings in the process.

However, competition is becoming fiercer and customer tastes are becoming more selective. If companies do not meet these challenges effectively through SCM, they will inevitably lose their competitive edge. To address the drawbacks of both JIT and JIS management, we propose a new type of SCM called decentralized SCM and have implemented a prototype named MASSOP (Multi-Agent Simulation-based SCM Optimization Platform) to model it. As the main vehicle for MASSOP, a general Bayesian network (GBN) was adopted to estimate sales levels more intelligently, and multi-agent simulation (MAS) was applied to incorporate all the factors related to the optimization of SCM, leading to an effective SCM optimization platform.

By using real dataset obtained from a motor company located in South Korea, initial parameters necessary to initiate MASSOP were built. Experiment reults from MASSOP clearly showed that compared with JIT and JIS, our approach is very robust and lenient in terms of controlling risks and costs facing unexpected turbulence that often occurs in the market. Details are addressed in the following sections.

2 Multi-Agent Simulation and Bayesian Network

2.1 Multi-Agent Simulation (MAS)

The world in which we live is an environment composed of sophisticated causal relationships. According to the theory of complex systems, we can predict the future if we can determine the mechanisms or principles underlying changes in the complex phenomena comprising those systems [6]. The subject of this study, the automotive industry, is itself a complex system.

When issuing orders to their factories, the leaders at company headquarters must consider production-related risks, such as natural disasters, factory downtime, and supply disruptions, as well as market-related risks, such as recessions and tariff changes. They must also consider periodic costs, such as mean time before failure (MTBF) and factory installation. Despite these efforts, it is difficult to determine the influences of many events on production targets and sales. However, we can analyze these problems using MAS.

MAS can illustrate the result of interactions among many intelligent agents within an environment, also known as emergent behavior. The emergent behavior that arises from the simple rules of behavior governing individual agents and the interactions among them can be useful tools in determining causality. We formulated a SCM model for hedging a variety of risks in a cost-effective manner by declaring the following items to be agents: economic indicators, the leadership at auto company headquarters, factories, markets, manufacturing risks, and market risks. We implemented our system using Repast Simphony (available at http://repast. sourceforge.net/) and the Java programming language.

2.2 Bayesian Network

A Bayesian network (BN), represented as directed acyclic graph (DAG) based on conditional probability tables (CPTs), identifies causal relationships in the simplest way by using a Markov blanket (MB) [8]. The MB consists of the target node, the direct parents of the target node, the direct successors of the target node, and all direct parents of the target node's direct successors in a given BN. The MB is the smallest set of nodes that has meaning. If a node is absent from the target node's MB, its value is completely irrelevant to the prediction.

In our model, we represent the causal relationships among a variety of economic indicators, the conditions of an automotive company, and car production. Specifically, we used raw data from 40 years of car production information obtained from a global automotive company and the economic indicators from that same period. With these data, we constructed and evaluated a GBN and an unrestricted BN, assisted by a Markov blanket.

We used the BN to implement the role of company leadership in a MAS that designed a SCM model of the automotive industry. We also used the WEKA API [4] (available at http://www.cs.waikato.ac.nz/ml/weka/) to combine the GBN and the MAS. Programming was performed using the Java language.

3 Experiments

3.1 Overview

This study compared the decentralized SCM with the two most common SCM approaches used in the automotive industry by examining them all in the same environment. Production achievement rate was used as an indicator to determine which SCM approach was the most robust for hedging various risks. In this case, the complexity of the SCM is determined by the number of factories. We conducted a simulation, adjusting the number of factories and observing the change in the production achievement rate. At the same time, we had to consider costs because the available resources were limited. In the proposed system, the higher sales SCM approach is the most cost-effective SCM approach because it results in a higher return on investment (ROI) despite its increased cost. The system was designed to work as follows:

First, economic indicators such as gross domestic product (GDP), exchange rates, the consumer price index (CPI), and unemployment rates are randomly generated (Step 1). The leadership of the automotive company instructs each factory to produce cars, taking into consideration the previous year's production, sales, production capacity, and other factors (Step 2). Each factory is affected by manufacturing risks such as natural disasters, factory downtime, and supply disruptions (Step 3). The impact size and probability of occurrence of each individual risk are set. The products produced in the factory are delivered to the market (Step 4). Each market is affected by market risks, such as worsening of the economy, tariff changes, and declines in the CPI (Step 5). Market agents calculate the ROI, taking into consideration facility installation and maintenance costs and the selling price of the car. When the process is complete, the simulation proceeds to the next year (Step 6).

3.2 JIT, JIS and Decentralized SCM

The proposed system takes JIT, JIS, and decentralized SCM into account. The company leadership at headquarters gives the same production orders for each SCM approach. We can determine the structural differences in the SCM approaches between the factories that are able to produce the key, irreplaceable components and the factories that cannot. In the simulation environment, the production capacity of each factory and the price of the cars produced using each SCM approach are set identically. Additionally, the number of factories is adjusted equally in each SCM approach. SCM becomes more complicated when the number of factories increases. However, JIT is the most cost-effective approach with respect to MTBF costs.

Table 1. Comparison of SCMs

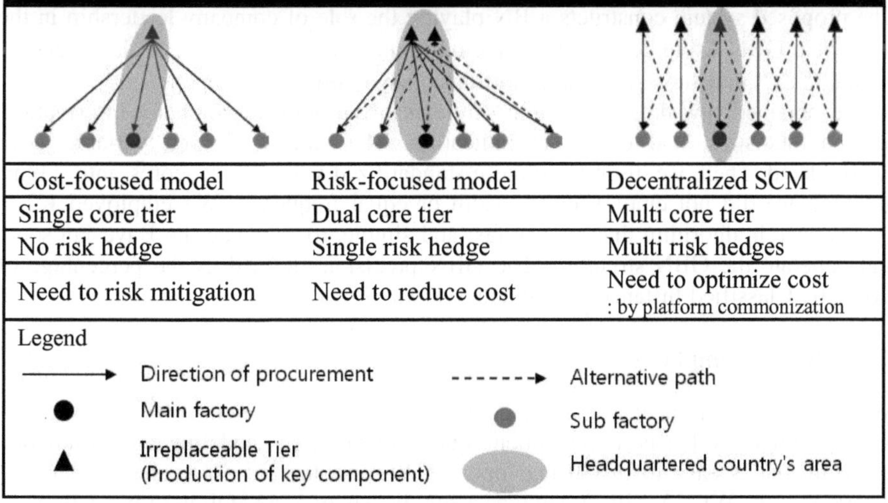

Just-In-Time	Just-In-Sequence	Decentralized SCM
Cost-focused model	Risk-focused model	Decentralized SCM
Single core tier	Dual core tier	Multi core tier
No risk hedge	Single risk hedge	Multi risk hedges
Need to risk mitigation	Need to reduce cost	Need to optimize cost : by platform commonization

Legend

→ Direction of procurement
- - - → Alternative path
● Main factory
● Sub factory
▲ Irreplaceable Tier (Production of key component)
Headquartered country's area

3.3 Agents

The proposed system contains six types of agents. Based on the setting, the study generated a large number of agents to interact with each other, resulting in emergent behavior. The agents are defined as follows:

- **Economic Indicator Agent:** This agent determines changes in economic indicators. For instance, we changed the exchange rates, GDP, and economic growth rate to reflect changing economic conditions.
- **Headquarters Agent:** This agent plays the role of the automotive company's leadership. It analyzes the economic indicators and predicts sales, manufacturing risks, and market risks. Based on this analysis, it then issues production orders to each factory. For example, the company leadership would instruct the factories to lower their production when the economic situation worsens or to increase production in boom times.
- **Manufacturing Risk Agent:** This agent represents the risks that can affect production in a factory, including natural disasters, supply disruptions, and strikes.
- **Market Risk Agent:** This agent represents the risks related to market consumption, including changes in exchange rates and government policies.
- **Factory Agent:** This agent represents the production output requested by the company leadership. It includes both independent risks (e.g., changes in factory utilization) and dependent risks (e.g., ability to procure key parts).
- **Market Agent:** This agent examines the risks related to product consumption and determines the final sales of the products, feeding the data from product inventories back to headquarters.

3.4 GBN Structure

The proposed system constructs a BN playing the role of company leadership in the form of a GBN using 35 variables, including economic indicators, social overhead capital (SOC) indicators, and the conditions of an automotive company.

We obtained raw data combining 40 years of automotive company information, national statistics, and economic indicators. The values of each variable were standardized. Then, we discretized these standardized values, or z-scores, into 7 bins, although we did not employ equal width or equal frequency. We employed K2, a greedy search algorithm that is very fast and simple, to calculate the Bayesian score and generate the GBN structure. The GBN precision, defined as the percentage of Correctly Classified Instances in the data set, was 75.61%.

3.5 Repast Simphony

Multi-agent simulation can be implemented using several different software packages. Repast Simphony [7] is a free, open source agent-based modeling and simulation platform that is easy to install and operate. We use the Repast version of Java to incorporate the WEKA API. A sample screen display of MASSOP is shown below.

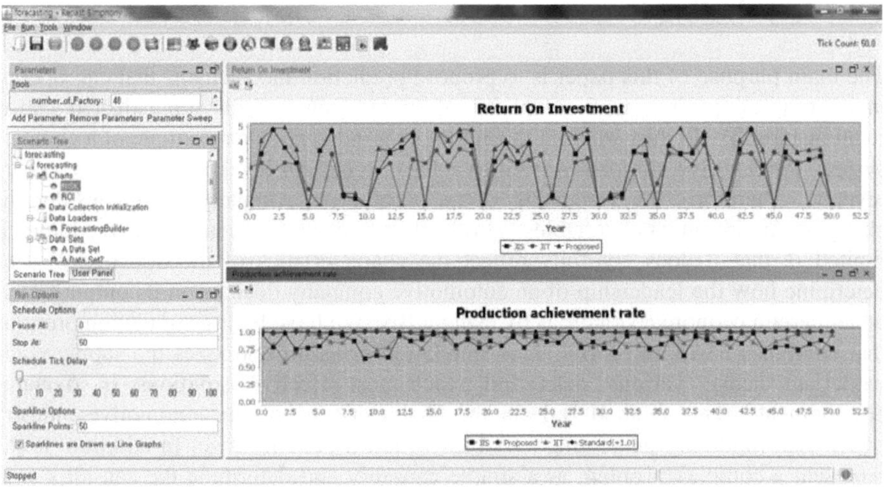

Fig. 1. MASSOP Screen Snapshot

4 Results

The proposed system compared the JIT, JIS, and decentralized SCM approaches. We determined that decentralized SCM is the most robust SCM approach because it hedges the various risks better than the other approaches. Moreover, it outperformed the other approaches with respect to ROI. This pattern was clearly apparent when the number of factories was increased.

Table 2. Experiment results

		F=6	F=12	F=24	F=48
PAR	JIT	0.9553	0.9371	0.9066	0.8496
	JIS	0.9532	0.9284	0.8878	0.8208
	Decentralized SCM	0.9842	0.9833	0.9822	0.9841
ROI	JIT	1.9404	1.9820	1.8864	1.8329
	JIS	2.4613	2.4405	2.3144	2.2054
	Decentralized SCM	2.5515	2.5915	2.5595	2.6586

Table 2 shows the results of the experiment. The average value was obtained after 15 iterations. The experiment was carried out for 50 clocks per iteration. The production achievement rate (PAR) value was 1.0, indicating that the total production amount matched the production instructions from headquarters. A PAR value greater than 1.0 indicates excess production; a value less than 1.0 indicates a production shortage. To calculate the ROI, the revenue is divided by the cost, and the result is expressed as a ratio. The price of the car is the same in all production methods.

5 Concluding Remarks

The main purpose of this paper is to propose prediction mechanisms that can operate in a complex environment composed of many factors with sophisticated causal relationships. To do this, we used the automotive industry as an example of a complex system. Automotive companies need to achieve a certain level of production to earn revenue. Therefore, the leadership of an automotive company must consider the changing environmental variables. However, the existing agent-based modeling is limited in that it does not fully reflect the characteristics of the domain. We can determine how the leadership of an automotive company decides on its output orders under certain economic situations by using a BN. We have built a simulation program that combines MAS and a BN. This simulation program optimizes the supply chain model to hedge various risks and reach cost-effective solutions in dynamic environments. This method reflects the characteristics of the automotive industry better than randomly generating variables within a certain range. In addition, it can represent a complex problem as a simple causality and determine the causality with emergent behavior — the outcome of the interactions among the intelligent agents.

Our experiments were carried out using data such as sales, production capacity, and factory utilization from just one automotive company. Therefore, it is difficult to generalize the outcomes to the entire industry. For example, we did not accurately identify the number of factories that had already adopted the JIT or JIS approach. Moreover, we did not use the car prices of each automotive company in the experiments. Instead, we adjusted the number of factories in each step and set the same price for each company's car.

In future research, we need to conduct an empirical analysis with data from several automotive companies to evaluate our prediction mechanism, which combines MAS and a BN, to prove the effectiveness and appropriateness of the system.

Acknowledgements. This research was supported by the World Class University (WCU) program through the National Research Foundation of Korea, funded by the ministry of Education, Science and Technology, Republic of Korea (Grant No. R31-2008-000-10062-0).

References

1. Bios, M.F., Quaddus, M., Wee, H.M., Watanabe, K.: Supply Chain Risk Management (SCRM): A Case Study on the Automotive and Electronic Industries in Brazil. Supply Chain Management: An International Journal 14(4), 247–252 (2009)
2. Blackhurst, J.V., Scheibe, K.P., Johnson, D.J.: Supplier Risk Assessment and Monitoring for the Automotive Industry. International Journal of Physical Distribution & Logistics Management 38(2), 143–165 (2008)
3. Giannakis, M., Louis, M.: A Multi-Agent Based Framework for Supply Chain Risk Management. Journal of Purchasing and Supply Management 17, 23–31 (2011)
4. Hall, M., Frank, E., Holmes, G., Pfahringer, B., Reutemann, P., Witten, I.H.: The WEKA Data Mining Software: An Update. ACM SIGKDD Newsletter 11(1), 10–18 (2009)
5. Kaihara, T.: Multi-Agent Based Supply Chain Modelling with Dynamic Environment. International Journal of Production Economics 85(2), 263–269 (2003)

6. Lazaric, N., Raybaut, A.: Knowledge Creation Facing Hierarchy: The Dynamics of Groups Inside the Firm. Journal of Artificial Societies and Social Simulation 7(2) (2004), http://jasss.soc.surrey.ac.uk/7/2/3.html
7. Collier, N., North, M.: Repast Java Getting Started, http://repast.sourceforge.net/docs/RepastJavaGettingStarted.pdf (accessed on September 30, 2012)
8. Shen, B., Su, X., Greiner, R., Musilek, P., Cheng, C.: Discriminative Parameter Learning of General Bayesian Network Classifiers. In: Proceedings of the 15th IEEE International Conference on Tools with Artificial Intelligence (ICTAI), pp. 296–305 (2003)
9. Tummala, R., Schoenherr, T.: Assessing and Managing Risks using the Supply Chain Risk Management Process (SCRMP). Supply Chain Management: An International Journal 16(6), 474–483 (2011)
10. Zolkos, R.: Supply Risks Take Priority. Business Insurance 45(31), 9–10 (2011)
11. Zolkos, R., Veysey, S.: Firms Rethink Supply Chain Risks. Business Insurance 45(45), 3–19 (2011)

Data Mining for Churn Prediction: Multiple Regressions Approach

Mohd Khalid Awang, Mohd Nordin Abdul Rahman, and Mohammad Ridwan Ismail

Faculty of Informatics,
Universiti Sultan Zainal Abidin, Gong Badak Campus,
21300 Kuala Terengganu, Terengganu, Malaysia
{khalid,mohdnabd}@unisza.edu.my,
ridwanewan@gmail.com

Abstract. The rapid development in the telecommunications industry contributed to the increased rivalry among the competitors. Customers switch to competitors or move out from the service provider become critical concerns for companies to retain customer loyalty. Churn prevention through churn prediction is one of the methods to ensure customer loyalty with the service provider. Detect and analyze early churn is a proactive step to ensure that existing customers did not move out or subscribe to the product from competitors. Selection of customer characteristics is one of the core issues to forecast customer churn in the telecommunications industry. This paper proposes multiple regressions analysis to predict the customers churn in the telecommunications industry based on recommended features. The results have shown that the performance of multiple regressions for predicting customer churn is acceptably good.

Keywords: Regression Analysis, Prediction, Churn, Churn Management, Data Mining.

1 Introduction

Predictions of future customers are one of the most important activities that form the foundation for all strategic decisions and planning in effective business operations. [3] stated that customer retention leads to improved sales and reduced marketing costs compared to selling to fresh customers. Maintain the right customer is the determinant of profitability for the long term, rather than finding new clients that will increase the cost. In the telecommunication industry, the issue of customer retention and loyalty management is becoming increasingly significant as competition from competitors that increasingly aggressive. Prediction on customer's behavior is very challenging to define due to human being and their satisfaction grounded on quality of customer service and product.

The rapid growth of wireless telecommunication has changed the trend of the Malaysian's telecommunication industries. Customers have the opportunity to select and switch from one package to another package offered by the different service providers. The behavior of customers who shift from one service provider to another

T.-h. Kim et al. (Eds.): EL/DTA/UNESST 2012, CCIS 352, pp. 318–324, 2012.

is known as churn and now has become a major concern of network providers in Malaysia. Finding the prospective churners can help the companies to retain their customers. Many researchers have tried to establish various models to predict customer churn, for example the decision tree, genetic algorithm, and regression analysis. Based on literature reviews and to the best of our knowledge, there are no researches found yet on doing churn prediction for a telecommunication company in Malaysia. Therefore, this paper proposed a multiple regression model to predict the customer churn in Malaysian's telecommunication industry.

2 Related Work

Churn management solution should not target the whole customer population, because not all customers are worth retaining and customer retention costs money. Instead, companies need to comprehend their customer's activities and find ways to maintain the existing customers. [1] indicated that trying to sell more to everyone is no longer a cost-effective sales plan.

2.1 Customer Churn in Telecommunication

Basically, there are three (3) types of churn: unavoidable churn, involuntary churn, and voluntary churn [9]. Unavoidable churn occurs when customer dies or moves out the provider's operating area. On the other hand, involuntary churn or forced churn occurs when a subscriber fails to pay for service and as a result the provider ends the customer's service. Our main focus is the voluntary churn whereby the service termination is on the customer's choice, leaving one operator for another. These three classifications can be divided further down into four categories defined by two variables; which are the financial and non-financial churn [5]. Financial churn is defined as bad debt subscribers who leave while non-financial churn refers to paying customers who leave. Customer churn is defined differently in different industries. In the telecommunication service industry, churn means customer attrition that can be classified into several types [7] [8] as describe in table 1:

Table 1. Four basic types of churn

Types of Churn	Description
Involuntary with Financial Churn	Force churn customers whereby the service provider removes the subscriber list because of bad payment and service suspended.
Involuntary with Non-financial Churn	Customers who moved to other place which is the provider cannot provide the services at the new area.
Voluntary with Financial Churn	Customer voluntary want to terminate due to lack of payment.
Voluntary with Non-financial Churn	Paying customer who defected because they were unhappy with the service or got a better offer from competitors.

Poor performance or inadequate coverage, pricing, competitor's promotion and satisfaction with customer service, these kinds of reasons should be taken into deep thought, because these reasons contribute to company's performance. Churn management define as developing techniques that empower firms to retain their profitable customers and it targets at increasing customer loyalty.

2.2 Regression Analysis

Regression analysis is regarded as one of the most popular techniques used by the researches to make prediction on customer satisfaction or churn [8]. The objective of regression analysis is to develop a statistical model that can be used to predict dependent variable from the value of at least one explanatory variable. Regression analysis is used to produce an equation that will predict a dependent variable using one or more independent variables. This equation has the form

$$Y = b1X1 + b2X2 + \ldots + A \tag{1}$$

Y is the dependent variable or the output to predict, while $X1$, $X2$ and so forth are the independent variables used to predict it. Whereas $b1$, $b2$ and so on are known as the coefficients or multipliers that describe the size of the effect the independent variables are having on the dependent variable Y, and A is the value Y is predicted to have when all the independent variables are equal to zero.

3 Research Method

This paper proposed regression analysis as a technique to predict customer churn. The independent variables which are known as the input data are extracted from four (4) different categories, which are the customer profile, customer demographic, call usage and billing data.

3.1 Data Preparation and Features Extraction

Data preparation is considered as the most time-consuming activity in the data mining processes. We have collected data from one of the most popular telecommunication companies in Malaysia. The raw data has been extracted manually based on the proposed features which are the billing data, customer relationship data, customer demographic data and usage data. The billing data consist of customer's usage and payment, and account receivable (AR) data. Customer relationship data consists of the internet and call packages they subscribes and monthly commitment that they have to pay. Customer demographic will explain about their age and gender. Usage data consists of number of national and international calls along with their usage period. The proposed features for churn analysis can be summarized as follows:

Table 2. Proposed Features

Features	Extracted Features
Customer Demographics	-Age -Gender
Customer Relationship Data	-Internet speed -Monthly commitment for internet -Call packages
Billing Data	-Account Receivable (AR) days -Total usage bill -Total payment
Usage Data	-Total number of National calls -Total number of International calls

3.2 Development of Regression Models

The data set was divided into two (2) sets, one set of 78 cases for training and 18 cases for testing the model. A model was built using a training set with multiple regressions. The development of the regression model began with the selection of the input features of independent variables. We have selected twenty (20) variables in our initial model. The multiple regressions analysis was performed using MINITAB for Windows, version 16.

3.3 Evaluation Criteria

The result from the model was measure based on accuracy, sensitivity and specificity. Accuracy is defined as the percentage of the model correctly makes prediction. Sensitivity of a classifier is the percentage of correctly predict churn (True Positive) based on total number of churn whereby specificity defined as the percentage of model to correctly predict non-churner (True negative) divided by total number of non-churn.

$$\text{Accuracy} = ((TP + TN) / (TP + TN + FN + FP)) \times 100\% \tag{2}$$

$$\text{Sensitivity} = (TP / (TP + FN)) \times 100\% \tag{3}$$

$$\text{Specificity} = (TN / (TN + FP)) \times 100\% \tag{4}$$

Table 3. Four Categories of Churn Prediction

	Actual Churns	**Actual Non- Churners**
Predicted Churns	True Positive (TP)	False Positive (FP)
Predicted Non-Churners	False Negative (FN)	True Negative (TN)

4 Result and Discussion

From the data set of 96 cases, 62 cases were classified as churners and another 34 as non-churners. For the training purposes, 78 cases were used as training data set which consists 50 and 28 for churners and non-churners respectively. The others data were used as testing set. The analysis was based on the third quarter years of customer usage.

Table 4. Result of Regression Analysis

	Actual Churns	**Actual Non-Churners**	**Total**
Predicted Churns	53	15	68
Predicted Non- Churners	9	19	28
Total	**62**	**34**	**96**

Based on Table 4, total accuracy of the development prediction system is about 75.00%, sensitivity: 85.48% and specificity: 55.88%. The result above concludes that the capability of prediction system to detect churners and non-churners customers is acceptable.

In order to improve the prediction system, stepwise regression was applied based on the same input variables. [2] stated that the independent variables in the regression model could be added or removed from the model at each step of the building process.

Table 5 shows the result after doing the Stepwise Regression Analysis. The accuracy of the development prediction system is about 76.04%, sensitivity: 87.10% and specificity: 55.88%. Based on the result in Table 4 and Table 5, the accuracy and the sensitivity of the prediction system have improved after performing stepwise regression.

Table 5. Result of Stepwise Regression Analysis

	Actual Churns	**Actual Non-Churners**	**Total**
Predicted Churns	54	15	69
Predicted Non- Churners	8	19	27
Total	**62**	**34**	**96**

5 Conclusion

Churn prediction system is crucial in saturated telecommunication markets. To be competitive, the service providers have to be able to predict possible churners and take proactive actions to retain their valuable customers rather than looking for new customers. Therefore, churn prediction model has become an important research problem for both academics and service provider companies in recent years.

This research has provided some interesting results for predicting customer churn. This study has addressed four features that focused on usage, billing, profile and demographic data as the independent variables in the regression model. The multiple regressions analysis has been employed and proven to be one of the best tools to predict customer churn. The accuracy of the prediction is acceptably good. However, there are some limitations with our proposed models. For future work, several issues can be considered. Other important features such as complaint information, fault reports, etc. should also been taken into consideration to improve the performance of the prediction. The study should also consider other modeling techniques available for prediction such as artificial neural network, support vector machine, decision tree, fuzzy logic and etc.

References

1. Canning, G.: Do A Value Analysis of Your Customer Base. Industrial Marketing Management 11, 89–93 (1982)
2. Levine, D.M., Ramsey, P.P., Smidt, R.K.: Applied Statistics For Engineers and Scientists Using Microsoft Excell and Minitab. Prentice Hall (2001)
3. Eriksson, K., Vaghult, A.L.: Customer Retention, Purchasing Behavior and Relationship Substance in Professional Services. Industrial Marketing Management 29, 363–372 (2000)
4. Song, G., Yang, D., Wu, L., Wang, T., Tang, S.: A Mixed Process Neural Network and its Application to Churn Prediction in Mobile Communications. In: IEEE International Conference on Digital Object Identifier, vol. 6, pp. 798–802 (2006)
5. Hadden, J.: A Customer Profiling Methodology for Churn Prediction. School Of Applied Sciences Manufacturing Department, Cranfield University. Doctor of Philosophy (2008)

6. Hyeseon Lee, Y.L., Cho, H., Im, K., Kim, Y.S.: Mining Churning Behaviors and Developing Retention Strategies Based on A Partial Least Square (PLS) Model. Decision Support Systems (2011)
7. John Hadden, A.T., Roy, R., Churn, D.R.: Prediction Using Complaints Data. World Academy of Science, Engineering and Technology 19, 1–6 (2006)
8. Hadden, J., Tiwari, A., Roy, R., Ruta, D.: Churn Prediction: Does Technology Matter? World Academy of Science, Engineering and Technology 16, 193–199 (2006)
9. Modisette, L.: Milking Wireless Churn for Profit, Telecommunicitions, Dedham, International Edition, vol. 33(2), p. 73, 2 pgs Appendix: Springer-Author Discount (1999)

It Is Time to Prepare for the Future: Forecasting Social Trends

Soyeon Caren Han, Hyunsuk Chung, and Byeong Ho Kang

School of Computing and Information System,
Tasmania 7005, Australia
{Soyeon.Han,hchung,Byeong.Kang}@utas.edu.au

Abstract. A social issue is what arises when the public discuss a specific event. Recently, many large Internet based service companies provide new trends services that display the emerging issues based on their data, for example, Google displays "top 10 most searched topics" every hour. Those emerging issues reflect the trend of public interest. Forecasting those issues helps the user to prepare for the future. In this paper, we present our research on proposing the social issue-forecasting model. To do so, we first collected social issue keyword from Google Trends for 3 months since it is based on the large scale of public data. We apply the k-nearest neighbor algorithm, which is the pattern recognition technology for recognizing the complex patterns and trends. To improve the accuracy, we applied Ripple Down Rules.

Keywords: Google Trends, Social Issue forecasting, Social Networking Sites, Web Trends Forecasting.

1 Introduction

Recently, many interned-based service companies provide new social trends analytic services, which displays the emerging public issue based on their data. Those services designed to entice and integrate people to notice the emerging issues much faster and discuss about the issue further. For example, Google provides the list of the popular search terms among people, called 'top 10 most searched terms'. However, it is a question how to use this information beyond just "interests" or "fun".

Most social trends analytic services are oriented for the interests of users. It seems to be a right direction but it is found that popular social issues are often ignored. It is because the software designed to monitor predefined keywords or issues. In most social analytics tools or services requires the target keyword to be monitored. It is unavoidable due to the size of information to be monitored. Therefore, a set of social issue keywords to be monitored is identified first. Then the lifecycle of these target keywords in social trends analytic services on the Web are monitored. This study proposes to monitor and develop the lifecycle forecasting model of social issues published by the service providers. By having this model, we can predict the trends of these issues.

T.-h. Kim et al. (Eds.): EL/DTA/UNESST 2012, CCIS 352, pp. 325–331, 2012.

For this study, we have collected about 3 months social issue keywords from 'Google Trends'. Then, we monitored the lifecycle of each social issue keywords. To forecast the lifecycle of social issue, we applied k-nearest neighbour algorithm, which is commonly used in the pattern matching area. We also consider not only the pattern matching but also the relations in different trending social issues so we applied ripple down rules for the adopted system.

The paper is structured as follows: Section 2 presents the related work, followed by the methodology of this proposed system in Section 3. In Section 4, we describe the evaluations conducted and discuss the results. Finally, we conclude this paper in Section 5.

2 Related Work

There is no doubt that recent years have shown a spectacular surge in the popularity of web-based services. People find and share information by using web-based service, especially search engines, social networking services, and Internet-news-services. By using those three services, people can obtain and share information faster than ever. Those services can be used to search or share real-time information. A great deal of research carried out on various aspects, such as the characteristics of each service, growth and evolution of each service, their activities, and the users' behavior.

Social trends analytic services become the important issue in every field, such as knowledge acquisition or software engineering recently [13]. Many large internet-based companies have provided trend-services, which display the list of the most popular topic, based on the data from their services. Those trends services have received a great amount of attention [9]. Google Trends and Yahoo Trending Topics are search-trends-services, which are provided by Google and Yahoo. Google Trends has been used to detect disease outbreaks [3, 6], suicide risk [10, 11]. For social networking service, there are only a few trend-services. The most popular trend-service is Twitter Trending Topic. It has been used to analyse social issue characteristics [9, 15], and detect natural disaster [5, 8].

There is little research on forecasting approaches in the social trends prediction. Thus, it is necessary to investigate the forecasting technologies in other areas, including weather forecasting, sales prediction, and stock forecasting. Many basic pattern recognition techniques, such as k-NN, have been used for short-term weather forecasting [4]. Atsalakis and Valavanis [2] indicated that many machine learning technologies used in the stock forecasting area, including Feed Forward Neural Network (FFNN) [1, 14], and Support Vector Machines (SVM) [7, 12]. Neural Network is also the most popular forecasting technology in the weather [16]. While the financial/stock forecasting area is focusing on the FFNN, recurrent neural network received a lot of attention in the weather forecasting area [17].

3 Social Trends Forecasting

We present our research on developing the system that predicts the lifecycle of social issues in the future. The social issue lifecycle forecasting system consists of two main components as follows:

(1) Social issue monitoring
(2) Social issue lifecycle forecasting

3.1 Social Issue Monitoring

First of all, the system monitors the trending social issue keywords, which present the public interests in the real time. As mentioned before, there are new social trends analytic services, which are provided by different internet-based service. There are three types of trends service, search-based, social networking service (SNS)-based, and Internet news-based trends service. For example, Google provide the search-based social trends analytics service, called 'Google Trends'. Google Trends presents the 10 fastest-rising search terms on an hourly basis. Compare to other trends analytic services, Google Trends provide the most objective social issue keywords since search results are affected not just by celebrities but also by the general users. However, SNS and Internet news based trends services are often affected by celebrities or specific groups. Therefore, we chose Google Trends as the social issue keywords provider in this study.

3.2 Social Issue Lifecycle Forecasting

To develop the social issue lifecycle forecasting model, we monitored social issue keywords and their lifecycle. Now, it is time to do the social issue lifecycle prediction. Since the size of data is getting increasing from time to time, it is necessary to find meaningful clusters in data. K-means clustering is a method commonly used to automatically partition a data set into k groups. It proceeds by selecting k initial cluster centres and then iteratively refining them [21]. In this paper, we clustered 10 initial clusters because of the forecasting speed.

After clustering, we applied the k-Nearest Neighbour algorithms, which is commonly used in pattern recognition. While the pattern matching algorithms provides looks for the exact matches in the training data, the pattern recognition algorithms search all similar results of input data. As we applied k-nearest neighbour algorithm (k-NN), it is necessary to decide to choose the number of k. The system classifies each lifecycle patterns based on 20 closest training examples in the feature space.

However, it is not perfect if we apply only artificial intelligence approaches for forecasting the lifecycle of social issues. This is because it is necessary to consider not only the pattern of the lifecycle of one specific social issue but also its relations with other social issues. This is totally different from basic time-series forecasting. Thus, we applied the Ripple-Down Rules (RDR) as a heuristic method, which is the case based reasoning technology. We created various cases and rules, such as topic, day, and specific periods (e.g. election period).

3.3 System Design

We developed a social issue lifecycle forecasting system using the proposed forecasting model. The system presents various factors, including the time the social issue keyword first appeared, ranking changes in an hour and three hours.

THE LIST OF TRENDING ISSUES FROM GOOGLE TRENDS

Rank	Keyword	Past			Forecast	
	Current	Appearance (ago)	Changes (3 hours)	Changes (1 hour)	Remaining time	Trend
1	paula deen	13 hr(s)	–	–	1 hr(s)	–
2	seattle weather	20 hr(s)	↑1	–	4 hr(s)	–
3	jenelle evans	8 hr(s)	↑4	↑1	7 hr(s)	↑
4	jerry yang	5 hr(s)	↓2	↓1	0 hr(s)	↓
5	justified	2 hr(s)	new	–	2 hr(s)	–
6	wisconsin recall	3 hr(s)	↑2	–	0 hr(s)	–
7	wikipedia blackout	23 hr(s)	↑2	–	1 hr(s)	–
8	scott walker	1 hr(s)	new	↑2	1 hr(s)	↑
9	girl scout cookies	16 hr(s)	reappear	–	6 hr(s)	–
10	school closings	13 hr(s)	–	↓2	1 hr(s)	↓

Fig. 1. The main table in the social issue forecasting system

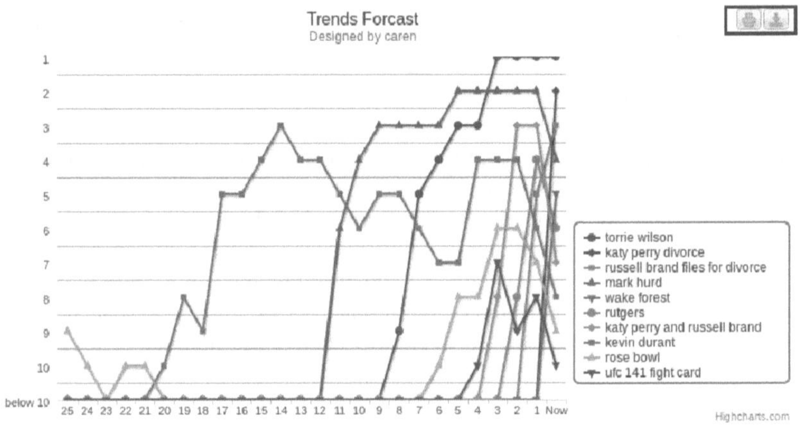

Fig. 2. The lifecycle graph in the social issue forecasting system

As you can see in Figure 1, the system also forecast how much hours each social issue keyword will remain in the Google Trends, and the trends whether the rank rise or fall in next hour.

Figure 2 displays the lifecycle of top 10 social issue keywords in Google Trends. X value indicates the time, and Y value indicates the ranking of each social issue keywords. It enables users to see how the lifecycle will be changed, as well as when the social issue disappeared and reappeared. Users enables to download and print the the lifecycle of top 10 social issue keywords in the real time.

4 Evaluation

We monitored social issues keywords for over 3 months, 109 days. We collected 26160 keywords totally. We pre-processed the collected data and obtained 4436 unique lifecycle patterns. In this paper, we applied k-NN as a pattern recogniser and Ripple Down Rules. We conducted an experiment to justify the efficiency of the proposed forecasting model by comparing with other three different artificial intelligence technologies, which are commonly used in stock forecasting area. The selected technologies include Feed-Forward Neural Network, Linear Regression, and k-star. In conclusion, combining k-NN and Ripple Down rules achieves the highest accuracy.

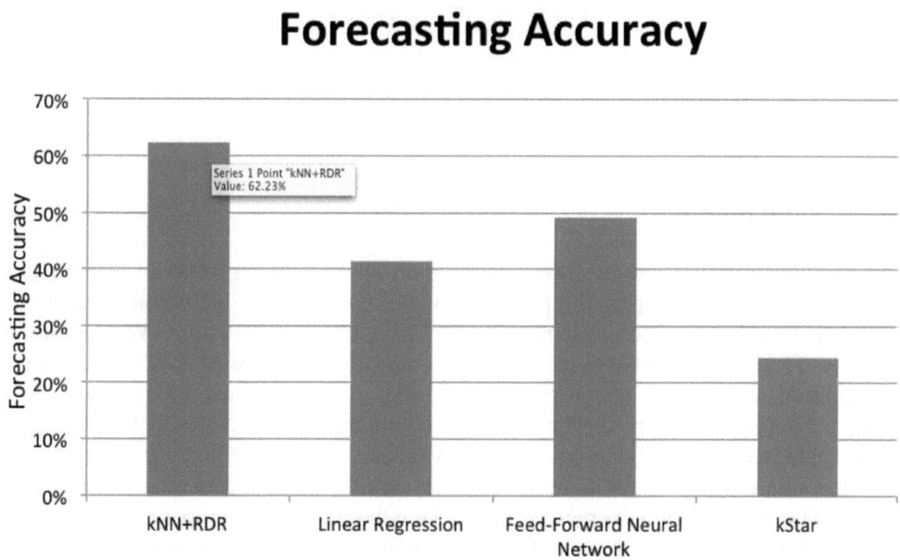

Fig. 3. Forecasting accuracy comparison among 4 technologies

As you can see the figure 4, we examined how the inclusion of RDR affects the accuracy of the forecasting model (k-NN). If we apply only k-NN, the forecasting accuracy is almost 50%, which is slightly higher than other forecasting technologies, as figure 3. However, with Ripple Down Rules, the accuracy is over 60%, which means it improves almost 10% accuracy by using Ripple Down Rules. From this experiment, it is proved that we can predict much accurate future by using the proposed method.

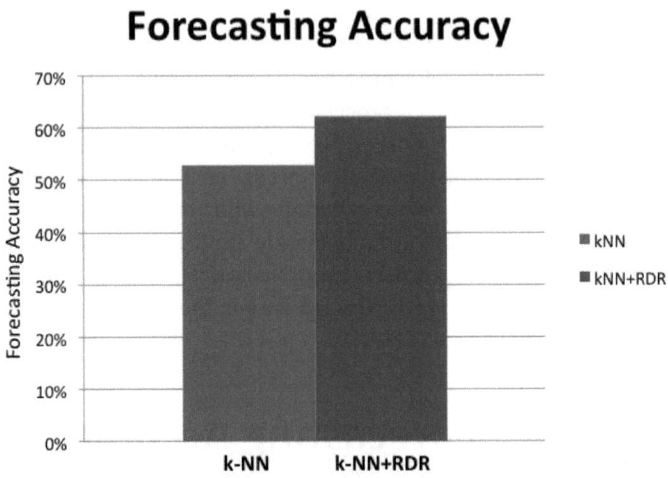

Fig. 4. Difference between k-NN and k-NN+RDR

5 Conclusion

As mentioned earlier, we propose our research on developing a model that predicts social trends. In this paper, the proposed model consists two main components: (1) trending social issue monitoring, and (2) Social trends forecasting. We monitored Google Trends as a social issue keyword collector. We applied k-NN, the pattern recognition technology, and Ripple Down rules to forecast the lifecycle of social issues. The evaluation results proved that combination of k-NN and Ripple Down Rules achieved much higher accuracy than other artificial intelligence technologies. For the future work, we will monitor other various social trends analytic services, such as Twitter Trending Topics or Yahoo Trending Now and compare them. We will analyse the collected social issue data and propose the crucial parameters and the case to improve the forecasting accuracy.

Acknowledgements. This paper was supported by Asian Office of Aerospace Research and Development (AOARD), Japan. This paper was also supported by Korea Association of Industry, Academy and Research Institute with the project called "Business support for academic-industrial common technology development". We are grateful to Hee-Geun Yoon for helpful discussions.

References

1. Ajith, A., Baikunth, N., Mahanti, P.K.: Hybrid intelligent systems for stock market analysis. In: Proceedings of International Conference on Computational Science (2003a)
2. Atsalakis, G.S., Valavanis, K.P.: Surveying stock market forecasting techniques–Part II: Soft computing methods. Expert Systems with Applications 36(3), 5932–5941 (2009)
3. Carneiro, H.A., Mylonakis, E.: Google trends: a web-based tool for real-time surveillance of disease outbreaks. Clinical Infectious Diseases 49(10), 1557–1564 (2009)

4. Chatfield_Ch_Tim_Series_Forecasting, 1st edn. (280) (2000)
5. Earle, P., et al.: OMG Earthquake! Can Twitter improve earthquake response? Seismological Research Letters 81(2), 246–251 (2010)
6. Ginsberg, J., et al.: Detecting influenza epidemics using search engine query data. Nature 457(7232), 1012–1014 (2008)
7. Huang, W., Nakamori, Y., Wang, S.-Y.: Forecasting stock market movement direction with support vector machine. Computer and Operations Research 32, 2513–2522 (2005)
8. Hughes, A.L., Palen, L.: Twitter adoption and use in mass convergence and emergency events. International Journal of Emergency Management 6(3), 248–260 (2009)
9. Kwak, H., et al.: What is Twitter, a social network or a news media? ACM (2010)
10. McCarthy, M.J.: Internet monitoring of suicide risk in the population. Journal of Affective Disorders 122(3), 277–279 (2010)
11. Page, A., Chang, S.S., Gunnell, D.: Surveillance of Australian Suicidal Behaviour Using the Internet? Australian and New Zealand Journal of Psychiatry 45(12), 1020–1022 (2011)
12. Pai, P.-F., Lin, C.-S.: A Hybrid ARIMA and support vector machines model in stock price forecasting. Omega 33(6), 497–505 (2005)
13. Rech, J.: Discovering trends in software engineering with google trend. ACM SIGSOFT Software Engineering Notes 32(2), 1–2 (2007)
14. Thawornwong, S., Enke, D.: The adaptive selection of financial and economic variables for use with artificial neural networks. Neurocomputing 56, 205–232 (2004)
15. Twitter study. Technical report, Pear Analytics (August. 2009)
16. Taylor, J.W., Buizza, R.: Neural network load forecasting with weather ensemble predictions. IEEE Transactions on Power Systems 17(3), 626–632 (2002)
17. Barbounis, T.G., Theocharis, J.B., Alexiadis, M.C., Dokopoulos, P.S.: Longterm wind speed and power forecasting using local recurrent neural network models. IEEE Trans. Energy Convers 21(1), 273–284 (2006)

Vague Normalization in a Relational Database Model

Jaydev Mishra[1,*] and Sharmistha Ghosh[2]

[1] College of Engineering and Management, Kolaghat,
West Bengal, India, Pin: 721171
jsm02@rediffmail.com
[2] Vellore Institute of Technology University, Vellore,
Tamilnadu, India, Pin: 632014
sharmisthaghosh@vit.ac.in

Abstract. Vague relational database models generalize the classical relational database model by allowing uncertain and imprecise information by means of vague set theory. In this paper, we have introduced vague extensions of the normal forms for a similarity based vague relational database model. Firstly, we have designed an algorithm to find the vague closure of an attribute set which can be utilized to find vague key. Next, with the concepts of α -**vfd** and partial α -**vfd** as introduced in [1], we have defined different vague normal forms in a vague relational database. We have also presented examples based on real life application to demonstrate how normalization based on α -**vfd**s of vague relation may be done.

Keywords: Vague set, similarity measure of vague sets, α -**vfd**, partial α -**vfd**, vague key, vague closure of attribute set, vague normal forms.

1 Introduction

It is well known that the classical relational data model introduced by Codd [2] in 1970 can handle only precise and exact data in an information source. However, information obtained from real life applications is more often imprecise and ambiguous. Fuzzy database models [3-12] based on fuzzy set theory proposed by Zadeh [13] in 1965 have been extensively studied and cultivated in literature to deal with such uncertain and vague information in relational databases.

Vague set theory has been subsequently introduced by Gau and Buehrer [14] in 1993 as a more efficient tool to treat ambiguous data and it has been successfully applied in many different fields such as fuzzy control, decision analysis, expert system etc. A vague set, conceived as a generalization of the concept of fuzzy set, is a set of decision objects, each of which has a grade of membership whose value is a continuous subinterval of [0,1]. It is characterized by a truth-membership function and a false-membership function and separates the positive and negative evidence for membership of an element in the set. Thus a vague set has more powerful ability to process imprecise information than traditional fuzzy sets. Therefore classical

* Corresponding author.

T.-h. Kim et al. (Eds.): EL/DTA/UNESST 2012, CCIS 352, pp. 332–344, 2012.

relational databases may also be extended to represent and deal with uncertain data in a more effective manner with the idea of vague set theory. Such an extended database model is then called a vague relational database model. Research in this direction has attracted some attention in recent years. However, till date very limited number of references is available in this area.

One of the primary objectives of any good database design is to decrease data redundancy and provide data reliability. Such data redundancies and insertion, deletion and update anomalies have been of great concern in a relational database. Like integrity constraints, normalization process also plays an important role in designing a good relational database. Studies related to normalization process minimizing redundancies and different anomalies for fuzzy relational database models are accounted in references 6,7,11,12. However, no such work has been reported so far in literature for a vague relational model.

So far, there had been some studies on extension of data dependencies to a vague relational database model. In particular, **Lu** and **Ng** [15] in 2004 and **Zhao** and **Ma** [16] in 2006 have defined vague functional dependency (**vfd**) based on similarity measure of vague data. In 2009, **Lu** and **Ng** [17] have again defined a **vfd** based on mi-overlapping of attributes values. The present authors [1] have also introduced a new definition of **vfd,** called α - **vfd,** based on α -equality of tuples in 2012.

In this paper, our objective is to design a vague relational database model by minimizing data redundancies and also by minimizing the insertion, deletion and update anomalies. For this purpose, vague closure of an attribute set has been presented to find vague key. Next, we have introduced a number of vague normal forms such as vague first (**1VNF**), vague second (**2VNF**), vague third (**3VNF**) and vague BCNF (**VBCNF**) based on **vfd**. Finally, all these concepts have been verified with an example.

The organization of the paper is as follows: The basics of vague set theory have been reviewed in the following **section 2**. In **section 3**, we have proposed an algorithm to find vague closure of an attribute set. **Section 4** discusses different vague normalization techniques, namely **1VNF**, **2VNF**, **3VNF**, and **VBCNF** of a vague relational database model by giving a real-life application. The final conclusions are reported in **section 5**.

2 Basic Definitions

In this section, we first review some basic definitions from vague set theory that will be useful throughout the paper and then define vague functional dependency as introduced in [1] (α -**vfd**).

2.1 Basic Preliminaries on Vague Set Theory

Here, we present definition of vague set and some basic definitions related to vague relational database model. Let U be the universe of discourse where an element of U is denoted by u .

Definition 1

A **vague set** V in the universe of discourse U is characterized by two membership functions given by:

(i) a truth membership function $t_V : U \rightarrow [0,1]$, and

(ii) a false membership function $f_V : U \rightarrow [0,1]$,

where $t_V(u)$ is a lower bound of the grade of membership of u derived from the 'evidence for u', and $f_V(u)$ is a lower bound on the negation of u derived from the 'evidence against u', and $t_V(u) + f_V(u) \leq 1$.

Thus, the grade of membership $\mu_V(u)$ of u in the vague set V is bounded by a subinterval $[t_V(u), 1 - f_V(u)]$ of [0,1] i.e., $t_V(u) \leq \mu_V(u) \leq 1 - f_V(u)$.

Then, the **vague set** V is written as $V = \{\langle u, [t_V(u), 1 - f_V(u)]\rangle : u \in U\}$.

Here, the interval $[t_V(u), 1 - f_V(u)]$ is said to be the vague value to the object u and is denoted by $V_V(u)$. For example, in disease diagnosis process of a medical system, the vague value [0.3, 0.6] can be interpreted as "the report of disease in favour is 30%, in against is 40% and another 30% is undeterminable."

The precision of knowledge about u is clearly characterized by the difference $(1 - f_V(u) - t_V(u))$. If this is small, the knowledge about u is relatively precise. However, if it is large, we know correspondingly little. If $t_V(u)$ is equal to $(1 - f_V(u))$, the knowledge about u is precise, and vague set theory reverts back to fuzzy set theory. If $t_V(u)$ and $(1 - f_V(u))$ are both equal to 1 or 0, depending on whether u does or does not belong to V, the knowledge about u is exact and the theory goes back to that of ordinary sets. Thus any crisp or fuzzy set may be considered as a special case of vague set.

2.2 Vague Relational Database Model (VRDB)

In this section, we present an extension of the classical relational database model that can incorporate imprecise or vague data by means of vague set theory and is termed as a Vague Relational Database Model (**VRDB**).

Definition 2

Let $A_i, i = 1,2,\ldots,n$ be n attributes defined on the universes of discourse sets U_i, respectively. Then, a **vague relation** r on the relation schema $R(A_1, A_2, \ldots, A_n)$ is defined as a subset of the Cartesian product of a collection of vague subsets:

$r \subseteq V(U_1) \times V(U_2) \times \ldots\ldots \times V(U_n)$ where $V(U_i)$ denotes the collection of all vague subsets on U_i.

Each tuple t of r consists of a Cartesian product of vague subsets on the respective U_i's, i.e., $t[A_i] = \pi(A_i)$, where $\pi(A_i)$ is a vague subset of the attribute A_i defined on U_i for all i. The relation r can thus be represented by a table with n columns. It may be observed that the vague relation can be considered as an extension of classical relations (all vague values are [1, 1]) and fuzzy relations (all vague values are $[a, a]$, $0 \le a \le 1$). It is clear that the vague relation can capture more information about vagueness.

2.3 Similarity Measure of Vague Data

The following similarity measure proposed by Lu et al. [15] has been used in the present study

Definition 3. *Similarity Measure between two vague values*
Let x and y be any two vague values such that $x = [t_x, 1 - f_x]$ and $y = [t_y, 1 - f_y]$, where $0 \le t_x \le 1 - f_x \le 1$, and $0 \le t_y \le 1 - f_y \le 1$. Let $SE(x, y)$ denote the similarity measure between x and y. Then,

$$SE(x, y) = \sqrt{\left(1 - \frac{\left|(t_x - t_y) - (f_x - f_y)\right|}{2}\right)\left(1 - \left|(t_x - t_y) + (f_x - f_y)\right|\right)}$$

Definition 4. *Similarity Measure between two vague sets*
Let $U = \{u_1, u_2, u_3, \ldots\ldots u_n\}$ be the universe of discourse. Let A and B be two vague sets on U, such that

$A = \{< u_i, [t_A(u_i), 1 - f_A(u_i)] >, \forall u_i \in U\}$, where $t_A(u_i) \le \mu_A(u_i) \le 1 - f_A(u_i)$ and $1 \le i \le n$.

$B = \{< u_i, [t_B(u_i), 1 - f_B(u_i)] >, \forall u_i \in U\}$, where $t_B(u_i) \le \mu_B(u_i) \le 1 - f_B(u_i)$ and $1 \le i \le n$.

Now, the similarity measure between A and B, denoted by $SE(A, B)$ is defined as:

$$SE(A, B) = \frac{1}{n}\sum_{i=1}^{n} SE([t_A(u_i), 1 - f_A(u_i)], [t_B(u_i), 1 - f_B(u_i)])$$

$$= \frac{1}{n}\sum_{i=1}^{n}\sqrt{\left(1 - \frac{\left|(t_A(u_i) - t_B(u_i)) - (f_A(u_i) - f_B(u_i))\right|}{2}\right)\left(1 - \left|(t_A(u_i) - t_B(u_i)) + (f_A(u_i) - f_B(u_i))\right|\right)}$$

2.4 Vague Functional Dependency (vfd)

The new definition of α -**vfd** proposed by the present authors in [1] is based on the idea of α -equality of two vague tuples defined as follows:

Definition 5. α - *equality of two vague tuples*
Let $r(R)$ be a vague relation on the relational schema $R(A_1, A_2, \ldots\ldots, A_n)$. Let t_1 and t_2 be any two vague tuples in r. Let $\alpha \in [0,1]$ be a threshold or choice parameter, predefined by the database designer, and $X = \{X_1, X_2, \ldots\ldots, X_k\} \subseteq \mathrm{R}$. Then the vague tuples t_1 and t_2 are said to be α -equal on X if $SE(t_1[X_i], t_2[X_i]) \geq \alpha, \forall i = 1,2,3\ldots.k$. This equality is denoted by the notation $t_1[X](VE)_\alpha t_2[X]$.

Definition 6. *Vague Functional Dependency (* α *-vfd)*
Let $X, Y \subset R = \{A_1, A_2 \ldots A_n\}$. Choose a threshold value $\alpha \in [0,1]$. Then a vague functional dependency (**vfd**), denoted by $X \xrightarrow[\alpha]{vfd} Y$, is said to exist if, whenever $t_1[X](VE)_\alpha t_2[X]$, it is also the case that $t_1[Y](VE)_\alpha t_2[Y]$.

We may read this **vfd** as follows: the set of attributes X vague functionally determines the set of attributes Y at α -level of choice. In another terminology, the set of attributes Y is vague functionally determined by the set of attributes X at α -level of choice. During the course of analysis, different α values may be set by the database designer so, that the above **vfd** may be termed as α **-vfd**.

2.5 Partial Vague Functional Dependency (partial α -vfd)

Partial vague functional dependency (**partial** α **-vfd**) for vague relational database is defined below:

Definition 7
Y is called partially vague functionally dependent on X at α -level of choice, i.e., $X \xrightarrow[\alpha]{vfd} Y$ partially, if $X \xrightarrow[\alpha]{vfd} Y$ hold and also there exists a non-empty set $X' \subset X$, such that, $X' \xrightarrow[\alpha]{vfd} Y$. The concept of **partial** α **-vfd** then expresses the fact that after removal of an attribute X_i from X, the dependency still holds i.e., for an attribute $X_i \in X, X - \{X_i\}$ still vague functionally determines Y at α -level of choice. The notion of **partial** α **-vfd** is needed to define vague key.

2.6 Vague Key

Extending the idea of classical key in the vague environment we have defined vague key in [1] as follows:

Definition 8
Let $K \subseteq R$ and V be a set of **vfd**s for R. Then, K is called a **vague key** of R at α-level of choice where $\alpha \in [0,1]$ iff $K \xrightarrow[\alpha]{vfd} R \in V$ and $K \xrightarrow[\alpha]{vfd} R$ is not a **partial** α**-vfd**.

3 Vague Closure of Attribute Set

To find the vague key of a relation scheme R, we should find the vague closure of an attribute or set of attributes. Vague closure of attribute set X denoted by X^+ is the set of attributes which are vague functionally determined by the attributes X. If the closure set X^+ is the minimal set which contains all the attributes of the relation scheme R then X is called vague key of the relation R. Below we explain an algorithm to find the vague closure of an attribute or a set of attributes.

Algorithm 1. *Computation of vague closure of an attribute or a set of attributes*

Input: A vague relational scheme R, a set of **vfds** V on R and an attribute or a set of attributes X.

Output: A set of attributes X^+, the vague closure set of X.

Method:
Let $X^+ = X$.
i.e., $X^+ = (X, \alpha_1)$ where $\alpha_1 = 1 [\because X \xrightarrow[1]{vfd} X]$
repeat
$X^* = X^+$.
for each **vfd** $Y \xrightarrow[\alpha_2]{vfd} Z$ in V
do
if $Y \subseteq X^+$ then $X^+ = (X^+ \cup Z, \alpha_3)$ where $\alpha_3 = \min(\alpha_1, \alpha_2)$.
$\alpha_1 = \alpha_3$.
end for
until $(X^* = X^+)$.

Example 1: Let $R(A,B,C,D)$ be a relational scheme and a set of **fd**s and **vfd**s V on R is given as $V = \{A \xrightarrow[.8]{vfd} C, B \xrightarrow[.8]{vfd} D, C \xrightarrow[.9]{vfd} B\}$. Find closure of A.

Solution:
Let $X^+ = A$ i.e., $X^+ = (A,1)$
Repeat Case-I
$X^* = (A,1)$
for $A \xrightarrow[.8]{vfd} C$, $X^+ = (AC,.8)$ $[\because A \subseteq X^+]$
for $B \xrightarrow[.8]{vfd} D$, $X^+ = (AC,.8)$ $[\because B \not\subset X^+]$
for $C \xrightarrow[.9]{vfd} B$, $X^+ = (ABC,.8)$ $[\because C \subseteq X^+]$
Since $X^* \neq X^+$ do the following repeat case
Repeat Case-II
$X^* = (ABC,.8)$
for $A \xrightarrow[.8]{vfd} C$, $X^+ = (ABC,.8)$ $[\because A \subseteq X^+]$
for $B \xrightarrow[.8]{vfd} D$, $X^+ = (ABCD,.8)$ $[\because B \subseteq X^+]$
for $C \xrightarrow[.9]{vfd} B$, $X^+ = (ABCD,.8)$ $[\because C \subseteq X^+]$
Since $X^* \neq X^+$ do the following repeat case
Repeat Case-II
$X^* = (ABCD,.8)$
for $A \xrightarrow[.8]{vfd} C$, $X^+ = (ABCD,.8)$ $[\because A \subseteq X^+]$
for $B \xrightarrow[.8]{vfd} D$, $X^+ = (ABCD,.8)$ $[\because B \subseteq X^+]$
for $C \xrightarrow[.9]{vfd} B$, $X^+ = (ABCD,.8)$ $[\because C \subseteq X^+]$
Repeat case will stop since $X^* = X^+$.
Hence the vague closure of A i.e., $X^+ = (ABCD,.8)$ which means $A \xrightarrow[.8]{vfd} ABCD$.

4 Vague Normalization

An important problem of relational database design is how to obtain relation schemes in which the so called storage anomalies [18-20] can be avoided as much as possible. Storage anomalies occur during updating operations and cause inconsistency of data. In order to avoid storage anomalies as much as possible, Codd [18] introduced a series of normal forms, such as first (**1NF**), second (**2NF**), third (**3NF**) and **BCNF** normal forms.

For a good database design any relation must follow at least **3NF** normal form but **BCNF**, a stricter form of **3NF** is the most desirable normal form from the point of view of redundancy. Hence, in a vague relational model, we introduce the normalization techniques for vague relation schemes called vague normalization up to vague **BCNF** normal forms. We will discuss step by step different normalization forms of vague relational database say, vague first (**1VNF**), vague second (**2VNF**) vague third (**3VNF**) and vague BCNF (**VBCNF**) normal forms. To discuss the above theory we consider the vague relation scheme $EMP(Name, City, City\_Status, Experience, Salary)$ as given below in **Table 1**.

Table 1. A vague relational instance *r* of EMP relation

$Name$	$City$	$City\_Status$	$Experience$	$Salary$
Smith	Delhi	30	{ <13, [.95, 1]>, <15, [.8, .95]>, <23, [0, 0]> }	{ <50000, [.85, .95]> }
David	Kolkata	20	{ <13, [.85, .95]>, <15, [.95, 1]>, <23, [.25, .3]> }	{ <50000, [.95, 1]>, <95000, [.1, .2]> }
John	Delhi	{ <10, [.2, .3]>, <20, [.5, .6]>, <30, [.95, .95]> }	{ <13, [.1, .15]>, <15, [.2, .3]>, <23, [.95, 1]> }	{ <95000, [1, 1]> }
Smith	Mumbai	10	{ <23, [.95, 1]> }	{ <50000, [.2, .3]>, <95000, [.95, .95]> }

Now we find the Similarity Measures for the domain $Experience$, $Salary$ and $City\_Status$ in **Table 1** using **Definition 4**. The results are shown below by the matrices E, S and CS respectively in **Table 2.**

Table 2. Matrices E, S and CS showing Similarity Measures

E

	t_1	t_2	t_3	t_4
t_1	1	.9	.37	.21
t_2	.9	1	.51	.33
t_3	.37	.51	1	.91
t_4	.21	.33	.91	1

S

	t_1	t_2	t_3	t_4
t_1	1	.91	.15	.41
t_2	.91	1	.25	.47
t_3	.15	.25	1	.9
t_4	.41	.47	.9	1

CS

	t_1	t_2	t_3	t_4
t_1	1	0	.82	0
t_2	0	1	.58	0
t_3	.82	.58	1	.44
t_4	0	0	.44	1

Now from the above **Table 1** and **Table 2** **vfd**s and **fd**s for the relation scheme $EMP(Name, City, City\_Status, Experience, Salary)$ is defined as follows:

$$V = \{City \xrightarrow[0.8]{vfd} City\_Status, Experience \xrightarrow[0.9]{vfd} Salary, NameCity \rightarrow Experience\}$$

The **fd** $NameCity \rightarrow Experience$ can be express in **vfd** as $NameCity \xrightarrow[1]{vfd} Experience$. So the above V set can be rewritten as follows:

$$V = \{City \xrightarrow[0.8]{vfd} City\_Status, Experience \xrightarrow[0.8]{vfd} Salary, NameCity \xrightarrow[1]{vfd} Experience\}$$

Next we have to find the vague key of the relation EMP. Using **Algorithm1** the vague closure of $NameCity$ is obtained as

$$(NameCity)^{+} = (Name \quad City \quad City\_Status \quad Experience \quad Salary, 0.8)$$

which means $NameCity \xrightarrow[0.8]{vfd} NameCityCity\_StatusExperienceSalary$. Therefore, $NameCity$ is the vague key of EMP-relation at **0.8**-level of choice.

4.1 Vague Prime and Non-prime Attributes

To state the condition for vague 2NF, it is also necessary to define vague prime and non-prime attributes for a relation.

Definition 9

Let $A \in R$ and K be a vague key set for R. A is called vague prime attributes if and only if $A \in K$. Those attributes which are not vague prime are called vague non-prime.

For an attribute to be vague prime attribute, it should be a part of at least one of the vague candidate keys of the relation. Similarly, for an attribute to be a vague non-prime attribute, it should not appear in any of the vague candidate keys of the relations.

Example 2

Let us consider the $EMP(Name, City, City\_Status, Experience, Salary)$ relation with **vfd** set $V = \{City \xrightarrow[0.8]{vfd} City\_Status, Experience \xrightarrow[0.9]{vfd} Salary, NameCity \rightarrow Experience\}$ of **Table 1**.

Here $NameCity$ is a vague key at **0.8**-level of choice. Therefore, we conclude that the attributes $Name$ and $City$ are vague prime attributes at **0.8**-level of choice and attributes $City\_Status$, $Experience$ and $Salary$ are vague non-prime attributes.

4.2 Vague First Normal Form

The first one of the classical normal forms that is extended and generalized within the framework of α-cut similarity-based vague relational model is the **1NF**.

Definition 10

Let D_k be the domain of attributes A_k, a relation schema R is called to be in first vague normal form i.e., **1VNF** if and only if for any relation r in R, none of the attributes contained multi-valued. **Table 1** defined above is in **1VNF**.

4.3 Vague Second Normal Form

The vague second normal form, **2VNF,** is based on the concept of the full **vfd**. By using the concepts of vague key and partial vague functional dependence, we can define the **2VNF**.

Definition 11

Let V be the set of **vfd**s for relation schema R and K be a vague key of R at α–level of choice. R is called to be in vague second normal form i.e., **2VNF**, if and only if for none of the nonprime attributes is partially vague functionally dependent on the vague key.

Example 3

Let us consider the EMP relation and **vfd** set V of **Table 1**.

i.e., $EMP(Name, City, City\_Status, Experience, Salary)$ and

$$V = \{City \xrightarrow[0.8]{vfd} City\_Status, Experience \xrightarrow[0.9]{vfd} Salary, NameCity \rightarrow Experience\}.$$

Vague Key: $NameCity$ at **0.8**-level of choice.

Here we have the nonprime attributes $City\_Status$ which is vague partially dependent on vague key $NameCity$ at **0.8**-level of choice. So, **Table 1** is not in **2VNF**.

To satisfy **2VNF** we have to decomposed the above **Table 1**. Since **vfd** $City \xrightarrow[0.8]{vfd} City\_Status$ is the only **vfd** violating the **2VNF** condition, so the two **2VNF** decomposed relations (using the decomposition concept for classical relational database) are

$EMPCityStatus(City, City\_Status)$ with **vfd**s $V1 = \{City \xrightarrow[0.8]{vfd} City\_Status\}$

Vague Key: $City$ at **0.8**-level of choice.

$EMP\_INFO(Name, City, Experience, Salary)$ with **vfd**s

$$V2 = \{Experience \xrightarrow[0.9]{vfd} Salary, NameCity \rightarrow Experience\}$$

Vague Key: $NameCity$ at **.9**-level of choice.

4.4 Vague Third Normal Form (3VNF)

The normalization process takes a relation schema through a series of tests to certify whether it satisfies a certain normal form. The process proceeds in a top-down fashion. In a database design satisfying the vague third normal form i.e., **3VNF**, insertion, deletion and update anomalies will be minimum.

Definition 12
Let V be the set of **vfd**s for relation schema R and K be a vague key of R at α-level of choice. R is called to be in vague third normal form i.e., **3VNF**, if and only if R is in **2VNF** and R should not contain any **vfd** among vague nonprime attributes i.e., for any non-trivial **vfd** $X \xrightarrow[\alpha]{vfd} A$ in V either X contains the vague key or A is vague-prime.

Example 4
From this definition of **3VNF** we can say that the above relation $EMPCityStatus(City, City\_Status)$ is in **3VNF**, but relation $EMP\_INFO(Name, City, Experience, Salary)$ is not in **3VNF**. In relation EMP_INFO the **vfd** $Experience \xrightarrow[0.9]{vfd} Salary$ is violating the **3VNF** condition. So, we decompose the relation EMP_INFO into **3VNF** relations as follows:

$EMPExpSal(Experience, Salary)$ with **vfd**s
$$V3 = \{Experience \xrightarrow[0.9]{vfd} Salary\}$$
Vague Key: $Experience$ at **.9**-level of choice.

$EMP\_MAIN\_INFO(Name, City, Experience)$ with **vfd**s
$$V4 = \{NameCity \rightarrow Experience\}$$

Vague Key: $NameCity$ at **1**-level of choice. Here vague key is also the classical key.

4.5 Vague Boyce Codd Normal Form (VBCNF)

Like its classical counterpart, vague boyce codd normal form i.e., **VBCNF**, is a stricter form of **3VNF**. **VBCNF** ensures that there is no redundancy that can be detected using **vfd** information alone. It is the most desirable normal form from the point of view of redundancy. The formal definition of the **VBCNF** can be given as follows.

Definition 13
Let V be the set of **vfd**s for relation schema R and K be a vague key of R at α-level of choice. R is called to be in vague BCNF normal form i.e., **VBCNF**, if and only if R is in **3VNF** and for any non-trivial **vfd** $X \xrightarrow[\alpha]{vfd} A$ in V, X must be a vague key or super vague key of R i.e., $X \supseteq K$.

Example 5
The following decomposed relations satisfying **3VNF** are also in **VBCNF**.

$$EMPCityStatus(City, City\_Status),\ V1 = \{City \xrightarrow[0.8]{vfd} City\_Status\}$$
$$EMPExpSal(Experience, Salary),\ V3 = \{Experience \xrightarrow[0.9]{vfd} Salary\}$$
$$EMP\_MAIN\_INFO(Name, City, Experience),$$
$$V4 = \{NameCity \rightarrow Experience\}$$

5 Conclusion

Like the classical relational database, a vague relational database may also suffer from data redundancy and different data anomalies if it is not designed properly. Vague normalization based on α-**vfd,** as defined in this work, plays an important role in the design of a good vague relational database.

In this paper, firstly we have designed an algorithm to find vague closure of an attribute set which helps in finding vague key and then the normalization process for vague relation has been discussed by defining different vague normal forms i.e., **1VNF**, **2VNF**, **3VNF**, and **VBCNF**. We have also introduced the definition of vague prime and vague non-prime attributes in order to state the condition for vague normal forms. We have illustrated with an example that how these vague normal forms can be used to decompose an unnormalized vague relation into a set of vague normalized relations.

References

1. Mishra, J., Ghosh, S.: A New Functional Dependency in a Vague Relational Database Model. International Journal of Computer Applications 39, 29–36 (2012)
2. Codd, E.: A Relational Model for Large Shared Data Banks. Comm. of ACM 13, 377–387 (1970)
3. Mishra, J., Ghosh, S.: A Multivalued Integrity Constraint in Fuzzy Relational Database. International Journal of Computational Cognition 9, 72–78 (2011)
4. Sözat, M.I., Yazici, A.: A complete axiomatization for fuzzy functional and multivalued dependencies in fuzzy database relations. Fuzzy Sets and Systems 117, 161–181 (2001)
5. Ma, Z.M., Zhang, W.J.: Multivalued dependencies in extended possibility-based fuzzy relational databases. In: IFSA World Congress and 20th NAFIPS International Conference, vol. 1, pp. 352–356 (2001)

6. Chen, G., Kerre, E.E., Vandenbulcke, J.: Normalization Based on ffd in a Fuzzy Relational Data Model. Information Systems 21, 299–310 (1996)
7. Raju, K.V.S.V.N., Majumdar, A.K.: Fuzzy functional dependencies and lossless join decomposition of fuzzy relational database system. ACM Transactions on Database Systems 13, 129–166 (1988)
8. Liu, W.Y.: Fuzzy Data Dependencies and Implication of Fuzzy Data Dependencies. Fuzzy Sets and Systems 92, 341–348 (1997)
9. Bosc, P., Dubois, D., Prade, H.: Fuzzy functional dependencies and redundancy elimination. Journal of the American Society for Information Science 49, 217–235 (1998)
10. Yazici, A., Sozat, M.I.: The Integrity Constraints for Similarity-Based Fuzzy Relational Databases. International Journal of Intelligent Systems 13, 641–659 (1998)
11. Shenoi, S., Melton, A.: Functional dependencies and normal forms in the fuzzy relational database model. Information Sciences 60, 1–28 (1992)
12. Bahar, O., Yazici, A.: Normalization and Lossless Join Decomposition of Similarity-Based Fuzzy Relational Databases. International Journal of Intelligent Systems 19, 885–917 (2004)
13. Zadeh, L.A.: Fuzzy Sets. Information and Controls 8, 338–353 (1965)
14. Gau, W.L., Buehrer, D.J.: Vague Sets. IEEE Trans. Syst. Man, Cybernetics 23, 610–614 (1993)
15. Lu, A., Ng, W.: Managing Merged Data by Vague Functional Dependencies. In: Atzeni, P., Chu, W., Lu, H., Zhou, S., Ling, T.-W. (eds.) ER 2004. LNCS, vol. 3288, pp. 259–272. Springer, Heidelberg (2004)
16. Zhao, F., Ma, Z.M.: Functional Dependencies in Vague Relational Databases. In: IEEE International Conference on Systems Man and Cybernetics, pp. 4006–4010 (2006)
17. Lu, A., Ng, W.: Maintaining consistency of vague databases using data dependencies. Data and Knowledge Engineering 68, 622–641 (2009)
18. Codd, E.F.: The relational Model for Database Management. Addison-Wesley (1990)
19. Date, C.J.: An introduction to Data Base Systems 8/E. Addison Wesley (2004)
20. Elmasri, R., Navathe, S.B.: Fundamentals of Database Systems. Pearson Education (2007)

Unrolling SQL: 1999 Recursive Queries

Aleksandra Boniewicz, Krzystof Stencel, and Piotr Wiśniewski

Faculty of Mathematics and Computer Science
Nicolaus Copernicus University
Toruń, Poland
{grusia,stencel,pikonrad}@mat.uni.torun.pl

Abstract. Hierarchical and graph data structures are common in practical application development. In order to query such data, one can use SQL:1999 recursive queries based on Common Table Expressions. Nowadays, numerous relational database management systems implement them. However, some popular systems, e.g. MySQL, still lack this useful feature. In this paper we show three methods to circumvent this situation: (1) the direct loop, (2) horizontal unrolling and (3) vertical unrolling. We analyze them and present a report on tests of their efficiency. We also describe our implementation of these methods as a prototype extension to Hibernate, a major object-relational mapping system. This extension allows running SQL:1999 recursive queries directly from an application code, even when the underlying DBMS does not support them.

1 Introduction

Recursive database structures are ubiquitous. Some of them are hierarchical, like corporate hierarchies, subject classifications in libraries or product categorization in online shops. There are also arbitrary graphs like a road network, a railway system or a bill of material. A number of ways to persist them in a database has been proposed [1]. The need to query such structures has also been recognized. In 1999 it resulted in augmenting the SQL standard with recursive queries based on Common Table Expressions. Such queries have already been implemented in a significant number of database systems, both commercial and open-source [2]. Researchers developed optimization methods for recursive queries [3–5]. However, there are still database management systems that do not implement SQL:1999 recursive queries, e.g. MySQL. Since this DBMS is widely used in web application development, numerous projects must be lacking this feature. Therefore, developers have to code it by hand in the application layer instead of employing native database facilities.

Object-relation mapping systems (ORM) [6, 7] are to bridge the gap between relational storage and object-oriented code known under collective name *impedance mismatch.* Of course they do [8, 9], but since they provide an object-oriented abstraction layer, they can be used to map additional features. In our research, we struggle to exploit this possibility. We have developed designs and

T.-h. Kim et al. (Eds.): EL/DTA/UNESST 2012, CCIS 352, pp. 345–354, 2012.

prepared prototype implementations of a number of novel features in ORMs. They are recursive queries [10–12], partial aggregation [13] and functional indices [14].

In this paper we describe a follow-up of our results with recursive querying through an ORM. We propose an extension to Hibernate, a major ORM. This extension allows an application to pose recursive queries even when the underlying DBMS does not provide SQL:1999 recursion. We have prepared a proof-of-concept implementation of this extension and conducted preliminary efficiency testing.

We have designed and implemented three methods to run a user recursive query inside Hibernate: direct loop, vertical unrolling and horizontal unrolling. The first method performs the query in a naïve user loop. The second method is similar to the standard compiler technique of loop unrolling. It simply unrolls the recursive query into a cascade of self-joins up to a specified depth. The third method is novel. It unrolls the query horizontally into the `SELECT` clause and a sequence of left outer joins. With this method the answer to a recursive query contains whole path records for output tuples. Although horizontal unrolling provides more data to the application, it appears to be the fastest method in our tests.

The contributions of the paper are:

- three methods to run recursive queries without using SQL:1999 recursive database facilities,
- a design of an extension to Hibernate that allows applications to run direct SQL:1999 recursive queries, even if the underlying DBMS does not support them,
- a proof-of-concept implementation of this extension.

The paper is organized as follows. In Section 2 we discuss querying recursive data structures using SQL:1999 queries. In Section 3 we present the three methods to run recursive queries without usage of native DBMS's recursion. Section 4 describes the design of the proposed extension to Hibernate. Section 5 reports our experiments with MySQL, a major database system that does not provide SQL recursion. Section 6 concludes.

2 Recursive Data Structures

A recursive data structures can be a hierarchy or an arbitrary graph. Such structures can be the subject of interesting queries like: finding all subordinates of a given employee or identifying possible railway connections between two cities. If the actual graph data contains a cycle, a recursive query to these data can loop forever. Although it is a known problem, it lacks a uniform solution in contemporary database systems and query languages. In this paper we assume that an application programmer is aware of the queried data and the stop condition for her queries.

The ideas discussed in this paper are well-suited even for arbitrary graphs. However, it is best to present them using hierarchical structures, like a corporate hierarchy. Let us consider the following sample table `emp`:

```
> SELECT * FROM emp;

 empId |   fname    |   sname    | bossId
-------+------------+------------+--------
     1 | John       | Travolta   |
     2 | Bruce      | Willis     |      1
     3 | Marilyn    | Monroe     |
     4 | Angelina   | Jolie      |      3
     5 | Brad       | Pitt       |      4
     6 | Hugh       | Grant      |      4
     7 | Colin      | Firth      |      3
     8 | Keira      | Knightley  |      6
     9 | Sean       | Connery    |      1
    10 | Pierce     | Brosnan    |      3
...
```

In order to find the employees that are direct and indirect subordinates of `Travolta`, an application can send the query from Listing 1.1 to a database system. According to [2] this query conforms to SQL dialects of most database managements systems that support SQL:1999 recursion.

Listing 1.1. A query to list Travolta's subordinates

```
WITH RECURSIVE rcte (
  SELECT empId, fname, sname, bossId
    FROM Emp WHERE sname = 'Travolta'
 UNION
  SELECT e.empId, e.fname, e.sname, e.bossId
    FROM Emp e JOIN rcte r ON (e.bossId = r.empId)
)
SELECT sname, fname
  FROM rcte;
```

Unfortunately, some database systems do not implement such queries. The most profound example of such a DBMS is MySQL, the preferred database system for web application development in the LAMP model.

3 Using Recursive Data without Recursive Queries

Assume an application development project such that its data model contains recursive data. In fact most of practical projects contain such data. If the chosen DBMS does not support recursive queries neither SQL:1999 nor any other form, recursive queries are to be implemented as a part of the application code. In this Section we discuss three methods how to do it.

3.1 Direct Loop

This methods consist in sending a separate database query for each encountered node. Its sketch for the query from Listing 1.1 is presented as Algorithm 1. First we initialize the list L with all employee records of Travoltas. Then for each employee on the list we query the database for her subordinates and append them at the end of L.

```
L ← get("SELECT * FROM emp WHERE sname = 'Travolta'");
i ← 0;
while i < len(L) do
    id ← L[i].empId;
    L ← L + get("SELECT * FROM emp WHERE bossId = $id");
    i++;
end
return L;
```

Algorithm 1: The direct loop

Algorithm 1 is inefficient, since it requires sending as many queries as the final size of the list L. This means a significant number of expensive roundtrips and substantial effort at the database server side. Each query instance must be parsed, optimized and verified against the access rights. We can improve the direct loop by using prepared statements. However, it will not be a noteworthy change.

3.2 Horizontal Unrolling

Horizontal unrolling is applicable provided we know the maximum recursion depth. Instead of sending separate queries for each employee, we construct a single cascade left outer self-join. In order to query for subordinates of Travolta up to the third level we send the query from Listing 1.2

Listing 1.2. Horizontal unrolling up to the third level

```sql
SELECT *
  FROM Emp l0
    LEFT JOIN Emp l1 on (l0.empId = l1.bossId)
    LEFT JOIN Emp l2 on (l1.empId = l2.bossId)
    LEFT JOIN Emp l3 on (l2.empId = l3.bossId)
  WHERE l0.sname = 'Travolta'
```

As the result to this query we obtain a wide table. Each of its rows represents a single path from the data. It contains 16 columns, i.e. the number of columns of the table `emp` multiplied by the number of levels to traverse plus one. SQL:1999 recursive queries can be algorithmically unrolled this way, by expanding its recursive section into subsequent left outer joins up to the specified level. The drawback of horizontal unrolling is the rapid growth of the size of the answer, when the required query depth increases. On the other hand, this method is fast even for moderate hierarchy depths (see Section 5.3). Furthermore, horizontal unrolling produces not only the set of reachable nodes but also records and outputs the paths used to reach it. Below we present a sample result to the query from Listing 1.2. For the sake of brevity we show only the column sname.

```
 l0.sname | l1.sname | l2.sname | l3.sname
----------+----------+----------+----------
 Travolta | Willis   | Schmidt  | Foremann
 Travolta | Willis   | Schmidt  | Flinch
 Travolta | Willis   | Ivanov   | null
 Travolta | Connery  | null     | null
...       |          |          |
```

3.3 Vertical Unrolling

We can also unroll a recursive query vertically. We simply compute the result level by level like in the textbook algorithm for fixed points. We could construct a single query that is a union of self-joins for subsequent levels $(1, 2, 3, \ldots)$. However, it is more efficient to store previously computed levels in temporary tables and compute the next level by joining to the previous level. With the single query approach, being at level n, in fact we have to compute again all levels $1, 2, \ldots, n-1$ from scratch.

An implementation of vertical unrolling requires three steps, with the second step possibly performed repeatedly. They are the seed step, the recurrence step and the result step.

Seed Step. In this step we simply run the seed query of the recursive query. The result is put into the table tmp(0). The seed step for our example query from Listing 1.1 is presented as Listing 1.3.

Listing 1.3. The seed step

```sql
CREATE TEMPORARY TABLE tmp(0)
  SELECT empId, fname, sname, bossId
  FROM emp
  WHERE sname = 'Travolta';
```

Recurrence Step. In this step we perform the recursive step of a query. For each $n = 1, 2, \ldots, L$ where L is the depth limit, we construct the temporary table tmp(n) using temporary table tmp($n-1$). We simply take the recursive subquery and replace the name of the recursive CTE with tmp($n-1$). The recurrence step for the example query from Listing 1.1 is shown on Listing 1.4.

Listing 1.4. The recurrence step

```sql
CREATE TEMPORARY TABLE tmp(n)
  SELECT e.empId, e.fname, e.sname, e.bossId
  FROM Emp e, tmp(n - 1) t;
```

If the maximum recursion level is set to L, we run the recurrence step L times. If it is not known, we run this step as long as the obtained temporary table is not empty.

Result Step. In this step we run the outer subquery from the recursive query on the union of the computed temporary tables. Listing 1.5 contains the result step for our sample query from Listing 1.1.

Listing 1.5. The result step

```
SELECT sname, fname
FROM (
     SELECT * FROM tmp(0)
   UNION
     SELECT * FROM tmp(1)
   UNION
     ...
   UNION
     SELECT * FROM  tmp(N)
);
```

Here N is the last step of recursion that produces a nonempty temporary table.

Vertical unrolling requires a number of queries to be sent to the database. However, this number is significantly smaller than in case of the direct loop (see Section 3.1). It is equal to the maximum recursion depth and not the number of returned records as in the direct loop. Therefore, vertical unrolling is notable faster. Furthermore, since it does not cause expansion of the width of the result, it can be used for larger recursion depths than horizontal unrolling (see Section 3.2. It is also more suitable for aggregate queries on trees.

4 Integration of Recursive Queries and ORM

If an application exploits some ORM and processes recursive data, it is almost certain that it implements the direct loop approach (see Section 3.1). Although it is notably inefficient, it is simple and can be easily implemented by hand. If the underlying database system offers SQL:1999 recursion, the application can address the database directly. However, it is not recommended, since it breaks the architecture and thus raises future maintenance cost.

As a remedy, we proposed to enhance object-relational mapping systems with interfaces and generators that that automatically map recursive object queries of an application onto SQL:1999 recursive queries of the database system. The results of this research have been published in [10–12]. Listing 1.6 shows a sample configuration file for the mapping of a recursive query to the corporate hierarchy stored in the table `emp`.

Listing 1.6. The configuration of the mapping for a query to a corporate hierarchy

```
<rcte>
  <rcteTable name="Subordinates" max-level="3"/>
  <tables>
    <table>Emp</table>
  </tables>
  <recursive-condition>
    <on>Emp.bossId</on>
    <to>rcte.empId</to>
  </recursive-condition>
  <filter section="seed">
    Emp.sname = $Param(sname)
  </filter>
  <select section="outer">
    sname, fname
  </select>
</rcte>
```

The elements in this XML snippet have the following meaning:

`tables`
: The list of tables used in the generated query.

`recursive-condition`
: The condition used to attach new nodes to the spanning tree beign built. The element `on` indicates the column of the new row added to result. The element `to` contains the column of the result constructed so far.

`filter`
: The conditions that are used in the evaluation. Depending on the value of the attribute `section` they are attach to: the seed query (`seed`), the recurrence query(`loop`) or the outer query (`outer`).

`select`
: The list of columns selected at each level. The value of the attribute `section` has the same meaning as in the element `filter`. If the list is not specified for a given section, all columns are considered to be selected. The lengths of select lists for the seed query and the recurrence query must be equal since they are merged by the `UNION` operator. Furthermore, the data types of corresponding columns on these lists must be conformant.

If the underlying database is PostgreSQL, the object-relational mapping system will issue exactly the query from Listing 1.1. Even if the table `emp` contains a couple of thousands of rows, such a solution will be more than one hundred faster than the equivalent direct loop. More information is given in our prequel papers, e.g. [12]. In that paper we have also shown a way to define this mapping using Java annotations.

In this paper we discuss what happens, when the underlying database system does not support SQL:1999 recursion, e.g. MySQL. The same mapping interfaces are used. However the underlying query generators use one the methods presented in Section 3.

5 Recursive Queries and MySQL

The goal of our research group is the introduction of additional useful features into object-relational mapping systems. Recursive queries on hierarchies and graphs constitute one of such features. Previous results consists in the integration recursive querying and ORM [10–12]. However, they cannot be used directly with databases like MySQL whose SQL dialects do not support recursion. Recursive data stored in MySQL can obviously be queries through a standard ORM using the direct loop (see Section 3.1). Such an approach is though remarkably inefficient. In this paper we describe our research on the integration of programmer interfaces from [12] with unrolling methods from Section 3.

5.1 Implementation of Vertical Unrolling

If Hibernate augmented with the proposed extension is run with MySQL as the underlying database, it will check the value of the attribute `unrolling` in the XML configuration element `rcte`. Its default value is `vertical`.

If the vertical unrolling is chosen, Hibernate will send the seed query first. Then it will send subsequent recurrence queries and check the cardinality of the result. The computation stops when the maximum recursion level is reached (defined by the attribute `max-level` of the tag `rcte`) or the recently created temporary table is empty. Then the contents of all temporary tables are collected and subjected to the outer query that is to generate the eventual result.

5.2 Implementation of Horizontal Unrolling

If the attribute `unrolling` of the tag `rcte` has the value `horizontal`, Hibernate will generate a single query according to the method described in Section 3.2. With this unrolling method the parameter `max-level` is mandatory, e.g.

```
<rcteTable name="subordinates"
           unrolling = "horizontal"
           max-level="3" />
```

Horizontal unrolling generates a significantly richer result. Each of its records represents a path from the member of the seed to a leave in the resulting spanning tree. This result is available as a matrix of records.

5.3 Performance

We have tested the performance of our unrolling methods and compared it with the direct loop. We used four instances of the table `emp`:

1. with 5 000 records and 5 levels of hierarchy depth,
2. with 5 000 records and 20 levels of hierarchy depth,
3. with 10 000 records and 5 levels of hierarchy depth,
4. with 10 000 records and 5 levels of hierarchy depth.

Table 1. Comparison of average execution time on MySQL

Record count	Hierarchy depth	Direct loop	Horizontal unrolling	Vertical unrolling
5000	5	18.1s	0.6s	1.1s
5000	20	10.1s	1.2s	5.4s
10000	5	17.1s	0.7s	1.3s
10000	20	19.3s	2.7s	8.9s

For all four instances we have created single-column B+tree indices on `empId` and `bossId`.

The results are summarized in Table 1 and Figure 1. Apparently, both unrolling methods caused a significant improvement when compared to the direct loop approach. From the two unrolling methods the horizontal one has proven to be faster. It has amounted to be even four times faster than the vertical method. Note that the improvement factor of four has been achieved for the scenario with relatively deep hierarchy of 20 levels. Large number of resulting columns has not constituted an obstruction.

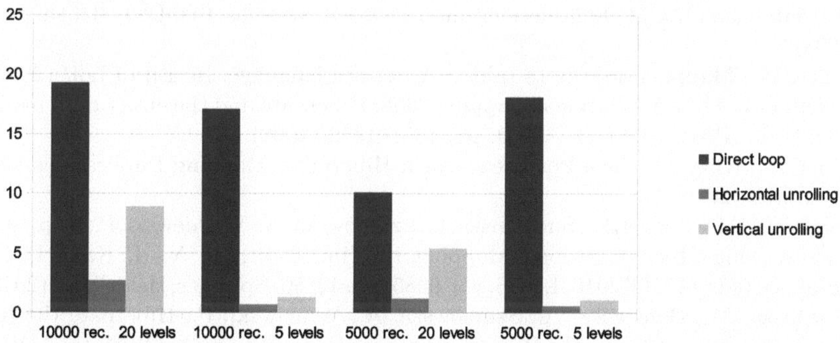

Fig. 1. Result of the performance tests for three mapping methods

6 Conclusions

In this paper we considered the problem of recursive querying a database whose SQL dialect does not support recursion, e.g. MySQL. Since object-relational mapping systems provide an abstraction layer over database management systems, it is natural to introduce query enhancements into this layer. We have identified three methods to run the recursive query without native SQL:1999 recursion: the direct loop, vertical and horizontal unrolling. We have implemented a prototype extension to Hibernate that works with MySQL. The implementation automatically maps application recursive queries to the unrolling method chosen by the software architect. We have tested all three methods using table instances with various volumetric characteristics. The results show that both unrolling methods are notably more efficient that the naïve direct loop approach. Horizontal unrolling has appeared to be superior over the vertical method.

References

1. Brandon, D.: Recursive database structures. J. Comput. Small Coll. 21(2), 295–304 (2005)
2. Przymus, P., Boniewicz, A., Burzańska, M., Stencel, K.: Recursive Query Facilities in Relational Databases: A Survey. In: Zhang, Y., Cuzzocrea, A., Ma, J., Chung, K.-I., Arslan, T., Song, X. (eds.) DTA/BSBT 2010. CCIS, vol. 118, pp. 89–99. Springer, Heidelberg (2010)
3. Ghazal, A., Crolotte, A., Seid, D.Y.: Recursive SQL Query Optimization with k-Iteration Lookahead. In: Bressan, S., Küng, J., Wagner, R. (eds.) DEXA 2006. LNCS, vol. 4080, pp. 348–357. Springer, Heidelberg (2006)
4. Ordonez, C.: Optimization of Linear Recursive Queries in SQL. IEEE Trans. Knowl. Data Eng., 264–277 (2010)
5. Burzańska, M., Stencel, K., Wiśniewski, P.: Pushing Predicates into Recursive SQL Common Table Expressions. In: Grundspenkis, J., Morzy, T., Vossen, G. (eds.) ADBIS 2009. LNCS, vol. 5739, pp. 194–205. Springer, Heidelberg (2009)
6. Melnik, S., Adya, A., Bernstein, P.A.: Compiling mappings to bridge applications and databases. ACM Transactions on Database Systems (TODS), 33(4), 1–50 (2008)
7. Keller, W.: Mapping objects to tables: A pattern language. In: EuroPLoP (2007)
8. O'Neil, E.J.: Object/relational mapping 2008: Hibernate and the entity data model (EDM). In: Proc. ACM SIGMOD, pp. 1351–1356 (2008)
9. Bauer, C., King, G.: Java Persistence with Hibernate. Manning Publications Co., Greenwich (2006)
10. Burzańska, M., Stencel, K., Suchomska, P., Szumowska, A., Wiśniewski, P.: Recursive Queries Using Object Relational Mapping. In: Kim, T.-H., Lee, Y.-H., Kang, B.-H., Ślęzak, D. (eds.) FGIT 2010. LNCS, vol. 6485, pp. 42–50. Springer, Heidelberg (2010)
11. Burzańska, M., Boniewicz, A., Szumowska, A., Winiewski, P.: Hibernate the Recursive Queries - Defining the Recursive Queries Using Hibernate ORM. In: ADBIS 2011, pp.190–199 (2011)
12. Szumowska, A., Burzańska, M., Wiśniewski, P., Stencel, K.: Efficient Implementation of Recursive Queries in Major Object Relational Mapping Systems. In: Kim, T.-H., Adeli, H., Slezak, D., Sandnes, F.E., Song, X., Chung, K.-I., Arnett, K.P. (eds.) FGIT 2011. LNCS, vol. 7105, pp. 78–89. Springer, Heidelberg (2011)
13. Gawarkiewicz, M., Wiśniewski, P.: Partial Aggregation Using Hibernate. In: Kim, T.-H., Adeli, H., Slezak, D., Sandnes, F.E., Song, X., Chung, K.-I., Arnett, K.P. (eds.) FGIT 2011. LNCS, vol. 7105, pp. 90–99. Springer, Heidelberg (2011)
14. Boniewicz, A., Gawarkiewicz, M., Wiśniewski, P.: Automatic Selection of Functional Indexes for Object Relational Mappings System. In: FGIT 2012 (2012)

Author Index

Ahn, Hyun-Sik 258, 298
Ameedeen, Mohamed Ariff 38
Awang, Mohd Khalid 318
Azmi, Zafril Rizal M. 38

Bae, Doo-Hwan 92, 107
Bae, Myung-Jin 184
Bae, Myungjin 246, 277
Bae, Seonggeon 246
Bae, Seoung-soo 252
Baek, Geumran 277
Boniewicz, Aleksandra 345

Chen, Cheng-ping 15
Chi, Pei-han 23
Cho, Chang-Suk 252
Cho, Eun-Byul 142
Cho, Seungyun 158
Choi, Gyoo-Seok 142
Choi, Han-Gil 44
Choi, Jinho 107
Choi, Ran 252
Chung, Hyunsuk 325

Defazio, Joseph 8

Erkollar, Alptekin 31

Ghosh, Sharmistha 332

Han, Dae-Yong 44
Han, Soyeon Caren 325
Hwang, Kyu-sung 239
Hwang, Young-Hwan 170

Ismail, Mohammad Ridwan 318

Jang, WonGyu 198
Jeong, Myeong-Jin 142
Jeong, Yeon-Man 134
Jung, Ji Won 233
Jung, Yong-Gyu 170

Kang, Byeong Ho 325
Kang, In-Su 80
Kang, Jeong-Jin 142, 158
Kil, Hyunyoung 72
Kim, Bonggyu 116
Kim, Byung-Kyu 80
Kim, DoHyeon 198
Kim, Haeng-Kon 58
Kim, Hangyu 116
Kim, Hyeon-Choel 252
Kim, Hyoseung 99
Kim, Jae-O 298
Kim, JeongAh 111
Kim, Jeong-Joon 134, 142
Kim, Jeong-lae 239
Kim, Jong-Dae 44, 265
Kim, Jung Tae 190
Kim, Kitak 99
Kim, Kyu-Ho 134
Kim, Milyoung 99
Kim, Mohan 272
Kim, Myongho 92
Kim, Myung-Sook 184
Kim, Seill 103
Kim, Seongwoo 116
Kim, Suntae 111
Kim, Yeong Gon 219
Kim, Yong-Kab 126
Kim, Yu-Doo 272
Kim, Yu-Seop 44, 265
Kwon, Jae-Hyun 126
Kwon, Young-Man 150, 170, 227
Kwun, Tae-Min 134

Lee, Dong Hoon 99
Lee, Eui Chul 219
Lee, Eun-Ser 150
Lee, HanKyu 219
Lee, Han Suk 204
Lee, Joohyun 92
Lee, Jung-Kuk 44, 265
Lee, Jung Woo 302
Lee, Ki-Young 134, 142
Lee, Kun Chang 302, 310
Lee, Kyung-Jung 258
Lee, Min-Ji 265

Lee, Sang-Hyun 289
Lee, Shinwon 177
Lee, SungHyup 198
Lee, Sungnam 111
Lee, Wonhee 177
Lee, Won Oh 219
Lee, Yoon-Jeong 265
Lee, Youngdae 158
Li, Yu 86
Lim, Jong-Han 289
Lim, Myung-Jae 150, 227
Lu, Hongyi 1

Minami, Toshiro 50
Mishra, Jaydev 332
Moon, Chan-Woo 298
Moon, Dosik 120
Moon, Il-Young 272
Moon, Kyung-Il 289
Moon, YouHyeong 198
Mun, Seong Mi 211

Nam, Wonhong 72

Oberer, Birgit J. 31
Oh, CheonIn 219
Oh, Yunghwan 116
Ohura, Yoko 50

Park, Chan-Young 44, 265
Park, Gun Yeol 233
Park, Hyung-Woo 184
Park, Jeongsik 116
Park, Jin Young 302
Park, Jon Hwan 99
Park, Kang Ryoung 219
Park, Keon-Jun 126
Park, Sooyoung 111
Park, Youngkyu 103

Qiu, Wenwei 1

Rahman, Mohd Nordin Abdul 318
Rho, Sunny 298
Ro, Sunny 258

Seong, Seung Chang 310
Shin, Kwang Yong 219
Son, Joo Young 211
Song, Hye-Jeong 44, 265
Stencel, Krzystof 345
Sun, Zhen 1
Sung-euk, Pakr 283

Wang, Chang-hwa 15, 23
Wiśniewski, Piotr 345

Xiao, Nong 1

Yeom, Ho Jun 204

Zhong, Sheng 86

MIX
Papier aus verantwortungsvollen Quellen
Paper from responsible sources
FSC® C105338

If you have any concerns about our products,
you can contact us on
ProductSafety@springernature.com

In case Publisher is established outside the EU,
the EU authorized representative is:
Springer Nature Customer Service Center GmbH
Europaplatz 3, 69115 Heidelberg, Germany

Printed by Libri Plureos GmbH
in Hamburg, Germany